AMERICA'S
FIGHTING
ADMIRALS

AMERICA'S
FIGHTING
ADMIRALS

WILLIAM TUOHY
PULITZER PRIZE WINNER

For Sarah, Sebastian, and Rose Marie

First published in 2007 by Zenith Press, an imprint of MBI Publishing Company LLC, Galtier Plaza, Suite 200, 380 Jackson Street, St. Paul, MN 55101 USA

Zenith Press titles are also available at discounts in bulk quantity for industrial or sales-promotional use. For details write to Special Sales Manager at MBI Publishing Company, Galtier Plaza, Suite 200, 380 Jackson Street, St. Paul, MN 55101 USA.

To find out more about our books, join us online at www.zenithpress.com.

Designer: Jennifer Maass

Front cover image:
Task Group 38.3 enters Ulithi anchorage in column, December 12, 1944, while returning from strikes on targets in the Philippines. Ships are (from front): *Langley* (CVL-27); *Ticonderoga* (CV-14); *Washington* (BB-56); *North Carolina* (BB-55); *South Dakota* (BB-57); *Santa Fe* (CL-60); *Biloxi* (CL-80); *Mobile* (CL-63); and *Oakland* (CL-95). *Official U.S. Navy Photograph*

Library of Congress Cataloging-in-Publication Data

Tuohy, William, 1926-
  America's fighting admirals : winning the war at sea in World War II / by William Tuohy.
     p. cm.
  ISBN-13: 978-0-7603-2985-6 (hardbound w/ jacket)
  ISBN-10: 0-7603-2985-0 (hardbound w/ jacket)
  1. World War, 1939-1945—Naval operations, American. 2. United States. Navy—History—World War, 1939-1945. 3. World War, 1939-1945—Campaigns—Pacific Area. 4. Admirals—United States—Biography. 5. United States. Navy—Officers—Biography. 6. United States—Biography. I. Title.
  D773.T757 2007
  940.54'59730922—dc22

                              2006034490

Printed in the United States of America

CONTENTS

But here are men who fought in gallant actions
As gallantly as ever heroes fought . . .
—Lord Byron

INTRODUCTION

admiral: Derived from Arabic, *amir-al-bahr*, "Lord of the sea."

The American naval actions of World War II comprise the most widespread, complex, and dramatic battles in the history of sea warfare. The fighting took place over vast distances in the Atlantic and Pacific oceans, and in the constricted spaces of the Mediterranean and Solomon seas. Each of the major actions had a commander in charge, an admiral who led the battle.

In the overall war, U.S. admirals played several roles: The senior flag officers ran the strategic planning and gave orders from Washington and Pearl Harbor. Some flag officers held various administrative, supply, and training posts, crucial to an expanding navy. But the fighting admirals were those who actually led warships in action against enemy formations. Their task: to plan and win naval operations at sea, inflicting maximum damage on the enemy and minimum damage to their own forces. In combat, the abilities and determination of these commanders at sea were put to the most severe test.

The fighting admirals were a diverse lot. Some were impetuous and headstrong, charging almost heedlessly into battle while projecting a flamboyant, charismatic public personality: The exemplar was William F. Halsey, Jr. Others were calm, thoughtful, publicity-shy and wary of taking unnecessary risks, like Raymond A. Spruance. Some were rough tongued and abrupt, like Richmond Kelly Turner. Others were charming and personable, like Richard L. Conolly. Some were drivers, some were leaders.

The finest fighting admirals combined various qualities: an eagerness to close the enemy, coupled with a cool ability to handle their ships expertly in the heat and confusion of combat. But it was impossible to predict who would prove successful in battle, who would have the rare "Nelson touch." Some admirals who seemed in peacetime to have all the necessary credentials did not measure up in the crucible of combat. The qualities that made for a fine flag officer in peacetime were not necessarily those that made for a fighting admiral in wartime. Some seagoing admirals seemed at first to shine, but then flagged and faded into obscurity as the war progressed.

This narrative describes the course of U.S. sea action in World War II and examines the skills, strengths, weaknesses, and personalities of the American admirals who fought the battles at sea. It examines the effect that stress, tension, and responsibility have on senior officers manning the bridges of their flagships, making vital decisions in the blaze of battle. And it reveals the changing nature of the responsibilities of flag officers as the war progressed and became enormously complex.

At the Tokyo raid, for instance, the carrier task force had aboard only two admirals: William "Bill" Halsey and Raymond Spruance. Toward the end of the war, the great armada that assembled for the invasion of Okinawa had no less than forty-four U.S. flag officers. Of the many admirals in the wartime U.S. Navy, some proved most able in the administrative, supply, and training commands, which were necessary to back the seagoing fighting forces. Such brilliant and famous admirals as Ernest King and Chester Nimitz never held command positions at sea in the war. Nor, in the nature of their jobs, could a brilliant air admiral like John H. "Jack" Towers or a submariner like Vice Admiral Charles A. Lockwood, Commander, Submarine Force, U.S. Pacific Fleet (ComSubPac), go to sea.

But a dozen or so flag officers had the good fortune, through time, place, and opportunity to stand out, and did so—America's greatest fighting admirals in World War II.

This account recognizes the tremendous courage, fortitude, and contribution of ordinary seamen, and that an admiral is only as good as his captains, his officers, and his men. Men matter most, but this book necessarily focuses on the fighting admirals who commanded the ships in battles at sea. In a modern age of missiles, World War II was probably the last conflict in which flag officers in warships would directly engage one another. Never again would admiral be pitted against admiral in sea battles. This is the story of those American admirals who won the great sea battles of World War II, and those who lost them.

One

THE RAID FROM SHANGRI-LA

January–April 1942

At dusk on January 31, 1942, the new aircraft carrier USS *Hornet* lay at anchor in Hampton Roads off the huge American naval base at Norfolk, Virginia. Her captain was Marc Andrew Mitscher, known throughout the navy as "Pete," a pioneer naval aviator, the thirty-third to win gold wings in 1916. As pilot of the flying boat, Navy-Curtiss (NC) 1, his first trans-Atlantic attempt fell just short of the Azores in 1919. Pete Mitscher—small, wiry, and weather-beaten, looking ten years older than his fifty-five years—had flown every type of naval aircraft and held a variety of aviation jobs. He commissioned *Hornet* in November 1941 and was conducting shakedown exercises from Norfolk, expecting soon to be assigned to the Pacific to fight the Japanese.

Mitscher waited to receive Captain Donald B. "Wu" Duncan, the air operations officer on the staff of Admiral Ernest J. King, the commander in chief of the U.S. Fleet. Wu Duncan, too, was a veteran naval aviator and brilliant planner, but Mitscher had no inkling of the purpose of his visit. Duncan came aboard *Hornet* on the afternoon of the next day, February 1, and got right to the point.

"Pete, can you put a loaded B-25 in the air on a normal deck run?" (The B-25 Mitchell was a twin-engine army bomber.)

Mitscher replied, "How many B-25s on deck?"

"Fifteen," Duncan replied.

Mitscher turned to his spotting board, a small-scale replica of *Hornet*'s flight deck, and calculated the possible arrangement of the medium bombers, which unlike carrier aircraft did not have folding wings. The largest navy carrier planes had a wingspan of 40 feet. The army planes had wingspans of 67 feet and were 53 feet long. Ironically, the B-25 was named for General William A. "Billy" Mitchell, a fierce opponent of carrier aviation.

"Yes, it can be done," Mitscher said.

"Good," Duncan said, "I'm putting two aboard for a test launching tomorrow."

The laconic Mitscher asked no questions as to why *Hornet* should carry army bombers aboard.

The next day, two B-25s were lifted aboard; Mitscher spotted one on the after part of the flight deck, while the second bomber was placed in the position from which it would take off when the other planes were in place. On February 2, *Hornet* steamed into Chesapeake Bay and through the Virginia Capes into the Atlantic. Normally, Mitscher figured a B-25 needed 1,200 to 1,500 feet of runway to take off. *Hornet's* deck was 780 feet long, so the bombers had little more than half that deck length to get airborne.

In the early afternoon, in near-freezing weather, Captains Mitscher and Duncan wore heavy weather gear on *Hornet's* bridge. Earlier in Washington, Duncan told Admiral King he thought that *Hornet* could successfully launch a B-25, but he wanted to see it done by Pete Mitscher.

Captain Mitscher ordered *Hornet* to be turned into the bitter, wet wind, followed by two destroyers acting as plane guards. *Hornet* was making more than 30 knots, and that speed together with the wind over the deck provided the lift needed. The first B-25, with an army pilot at the controls, revved up to full power. The chocks were pulled, and the bomber charged down *Hornet's* empty deck and rose into the air with space to spare. Mitscher smiled at Duncan. Their estimates had been correct. The second B-25 soon followed. Skipper Mitscher ordered *Hornet* back to Norfolk. Captain Duncan left for Washington to report.

Mitscher was still mystified by the experiment. He discussed the operation with his senior officers: Executive Officer George R. Henderson, who held seaplane flying records; Air Officer Apollo Soucek, who set a world altitude record for aircraft; and Navigator Frank Akers, the first pilot to make a blind landing aboard a carrier. Captain Duncan had said the tests were to determine the takeoff capabilities of the B-25, but that could have been established ashore. Mitscher was annoyed Duncan hadn't told him more in confidence. But Pete suggested to his officers that "the less you know, the better."

Unknown to Mitscher, Captain Duncan was supervising land tests with the B-25 at Eglin Field in the pine barrens of the Florida Panhandle. The training was conducted by a top-notch carrier pilot, Lieutenant Henry L. "Hank" Miller, from the nearby Pensacola Naval Air Station. A space the size of *Hornet's* deck had been parceled out at the base, with a volunteer squadron of B-25 pilots practicing short-runway takeoffs in the allotted length.

When Lieutenant Miller showed up at Eglin, he was asked, "Have you ever flown a B-25?"

"I've never ever seen one," Miller replied.

Miller quickly set about showing the army pilots the technique for a short takeoff from a carrier's deck length from his copilot's seat in the bomber. Among Hank Miller's students was Lieutenant Colonel James "Jimmy" Doolittle, one of America's top racing pilots in the 1930s who was an oil company executive and a reserve officer called into active service in 1940. The forty-five-year-old Jimmy Doolittle headed the all-volunteer squadron, selected from the 17th Bombardment Group. When Doolittle asked his group for volunteers for a hazardous mission, all stepped forward. Jimmy Doolittle picked twenty-four crews for sixteen planes.

Meanwhile, Admiral King alerted Admiral Chester W. Nimitz, Commander in Chief, Pacific Fleet (CinCPac), that he was dispatching Captain Duncan to discuss a top-secret project of high national importance. When Admiral Nimitz learned that the project involved carriers, he summoned Vice Admiral Halsey, the senior carrier flag officer in the Pacific. The colorful Halsey, at a robust age of fifty-nine, flew his flag aboard USS *Enterprise*, the famed "Big E." He reported to Nimitz's headquarters for a conference with Captain Wu Duncan.

Admiral King's Washington emissary spelled it out. President Franklin D. Roosevelt and Admiral King were anxious to launch a dramatic attack against Japan to retaliate for Pearl Harbor and boost American morale. Captain Duncan and another senior planner, Captain Francis B. Low, came up with idea of bombing Tokyo with the longer-range army B-25s from an aircraft carrier. It would be a one-way trip; since the bombers could not land on the carrier deck, they would have to fly to airfields in China. Some high-level officers called it a suicide mission. Others objected that it was a waste of planes, and a precious carrier would be diverted from other offensive operations for what amounted to no more than a publicity stunt.

But seventy officers and 130 airmen volunteered to fly and service the bombers. The B-25s would take up the after flight deck, with room for sixteen. *Hornet's* own planes would have to be stowed on the hanger deck, which meant another carrier would be necessary to provide air support for the task force. *Yorktown* and *Lexington* were busy in the South Pacific. Only the Big E was available. That was why Halsey was summoned.

Nimitz asked Halsey, "Do you think it would work, Bill?"

"They'll need a lot of luck."

"Are you willing to take them out there?"

"Yes, I am."

"Good," Nimitz said, "It's all yours."

Captain Duncan sent a dispatch to General Henry H. "Hap" Arnold, head of the Army Air Forces: "Tell Jimmy to get on his horse."

Doolittle began moving his squadron from Florida to California. He himself flew to San Francisco for a meeting with Vice Admiral Halsey and Captain Duncan to discuss the operation in Halsey's room at the Fairmont Hotel. Halsey was aware of the severe risks Doolittle's men would be facing, and how bleak their chances were of surviving. Doolittle, too, recognized the danger to the task force: putting in jeopardy two out of the four U.S. carriers in the Pacific, as well as fourteen other ships and the lives of several thousand sailors, including three of the best—Halsey, Mitscher, and Rear Admiral Raymond A. Spruance (age fifty-five), who would command the cruiser screen.

Bill Halsey, Jimmy Doolittle, and Wu Duncan agreed that the *Enterprise* and *Hornet* groups would meet at sea, steam to within 500 miles of the Japanese coast, and launch the B-25s at dusk for a night attack on Tokyo. If enemy warships discovered the task force en route, it would have to dump the B-25s overboard to free the flight deck for *Hornet's* own fighters. Halsey and Doolittle shook hands. The admiral prepared to return to Pearl Harbor. The colonel rejoined the B-25 squadron, now at McClellan Field near Sacramento, for a flight to the Alameda Naval Air Station, across the bay from San Francisco. Navy Lieutenant Hank Miller suggested to Colonel Doolittle that he come along in an extra B-25 and fly it off *Hornet* 100 miles offshore, just to show that a pilot with less B-25 time than anyone else could get the bomber off a carrier. Doolittle agreed.

Meantime, *Hornet* had transited the Panama Canal and had been tied up at San Diego to give additional training to the carrier pilots. Captain Duncan boarded *Hornet* at the North Island Naval Air Station and again consulted Captain Mitscher, who closed the door to his cabin.

"Pete," Duncan said, "you're going to take Jimmy Doolittle and fifteen army bombers to hit Tokyo."

"That's fine," the laconic Mitscher replied.

On March 31, *Hornet* docked at the Alameda Naval Air Station. Sixteen B-25s were hoisted aboard by crane. The bombers were lashed down on *Hornet*'s flight deck. Mitscher let the rumor spread that the planes were simply being transported to Pearl Harbor to beef up the Army Air Forces over there.

Early on the morning of April 2, *Hornet*, in company with the cruisers *Vincennes* and *Nashville*, the oiler *Cimarron*, and the ships of Destroyer Division 22, sailed through the Golden Gate. When *Hornet* cleared the Golden Gate and California began to recede in the distance, Pete Mitscher announced over the carrier's loudspeaker system: "This ship will carry the army bombers to the coast of Japan for the bombing of Tokyo."

A cheer greeted the announcement broadcasted on the *Hornet*'s blinker to the escorting ships.

On the flight deck, Doolittle asked Miller, "Well, Hank, how does it look to you?"

"This is a breeze," Miller said.

"Let's get up in the airplane and look," Doolittle said.

Doolittle got into the pilot's seat with Miller next to him in the copilot's position. There was about 500 feet forward for takeoff.

"This looks like a short distance," the colonel said.

"You see where that toolkit is way up the deck by the island structure?"

"Yes."

"That's where I used to take off in fighters on *Saratoga* and *Lexington*."

"Henry, what name do they use in the navy for bullshit?"

Back on deck, Captain Pete Mitscher wondered whether he could get Miller enough wind over the deck for his flight back home that afternoon.

"We've got plenty of wind, Captain," Miller said. "We won't have any bombs, and it'll be lighter than the other planes. I taught these guys how to take off in 300 feet, and I'll have about 395 feet to take this one off."

"Well, hell," Mitscher said, "then we'll take this extra plane."

Mitscher called Doolittle to the bridge and suggested saving the extra plane for the Tokyo mission. Doolittle was leery, believing a demonstration takeoff would improve his pilots' morale.

Mitscher argued, "They've got to fly them all off anyway, no matter whether this one takes off or not. This way, you've got an extra plane."

"Suits me," Doolittle said. The plane stayed aboard, and sixteen rather than fifteen planes were scheduled to raid Japan.

On April 13, *Hornet's* group linked up with Halsey's *Enterprise* force northwest of the Hawaiian Islands, which was escorted by the ebullient Captain Richard L. "Dick" Conolly, commodore of Destroyer Squadron 6 in *Balch*.

Early on April 16, the bombers were re-spotted aft of *Hornet's* island, with the rear planes, tails hanging over the ship's stern. On April 17, approximately 1,000 miles from Japan, the oilers topped off the carriers, and the tankers and destroyers, slowed down by rough seas, were left behind as the carriers and cruisers made a high-speed run toward Japan. According to the plan, *Hornet* would launch the Doolittle force 500 miles from Japan's coast on the afternoon of April 18. The main attack force would head for Tokyo, with individual bombers assigned to hit the cities of Yokohama, Nagoya, Osaka, and Kobe. The task force [it was the bombers, not the task force] would then cross the Sea of Japan, head for China, and try to get far enough inland on empty gas tanks to land at friendly airfields.

On April 17, Doolittle called a meeting of his eighty fliers who would make the trip to go over the plan.

"If all goes well, I'll take off so as to arrive over Tokyo at dusk. The rest of you will take off later and can use my fires as a homing beacon."

"Colonel," a pilot said, "what should we do if we lose an engine or something else goes wrong and we have to crash-land in Japan?"

Doolittle replied that it was an individual decision. He himself did not intend to be taken prisoner.

"If my plane is crippled beyond possibility of fighting or escape, I'm going to bail out my crew and then dive it, full throttle, into any target I can find that will do the most damage." He gave his men a final chance to back out of the hazardous mission. None did.

The plan changed suddenly on the morning of April 18, when the task force was spotted by Japanese picket boats, less than 700 miles from the Japanese coast, and steaming west. Surprise was presumed lost. Admiral Halsey could not risk his precious carriers to move much closer. He flashed a message to Pete Mitscher on *Hornet*: "Launch planes. To Colonel Doolittle and Gallant Command: Good luck and God bless you. Halsey."

On *Hornet*'s bridge, Doolittle shook hands with Mitscher and dashed below, declaring, "OK, fellas, this is it! Let's go!" *Hornet*'s loudspeaker blared, "Army pilots, man your planes!"

Mitscher turned *Hornet* steaming at 22 knots into the 18-knot wind, making a 40-knot headwind along the deck. The rough sea kicked up 30-foot waves. Spray drenched the flight deck on a gray day with intermittent rainsqualls. The pilots had planned to attack under the cover of night. Now they would arrive over the target in full daylight, with only darkness awaiting them in China. *Hornet* was now some 620 miles from Japan, which meant that the B-25s would have to fly longer to reach China and hope to find a friendly landing place.

Lieutenant Hank Miller worried. He had taught the army pilots to take off from a carrier, but now the deck was moving sharply up and down in the seas. Would they go through with it? To help the pilots, they would be started down the deck when the ship was in a trough, thus reaching the take-off point when the ship's bow headed up.

In the first plane, Doolittle waved goodbye. Mitscher saluted him. Doolittle revved the engines to a scream, released the brakes, and trundled down the deck, fighting to get into the air. He made it with yards to spare. He circled *Hornet* once and headed for Tokyo. The other planes took off at 4-minute intervals and, wasting no gas-consuming time getting into formation, each headed independently toward Japan.

"The wind and sea were so strong that green water was breaking over the carrier's ramps," Halsey said. "Jimmy led his squadron off. When his plane buzzed down *Hornet*'s deck, there wasn't a man topside in the task force who didn't help sweat him into the air."

All unaccompanied sixteen B-25s got off safely, and Halsey headed back toward Pearl Harbor with *Hornet* and *Enterprise*. Most of the Mitchell bombers flew over Tokyo around noon and aimed at military targets. Three other Mitchells dropped incendiary bombs on Nagoya, Osaka, and Kobe. None of the planes was lost over Japan. One crew landed in Vladivostok and was interned. Fifteen planes flew to China: four made crash landings; crews of eleven others parachuted into the night. One crewman was killed bailing out; four drowned; and eight men were captured, three of whom were executed and one died in prison. So seventy-one of the eighty fliers, including Jimmy Doolittle, survived the raid. Colonel Doolittle was awarded the Medal of Honor and promoted to brigadier general.

"In my opinion," Halsey said, "their flight was one of the most courageous deeds in all military history."

At the time, the U.S. Navy was given little credit for its central role in the Tokyo attack. Because of wartime secrecy, the source of the bombers was not disclosed. When warned that reporters would ask where the raid came from, the president said, "Tell them Shangri-La," after the fictional Tibetan city in the popular novel and movie, *Lost Horizon*. Roosevelt had given the name to his new hideaway in Maryland's Catoctin Mountain. In 1944, the navy commissioned a new fast carrier with the unusual name: *Shangri-La*.

The Tokyo raid fortuitously brought together four naval officers who would become among the foremost of the U.S. Navy's fighting admirals of the war: Bill Halsey, Raymond Spruance, Pete Mitscher, and Dick Conolly.

Two

THE EDUCATION
OF AN ADMIRAL

1900–1930

The name admiral dates back a thousand years, derived from the Arabic, *amir-al-bahr*, or lord of the sea, which worked its way into several other languages with little change. An admiral is the commander of a group of warships that can have anywhere from two battleships to four cruisers to a vast fleet. It is also a rank held by senior naval officers ashore, directing various operations, departments, and bases. Admirals fly their personal flags—white stars on a blue field—hence the expression "flag officers" and "flagships" for their vessels. Reaching flag rank is the apex of a naval officer's career, whether a two-star rear admiral, a three-star vice admiral, or the exalted four-star full admiral.

The American admirals who fought World War II were all products of the U.S. Naval Academy at Annapolis, Maryland. The Academy's campus, known as "the Yard," is graced by wide lawns, shade trees, and parade grounds on a promontory in the Maryland capital, where the Severn River empties into Chesapeake Bay. Then, Annapolis was a sleepy southern community known to the midshipmen, or "middies," as "Crabtown."

World War II's senior admirals graduated from Annapolis in 1900 to 1910; more junior admirals in the war were mainly in the graduating classes of 1911 to 1920. For example: Ernest King was in the Class of 1901; Bill Halsey, 1904; Chester Nimitz, 1905; Raymond Spruance, 1907; Pete Mitscher, 1910; and Dick Conolly, 1914.

The World War II admirals beginning their careers as Naval Academy midshipmen, usually at seventeen or eighteen, entered at a propitious time. It was the golden age of American sea power, when President Theodore Roosevelt was expanding the navy with warships, and officers and seamen to man them. Many buildings were added to the Naval Academy during this period. This renaissance fitted in with the Academy's motto, *Ex Scientia Tridens*, or From Knowledge, Sea Power. The expanding fleet's need for junior officers was such that the Classes of 1903 through 1906 graduated in the middle of their last year.

The fresh-faced middies shared experiences, training, and education. Most were from a broad spectrum of middle-class American society. They were appointed by congressmen from every state in the Union. The freshmen, or "plebes," were often given nicknames at the Academy, many of an esoteric nature. Some stuck throughout their naval carrier, like "Pete" Mitscher, named after a fellow Oklahoma plebe who bilged out; and "Wu" Duncan named after a play he saw as a midshipman in London called "Mr. Wu"; and Harold "Betty" Stark, for the wife of a general who happened to be in the news at the time. Other nicknames were soon dropped.

Entering-plebe classes ranged from 100 to 250 with graduates numbering about 70 to 200 as the size of the student body grew. Looking ahead, the midshipmen hoped to ascend the naval officer ladder step by step: ensign, lieutenant junior grade, lieutenant, lieutenant commander, commander, captain, commodore, and the grades of admiral. The competition was fierce, as the promotion pyramid narrowed sharply in the upper ranks, and only a few midshipmen would ascend to make flag rank.

In the navy, Annapolis students either personally knew or were aware of their classmates and many other midshipmen, particularly high flyers. In the early 1900s, there were rarely more than 700 midshipmen at the Naval Academy. Again and again, senior officers would refer to another officer as "a classmate," or "a class above of me" or "a class below me" at the Naval Academy.

During his four years at Annapolis, young Chester Nimitz numbered among his fellow midshipmen: Bill Halsey, Harold Stark, Husband E. Kimmel, Royal Ingersoll, Robert L. Ghormley, Frank Jack Fletcher, Raymond Spruance, Jack Towers, Herbert Fairfax Leary, Milo F. Draemel, Isaac C. "Ike" Kidd, John S. "Slew" McCain, Aubrey W. "Jake" Fitch, Thomas C. Kinkaid, Wilson Brown Jr., H. Kent Hewitt, and Richmond Kelly Turner—all of whom would play leading roles as admirals thirty-five years later.

So flag officers were not normally strangers to one another; over the years they had become aware of each other's reputations, of their strengths and weaknesses, reputed or otherwise. And coming from the same stratum of society, they mainly held the same values—a respect for tradition and a sense of their own place in the firmament.

Because of the process of appointment, they came from every state: Chester Nimitz haled from Fredericksburg, Texas; Ernest King from Marion, Ohio; Raymond Spruance, born in Baltimore, Maryland, and brought up in Indianapolis, Indiana; Richmond Kelly Turner, born in Oregon and raised in California; Jake Fitch from Michigan; Bill Halsey, a navy brat born in Massachusetts; Dick Conolly from Illinois; Willis A. "Ching" Lee from Kentucky; Jack Towers from Georgia; and Arleigh Burke from Colorado. Throughout their careers, they were part of a tight officer corps within the larger American society.

At the Naval Academy, midshipmen followed the same curriculum, which was based heavily on engineering-oriented studies. They were taught math, physics, ordnance and gunnery, navigation, seamanship, and English literature, with the only elective being modern languages. They read texts like Dandell's *Principles of Physics*, Slades' *Lessons in Applied Mechanics*, and Genung's *Outlines of Rhetoric*. The Academy had an intense course in naval history. The ratio of naval officers to civilian instructors was roughly two to one, and assignment to the Naval Academy as a teacher was considered a choice shore assignment for an ambitious officer.

The navy also attached a measure of importance to the training of midshipmen. Tom Kinkaid of the Class of 1908, for instance, was taught as a midshipman by four future Chiefs of Naval Operations (CNO) and four further commanders of the U.S. Fleet. Generally speaking, most midshipmen studied hard. They knew their rank in class determined seniority on graduation—their signal number. Whenever officers of the same rank and class were together, the man with the higher signal number would automatically assume command, being senior. Seniority played a critical role in the selection for higher rank in peacetime, a method of selection which was not always the best.

In naval history courses, midshipmen studied the careers and tactics of history's great fighting admirals. They learned how Sir Francis Drake and Sir John Hawkins defeated the Spanish Armada in 1588, and the exploits of Admiral Robert Blake in fighting Dutch Admiral Maarten

Tromp, and how Holland's Michiel de Ruyter turned the tables by defeating the English in the Thames Estuary.

In the eighteenth century, the premier English fighting admiral was Edward Hawke, who commanded the future admirals Charles Saunders, George Rodney, and Philip Saumarez. France's Pierre Andre de Suffren de Saint Tropez was a superb tactician and defeated the English in the Indian Ocean. The students learned of the fate of the hapless British Admiral John Byng, unfairly court-martialed for cowardice against the French and shot by firing squad. This travesty led the French philosopher Voltaire to comment dryly that the British thought it necessary to execute an admiral from time to time "to encourage the others."

The midshipmen studied the naval tactics of the days of fighting sail, culminating in the superb exploits of Admiral Horatio Nelson. Nelson was the victor in four great battles: Cape St. Vincent off Portugal; the Nile in Aboukir Bay; Copenhagen; and Cape Trafalgar, off the Spanish Atlantic coast. A slight, fragile figure, Nelson lost an arm and an eye during his stellar career, and finally his life at the zenith of his success, the victory of the Battle of Trafalgar in 1805 against the French and Spanish fleets. His naval philosophy could be summed up in his dictum: "No captain can do very wrong if he places his ship alongside that of an enemy."

The "Nelson" touch became a template for a successful admiral. Nelson treated every problem with a fresh look at the specific situation, casting aside traditional rules. He placed responsibility and trust in his senior officers, and gave them leeway to use their judgment and make snap decisions. He confided in his captains before battles, making sure everyone knew what he expected. Since they knew his mind, a minimum of signaling was needed, so much so that when Admiral Cuthbert Collingwood, Nelson's second in command, saw the flagship *Victory* raising the famous flag hoist, "England expects every man to do his duty," he grumbled, "I wish Nelson would stop signaling. We know well enough what to do." Actually, Nelson wished to make the signal "Nelson confides . . .," but that would have necessitated additional flags, and Nelson was advised to go with the simpler, less personal version.

Nelson imbued his officers and men with fighting spirit. He showed concern for his crews whose Hobbesian lives were often nasty, brutish, and short. In turn, Nelson's sailors loved him. Novelist Joseph Conrad, who knew as much about the sea as anyone, said, "In a few short years, he revolutionized not the strategy or tactics of sea warfare, but the very conception of victory itself. He brought heroism into the line of duty."

Annapolis students were steeped in the history of the American navy, from Revolutionary War days to the victories of the Spanish-American War. While the early American navy fought mostly small unit actions rather than fleet actions, the words and deeds of famous captains and commodores were inscribed in various halls at the Naval Academy.

"I want nothing to do with a ship that will not sail fast, for I mean to go in harm's way," the hot-tempered John Paul Jones informed his superiors. From his badly damaged ship, *Bonhomme Richard*, Jones declared, "I have not yet begun to fight," before conquering the English *Serapis* in sight of the English shore. Commodores John Barry and Thomas Truxton defeated French privateers in the Caribbean. Later, Commodores Edward Preble, Stephen Decatur, and William Bainbridge fought the Barbary pirates in the Mediterranean. In the War of 1812, Commodore Oliver Hazard Perry sent his short message after the Battle of Lake Eire: "We have met the enemy and they are ours." In the same conflict, Captain James Lawrence, as he lay mortally wounded aboard *Chesapeake*, pleaded, "Don't give up the ship."

Commodore Charles Stewart was a brilliant seaman whose career spanned sixty-two years, as a fighting captain and leader of men. He supported young and able officers like David Glasgow Farragut and Uriah Levy, who would become the first Jewish commodore in the American navy and strived to abolish flogging as a routine punishment.

In the Civil War, the outstanding admiral was the Union's David Farragut, who blockaded New Orleans. In the Battle of Mobile Bay, from his flagship *Hartford*, he ordered his ships: "Damn the torpedoes [mines]. Full speed ahead!" He was assisted by the equally competent Admiral David D. Porter, who served in the Mississippi River and in the final phase of the war on the Chesapeake Bay. Porter commanded a fleet of more than sixty ships, the largest to date in U.S. history. With the introduction of the ironclad ships—which were used in the inconclusive duel of the Union's *Monitor* and the Confederate's *Merrimack* on Chesapeake Bay—the historic shift began from wooden ships and canvas sails to steel ships with steam engines and explosive shells. The age of fighting sail was ending.

During the Spanish-American War, the American naval hero was Commodore George Dewey, who commanded the U.S. Asiatic Fleet.

Dewey trained his ships and sailors well. When war was declared between the United States and Spain, Dewey sailed into Manila Bay in 1898 and inflicted a devastating defeat on the Spanish fleet, led by Admiral Patricio Montojo y Pasaron. Dewey began the fateful battle— which would see the Philippines ceded to the United States—with these words to his flagship's captain: "You may fire when you are ready, Captain Gridley." All twenty-five Spanish warships were sunk or captured. The American navy lost not one man. Dewey was feted as a national hero and promoted to full admiral.

Of special interest to midshipmen was another battle in the Spanish-American War, which led to lasting recriminations. Admiral William Sampson commanded the U.S. blockading forces off the Cuban port of Santiago in May and June 1898, and devised the strategy for dealing with the Spanish fleet, under Admiral Pascual Cervera y Topete. When the Spaniards finally sortied from the harbor, Sampson was briefly away, meeting with the U.S. Army commander. In the pursuit of the Spanish ships, Sampson's second in command, Commodore Winfield Scott Schley, was technically in command aboard *Brooklyn*. But he gave few orders in the chase, and it was never clear what role he actually played in the eventual victorious battle. At first, Schley was given credit. Sampson arrived soon after, and later commanded the successful capture of Guantanamo Bay.

For obscure reasons, a running argument ensued between the supporters of the two naval commanders over credit for the victory at Santiago. The Naval Academy in the early twentieth century saw that controversy fueled by publication of the third volume of Edgar S. Maclay's *History of the United States Navy*, a standard text at Annapolis. Maclay charged that Schley lost his nerve at Santiago and never actually led the U.S. ships in pursuit of the Spanish. The rancorous debate did little for the prestige of the U.S. Navy or the participants.

The unsavory incident left a lasting impression among the Academy graduates of that era. In later years, U.S. flag officers, not wishing to get into public arguments with contemporaries, cited the Sampson-Schley feud as a prime example of what should be avoided— in the navy's interest. This caution, according to naval historians, tended to carry over into the memoirs of World War II admirals. Chester Nimitz, for one, vowed that he would never participate in washing the navy's dirty linen in public.

The Annapolis students noted the rise of Japanese naval power in studying the May 27, 1905, Battle of Tsushima Strait, where a Japanese force under Admiral Heihachiro Togo "crossed the T" of a Russian force heading for Vladivostok—after steaming halfway around the world from St. Petersburg. This was a classic maneuver, also called "capping the T," where the Togo force turned broadside to the oncoming Russians. Thus, the Japanese ships could train all their turrets on the approaching enemy, while the Russians were confined to firing only their forward guns. Furthermore, the forward guns of the rearward ships were masked by the vessels ahead and nullified. Admiral Togo sank or captured almost all of the thirty-eight-ship Russian fleet, headed by Admiral Zinovy Rozhestvensky, and the victory ensured Japanese hegemony in the northeastern Pacific. Japan would become the most obvious rival of the United States in the Pacific.

With the commissioning of HMS *Dreadnought* in 1906, the Annapolis students witnessed the introduction of the big-gunned capital ship, which would guide naval thinking in the years to come. *Dreadnought* mounted ten 12-inch guns with an 11-inch armor belt and was capable of making 21 knots with new steam turbines. The powerful *Dreadnought* gave her name to an entire class of capital ships and was quickly emulated by the Americans, French, Italians, Germans, and Japanese. Overnight, existing battleships were obsolete and the *Dreadnought* design became standard for all the world's navies.

The Annapolis midshipmen were introduced to theoretical writings on naval strategy by one of their own, Captain Albert Thayer Mahan, Class of 1859. Mahan served as a young officer aboard blockading ships during the Civil War. He later wrote on naval history and strategy, including the seminal *The Influence of Sea Power on History* in 1890. Mahan became the navy's most eminent historian. His works stressed the paramount importance of sea power in establishing national supremacy. He also emphasized—some strategists thought wrongly—battleship strength and significance, and he underplayed the role of anti-commerce warfare and amphibious operations. Some close followers of Mahan's teaching in future years became blinkered, applying lessons of the past that did not relate to the changing nature of naval warfare. A remark attributed to Henry L. Stimson, President Taft's secretary of war (and again secretary of war in World War II), referred to "the peculiar psychology of the Navy Department, which frequently seemed to retire from the realm of logic into a dim, religious world in which Neptune was god, Mahan his prophet, and the U.S. Navy the only true church."

The Annapolis graduates of the Classes of 1900–1919 saw sea duty before the lessons of World War I could be absorbed. By the time of World War I, most of those who later became senior officers of World War II were serving in the fleet; some were assigned to warships that participated in convoy duty and other naval activities based in the British Isles. No major fleet actions were fought after America's entry into the war.

The careers of American navy line officers between the wars followed the same rough progression. New ensigns generally were assigned to capital ships—battleships and heavy cruisers. In the U.S. Navy of the first third of the twentieth century, these were considered the most desirable assignments since big-ship duty was thought to enhance career prospects for ambitious officers. The battleship was the queen of battles, the battle line, the fighting core of the navy. Naval aviation was still in its infancy, still an unknown element.

In higher circles, submarine duty was scorned as the "hooligan navy," tiny boats with grimy conditions. The spit and polish of the capital ships was the order of the day. Most officers were then assigned a tour of destroyer duty. With all its dash and élan, though, destroyers were thought not quite mainstream navy, but simply escorts to the big boys, the battleships, and cruisers. Along the way, the officers picked up the slang terminology for warships: battleships were "battlewagons," or simply "wagons"; carriers—when they came into service—were "flattops"; destroyers were "tin cans," or "cans"; and submarines were "boats."

After a couple of tours at sea, young officers could volunteer to qualify as naval aviators or submariners. Sea duty alternated with shore assignments as an officer moved up the ladder in seniority and experience: commanding destroyers, becoming executive officers of battleships or cruisers, and eventually commanding a capital ship. The command of a battleship or cruiser was considered essential for selection to rear admiral.

Admiral Spruance's career, for example, might be considered typical after graduation in 1906: the old battleships *Iowa* and *Minnesota* as an ensign; instruction in electrical engineering in Schenectady, New York; the battleship *Connecticut*; senior engineer of cruiser *Cincinnati* as a lieutenant junior grade; command of old destroyer *Bainbridge*; electrical officer of battleship *Pennsylvania* as a full lieutenant; assistant engineer officer at New

York Navy Yard as lieutenant commander; executive officer of troop transport *Agamemnon* as a commander; captain of destroyers *Aaron Ward* and *Percival*; head of the electrical division at the Bureau of Engineering; assistant chief of staff to Commander U.S. Naval Forces in Europe; executive officer of the battleship *Mississippi*; chief of staff to Commander Destroyers Scouting Force; and commanding officer of battleship *Mississippi* as a captain. Promotion was slow in peacetime.

Early on, some officers seemed to show potential for high rank. Bill Halsey, an expert ship-handler, was the highly popular, highly colorful commander of the destroyer *Osborne* in the early 1920s in the Mediterranean. His ships, and later his division of tin cans, were always top rated. The high-spirited Halsey was due to be relieved in *Osborne* by low-geared Raymond Spruance. Halsey warned his officers not to be deceived by Spruance's quiet manner, for there was no more capable commanding officer. As a result, Spruance commanded the outstanding destroyer in Halsey's outstanding division of the outstanding destroyer squadron in the Pacific Fleet. Halsey and Spruance, despite the marked differences in personality and leadership style, became fast friends for life.

The officers soon learned that Spruance preferred a "quiet" bridge; he addressed the officers by their last names rather than their first, as was Halsey's practice. Spruance soon achieved a quiet bridge, where there was no superfluous chatter. He gave quick, clear orders. His officers knew what was expected of them. Once in the harbor of Bizerte in French Tunisia, *Osborne* was anchored in 6 fathoms, or 36 feet, of water. A distraught torpedo officer rushed to the bridge and reported, "Captain, we've just dropped a depth charge over the stern!"

"Well, pick it up and put it back," was Spruance's measured response.

The crew safely recovered the charge, thereby avoiding what could have been an embarrassing international incident.

Where Raymond Spruance's career differed from his contemporaries was the three tours, rather than one, at the Naval War College, first as a student and later faculty member. The prestigious Naval War College was an important career stepping stone to flag rank. This was where aspiring senior officers shifted into high gear. This was the finishing school for prospective admirals.

Three
NAVAL WAR COLLEGE

The Naval War College is the U.S. Navy's institution of advanced tactical and strategic thinking, located on a beautiful site on Coasters Harbor Island in Narragansett Bay in Newport, Rhode Island. The primary mission of the Naval War College is to prepare officers, intellectually and practically, for higher command—in effect to exercise flag rank. The Naval War College was founded in 1884 by Commodore Stephen B. Luce to develop naval philosophy, which would include tactics and strategy. Its motto is: *Viribus Mari Victoria*, or Victory through Strength at Sea.

From the first, the Naval War College held a controversial place in the navy, characterized by running arguments about its role and curriculum. Some senior officers questioned its very existence on the grounds that officers could better learn their trade at sea. When Admiral Mahan, who would join the teaching staff, first asked for shore duty to write a book, he was told that a naval officer's duty was aboard a ship.

In the 1920s and 1930s, after many changes in emphasis, the length of the courses, and the size of the student body, the institution settled on both junior and senior courses. So officers entered at various ages and levels of rank for a ten-month program. Most found the experience valuable; it gave them time to study and to think about the art of war. They read Carl von Clausewitz's *On War*, Admiral Mahan's works (particularly the ramifications of his dictum Communications dominate war), and Sir Julian Corbett's *Some Principles of Maritime Strategy* on the philosophy and conduct of war. They studied naval history, maritime law, and communications and logistics. They distilled their knowledge in tactical and strategic problems worked out on a huge war games board on the upper floor of Luce Hall. These war games were the essence of the Naval War College experience.

The principal naval battle studied closely was the Battle of Jutland, the World War I engagement that pitted the British Grand Fleet against the German High Seas Fleet in the North Sea off Denmark's Jutland area. Admiral Nimitz said that as a student he learned Jutland by heart. The sprawling battle was waged over two days, May 31–June 1, 1916, and involved the largest number of warships in history; the British deployed 148 ships with sixty thousand men; the Germans some hundred ships with forty-five thousand sailors.

The British battle fleet was led by Admiral Sir John Jellicoe, a competent, highly respected, and admired officer. Jellicoe was short and with a prominent nose and weathered face. He looked unprepossessing. He was also cautious, as befitted an officer with the major responsibility for keeping the German fleet at bay. Jellicoe's battle cruiser squadron was commanded by the dashing, impetuous Vice Amiral David Beatty, a handsome daredevil who tilted his admiral's hat at a rakish angle. Beatty had developed a reputation as a hell-for-leather flag officer who was aggressive and fearless in action. He caught the attention of the British press, which characterized him as a modern Nelson.

The Germans were headed by Admiral Reinhard Scheer, a schoolmaster's son who was a torpedo specialist and had developed an enviable reputation as an alert, confident tactician in the German Imperial Navy. His battleships were preceded by a scouting force of battle cruisers, commanded by Vice Admiral Erich Hipper, David Beatty's counterpart. Hipper was an offensive-minded admiral, who had sought ways to engage part of the British fleet without getting his lighter ships caught by the bigger British Grand Fleet battleships.

The Germans sortied initially, hoping to lure a part of the British fleet into battle, rather than seeking a full-scale action. They had vainly stationed U-boats off British naval harbors to ambush enemy warships. Admiral Beatty sighted Hipper's battle cruisers first in the afternoon. Both squadrons opened fire and Beatty pursued Hipper, who turned back toward the German battleships with Scheer. Superior German gunnery quickly sank lightly armored *Queen Mary* and *Indefatigable*, and badly damaged Beatty's flagship *Lion*. This prompted Beatty's trenchant comment on his bridge, "There seems to be something wrong with our bloody ships today."

Beatty failed to inform Admiral Jellicoe of the enemy's whereabouts as he pursued them. He also failed to properly signal four battleships assigned to him to follow his lead. Then, Beatty's force spotted the German main body, and reversed course, planning to lead Scheer's battleships into the oncoming guns of Jellicoe. Finally, Jellicoe was apprised of the enemy's presence and location and joined the battle with a superior tactical position. The Germans were heading Jellicoe's way, and he turned his fleet to cross the T and commenced firing. But the Germans rapidly reversed course and shot their way out of a potential trap. Then Admiral Scheer, for reasons he never made clear, decided to attack again and turned back toward Jellicoe, who was still in position to cap Scheer's T. Once again, Admiral Scheer turned away but sent his destroyers to launch torpedoes. Jellicoe swung his ships away from the deadly war fish to thread them—as current fleet doctrine prescribed—thereby missing the chance to engage the German battleships.

Before the British fleet could reform, smoke from 250 ships, swirling thick mists, and gunpowder obscured the main bodies of both fleets, foreclosing decisive action. During the night, both formations steamed on parallel southerly courses, though the admirals did not know it. Disgracefully poor and misleading radio communications from the British Admiralty, and difficulty in signaling between his ships, left Admiral Jellicoe with little tactical information. The Germans made good their retirement to homeports.

In the sporadic fierce fighting, the British lost three battle cruisers, three cruisers, and eight destroyers, as well as 6,097 sailors. The Germans lost a battleship, a battle cruiser, four cruisers, five destroyers, and 2,551 men. Both sides claimed victory; the Germans tactically because they sank more ships and their seamanship and gunnery were superior; the British strategically because they retained control of the North Sea and the Germans never again sortied in serious force. As one newspaper summarized, "The German fleet has assaulted its jailor, but it is still in jail."

At the Naval War College, lecturers stressed the lessons of Jutland: the messy communications in handling large formations of warships; the breakdown of contact with the admiralty; the lack of night fighting capability; the poor visibility caused by mist and smoke; the vulnerability of lightly armored battle cruisers; and the cautious performance of several of the admirals. Jutland exposed weaknesses in the seniority promotion system. Officers were promoted by age and their abilities in ship-handling, navigation, and gunnery, rather than on command, tactical, and communication skills.

Jellicoe was criticized for caution, for turning away from the German torpedo attack, and for losing contact. Winston Churchill maintained that Jellicoe was "the only man on either side who could lose the war in an afternoon." It was, however, difficult for Jellicoe to exercise taut command and control, given the number of ships, the violent maneuvers, the poor visibility, and the lack of information. At one point, an armored cruiser force, under Rear Admiral Sir Robert Arbuthnot, spotted the disabled German cruiser *Wiesbaden* and heedlessly cut across Beatty's formation. Beatty had to make an emergency turn in *Lion* to avoid a collision. Arbuthnot's flagship *Defence* was hit and her magazines exploded, killing the admiral and almost all of the nine-hundred–man crew. His action was called "berserk," and historian Andrew Gordon wrote, "While center stage should have been clearing for the leading contenders to engage, here was a supporting actor, getting in the way and babbling his own nonsensical lines."

For his role, Beatty was faulted for his rashness and failure to notify his senior officer of his actions and the location of the enemy, which was the primary task of the battle cruiser squadron. After the Battle of Jutland, the adherents of Admirals Jellicoe and Beatty argued heatedly over who deserved the most credit—or blame. Beatty's audacious style seemed to win popular approval, while Jellicoe's performance won the favor of most senior officers and later historians. As one historian, Cyril Falls, put it of Jellicoe's role: "He fought to make a German victory impossible rather than to make a British victory certain."

The feud reminded some American naval officers of the Sampson-Schley controversy that was still reverberating in U.S. Navy circles. In fact, of the four principal commanders at Jutland—Jellicoe, Scheer, Beatty, and Hipper—only Erich Hipper came away with a widely enhanced reputation.

Jellicoe and Beatty's differing styles of flag command would carry over to World War II, where there were running arguments over whether large-force commanders should rely on dash and élan or be more concerned with the ultimate mission of the operation. But many historians and senior officers, and thus their students, misread the ultimate lesson of Jutland. A generation of young officers in all navies was taught the supremacy of the battleship with the big naval gun, the final arbiter of battle. Furthermore, this conventional wisdom dictated that the course of naval war would be determined by the major decisive sea fight between opposing battle lines led by the big ships with big guns. Aviation played no significant role at Jutland, and so the possibilities involving carriers were overlooked in the various analyses of the seminal battle.

In the 1920s, and to a lesser degree the 1930s, naval aviation took a back seat to the primacy of the battle line in the studies and gaming boards at the Naval War College. Moveover, naval aviators were underrepresented in the War College student body, partly because the Bureau of Aeronautics (BuAer) was loath to assign aviators outside of the aviation organization.

The naval conferences in the 1920s and 1930s limited the number of battleships and cruisers and their guns. The largest naval gun with the longest range then was 16 inches (in diameter) with a rifled barrel and was carried by the latest battleships. Heavy and light cruisers were differentiated not so much by tonnage but by armament. U.S. heavy cruisers ran slightly less than 10,000 tons but carried 8-inch main batteries, while light cruisers ran to 10,000 tons with 6-inch guns. The range of these capital ships' guns generally determined the nature of their seagoing tactics against a similar enemy. It was usually considered tactically favorable to maneuver in such a way to outrange enemy ships with one's own guns. It was better to operate with ships of the same class because they had similar capabilities in armament, speed, and maneuverability.

Another form of warfare taking a back seat, like aviation, was amphibious operations, though the disastrous World War I British landing and campaign against the Turks at Gallipoli was reviewed. One diligent student of the subject, studying it in as far back as 1921, was Major Holland M. "Howlin' Mad" Smith of the U.S. Marine Corps. He was concerned with developing a doctrine for amphibious operations, at which the marines excelled. Smith, who picked up his nickname as a headstrong, young officer in the Philippines, complained that nobody—from War College President Admiral William S. Sims on down—paid much attention to landing troops on a hostile shore. "Under the old Navy doctrine," he wrote, "a landing was a simple and haphazard affair, involving no planning and very little preparation. Assault forces were stowed in boats 5,000 yards off the beach and given a pat on the back with the hope that all would go well. Warships threw a few shells into the beach and that was all." General Smith was one of those instrumental in promulgating the Marine Corps doctrine that "the special role of the Marine Corps within the military establishment was to provide a small, well-trained amphibious assault force to seize and occupy overseas bases for fleet operations."

Throughout the interwar period, the Naval War College developed contingency plans in the event of hostilities, focusing on a conflict with Japan, the likeliest foe in the Pacific. As a student, Commander Chester Nimitz noted that the enemy in the war games was always Japan, so in World War II when this prediction became reality, nothing that happened in the Pacific was "strange or unexpected." But his class, which included future admirals Thomas C. Hart and Harold Stark, also wrote papers on the Battle of Jutland until Nimitz "knew it by heart." Evolving theory at the War College was often transmuted into fleet strategy, through fleet exercises, and through recommendations of the U.S. Navy's General Board, which tried to develop fleet doctrine. Curiously, in 1924, a Japanese delegation visited Newport and the War College, which included Captain Isoruko Yamamoto, who would command the Japanese fleet seventeen years later.

Plan Orange was the core strategic plan, foreseeing an attack by Japan on U.S. possessions or allies in the Western Pacific and the United States' Plan Blue response. Most scenarios involving Blue versus Orange called for the U.S. Fleet to steam across the Pacific and take on the Japanese fleet in a kind of massive Jutland showdown battle. There were many revisions to Plan Orange, but they all involved U.S. capital ships crossing the Pacific; hence War College students became familiar with the names of the obscure islands that were to become headlines during World War II.

In tackling solutions, students were given specific fleet problems, then required to provide an estimate of the situation and to draft ensuing orders to deal with it in clear and coherent form. The orders were executed in the war games. The faculty insisted that command required not just personal leadership and technical competence, but a systematic, disciplined cast of mind. As the War College faculty saw it, the aim was to teach naval officers how to make correct decisions when in command positions. The faculty believed the premier quality for such an officer was good judgment, which could be developed through study, reflection, and practice in war games based on practical problems.

Though not directly involving combat operations, the students were warned of a blind, follow-the-leader approach to naval command and leadership. A leading case in point was the U.S. Navy's greatest peacetime disaster: the destroyer pileup at Point Arguello in Santa Barbara County, in a remote stretch of rocky coast that is now part of Vandenberg Air Force Base. The destroyer commodore was leading a high-speed column of fourteen four-piper tin cans in fog about 2100 on September 8, 1923.

At 20 knots, the interval between ships was only 13 seconds. The flag navigator misinterpreted both radio bearings and his dead reckoning and turned too soon to the east to enter the Santa Barbara Channel between the coast and San Miguel Island. The lead destroyer *Delphy* steamed straight onto the rocky shore near the village of Lompoc. Eight more tin cans crashed ashore following the flotilla leader. Seven of the nine new ships were total wrecks; two managed to back off the rocks and remain afloat. Twenty-three sailors lost their lives in the blackest mark on the peacetime navy.

A court-martial found the destroyer flag officer and the flag captain of negligence. Other tin can captains were charged with negligence for following the leader, though it is difficult to see what else they could do, other than taking their own readings and notifying the squadron commander, which would probably be too late. There was another serious downside to the disaster. A chief practical lesson learned by officers was caution. Skippers—whether destroyermen or submariners—were imbued with undue caution: if you were involved in an accident or ran your ship aground, your career was ruined. Meanwhile, the Japanese navy trained in arduous, nighttime exercises, suffering its share of accidents but instilled an offensive spirit in its cruiser and destroyer captains, which would pay off in World War II.

Future Admiral Ernest King recalled his War College years, 1932–1933, as "refreshing and valuable." Newport was a pleasant place to live. In the summer, some of the richest and most fashionable Americans gathered at their mansions there. The America's Cup races were held offshore, the sails of the huge J-boats billowing in the wind. The navy often used Narragansett Bay as an anchorage. In 1934 the U.S. Fleet arrived, the first East Coast visit since 1927. Among the War College students that summer was the up-and-coming Commander Norman Scott, who was to make an enduring reputation as a flag officer. Newport was a lively combination of an elegant resort and a navy town that year, as most years. The *Daily News* commented, "Newport loves the Navy, and at last it has come back."

Ernie King found he had "in addition to the prescribed course of study, time to browse in the excellent library, to reflect upon . . . and consider the world situation, particularly in those aspects that appeared to be leading to war." In his thesis, Captain King accepted Albert Thayer Mahan's opinion that Great Britain's tradition suppressed maritime competition. Thus the British would always be against any perceived naval competition from the United States, whatever the state of their alliance. This mindset led Ernest King to harbor a deep mistrust of British motives that carried well into World War II. During a War College major war game, King served as commander of the Blue fleet seeking to recapture the Philippines, which had been seized by Orange.

For his part, Captain Bill Halsey, a student in 1933, remembered the experience as "stimulating because of the instruction, the exchange of ideas, the chance to test your pet theories on the game board, and the opportunity to read up on professional publications."

Tom Kinkaid, whose experience was centered on the Atlantic, found the tactical problems associated with the theoretical enemy in the Pacific (Japan) fascinating. He was exposed to the reality of moving warships across the Pacific in Plan Orange, and it left him with some concepts of managing naval operations across the broad Pacific.

Student interest was wide-ranging, as evidenced in the various papers and theses some future admirals wrote. Commander Husband Kimmel argued against the general view that Japan was a likely future enemy of the United States. Commander Royal Ingersoll recognized the role of economics in helping to shape American foreign policy. His classmate Raymond Spruance, one of the brightest of the students, wrote that America had become unpopular abroad because of its insistence on collecting World War I debts and failure to help settle postwar problems. Spruance also wrote about Japanese Admiral Togo at Tsushima, who had given his subordinate commanders freedom of initiative and action, and who himself was calm, patient, and cool-headed in the stress of battle. Commander Jesse B. "Oley" Oldendorf focused on Europe rather than the Pacific. Commander Alan G. Kirk thought that while American isolation might have been admirable in the past, the United States must now play an international role. On the other hand, Commander Slew McCain argued that U.S. policy must avoid "entangling alliances."

The aim of the War College was distilled in the 1930s. It was for prospective flag officers to seek strategic goals and conduct the tactical exercises to achieve them, to make sound naval decisions through the use of good judgment, based on available facts. As Rear Admiral William D. Leahy, chief of the Bureau of Navigation (which soon was renamed the Bureau of Naval Personnel) put it to a graduating class: "To survive at sea, study and knowledge of history are helpful—plans for the future are necessary—and with these, with which you are now well provided, you should more easily acquire that facility of meeting unanticipated changes in conditions which is the final essential to success at sea. My closing advice is that you should assiduously cultivate this facility."

Toward the end of the 1930s, naval aviation made great strides in the fleet, and aircraft carrier operations were introduced into the Naval War College's courses. Commander Jack Towers, the navy's senior aviator, as a student wrote a thesis on "The Influence of Aircraft on Naval Strategy and Tactics."

Some bright students like Dick Conolly were asked to join the staff immediately after graduating. Other students returned later as instructors. Faculty members were not beholden to doctrine but engaged in spirited exchanges about tactics and strategy. In 1935, War College president, Rear Admiral Edward C. Kalbfus, asked Captain Raymond Spruance to join the faculty. Spruance became head of the Operations Department, with an old shipmate, Commander Charles J. "Carl" Moore, on his staff.

Spruance's friend, Captain Richmond Kelly Turner, who went by his middle name, was head of Strategy. The decisive, combative Kelly Turner engaged in fiery debates with another stormy intellectual, Captain Robert A. "Fuzzy" Theobald. Turner developed into a brilliant teacher of naval strategy. His lectures emphasized naval aviation and amphibious operations as the predominant future forms of naval warfare. But his was almost a solitary voice. The battle line was still God at Newport. Turner realized that among the lessons of World War I's Gallipoli operation were that there should be a clear chain of command under a single forceful commander. Moreover, Turner decided there were two major requisites for a successful amphibious operation: secure lines of communication and supplies to the area of conflict, and maintaining command of the sea and air around an invasion site. Kelly Turner's interest in amphibious doctrine was to bear great dividends for the U.S. Navy.

Though normally calm and scholarly, Raymond Spruance, in criticizing Admiral Kalbus' treatise, "Sound Military Decision," got into a bitter row with a superior, Captain John W. Wilcox. Spruance had been friendly with the difficult, distant Wilcox over the years, however, this argument ended their relationship. Among the other members of the senior faculty at the time were Captain Milo Draemel and Commanders Walden L. "Pug" Ainsworth, Lawrence F. Reifsnider, Alvin D. Chandler, and Bernard H. Bieri, all of whom would become flag officers.

Kelly Turner had many of the physical and mental qualities—attractive and unattractive—of Ernie King. Tall, erect, and lean, Turner was highly intelligent with a keen, analytic mind and encyclopedic memory. He was tough, mean, self-assured, sharp-tongued, forceful, and extremely competent. He was a profane, hard-drinker but deadly serious about his profession and an inexhaustible worker. He had been executive officer of the carrier *Saratoga*. Turner had won his aviator's gold wings in 1927 at age forty-two and was one of the few Newport faculty members with wings. A vigorous proponent of naval aviation, he believed the War College "damage rules," which were used in judging all fleet problems and tactical exercises, underrated the effectiveness of carrier aviation, particularly dive-bombing. He criticized his predecessor as head of the strategic section, Fuzzy Theobald, for being unimaginative and unaware of the importance of naval aviation. He also urged that the veteran Plan Orange be updated to include aircraft carrier and amphibious operations.

In their different ways, their tours at Newport marked Raymond Spruance and Kelly Turner as among the navy's foremost strategists. Thanks to Turner, attention at the War College began focusing on aircraft carriers and their tactical and strategic potential in implementing Plan Orange. Naval aviation, at long last, was on the agenda.

By the late 1930s, the War College had developed a clear philosophy. It was to groom senior naval officers in practical discipline to command forces at sea, rather than making policy or managing naval bureaucracies. The aim was to teach officers how to develop good judgment to make sound decisions when in command. The Naval War College would teach strategy and tactics and elements of command, and develop naval thinkers. But the ability to think was not enough. A flag officer in combat needed a fighting spirit. And that was something the Naval War College could not teach.

Four

RISE OF THE AIR ADMIRALS

In the peacetime navy between the wars, aviation was playing a significant and increasing role at sea. Navy pilots had been trained in World War I, many of whom were reservists, under the redoubtable Lieutenant Jack Towers, who was designated Naval Aviator No. 3 in 1911. He was a feisty, vocal, sometimes abrasive supporter of naval aviation. The crusty Admiral William Sims, who had commanded U.S. naval forces in Europe during World War I, foresaw the potential of the aircraft carrier and, while he was president of the War College, instituted aviation studies.

Naval aviation made history in the first flight across the Atlantic of the wartime NC flying boats. NC-1, NC-3, and NC-4 took off from Newfoundland on May 16, 1919, planning to stop at the Azores en route to Lisbon, Portugal, and thence to England. The formation was headed by Commander Jack Towers, commander of Seaplane Division One, and the pilots included Lieutenant Commander Patrick N. L. "Pat" Bellinger, Lieutenant Commander Albert C. "Putty" Read, and Lieutenant Commander Pete Mitscher. (One of the U.S. destroyers stationed along the route, *Aaron Ward*, was commanded by Lieutenant Commander Raymond Spruance.)

Towers' plane, NC-3, was low on fuel and landed in the sea, 200 miles short of the Azores. By taxiing and with an eventual tow, NC-3 reached port but was badly damaged and in no shape to continue. NC-1, with Pete Mitscher, also landed in the sea west of the Azores and sank while towed by a passing Greek merchantman. But NC-4, with Putty Read as pilot, made it into the Azores and, when the weather finally lifted, took off for Lisbon, arriving on May 27 and completing its trans-Atlantic crossing. The feat of the navy flying boats was somewhat overshadowed a few days later by the nonstop flight from Newfoundland to Ireland by British challengers, John Alcock and Arthur W. Brown, but both flights provided vast popular support for aviation enthusiasts.

In 1922, a former coal collier was converted into the navy's first aircraft carrier, *Langley*, after Samuel Langley, an aviation pioneer. Navy aviation faced obstacles from within and without. Admiral William S. Benson, CNO, thought naval air should be administered at a low level. Brigadier Billy Mitchell argued that navy aviation should be combined with the Army Air Forces into a separate service. But in 1921, the Bureau of Aeronautics (BuAer) was established as the first new naval bureau in sixty years, with Rear Admiral William A. "Billy" Moffett as chief. A courtly but resolute South Carolinian, Billy Moffett was a pioneer aviation advocate who accumulated the necessary one hundred hours of passenger flight time to qualify for naval observer wings in 1922 at the age of fifty-two. He served three tours in the key post of chief of BuAer before dying in the crash of the dirigible *Akron* in a storm off New Jersey in 1933. He was justly called the father of naval aviation, and Moffett Field south of San Francisco was named for him.

In 1925, Admiral Sims informed a congressional committee: "A small, high-speed carrier alone can destroy or disable a battleship alone . . . a fleet whose carriers give it command of the air over the enemy fleet can defeat the latter." This was directly contrary to conventional fighting doctrine; the role of aviation and carriers, somewhat like submarines, was viewed strictly as a scouting force, the so-called eyes of the fleet.

In 1925, Captain Joseph Mason "Bull" Reeves, whose nickname came from his football days at the Academy, was fresh out of the Naval War College. He underwent flight training at Pensacola in 1925 at age fifty-three to qualify as a naval observer, and then took command of the first carrier *Langley*. A forceful, inspiring experimenter, Reeves thought that carriers should attack enemies with bombers and not merely scout for the fleet. He developed new techniques for dive-bombing and devised ways to spot planes on hanger and flight decks to increase *Langley*'s capacity to forty-two aircraft. He also invented the system of flight deck personnel wearing different-colored jerseys for their tasks: mechanics, ordnancemen, plane handlers, and plane directors. Bull

Reeves became an influential aviation admiral, promoting aggressive carrier tactics. Ultimately, he was raised to four stars and given command of the U.S. Fleet.

Several up-and-coming officers took time to qualify for naval observer wings, which ranked them technically as naval aviators. Congress decreed that commanding officers of aircraft carriers, seaplane tenders, and naval air stations had to be qualified aviators. So a short course was offered at Pensacola, the home of naval aviation, to qualify selected senior officers as naval observers.

Naval aviation was appealing. Pensacola was expanding, as was the San Diego Naval Air Station at North Island. Other airfields were under construction. The huge carriers *Saratoga* and *Lexington*, originally laid down as battle cruisers, were commissioned in 1927. Their christenings began the practice of naming carriers after early American battles or famous U.S. fighting ships—as battleships were named after states, cruisers after cities, destroyers after naval heroes, and submarines after fish or marine life. "Sara" and "Lady Lex" soon became key elements of the fleet, leading innovative raids in the annual exercises. Some latecomers to aviation as bona fide aviators included future admirals Ernest King, who won his wings at 48; Bill Halsey at 52; Slew McCain, 52; Kelly Turner, 42; Jake, or Jakie, Fitch, 46; and Frederick C. "Ted" Sherman, 47. Most served aboard *Saratoga* or *Lexington* in some senior capacity during the 1930s.

These older officers, in competition for senior aviator billets, were often resented by the early navy air pioneers who took up flying soon after Annapolis. These included their acknowledged leader: Jack Towers; Pat Bellinger (No. 8); George D. Murray (No. 22); Pete Mitscher (No. 33); Dewitt C. "Duke" Ramsey (No. 45); and later Forrest P. Sherman; Arthur W. "Raddy" Radford; Wu Duncan; John W. "Black Jack" Reeves; Ralph E. Davison; Alfred E. "Monty" Montgomery; Gerald F. "Gerry" Bogan; Thomas L. "Tommy" Sprague; Clifton A. F. "Ziggy" Sprague (no relation); and Joseph J. "Jocko" Clark, among others.

They all knew each other, served together in squadrons and on carriers, and drank together in officers clubs at naval air stations. Hard drinking and heavy smoking was not uncommon among young naval officers ashore, particularly aviators. The younger pilots referred to the newer but older aviators as Johnny-come-latelies, or JCLs. They themselves had to wait their turn to gain enough seniority to be considered for senior and flag command. Most aviators were heartened in 1934 when naval observer Bull Reeves was named commander in chief of the U.S. Fleet

Friction continued between aviators and non-aviators, and between pioneer pilots and the JCLs. Admiral King, a JCL, grumbled that many of the pioneer pilots seemed to believe "that if one were to fly, one had to be born with wings." The differences extended even to dress. Aviators, in addition to their dress blue uniforms, wore distinctive, forest-green uniforms with brown shoes. This led to describing the "brown shoe" aviation navy and the "black shoe" surface navy. Aviators sometimes referred disparagingly to "gun club" officers on surface ships. Some senior battleship officers argued that pilots were aviators first and naval officers only second. The aviators went so far as to insist that any admiral in command of aircraft carriers should be a naval aviator, since only pilots understood the intricacies of carrier operations.

The aviators thought that the urbane, sophisticated Jack Towers, now captain, deserved to succeed Moffett as chief of BuAer. But he was still too junior to rate flag rank. Rear Admiral King was selected instead, who was a fine choice but not popular with the veteran aviators. The appointment created ill feeling between two strong-minded officers, Jack Towers and Ernie King, which would extend well into World War II.

In the fleet, the importance of airpower was demonstrated in the annual maneuvers. Rear Admiral Harry Yarnell, an early proponent of naval aviation and a qualified naval observer, commanded *Lexington* and *Saratoga* and launched a successful dawn raid on Pearl Harbor in a fleet exercise—ten years before the Japanese attack. During these fleet maneuvers, a basic problem showed up. The carriers steaming at 25 to 33 knots were too fast for the fleet's battleships, which could make 21 knots at best. The question was how to combine these disparate elements in carrier operations.

In maneuvers, carrier commanders argued that they should be detached from close fleet support, though it was a gamble. Surface ship admirals insisted that the carriers should stay close to the fleet for the flattops' own protection. The airmen believed that tying carriers to battleships or landing operations restricted their mobility and offensive capability. This running argument continued into the war and was the subject of acrimony over tactics for the amphibious assaults in the Pacific. During this period, it was difficult for air admirals and aviator captains to agree on an overall carrier doctrine and on how best to use it, particularly over the objections of the battleship admirals.

Under the policies of navy-oriented President Franklin Roosevelt, a two-ocean navy began to take shape. The first U.S. carrier built from the keel up, *Ranger*, was commissioned in 1934, followed by two big, fast sister ships, *Yorktown* in 1937 and *Enterprise* in 1938. Next came *Wasp* in 1940 and a sister, *Hornet*, in 1941. The United States was also building fast battleships, *North Carolina* and *Washington*, which could keep up with the fast, new carriers. The command of the carriers, known as Aircraft Battle Force, went to Vice Admiral King and then to Vice Admiral Halsey. Jack Towers was captain of *Saratoga*. Slew McCain skippered *Ranger*. Leigh Noyes had *Lexington*. The aviators were moving up into choice commands.

Aircraft carriers, along with battleships and cruisers, were generally equipped with a flag bridge—where an admiral directed operations—while the navigation bridge, usually a deck higher, was the province of the ship's captain. The captain directed all operations pertaining to the ship itself; while the admiral issued operational orders—course, speed, gunnery firing, aircraft launching—to the captain and other captains in the force. Flagships had extra quarters for an admiral's staff. The admiral's chartroom, where he and his staff worked, was just aft of the flag bridge and called the flag plot. During the war, it evolved into the combat information center (CIC), the nerve center full of radar screens, navigation, and communications gear.

As war approached, the U.S. carriers were split between the Atlantic and the Pacific fleets. The two-ocean navy was still largely under construction. The U.S. Navy was not yet ready for hostilities, and its leaders—the admirals and captains, surface and air—untried in the crucible of combat.

Five

ADMIRALS
IN ACTION

1939–1941

In the late 1930s, attention at the Naval War College and the office of CNO followed the rise of German power wielded in Europe. Hitler marched into Poland on September 1, 1939, and the British and French declared war on Germany two days later. The unprepared Allies went on the strategic defensive on land to build up their military strength, leading to the so-called phoney war, a period of relative military inactivity. But the Germans moved quickly at sea, launching an aggressive war with their U-boat force and surface raiders. On the first day of the war, the *U-30* torpedoed and sank the British liner *Athenia*, the first of forty-one ships to go down in that month alone. The *U-47* torpedoed the battleship *Royal Oak* in the huge Scapa Flow anchorage, with 833 of her crew lost.

On September 5, President Franklin D. Roosevelt ordered the U.S. Navy to create a neutrality patrol in the North Atlantic to track any belligerent forces approaching the coasts of the United States or West Indies. By September 12, elements of the Atlantic squadron were assigned sectors to patrol, though the warships, mostly destroyers, were few and far between. The U.S. Navy, which had concentrated on the Pacific, began building strength in the Atlantic. A meeting of the Foreign Ministers of the American Republics in Panama declared on October 2 that its policy was to keep the European war from entering the entire Western Hemisphere.

In Berlin, Grand Admiral Erich Raeder, age sixty-three and head of the German Imperial Navy, was an intense, pragmatic veteran of Jutland who was largely responsible for building a modern fleet for the Third Reich. In late September, he sent the pocket battleships *Deutschland* (soon renamed *Lutzow* so that no warship bearing the name "Germany" could be sunk) into the North Atlantic and *Graf Spee* into the South Atlantic to sink merchantmen. After a successful cruise into the Indian Ocean, *Graf Spee* ran up against three British cruisers, under Commodore Henry Harwood, off the River Plate estuary between Argentina and Uruguay. *Graf Spee* suffered damage and Captain Hans Langsdorff decided to put into Montevideo to make repairs. But the Uruguayan officials gave Langsdorff only three days' grace, or else he would face internment. Langsdorff believed the waiting British warships had been reinforced and he decided to scuttle *Graf Spee*. He got his men off safely before blowing up the pocket battleship in the estuary. Then Langsdorff shot himself in his Buenos Aires hotel room. The Battle of the River Plate was a great lift to British morale. Harwood was knighted and promoted to rear admiral.

Morale soon fell, though. As American naval observers watched from long distance, aboard their ships in the Atlantic and at the Navy Department in Washington, the British were badly outmaneuvered by the Germans invading Norway. The failure to stop the German Imperial Navy covering the invasion showed endemic weaknesses that taught stark lessons to those observers: a mixed chain of command, failure to disseminate intelligence, and the need for air cover because of the vulnerability of ships to land-based air. The lessons indicated that some peacetime admirals did not adjust readily to wartime conditions.

The fall of France in May 1940 marked a dramatic shift in U.S. strategy. Admiral Harold Stark, now CNO, asked the U.S. Congress for $4 billion to implement the two-ocean navy. In a month's time, Congress approved construction of new, fast battleships, carriers, cruisers, destroyers, and submarines. But for two years, the United States would be markedly weak if the Germans defeated the British. Roosevelt, publicly preaching neutrality, cautiously adopted a policy of helping Britain "short of war." Caution was deemed necessary because the isolationist movement was still strong in the country.

In mid-1940, Roosevelt inaugurated the lend-lease program, swapping fifty old destroyers for rental of naval bases on British territory in the Western Hemisphere. Recently promoted Rear Admiral Raymond

Spruance became the first commandant of the new 10th Naval District—the Caribbean and West Indies—with headquarters in San Juan, Puerto Rico. One of the neutrality patrols based at San Juan was headed by Captain Pug Ainsworth, commodore of Destroyer Squadron 2. It kept an eye on the French Antilles, which were still under the control of the Vichy France regime.

Admiral Spruance's Caribbean command was often visited by the new commander of the Atlantic Fleet, Admiral Ernest King, who wished to observe the fleet amphibious landing exercises at Culebra, Puerto Rico. King invited Spruance aboard his flagship, the battleship *Texas*, and the two officers were able to size each other up. The U.S. Marines landing force was supervised by Brigadier General Smith, the tough, fractious officer who quarreled with King over amphibious procedures and the choice of landing beaches. His nickname, Howlin' Mad, was well chosen.

The U.S. Marines by now had made a specialty of amphibious operations. By 1933, the Fleet Marine Force was set up and annual maneuvers were held. Tactics and equipment slowly evolved. The technique of combat-loading transports was studied, and special land-ing craft were developed. With his eye for detail, King called for wide-spread improvements to establish an effective amphibious force with attack transports and modern landing craft. In the Culebra exercise, General Howlin' Mad Smith was eager to show King the marines' new "alligator" vehicles, or landing vehicles tracked (LVT), which could swim in water and crawl up over reefs and beaches carrying troops. Admiral Spruance decided Smith knew his business, and thought that if he were to need a marine amphibious commander some day, it would be Howlin' Mad Smith. Admiral King felt the same way about the marines' amphibious capabilities and Smith's capacity to lead them.

In Washington and in the U.S. Atlantic Fleet, naval officers were buoyed by the Royal Navy's successes in the Mediterranean. The British commander in chief was Admiral Sir Andrew Browne Cunningham, age fifty-seven and known to the fleet as "ABC." Under the short, stocky, aggres-sive Scot's leadership, the British successfully attacked the Italian fleet at its base at Taranto—in the heel of the Italian boot—in November 1940. The ancient Swordfish biplanes carrying torpedoes flew off the carrier *Illustrious* at night and caught the Italians unaware, sinking three battleships, which settled into harbor mud with negligible losses to the British strike aircraft. This marked the splendid debut of carrier warfare.

Admiral Cunningham backed up this victory with another successful attack on the Italian navy off Cape Matapan in Greece in March 1941. ABC ordered a daytime carrier strike against the Italian ships, damaging a battleship and cruiser and confusing the Italians. Then in a night battle, the British sank three Italian cruisers and two destroyers. Britain was in full control of the Mediterranean.

But ABC's luster was soon dimmed by the losses the Royal Navy suffered in the evacuation of the island of Crete, as well as other parts of Greece, in May 1940 when it came under withering attack by land-based German bombers. Cunningham's losses in Crete—three cruisers and eight destroyers sunk, with serious damage to two battleships, one aircraft carrier, five cruisers, and seven destroyers—crippled the Mediterranean fleet, though the flawed strategy of committing troops to Greece was Prime Minister Winston Churchill's. In defending the Royal Navy's gallant but vain performance, Cunningham declared, "It takes the navy three years to build a ship. It would take three hundred years to rebuild a tradition."

In the North Atlantic, German surface raiders still threatened vital shipping lanes between North America and the British Isles. The British and American high commands sent staff officers for a series of meetings and conversations for contingency planning in case the United States should enter the war. The U.S. naval officers included Rear Admiral Robert Ghormley, Rear Admiral Kelly Turner, and senior Captains Alan Kirk and Duke Ramsey. One key result was the decision that the U.S. Navy would provide escorts for trans-Atlantic shipping when it could do so. Kelly Turner, who was now Director of War Plans in the office of the CNO, estimated the navy would be ready to escort merchantmen from North America to Scotland by April 1, 1941.

In what some considered a risky move, in view of the growing Japanese threat, Admiral Stark transferred three battleships, an aircraft carrier, and four cruisers, as well as two destroyer squadrons, from the Pacific to the Atlantic to support the short-of-war effort to help the British. The danger to unprotected convoys shuttling between North America and the United Kingdom was underscored by the first and only cruise of the German battleship *Bismarck*.

*

On a standard Mercator projection map, the distances between the Norwegian coast, the Faroe Islands, Iceland, and Greenland seem vast. But seen on a globe, the distances shrink: the Denmark Strait, between Greenland and Iceland, and the Iceland-Faroe gap were readily accessible to fast German sea raiders setting out from Norway's north coast ports. The Germans had previously slipped pocket battleships and cruisers through those passages to sink Allied shipping in the North Atlantic. Now in May 1941, Admiral Raeder decided to send the mighty *Bismarck* on a raiding trip. *Bismarck* was a handsome powerhouse, 820 feet long, displacing 52,000 tons with heavy armor, eight 15-inch guns, and able to make 30 knots. Flying the flag of the formidable Vice Admiral Gunther Lutjens, *Bismarck* sailed from the Baltic Sea via Norway, accompanied by the cruiser *Prinz Eugen*.

The breakout took place in the Denmark Strait. But Lutjens' force was spotted by two British cruisers, under Rear Admiral William F. Wake-Walker, who radioed the vital news to the Admiralty. Admiral Sir John Tovey, commander in chief of the Home Fleet, alerted battleship *Prince of Wales* and battle cruiser *Hood* with Vice Admiral Lancelot E. Holland aboard. *Hood* was the showboat of the Royal Navy, but lightly armored and twenty years old. Admiral Holland placed *Hood* in the lead rather than the more powerful *Prince of Wales*. He failed to notify the cruisers or *Prince of Wales* of his battle plan—if he had one. *Bismarck's* gunners were fast and accurate. Five salvos ranged in on *Hood's* thin plating, causing instant, enormous explosions. The pride of the Royal Navy sank quickly in a mass of flame and smoke, taking down all but three of the 1,419-man crew; among the fatalities was Admiral Holland.

Prince of Wales was hit, too, but managed to strike *Bismarck* twice, which caused leaks in the fuel tanks, before breaking off the action. Admiral Lutjens rejected the advice of *Bismarck's* Captain Ernst Lindemann to first dispose of *Prince of Wales* and then head for home the way they came. Instead, Lutjens decided to continue into the North Atlantic. Admiral John Tovey had been slow to react and now attempted to deploy his ships to intercept *Bismarck*. Lutjens made a serious violation of radio security when he signaled a long message describing the battle and his present intentions to Berlin. They were picked up by British intelligence. Tovey was bombarded by a stream of suggestions from Admiral Sir Dudley Pound, First Lord of the Admiralty, who himself was being pressured by Prime Minister Churchill.

The next morning, *Bismarck* was spotted by a Catalina flying boat piloted by Ensign Leonard B. Smith of the U.S. Navy, one of nine Americans secretly sent to the Royal Air Force as observers. The sighting led Admiral James Somerville to dispatch his Force H's planes from his carrier *Ark Royal* out of Gibraltar to attack; otherwise *Bismarck* would get away. One of the old Swordfish planes put a torpedo into *Bismarck's* steering room, causing the behemoth to circle while divers tried to clear the rudder. The delay allowed British battleships to catch up. Salvos from *Rodney* and *King George V* and cruisers *Norfolk* and *Dorsetshire* rained down on the German warship. Lying dead in the water and helpless, *Bismarck's* crew opened the sea valves, and the ship went down with 2,200 men, including Admiral Lutjens and Captain Lindemann. With the exception of Somerville, British admirals and the Admiralty could not claim the Battle of the Denmark Strait as the Royal Navy's finest hour.

The Allies still faced the problem of German U-boats and aircraft attacking the ships that supplied Britain's vital artery to the American arsenal. In May 1941, President Roosevelt declared an Unlimited National Emergency. Three days later, a Nazi wolf pack sank nine ships in a convoy carrying lend-lease supplies to Britain. In July, the U.S. Marines landed in Iceland to take over occupation duties from the British. In September 1941, a U-boat fired two torpedoes at U.S. destroyer *Greer* near Iceland, but the old four-piper dodged them.
This led to an undeclared U.S. naval war against German U-boats in the Western Hemisphere. The U.S. Navy began active escort duty for convoys between North American ports and Iceland. Later, *U-568* torpedoed the U.S. destroyer *Kearny*, which was escorting a convoy, but inflicted only limited damage. On October 31, 1941, the USS *Reuben James* became the first American ship sunk in the war when *U-552* torpedoed the destroyer. During this tense period, convoy escort techniques were refined as the American effort increased. The overall operations were commanded by Rear Admiral Arthur Bristol Jr., a highly competent seaman and aviator whose abilities led to his promotion to vice admiral. But Bristol died of a heart attack aboard his flagship *Prairie* in Argentia, Newfoundland, on April 20, 1942.

*

In Washington during late 1941, senior naval officers, while busy organizing Atlantic convoys, were attempting to discern Japanese naval capabilities and intentions. American code-breaking efforts had gotten off to a shaky start when in 1929 then Secretary of State Henry Stimson ordered existing operations ceased because "gentlemen do not read each other's mail." By the late 1930s, American cryptologists in the Office of Naval Intelligence (ONI) had developed a machine that cracked the Japanese naval code in 1940. At first, U.S. officers labeled decrypted Japanese messages with the term "Magic." When the British broke the German code with the aid of the Enigma machine, they called the resultant intelligence "Ultra," for ultrasecret, which became the standard term for decrypted top intelligence. But the Japanese often changed their codes, so the United States needed to keep breaking them. In some periods, the United States could read Japanese naval and diplomatic codes, at other times it could not. In mid–late 1941, the United States had no precise knowledge of the Japanese fleet movements.

The valuable intelligence about the Japanese coming into the Navy Department was bedeviled by bureaucratic infighting over the collection and dissemination of intelligence about Japanese plans. The secret information was originally provided by the Department of Naval Communications, headed by Rear Admiral Leigh Noyes. This raw material was assembled and translated by the Director of Naval Intelligence, first led by Captain Alan Kirk, and then by Captain Theodore S. "Ping" Wilkinson.

But the real power—deciding on distribution of valuable intelligence—was wielded by Rear Admiral Kelly Turner, now Director of War Plans, who had been promoted to flag rank after his stint at the Naval War College and command of heavy cruiser *Astoria*. His post in the office of the CNO was one most influential in the navy. "Terrible Turner" remained the brightest officer around, however testy and self-confident.

The Director of Naval Intelligence, the forceful Captain Kirk, believed it was his department's job to distribute intelligence reports to interested parties in the navy. He stood up to Turner on the issue. Turner insisted that it was his department's responsibility to assess and evaluate the threat and alert fleet commanders. Kirk went head-to-head with Turner, and the matter was bucked to CNO, Admiral Stark, who considered Turner "invaluable." Hence, Turner won his point, and Captain

Kirk was shipped out to sea as commander of a destroyer squadron, later to achieve fame in the European theater. Turner laid down his law: "ONI make no estimate of prospective enemy intentions to CNO, but furnish information to War Plans who would make the required estimate." The officers in ONI deeply resented Kelly Turner's arrogant usurping of their role in interpreting and distributing key intelligence. There was bad feeling all around.

When the Japanese government warned its ambassador in Washington about deteriorating relations in the Far East, the import of the intercepts was not immediately recognized. There was some question over who should alert the Pacific and Asiatic Fleet commanders. There was confusion about what decryption facilities were in use at Pearl Harbor headquarters, and thus what Admiral Kimmel knew independently about the diplomatic traffic. The ball was fumbled in Washington as to what warnings should be sent to whom.

Admiral Kimmel in Pearl Harbor was never promptly apprised of Washington's concern that war was imminent. On November 27, Admiral Stark in Washington sent Admiral Kimmel a so-called "war warning," telling him to expect an aggressive move by Japan within the next few days . . . against the Philippines, Thailand's Kra Isthmus, or possibly Borneo. Stark told Kimmel to prepare "defensive deployment preparatory to carrying out" the existing war plans. But Stark did not cite Hawaii as a possible target. The next day, Stark followed up with another message stating, "Hostile action is possible at any moment," but also ordered the Pacific commander to "undertake no offensive action until Japan has committed an overt act." Neither Kimmel nor the army commander, Lieutenant General Walter Shore, believed Hawaii to be in immediate danger.

In Washington, army and navy reading Japanese radio intercepts thought war was likely to break out on the weekend of November 29 in the Far East. But when the weekend passed without incident, Washington relaxed. One senior intelligence office, on December 4, recommended sending Kimmel another war warning, but Stark thought this confusing and vetoed the suggestion. Kelly Turner later claimed that the November 27 war warning was sufficient to alert Pearl Harbor, but others believed that Washington's warning should have been more specific and alarming. On December 6, Tokyo began a long coded dispatch to the Japanese embassy in Washington on breaking off diplomatic relations with the United States. When Roosevelt began to read them that evening, he said, "This means war!"

But the long message gave no details of when and where any attack would take place. Furthermore, the army and navy intelligence officers failed to get the substance of the message to Admiral Stark or General George C. Marshall. It was not until the morning (Washington time) of December 7 when Admirals Stark and Kelly Turner received from Ping Wilkinson the substance of the final Part 14 of the long Tokyo message, which ordered a break in diplomatic relations. But this part still did not specify that war would be declared or an attack launched.

The message ordered that a diplomatic note be presented at 1300 Washington time, an odd hour on a Sunday afternoon for such a delivery. Wilkinson recommended that Stark immediately call Admiral Kimmel in Pearl Harbor and alert him. Stark believed that since General Short was in charge of the defense of Hawaii, General Marshall should alert him. Marshall was out for his usual Sunday morning horseback ride. Finally the top brass gathered at 1115 and agreed war was imminent, and Pearl Harbor and Manila should be informed at once. However, the army was entrusted with sending the message, and through a foul-up in communications, an officer sent it by Western Union! It did not reach Hawaii until after the attack. The whole mix-up was to be the subject of a bitter debate, which has continued over the years.

In the Western Pacific, the U.S. Asiatic Fleet was pitifully weak, except for submarines. The main U.S. naval base in Manila Bay at the province of Cavite was highly vulnerable. To keep from offending Japan's sensibilities, the United States did not reinforce potential bases in the Western Pacific, including Guam. Japan's sun was rapidly rising throughout the Far East.

Six

AMERICA ENTERS THE WAR

December 1941–March 1942

Early in 1941, Admiral Harold Stark, the CNO, ordered the commander in chief of the U.S. Fleet, Admiral James O. Richardson, to shift his base from San Pedro Bay in California to Pearl Harbor, located on the Hawaiian island of Oahu. Richardson, a highly professional officer who spoke his mind, had objected to the move in 1940, partly because it involved complicated logistics, and partly because he did not perceive Japan as a major threat. Even after the move, Richardson balked. He queried Stark, "Why are we here?" Stark wrote back, "You are there because of the deterrent effect which it is thought your presence may have on the Japs going into the East Indies."

Richardson continued to disagree with the fleet-basing policy set by President Roosevelt. On February 1, 1941, Roosevelt replaced Richardson with the relatively junior but highly regarded Admiral Husband Kimmel, Commander Cruisers Battle Force. On that day, the U.S. Fleet was renamed the U.S. Pacific Fleet, commanded by Admiral Kimmel. The U.S. Atlantic Fleet was so designated under Admiral Ernest King and the Far Eastern naval forces were upgraded to the U.S. Asiatic Fleet commanded by Admiral Thomas Hart.

In Tokyo, the Japanese military prepared for war. The army drew up secret plans for striking Southeast Asia, the Dutch East Indies, the Philippines, Hong Kong, Singapore, Guam, and Wake Island. The navy developed plans to attack the American fleet at Pearl Harbor under the direction of Admiral Isoruka Yamamoto, the fifty-seven-year-old commander in chief of the Combined Fleet. Yamamoto fought at Tsushima, studied at Harvard University, and was aware of Western industrial prowess. He was not keen about going to war with the United States. But once war began, he believed Japan should strike hard and quickly, seizing as much as the army and navy could take in the Western Pacific, and then negotiate a peace on favorable terms.

Yamamoto picked Vice Admiral Chuichi Nagumo, age fifty-four and an advocate of combining sea and air power, to lead the Pearl Harbor Striking Force. Nagumo was conservative minded and a non-aviator, not given to initiatives. But Nagumo had the services of the superb pilot and tactician, Commander Minoru Genda, as his air specialist. The striking force sortied in echelons from the Kure Naval Base in the Seto Inland Sea in November, keeping radio silence as the ships headed for the Kurile Islands to the north. Then it raced across the North Pacific.

On December 1, the Cabinet Council ratified Prime Minister Hideki Tojo's decision to begin hostilities. The next day Yamamoto radioed from his flagship battleship *Nagato*, "Climb Mount Niitaka," the signal confirming the attack. Admiral Nagumo reached his launch point 275 miles north of Oahu promptly at 0600 on December 7. He ordered the first of a 355-plane force against the American bastion.

On the Sunday morning, seven of the Pacific Fleet's battlewagons were moored along "battleship row" at Ford Island in the middle of Pearl Harbor. The flagship of the Pacific Fleet, the battleship *Pennsylvania*, was undergoing a refit in dry dock at the navy yard. There were several U.S. admirals present in the area. But as was customary in peacetime weekend routine, many were ashore, along with ship captains.

Admiral Kimmel (age fifty-nine) was at his spacious home in Makalapa near his fleet headquarters at the Pearl Harbor Submarine Base. Rear Admiral Claude C. Bloch (age sixty-three), commandant of the 14th Naval District with responsibility for the Hawaiian Islands, was at his home ashore. Vice Admiral William S. Pye (age sixty-one), Commander Battle Force, whose flagship was the battleship *California*, was also ashore. Rear Admiral William R. Furlong, Commander Mine Force, Pacific Fleet, was aboard his flagship *Oglala*, an elderly minelayer tied up outboard of the light cruiser *Helena* at the long "ten-ten" dock, named for its length, 1,010 feet.

Rear Admiral Ike Kidd (age fifty-seven), commander of Battleship Division One, was on his flagship *Arizona* in battleship row. Rear Admiral Milo Draemel, Commander Destroyers Battle Force, was aboard his flagship, the old light cruiser *Detroit*, moored at a buoy on the north side of Ford Island. Rear Admiral Pat Bellinger (age fifty-six), commander of patrol planes, was at his headquarters on Ford Island. Rear Admiral Walter S. Anderson, Commander Battleships Battle Force, flew his flag aboard *Maryland*, but he was ashore staying at the Halekulani Hotel with several senior officers, including Rear Admiral Leary, Commander Cruisers Battle Force, whose flagship was USS *Honolulu*. Rear Admiral Fuzzy Theobald, Commander Destroyer Flotilla 1, and Kelly Turner's old antagonist, was ashore at home.

Several forces were at sea, commanded by admirals who would play leading roles in the war. Vice Admiral Bill Halsey, the rough-hewn fighting sailor of fifty-nine who came late into naval aviation, was aboard his flagship *Enterprise*, which had delivered twelve marine fighter aircraft to Wake Island, 2,000 miles west of Oahu and was returning to Pearl. With Halsey was a cruiser-destroyer group under command of his old friend, Rear Admiral Raymond Spruance (age fifty-five), the quiet, thinking-man's admiral who was a keen student of tactics and strategy.

En route to Midway Island to deliver marine scout-bombers, a carrier task force was built around *Lexington* under the temporary command of Rear Admiral John H. Newton (age sixty), Commander Cruisers Scouting Force, who was a fine administrator but had no aviation experience. Another force under Vice Admiral Wilson Brown (age fifty-nine), Commander Scouting Force, in the heavy cruiser *Indianapolis* was conducting exercises near Johnston Island, 700 miles southwest of Pearl Harbor. Rear Admiral Frank Jack Fletcher, a well-liked fifty-six-year-old sailor who won a Medal of Honor for action in Veracruz, Mexico, in 1914, was conducting maneuvers with the heavy cruiser *Minneapolis* and an escort of destroyers. The third Pacific Fleet carrier *Saratoga* was in San Diego, flying the flag of Rear Admiral Jake Fitch (age fifty-eight), a midcareer aviator and popular officer, experienced in carrier operations.

At 0755 as morning colors were being readied to be raised on ships, the moored U.S. Fleet was caught by surprise as Japanese fighters, bombers, and torpedo planes swept over Oahu in waves. Rear Admiral Furlong was pacing the quarterdeck of *Oglala* at the navy yard, when he noticed a plane flying low over the air station. He heard explosions, saw debris rise in the air, and believed it was a mistaken bomb drop by friendly aircraft. As the plane pulled up, Furlong saw the red sun on the fuselage. He ordered General Quarters. When admirals and captains are absent from their ships, pennants are hoisted to yardarms so indicating. Furlong checked the various flagship masts and realized he was senior officer present afloat (SOPA) and thus in command. He ordered the flag signal hoisted: "All ships in harbor sortie."

At the same time, signalmen in the navy yard tower phoned Admiral Kimmel's headquarters at the adjacent Pearl Harbor Submarine Base: "Enemy air raid. Not a drill." At 0758, Rear Admiral Pat Bellinger at Ford Island broadcast a message that, when intercepted, rattled the world: "Air raid Pearl Harbor. This is no drill." It was followed two minutes later by a message from Admiral Kimmel: "This is not a drill."

There were ninety-four naval ships in Pearl Harbor's various reaches and lochs, but the Japanese concentrated on battleship row and the other major ships tied up at Ford Island, or in dry dock and alongside piers at the navy yard.

Aboard *Arizona*, Rear Admiral Kidd, a native of Cleveland who had previously skippered the flagship, was on the signal bridge as General Quarters sounded. *Arizona* quickly suffered several lethal torpedo and bomb hits, which blew up her forward magazines. In the enormous explosion, Admiral Kidd was killed while directing anti-aircraft gun crews nearby. Ike Kidd was the first American admiral to lose his life in action against a foreign enemy. Killed too was Captain Franklin Van Valkenburgh, who was on the navigation bridge organizing the flagship's defenses. The proud battleship settled quickly. The navy established that 1,177 of the crew of 1,731 went down with the ship, the worst single disaster in U.S. Navy annals.

On the bridge of *Detroit*, Rear Admiral Draemel ordered the various nests of destroyers to get underway, but they needed time to get up steam. They opened fire with their machine guns at the low-flying Japanese planes. On the flag bridge of *Oglala*, Admiral Furlong watched as a torpedo from a plane raced toward his creaky flagship, passed under the keel, and exploded in *Helena* alongside. An engine room and boiler room in *Helena* flooded, but rapid damage control saved the light cruiser.

Oglala's side plates were ruptured by the *Helena* blast, and the old minelayer rolled over.

By 1000, the Japanese had ceased their attacks and returned to their aircraft carriers. Admiral Nagumo's staff air officer, Commander Genda, urged him to launch another strike to finish the job against Pearl Harbor. Commander Mitsuo Fuchida argued that the naval base's factories and destroyer flotillas had been little damaged. But Nagumo and his chief staff officer were worried that a second attack would lead to serious losses. Nagumo called off the possible follow-up attack. He was criticized by Admiral Matome Ugaki, chief staff officer for the Combined Fleet, who declared, "He was like a robber fleeting the scene, happy with small booty."

The U.S. Navy's battle line lay in the mud of Pearl Harbor: *Arizona*, *Oklahoma*, *West Virginia*, *California*, *Tennessee*, and *Maryland*. *Nevada* made a break for the harbor entrance but was hit and beached at Hospital Point. *Pennsylvania* suffered heavy damage in dry dock. A total of 2,403 sailors, soldiers, marines, and civilians were killed, and 1,178 wounded. But the Japanese planes missed Pearl's vital repair shops, the fuel tank farms, and the submarine base. All but two of the battlewagons would be repaired and would fight at sea.

The Pearl Harbor inquests and arguments have lasted for years: Who bore the most responsibility for the surprise attack? Why had not Washington gathered the obvious evidence of Japanese intentions? More importantly, why was that information with warnings not promptly transmitted from Washington to the Pacific Fleet? Secretary of the Navy Frank Knox called for a major shakeup.

Admiral Husband Kimmel was singled out by Washington for the most blame—possibly unjustly—and quickly beached. Others in Washington and Pearl who were senior planning, intelligence, and operations officers survived to lead forces into battle in the Pacific war. Chief among them were Rear Admiral Kelly Turner, war plans officer; Rear Admiral Ping Wilkinson, Director of Naval Intelligence; and Captain Charles H. "Soc" McMorris, CinCPac war plans officer. As Admiral King observed, "An unwarranted feeling of immunity from attack . . . seems to have pervaded all ranks at Pearl Harbor, both army and navy." The same could be said, even more bluntly, about the top echelon in the Navy and War Departments in Washington, which had much better intelligence readily available.

*

In the Far East, the U.S. forces were equally unprepared for the Japanese onslaught. The U.S. Asiatic Fleet was headed by Admiral Thomas Hart, a tough, taut, stern disciplinarian and a competent submariner who had taken over the force in Shanghai in 1939. Hart knew his fleet's weaknesses. He once remarked that all of his ships were old enough to vote. In the autumn of 1940, he began shifting his ships from China to Manila Bay in the Philippines, flying his flag in the heavy cruiser *Houston*. He left behind Rear Admiral William A. Glassford as commander, Yangtze Patrol, in Shanghai to run the river gunboat flotilla. In early 1941, Washington decided to give Admiral Hart responsibility for the defense of the Philippines. Admiral Hart was permitted, if required, to move his command south to a British or Dutch base to carry on a fight.

In July 1941, the Japanese military moved into French Indochina and, in reply, the United States froze Japanese assets. In the Philippines, General Douglas "the General" MacArthur, head of the Philippines defense force, was recalled to active U.S. service. His Filipino army command was absorbed into the new U.S. Army Forces Far East, which he headed. Washington and MacArthur believed the Philippines could be defended with the projected land force of two hundred thousand soldiers—mostly local defense—and several squadrons of the new B-17 Flying Fortress long-range bombers.

The American defense plan called for basing naval forces at Cavite in Manila Bay and in the southern Philippines in the event of war. In late 1941, Admiral Hart started deploying some of his forces to ports in the southern Philippines and in the Dutch East Indies. Admiral Glassford moved from China to command the U.S. Asiatic Fleet cruisers and destroyers at sea, which were designated the striking force. The senior U.S. naval command consisted of Admiral Hart; Admiral Glassford; Rear Admiral William R. Purnell, Hart's chief of staff; and Rear Admiral Francis W. Rockwell, commander of the 16th Naval District—the Philippines.

The U.S. Asiatic Fleet was fortunate in having twenty-nine submarines—six old S-boats and twenty-three more modern fleet boats, under Captain John Wilkes, Commander Submarines Asiatic Fleet. It was the largest single submarine force in the U.S. Navy, but it was not to perform well. Other Asiatic Fleet warships and supply vessels were scattered around Southeast Asia.

At 0300 (local time) on December 8, a marine duty officer delivered a message to Admiral Hart in his quarters at the Manila Hotel, where MacArthur and his family occupied the penthouse. It was not addressed to Hart, but rather it was an intercept by an alert navy radioman: "Air raid on Pearl Harbor. This is no drill." Hart drafted a message to the Asiatic Fleet: "Japan started hostilities. Govern yourselves accordingly." Admiral Purnell arrived and drove to army headquarters to hand the message to Major General Richard Sutherland, MacArthur's chief of staff, which was his first news of the momentous event. That afternoon, Japan began an air assault against Clark Field—north of Manila—then Cavite and the rest of the Philippines with immediate destructive results. The much-vaunted B-17 force was caught on the ground and destroyed at Clark Field. Enemy main invasion forces landed on Luzon on December 22 with little or no opposition at sea or on the beaches.

Historians have never found satisfactory explanations as to why MacArthur and Sutherland did not permit Army Air Corps General Lewis Brereton to send his bombers against Japanese airfields on Formosa (Taiwan). Nor why most of his air force was destroyed on the ground nine hours after he received word about Pearl Harbor. Nor why the combined land forces of the U.S. and Filipino armies were not better able to defend themselves and the capital Manila. MacArthur was wildly optimistic in his assessment of the military capability of the Filipino troops in his command and of his ability to repulse a Japanese land attack.

To some, the general seemed mentally paralyzed, as if in a state of shock. General Sutherland, supposedly MacArthur's strong right arm, was no help at all. A MacArthur biographer, D. Clayton James, noted that MacArthur's supreme "overconfidence and unjustified optimism as to the abilities of himself, his staff, and the untried Filipino soldiers . . . became a contagion which ultimately affected even the War Department and the Joint Army-Navy Board." MacArthur, who prided himself on understanding the Asian mind, told Admiral Hart and High Commissioner Francis Sayre that "the existing alignment and movements of Japanese troops convinced him that there would be no attack before the spring."

Admiral Hart, constantly snubbed in his efforts to work out joint army-navy policy with MacArthur, wrote his wife: "The truth of the matter is . . . that Douglas is, I think, no longer sane. . . . He may not have been for a long time."

From the roof of his Manila office building headquarters, Admiral Hart watched in despair the bombing of the Cavite naval base, home of his submarines and repair facilities. He soon gave the order for all ships, except submarines, to move to safer bases to the south. In effect, the U.S. surface navy was pulling out of the Philippines, led by Admiral Glassford in *Houston*, heading for Balikpapan in Borneo. Two weeks later, Admiral Rockwell moved his naval district command post to Corregidor Island in Manila Bay, off Bataan Peninsula. Admiral Hart turned over the remaining naval units to Rockwell, and he and his staff left by the submarine *Shark* for Java.

In seventeen days, the Japanese completed nine separate landings in the Philippines and were well on their way to control. Eventually, General MacArthur and his family moved to Corregidor, from where he sent agonizing messages to Secretary of War Henry Stimson. An army officer, Dwight D. Eisenhower, who worked for MacArthur earlier in the Philippines, joined Stimson in questioning MacArthur's performance and motives, and why he had not "made a better showing on the beaches" or "saved his planes." MacArthur, Eisenhower believed, "had lost his nerve," could not accept the reality in front of him, and was forwarding plans more suitable for "plebes at West Point" than for the present war.

But President Roosevelt was well aware of MacArthur's glorified reputation in some American quarters, among Republicans in Congress and in the anti–New Deal press: the Henry Luce magazines and the newspapers of William Randolph Hearst, Colonel Robert R. McCormick, and Roy Howard. All were desperate for a military hero and MacArthur with his self-serving communiqués seemed tailor-made for role. Eventually, Roosevelt ordered MacArthur to Australia to command the Allied forces assembling there. In early March, MacArthur with his wife Jean, four-year-old son Arthur, Chinese nanny Ah Cheu, military aides, and Admiral Rockwell left Bataan by PT boat to Mindanao, and B-17 to Australia.

On the western side of the South China Sea, the Japanese attacked Malaya, landing troops at several locations along the peninsula. The British vastly overestimated the defensive capability of their main base at Singapore. Japanese moved quickly through the jungles of Singapore from the land approaches, while Singapore's big artillery was facing seaward. In November 1941, Admiral Sir Tom Phillips, a bright, dogmatic bantam of a flag officer of fifty-three, was given command of the British

Far East Fleet. He arrived in Singapore on December 2. On December 8, he led his flagship, the battleship *Prince of Wales*, and the old battle cruiser *Repulse*, with only four destroyers, up the east coast of Malaya seeking Japanese invasion forces. Admiral Sir Tom Phillips' force had no air cover.

On December 10, Japanese land-based aircraft attacked the capital ships with bombs and torpedoes, quickly sinking both battleships. Admiral Phillips went down with *Prince of Wales*, as did skipper Captain John Leach, who had fought *Bismarck*. The disaster was soon overshadowed by the abject surrender of the supposedly impregnable Singapore on February 15, Britain's most humiliating defeat in World War II.

The Allies fell back trying to regroup around the island of Java, the center of the Dutch East Indies. They improvised the American, British, Dutch, and Australian (ABDA) Command. It was a confused setup with each national group answering to superiors in their capitals. Hart was ABDA naval commander and remained Commander U.S. Asiatic Fleet. Task Force 5 was his U.S. striking force under Rear Admiral Glassford in heavy cruiser *Houston*, with cruisers *Boise* and *Marblehead*, and assorted destroyers, submarines, and patrol aircraft. The Commonwealth naval forces were under Admiral Sir Geoffrey Layton with cruisers *Exeter*, *Hobart*, and *Perth*. The Dutch naval units were commanded by Vice Admiral Conrad Helfrich, with three cruisers and a half-dozen destroyers. Rear Admiral Karel Doorman was commander of the Dutch strike force.

From the naval base of Surabaya in northern Java, Admiral Hart tried to pull together his forces. At sixty-four, he seemed at first weary and spent. But he snapped back physically, though with little time to organize his far-flung, retreating fleet. The Japanese moved rapidly to consolidate their grasp on the oil, rubber, and minerals of the rich East Indies. When the Japanese landed at Balikpapan in eastern Borneo, Hart ordered Glassford to interdict. But Glassford's flagship *Boise* hit an uncharted reef, and he transferred his flag to the weaker *Marblehead*, which lost a turbine and had to turn back. Hart signaled the commodore of the remaining old four-piper destroyer division, Commander Paul H. Talbot: "Attack!"

Commodore Talbot launched a night torpedo attack at Japanese transports, the first U.S. surface action in the Pacific war. Four transports and a patrol craft were sunk, and others damaged. At the time, the action was hailed as a tremendous victory. But it failed to halt the Japanese advance.

Dutch Rear Admiral Doorman was placed in charge of a mixed force, which suffered severe damage from Japanese air attacks. Doorman retired to Batavia, a move that incurred Admiral Hart's displeasure. Hart considered relieving Doorman of command but realized it would complicate an already confused international force with political overtones. For their part, the Dutch argued that Hart be replaced by a Dutch admiral as naval commander. Admiral King in Washington at first demurred, since he had little confidence in the Dutch naval command. But the United States finally agreed, probably on the grounds that it would be better to leave the leadership of a hopeless struggle to the Dutch. On February 16, Hart left Java, replaced by Admiral Helfrich. Hart was succeeded within the U.S. naval command by newly promoted Vice Admiral Glassford.

Glassford ordered his remaining supply vessels to Exmouth Gulf in northwest Australia. The Japanese whittled away, overrunning Sumatra, Borneo, Celebes (now Sulawesi), Ambon, and Timor. The enemy then closed in on Java. Various senior Allied officers began departing Java for Ceylon (now Sri Lanka) and Australia. On February 27, Admiral Helfrich ordered Admiral Doorman to sail worn and ailing ships to intercept a Japanese force northwest of Surabaya in the Java Sea. Doorman left in haste with cruisers—the Dutch *De Ruyter* and *Java*, the U.S. *Houston*, the British *Exeter*, and the Australian *Perth*—without working out a plan of operations. ABDA never devised a common communications code for the mixed naval forces.

In a series of actions in the next two days, the Allies ran into Japanese forces led by Rear Admirals Takeo Takagi, Shoji Nishimura, and the redoubtable Raizo Tanaka. The Japanese used the tactic of leading a destroyer force by a light cruiser, in this case Tanaka's *Jintsu*. In the first action, Tanaka's destroyers sank a Dutch destroyer and damaged the British cruiser *Electra*. Another torpedo spread hit the Dutch cruisers *De Ruyter* and *Java*, both of which soon sank. Admiral Doorman went down with his flagship *De Ruyter*.

Later, cruisers *Houston* and *Perth* opened fire on transports landing on Java, sinking four small transports. The Allied warships, in turn, were spotted by a heavier force of Japanese cruisers and destroyers. Gunfire and torpedoes soon dispatched *Perth* early on March 1. Minutes later the graceful *Houston*—favorite ship for the seagoing vacations of President Roosevelt—with her ammunition exhausted, was pounded into the depths of the Java Sea. Her skipper, Captain A. H. Rooks, died with his ship. Later that morning, the cruiser *Exeter* with destroyers *Pope* and *Encounter* en route to Ceylon, were found by Japanese surface ships near the Sunda Strait. Four Japanese heavy cruisers overpowered the Allied force, sending the three ships to the bottom.

In Bandung, Java, on March 1 Admiral Helfrich informed Admiral Glassford that the ABDA Command was dissolved and he was free to leave Java. Glassford drove to Tjilatjap (now Cilacap) on Java's south coast and took off in a Catalina flying boat for Australia. So ended the U.S. Asiatic Fleet's efforts against the Japanese. The fleet had suffered a bitter defeat, though it showed grit and fortitude in its unequal, hopeless struggle against a superior and well-led foe.

Seven

THE CARRIERS STRIKE BACK

December 1941–April 1942

In Pearl Harbor, the U.S. Navy began to pull itself together, though Admiral Nagumo's carrier strike force made good its retirement without being seen by a U.S. ship or plane. If the shambles left by the Japanese attack weren't enough, the news coming in from the Western Pacific was totally negative. The Japanese Empire now virtually extended eastward in the Pacific to the 180th meridian. But the U.S. Navy's shore installations at Pearl were intact, and three aircraft carrier groups were operating at sea. One of the most pressing problems was the imminent Japanese attack on Wake Island, and its tiny marine garrison.

An isolated atoll that served as a stop for the trans-Pacific service of Pan American Airway's China Clippers, Wake Island was strategically placed in the central Pacific. The Japanese Fourth Fleet, based at the Truk (also known as Chuuk) island bastion, was selected by Admiral Yamamoto to take Wake Island. From December 8 on, Japanese bombers based on Kwajalein Atoll began striking Wake Island, smashing the few American fighter planes on the airstrip and destroying facilities.

Admiral Kimmel decided to dispatch an expedition to relieve Wake Island with troops and aircraft. He planned to use all three available carrier groups. The *Lexington* group under Vice Admiral Wilson Brown (age fifty-nine) would act as a diversionary force to pin down Japanese air and surfaces in the Marshall Islands. *Enterprise* group with fifty-nine-year-old Vice Admiral Bill Halsey at the helm would serve to support the strike. The main carrier attack was to be led by Rear Admiral Jake

Fitch (age fifty-eight), which carried a marine fighter squadron to land on Wake Island.

Kimmel chose perhaps unwisely in selecting the flag officer to head the assault phase of the operation. Rear Admiral Frank Jack Fletcher (age fifty-six), commanded a cruiser division in the heavy cruiser *Astoria* with sister ships *Minneapolis* and *San Francisco*. Fletcher and Jake Fitch were classmates at Annapolis, but Fletcher graduated well ahead of Fitch, made flag rank earlier, and was thus senior. Fletcher was a non-aviator with no carrier experience. In contrast, Fitch was one of the more experienced carrier admirals in the navy. Kimmel opted for seniority and appointed Fletcher task force commander, apparently without discussing details of the mission or the carrier attack plan.

An observer aboard Fletcher's flagship *Astoria* was newly promoted Rear Admiral Tom Kinkaid, who was scheduled to take over from Fletcher after the operation. Kinkaid was fifty-three years old and riding as a "makee-learn," or a prospective commanding officer, to get the hang of the job before assuming command. The makee-learn practice would become common in the Pacific Fleet, ranging from submarine commanders to carrier admirals.

The *Saratoga* task force departed Pearl on December 16. The next day, Admiral Kimmel was fired by Secretary of the Navy Knox as CinCPac, to be replaced by Admiral Chester Nimitz, who was still in Washington. Vice Admiral William Pye, a competent but hesitant sixty-one-year-old officer who had lost his flagship *California* on December 7, was named acting commander in chief, pending Nimitz's arrival. Rear Admiral Milo Draemel replaced Captain W. W. "Poco" Smith as Pye's chief of staff. Fletcher's force was apprised of the parlous situation facing the outnumbered marine and navy defenders of Wake Island. But Fletcher was a cautious man and did not proceed at high speed, delaying his advance to refuel the destroyers in his task force. Refueling at sea was not yet the accomplished art it would become, and often took hours.

By 2000 on December 21, Saratoga was 600 miles east of Wake Island, in position for a fast run-in to surprise the Japanese invaders with an air strike at dawn on December 23. But Admiral Fletcher delayed to refuel his destroyers the next day, which took hours to complete. Fletcher developed a negative reputation for taking his time to refuel.

Meanwhile, Pearl Harbor received word from navy Commander W. S. Cunningham, in charge of the island's defenses: "The enemy is on the island.

The issue is in doubt." Fletcher's laggardly approach was too late. Admiral Pye sent Admiral Fletcher several conflicting dispatches to launch an air attack, which was then countermanded. With irresolution prevalent in Pearl Harbor, Frank Jack Fletcher could have pressed an attack on his own.

In Pearl Harbor, Pye held a long meeting with his new chief of staff, Rear Admiral Draemel, and operations officer, Captain Soc McMorris to decide what to do. Though by now the Japanese had taken Wake Island, *Saratoga* could still launch a serious attack against the invasion force, backed up by *Lexington* and later *Enterprise*. But Admiral Pye ordered Admirals Fletcher and Brown to retire.

Aboard *Saratoga*, the order was received with disbelief and anger. Some of Admiral Fletcher's staff on *Astoria* suggested he ignore the order and press ahead. A cruiser captain said, "Frank Jack should have placed the telescope to his blind eye, like Nelson." The *Saratoga's* skipper, Captain Archibald H. Douglas, urged Admiral Fitch on the flag bridge to request Fletcher that the carrier be permitted to launch air strikes. Admiral Fitch reported privately that the mood on the bridge was so mutinous that he walked away, though he agreed with the sentiments.

In his dispatch to Washington, Admiral Pye declared: "The use of offensive action to relieve Wake had been my intention and desire. But when the enemy had once landed on the island, the general strategic situation took precedence, and the conservation of our naval forces became the first consideration. I ordered the retirement with great regret."

Many officers considered Pye's decision a black mark on the escutcheon of the U.S. Navy. But Tom Kinkaid defended the action, later writing: "I am extremely glad that Pye and Fletcher made what I consider to be sound decisions in those very difficult circumstances. . . . By their decisions they prevented the useless sacrifice of valuable ships which later saw action with our enemy in circumstances of vital importance."

By now, the U.S. Fleet was undergoing a major shakeup. The top two naval appointments were crucial and the choices were fortunate indeed. Admiral Ernest King, the sixty-three-year-old, abrasive, brilliant commander in chief of the Atlantic Fleet, was appointed commander in chief of the U.S. Fleet and would soon take over the additional job as CNO. He replaced Admiral Stark, who was sent to London in charge of U.S. Naval Forces Europe. Chester Nimitz, a cool, intelligent experienced administrator at the age of fifty-six, jumped over many flag officers—from rear admiral in charge of the Bureau of Navigation (Personnel)—to four stars as CinCPac.

King was to run the navy with an iron fist, and no velvet glove. He was tall, lean, and short-tempered. He had a domineering personality—some called him a bully—but an incisive mind and an even sharper tongue, with a deft command of strategy. While he was a latecomer to naval aviation, he had commanded aircraft carriers and carrier forces, and was a fervent believer in naval airpower. He liked hard liquor and attractive women. Whether it was a strength or weakness, Ernie King believed that he could do any job in the U.S. Navy better than anyone else.

As CNO, Admiral King was soon to become a leading member of the newly created Joint Chiefs of Staff (JCS), comprising King, U.S. Army Chief George Marshall, and Army Air Forces General Hap Arnold. This summit group was headed by a chairman, Admiral William Leahy, chief of staff to President Franklin Roosevelt, in his role as commander in chief of the Armed Forces. Leahy was a trusted friend of the president and a fine administrator who acted as an adjudicator among the strong-minded service chiefs.

The JCS served as the highest strategic policy board in the U.S. armed forces. It had the final say in deciding on operations, and its planning staff had a hand in nearly every major military and naval operation. It often had fierce debates among the members, but President Roosevelt wanted it to come to a unanimous conclusion before presenting major strategic decisions to him for approval. King soon earned a reputation for pressing his case for naval strategy in the Pacific, and his views on targets and timing usually carried the other four-stars with him. His time at the Naval War College spent developing Plan Orange served him well.

Admiral Nimitz arrived in Pearl Harbor on December 25 and raised his new four-star flag symbolically aboard the submarine *Grayling*—since there were no operative battleships—but maintained his headquarters ashore at the sub base. Though Nimitz preferred a seagoing command, he realized that the CinCPac job was geographically too widespread and communications too complex to be run from a warship. In many ways Ernie King's opposite, Chester Nimitz was quiet, thorough, and thoughtful—a natural diplomat, with fatherly white hair and a pink complexion. Nimitz immediately bucked up morale by hanging on to the CinCPac staff and encouraging Admiral Pye to serve as an unofficial adviser. Chester Nimitz turned out to be the ideal flag officer to run the naval war in the Pacific. His first task was to assign admirals in command of strike forces and, more importantly, to determine which flag officers were best equipped for the arduous and demanding burden of leading combat forces in action.

King urged Nimitz to make early retaliatory strikes in the Pacific while holding, at all costs, a line that ran from the Aleutian Islands through Midway Island, Samoa, Fiji, to Australia. Nimitz was reluctant to accede immediately to King's anxious desire to go on the offensive, raiding Pacific Mandate islands under Japanese administration with all available forces. Nimitz wanted to be more selective in his approach to the hit-and-run "nuisance" strikes. At least in Bill Halsey he had a fighting admiral willing to go anywhere he was ordered. As vice admiral in charge of his carrier forces, the aggressive, outspoken Halsey was soon dubbed "Bull" by the press, though his friends and family, as well as Nimitz and other senior admirals, always called him Bill. Whatever his tactical shortcomings, Bill Halsey was a sailor's admiral, admired by everyone in the fleet.

Bill Halsey and Raymond Spruance attended a CinCPac meeting on January 8, which discussed possible strikes suggested by Nimitz against the Pacific Mandate islands—named for those ceded by the Germans to the Japanese after World War I. Halsey was surprised to find that Rear Admiral Draemel, Admiral Bloch, and others argued that the strikes would be ineffectual and would endanger precious carriers by exposing them to land-based bombers. Halsey roundly denounced such "defeatism" and offered to lead the strikes himself. Admiral Nimitz remained ever grateful for Halsey's support at this critical juncture. It would be Nimitz's job to look for this kind of leadership in flag officers, for men with fighting temperaments, which could rarely be discovered in advance.

At sea, Frank Jack Fletcher moved his flag to the new carrier *Yorktown*. He was relieved as commander of the *Saratoga* force by Vice Admiral Leary. Rear Admiral Tom Kinkaid was responsible for the cruisers and destroyers, riding heavy cruiser *Astoria*. After a fruitless mission, *Saratoga* ran afoul of a Japanese submarine, which struck the carrier with a torpedo 500 miles southwest of Oahu. She had to retire to Bremerton, Washington, for repairs, so the task force was broken up. Admiral Leary was transferred to Wellington, New Zealand, to command a new U.S.-Australia–New Zealand force known as the Australian and New Zealand Army Corp (ANZAC), which was directly under Admiral King in Washington. Leary then moved to Melbourne to become General MacArthur's naval chief. (During the war, designators for fleet, task forces, and task groups changed often, leading to some confusion over terminology.) Admiral Kinkaid shifted his flag to *Minneapolis*, and his cruisers became attached to Vice Admiral Wilson Brown's *Lexington* task force.

Nimitz ordered Halsey's *Enterprise* task force to strike the Marshall Islands. Halsey divided his task force into three groups: the carrier and destroyers to hit Wotje Atoll, Maloelap Atoll, and Kwajalein Atoll; the cruisers under Spruance in *Northampton* to bombard Wotje Atoll. Rear Admiral Fletcher in *Yorktown* was assigned to strike three smaller islands of the Marshall Islands. In heading his group, Spruance insisted on remaining on the open flag bridge without a steel helmet. He believed an admiral should show a disregard for personal danger, though he instructed others to wear regulation protective gear.

On February 1, Halsey launched his planes from the Big E, the first U.S. offensive in the Central Pacific, which caused serious damage to Kwajalein Atoll's installations and ships in the lagoon. Eighteen enemy planes were destroyed on the ground and some ninety Japanese servicemen were killed, including Rear Admiral Yashiro, the area commander. After his third strike, one Big E flight leader reported to the flag bridge and said impertinently, "Admiral, don't you think it's about time we got the hell out of here?"

"My boy," Halsey replied, "I've been thinking the same thing myself." So was formed the exclusive club called "Haul Ass with Halsey!"

The news was released to the American press, which went wild over the vastly overestimated accounts of battle damage. "Pearl Harbor Avenged!" screamed one headline. However, Raymond Spruance was less than happy with his own performance with the cruiser bombardment. A false sub sighting by one of his skippers led the ships individually to turn away. Typically, Spruance blamed himself, telling Flag Lieutenant Robert J. Oliver, "The ships scattered in all directions and no amount of signaling got them back. I had lost control."

Captain Dick Conolly, commodore of Destroyer Squadron 6 and an outstanding officer, was assigned a bombardment mission in the Marshall Islands with the heavy cruiser *Chester* in command, under Captain

Thomas M. Shock. An affable forty-nine-year-old Irishman and master ship-handler, Conolly was disappointed in the bombardment results. "I wanted to go in closer to the island," he said, "steam across the end of it, and put the airfield out of commission. We could have steamed across the end of it at high speed about five or six thousand yards away, and could have knocked that airfield practically off the island. But the fellow on the cruiser [Captain Shock] didn't want to."

On February 5, when the Big E entered Pearl with her oversized battle flag flying, welcoming sailors aboard ships and shore cheered—as the ships sounded their sirens in congratulations. Nimitz greeted Halsey in the harbor, with a "nice going," as he pumped Halsey's hand. Nimitz called a rare press conference. Admiral Halsey impressed the journalists and made great copy. The quiet Raymond Spruance was overlooked. The legend of "Bull" Halsey was launched. Halsey received the Distinguished Service Medal and much publicity, and his chief of staff, Miles Browning, got a rare spot promotion to Captain.

Frank Jack Fletcher's *Yorktown* group had less success in attacking the southern Marshall Islands. Fletcher launched a strike but bad weather precluded an effective one, and a half-dozen planes failed to return. Because of the weather, Fletcher decided to cancel a second strike on the atoll and return to Pearl.

Meanwhile, in the South Pacific, *Lexington's* task force, under Vice Admiral Wilson Brown and with Tom Kinkaid handling a cruiser escort and new Rear Admiral Poco Smith leading another screen, made a risky attack on Rabaul, the Japanese stronghold 3,000 miles from Pearl Harbor. While still some distance from the launch point on February 20, *Lexington* ran into Japanese planes out from Rabaul. A series of intermittent dogfights ensued; Lieutenant Edward H. "Butch" O'Hare shot down five Nakajima B5N torpedo bombers, or "Kates," in one engagement, an action that boosted carrier morale throughout the navy. He was awarded the Medal of Honor, and Chicago's international airport was named after him some years later. The crews on the ships could see many of the air fights and cheered on the home team. "I had to remind some members of my staff that this was not a football game," Admiral Brown commented.

Because surprise was lost, Admiral Brown called off the attack on Rabaul. On February 23, Admiral Halsey's *Enterprise* force hit Wake Island and then Marcus Island, less than 1,000 miles southeast of Tokyo.

Admiral Brown's *Lexington* task force, aided by Frank Jack Fletcher's *Yorktown* group, went back into action with Rabaul again the intended target. But news came in that the Japanese were conducting amphibious landings at Lae and Salamaua on the northern coast of New Guinea. Admiral Brown ordered Captain Ted Sherman—the skilled, outspoken, fifty-three-year-old skipper of Lady Lex—to steam from the Coral Sea to the Gulf of Papua and launch planes with *Yorktown*. With little carrier experience, Admiral Brown appointed Captain Ted Sherman as his "air commander." Sherman had faith in multicarrier operations and believed in keeping the flattop groups together for mutual support and protection.

The American carrier planes cleverly approached from the south, crossing New Guinea's high Owen Stanley Range and surprised the Japanese unloading operations at Lae and Salamaua on March 10. They sank a 6,000-ton transport, a 6,500-ton converted light cruiser, and a large minesweeper. These carrier actions were not militarily significant, and in the early days, many damage claims were vastly inflated. But the strikes served to blood carrier pilots and boost morale back home. However, Vice Admiral Wilson Brown was a loser in the operation.

Admiral King indicated he was not pleased with what he perceived was Wilson's lack of aggressiveness. Nimitz detached Brown from the carriers and made him commander of the new Pacific Amphibious Force based in San Diego. Not long after, Brown became ill, which gave Admiral King the chance to shift him back to Washington as President Roosevelt's naval aide, a job he previously held with distinction, and continued to do so. In the trial-and-error search for fighting admirals to command Pacific task forces, the demanding Ernie King tended to be much harsher in his judgments on a flag officer's competence than the easier-going Chester Nimitz. Other admirals after fighting at sea would fail to measure up to King's stern standards and, often to their surprise and chagrin, would be shuffled to lesser postings ashore.

Eight

CORAL SEA CLASH

March–May 1942

By the spring of 1942, Admiral Nimitz and his staff were sorting out the lessons learned in the first scattered offensive strikes of the war. There was still no agreed carrier doctrine: whether carriers in a force should remain separated for safety and maneuvering room, or remain closer together for mutual protection, concentrating their anti-aircraft fire, defensive air patrols, and surface screening ships. There had not been enough carriers or actions to test various concepts in combat. Most operations were conducted with a single carrier, with its supporting escorts of cruisers and destroyers, and an oiler tagging along for at-sea refueling. There had been—with the exception of the Lae, New Guinea, strike— no two carriers operating within the screen of a single group of escorts.

In April 1942, Admiral Nimitz did away with the old battle force system of arranging forces at sea. He divided aviation units into carriers, patrol craft, and utility planes under separate commands. Vice Admiral Halsey thus became Commander Carriers Pacific. This new separation proved to be unworkable, but another reorganization would wait until later.

In prewar days, the role of a cruiser was to steam ahead of the battleship force to scout out the enemy, engage, and report back. To increase scouting range, cruisers would use their floatplanes carried aboard and launched by catapult. With their great range, cruisers were expected to protect sea communication lines across vast distances. Their 8- or 6-inch guns would protect merchant convoys from enemy surface attack. Their escort destroyers would protect them from hostile submarines.

But war and the sunken battleships at Pearl changed this doctrine. Now the carrier force was the main offensive weapon and the cruisers' job was to protect the flattops with their anti-aircraft batteries. So a fast-moving task group, steaming at 28 knots or more, consisted of a carrier, cruisers, and destroyers. An admiral aboard the carrier was generally in tactical command, with another junior admiral onboard in charge of the escort force. With the Pacific full of enemy-held islands, the cruiser force was expected to be detached from the carrier for bombardment missions. All admirals had their staffs, the size depending on the nature of the command, and a flag officer's preference. Flagships had special flag-country quarters to accommodate an admiral's staff.

The U.S. Navy's command system traditionally rested on seniority. Beginning at the Naval Academy, each graduate was ranked according to his place in his class, or signal number. Promotions in the lower officer ranks were often for a whole class, so that seniority continued in place. As officers moved higher and the selection process winnowed out many, the seniority system among those of equal rank still hinged on the higher signal number, which in time was dependent on date of promotion.

This meant that even as rear admirals, each officer knew precisely where he stood in relation to his peers: one was always senior, one always junior. This seniority system produced problems (as we have seen) when an aviation flag officer and a non-aviator were considered for command of a carrier task force. Logic would suggest that the aviator was better suited to take command, but seniority often dictated otherwise. Most battleships, carriers, and cruisers were fitted out to carry an admiral and staff aboard. Admirals had sea cabins, usually behind the bridge, and larger in-port quarters down below where they did their paperwork.

In many ways, any admiral was only as good as his staff—from the imperious Ernie King in Washington, to the newest cruiser division commander at sea. A bright, energetic staff handling operational detail and offering tactical advice enabled an admiral to devote his time to thinking and planning advance moves. An admiral had a chief of staff and various officers to supervise planning, operations, communications, and administration. As Admiral Kent Hewitt put it: "A commander can't do

all the thinking for himself. The commander has to make the decisions, but let his staff do some of the thinking for him, and present the situation to him for decision." Admiral Spruance left most detail to his staff, to keep his mind on major decisions. He was not a chain-smoking, coffee-drinking, round-the-clock bundle of nervous energy—like Bill Halsey—but believed a good night's sleep was necessary for a clear mind to make those decisions.

In the navy, admirals were appointed to head "type" commands, which were administratively in charge of battleships, carriers, cruisers, destroyers, submarines, mine craft, and service craft. For instance, Commander Destroyers Pacific (ComDesPac) had administrative control over all the Pacific Fleet tin cans. This meant that ComDesPac was responsible for manning the destroyers, replacing crewmembers, planning upkeeps and overhauls, and assigning destroyers to task units. But the actual operational command of the ships was invested in the division, squadron, or task group commander at sea.

Similarly, Commander Air Forces Pacific (ComAirPac) was administratively in command of carriers and patrol squadrons receiving planes and pilots from the States and combining them for service aboard carriers and air wings. Once the ships were assigned to a task force, they came under the command of the admiral heading the force. ComAirPac would participate in selecting admirals to handle carrier forces, but the decision was too important to leave to one officer alone. Admiral Nimitz usually had a say, and Admiral King was invariably involved in the selection of all flag officers and their assigned billets. Chief of the renamed Bureau of Naval Personnel also made recommendations. Unlike the assertive Ernie King, Chester Nimitz did not like to select personally his flag officers—though he made exceptions—possibly to save himself headaches and embarrassment over such choices. Nimitz could always blame a sudden transfer, unwanted by an admiral he had come to know, on "the Bureau," that is the Bureau of Personnel in Washington.

As Admiral King looked over the list of captains coming up for selection to rear admiral; the air officers pressed for more aviators to be promoted to flag rank. Rear Admiral Jack Towers, the early pilot who was chief of BuAer, prepared a list of air captains for Admiral King. They were picked for "ability, aggressiveness, stamina, and modern ideas." They included Pete Mitscher, Gerry Bogan, Wu Duncan, Ted Sherman,

Raddy Radford, Forrest Sherman, Ralph Davison, Arthur C. Davis, Charles P. Mason, and John D. Price.

In late April 1942, the Japanese proceeded with a plan to occupy Port Moresby—located on the south coast of New Guinea and across the northwest quadrant of the Coral Sea from northern Australia—and Tulagi in the lower Solomon Islands. The Rabaul stronghold in the Bismarck Archipelago was the jumping-off point. Admiral Nimitz, alerted by radio intercepts, decided to thwart the attack on Port Moresby with two carriers. The Lady Lex, commanded by Ted Sherman, flew the flag of Rear Admiral Jake Fitch (who had relieved Wilson Brown) whose air group had such renowned pilots as Butch O'Hare and John S. "Jimmy" Thach. Rear Admiral Frank Jack Fletcher still commanded the *Yorktown* task force. Under him were the cruiser screens, commanded by Tom Kinkaid in *Minneapolis* and Poco Smith in *Astoria*.

Vice Admiral Leary, who now commanded "MacArthur's Navy," sent a cruiser force under the Royal Navy's Rear Admiral John Crace in the Australian cruiser *Australia*. Admiral Fletcher was the officer in tactical command (OTC) of the forces. Admiral Halsey was still in Pearl Harbor with *Enterprise* and *Hornet* after the Tokyo raid but prepared to sail south to the Coral Sea.

On May 1, *Yorktown* and *Lexington* linked up in the Coral Sea under Admiral Fletcher with orders to "destroy enemy ships, shipping, and aircraft at favorable opportunities in order to assist in checking further advance by enemy in the New Guinea–Solomons Area." After refueling *Yorktown*, Fletcher planned to launch air searches to find the Japanese invasion force heading for Port Moresby. But the Japanese landed invasion forces instead at Tulagi across Sealark Channel from Guadalcanal Island. During the operation, Vice Admiral Takeo Takagi kept his big carriers, *Shokaku* and *Zuikaku*, well north of the Solomon Islands.

Admiral Fletcher gave Admiral Fitch in *Lexington* instructions to join up with him after refueling. But Fletcher received word of the Japanese landings at Tulagi. He decided to head north immediately without notifying Fitch, keeping radio silence. He ordered the nearby oiler *Neosho* to make a rendezvous with *Lexington* the next morning and inform Fitch that *Yorktown* was heading north to hit Tulagi. This failure to communicate immediately meant that only *Yorktown* could mount an air strike the next morning, May 4. Three attacks sank smaller ships and

damaged others, but not as many as the eager pilots thought. *Yorktown* lost three planes and Fletcher left two destroyers behind to search for survivors, the first such instance of what would become the air-sea rescue operation, which vastly improved the morale of the carrier pilots.

On the evening of May 5, Fletcher headed his two-carrier force northwest to blunt the Japanese move on Port Moresby. Fletcher intended to turn over tactical operations to Fitch, but word did not reach the air admiral until shortly before the operations began. By early on May 6, the two opposing carrier forces were 90 miles apart but unaware of each other. Unaccountably, Admiral Takagi failed to send out search planes, which could have caught the American carriers by surprise. Later that day, American bombers from Australia spotted the Japanese force heading for Port Moresby, which then held up its advance to await developments.

On May 7, a separate U.S. fueling group—oiler *Neosho* and destroyer *Sims*—were spotted by Takagi's search plane, which mistook the tanker for a carrier, so the entire air groups of the two big Japanese flattops promptly attacked, sinking *Sims* and leaving *Neosho* a drifting hulk. The same morning, *Lexington* launched an air strike, which found Admiral Aritomo Goto's force and the light carrier *Shoho*. In the first-ever American attack on a Japanese carrier, *Lexington*'s dive-bombers and torpedo planes piled on, and soon sent *Shoho* to the bottom. *Lexington*'s flight leader, Lieutenant Commander Robert E. Dixon, radioed from his dive-bomber: "Scratch one flattop."

Later, carrier air operations would try to avoid squadrons singling out only one ship like *Shoho* by employing a strike leader to direct air traffic and apportion targets. During the afternoon, Takagi, now south of the Solomon Islands, sent out attack planes. They failed to find the American carriers but tangled with fighters from *Lexington* and *Yorktown*, and several were shot down.

The second phase of the carrier duel began the morning of May 8, when an American search plane sighted *Shokaku* and *Zuikaku*. Only now did Admiral Fletcher properly inform the junior admiral, Jake Fitch, that he had tactical command of the carriers. A strike was launched with planes from *Lexington* and *Yorktown*, which aimed at several enemy ships. *Zuikaku* suffered severe damage to her flight deck, necessitating withdrawal. At the same time, the Japanese learned the location of the American carrier force and unleashed their planes. U.S. fighter director officers appear to have been caught off-guard, for not enough fighter planes were aloft in the combat air patrol. Fletcher and Fitch's ships had to rely on their own anti-aircraft fire against the attacking Japanese planes.

On the flag bridge of *Minneapolis*, or "Minnie," Admiral Tom Kinkaid watched the show as her gunners shot down four planes. Like other admirals, he tried to show coolness under fire. "There isn't time to emote," he said. "There isn't time. A commanding officer may be scared—in fact, if he has any sense he's scared—but he can't show it, with all the men around."

As the incoming planes approached the carriers, Kinkaid consulted his charts, declaring, "If Fletcher and Fitch were to be out of the picture, command would devolve on me, and I wanted to know what course was best to get the hell out of there, as the saying goes."

The Japanese torpedo planes bore in on both sides of *Lexington*'s bow and dropped their fish, scoring twice. This was followed by three more hits from enemy dive-bombers. Fires started and the carrier's deck elevators were damaged. *Yorktown* dodged eight torpedoes but was struck by a bomb, which killed or wounded sixty-six men but did not hamper flight operations. *Lexington*'s crew seemed to have the damage under control and planes were landed. But gasoline vapors accumulated below decks from leaking fuel lines. An electric motor generator left running by mistake set off severe explosions, which started uncontrollable fires.

For a while, *Lexington* maintained speed, but a second explosion doomed her. Captain Ted Sherman calmly directed damage control efforts, treatment of wounded, and removal of excess personnel. After four hours of vain effort, the wounded were lowered into whaleboats and picked up by destroyers.

Admiral Fitch suggested to Captain Sherman, "Well, Ted, it's about time to get the men off." Sherman ordered Abandon Ship. A marine orderly escorted Admiral Fitch to the forward port side, with Flag Secretary Lieutenant Paul D. Stroop, carrying the flag war diary. At deck's edge, Stroop semaphored a nearby cruiser to send a boat for the admiral. The marine orderly waited for his admiral to go down the line first, but Jake Fitch, balked—the admiral must be the last one to leave. By the time they got down the line, a boat was waiting for them. They never got their feet wet.

The last three men off were another marine orderly, Executive Officer Morton T. Seligman, and finally Captain Ted Sherman. Admiral Fletcher assumed tactical control and instructed destroyers to torpedo the much-loved Lady Lex, the queen of the U.S. Fleet, in a 2,400-fathom deep. It was a sorrowful day for the U.S. Navy. Admiral Kinkaid in *Minneapolis* took charge of rescuing the crew of 2,735. Everyone who got off was saved, though some 216 were killed in the fires and explosions. Jake Fitch wound up aboard *Minneapolis*, and the task force returned to Nouméa.

The Japanese lost an opportunity to follow up with more attacks but Vice Admiral Shigeyoshi Inouye, the indecisive overall commander of the Fourth Fleet in Rabaul, issued several contradictory orders that left the lesser Japanese admirals milling around before being ordered to retire.

The Battle of the Coral Sea was the first naval action in history fought solely by aircraft—with the opposing fleets never coming in sight of one another. The battle resulted in a tactical victory for the Japanese: one light carrier, *Shoho*, sunk and the new carrier, *Shokaku*, seriously damaged. The United States lost the mighty *Lexington*. But it was a strategic victory for the United States: the attack on Port Moresby was called off, and damage and casualties to the Japanese air groups kept the carriers out of action for the next two months.

Never again was Australia to fear a Japanese invasion. However, the Japanese move into Tulagi presaged future plans to take Samoa, Fiji, and Nouméa to the south. The action taught U.S. commanders the need for improvement of aerial gunnery and radio communications, as well as better coordination of attacking air squadrons, more fighters for air cover with improved fighter direction, and more effective tactics for the screening ships. As for tactics in the Coral Sea battle, many mistakes were made on both sides in this first sea battle in which neither side's ships saw each other. Luckily for the U.S. Navy, more mistakes were made by the enemy.

Nine

PRELUDE TO MIDWAY

May-June 1942

The next stage in the Japanese master plan was to capture Midway Island and gain a foothold in the western Aleutian Islands. A key element of winning Midway—as far as the Japanese commander in chief, Combined Fleet, Admiral Isoroku Yamamoto, was concerned—was to draw out the U.S. Pacific Fleet and annihilate it. Yamamoto, more aware of U.S. industrial capacity than most Japanese leaders, believed that Japan must force a decisive naval victory in 1942 to bring about a negotiated peace before the United States could gear up all-out war.

To carry out the plan, Yamamoto divided his fleet into several groups. These included: the Carrier Striking Force, composed of four of the six flattops that attacked Pearl Harbor, headed by Admiral Chuichi Nagumo in *Akagi*; the Midway Occupation Force under Admiral Nobutake Kondo in cruiser *Atago*, which comprised his covering group and Admiral Takeo Kurita's Close Support Group of four heavy cruisers; a transport group with five thousand occupation troops under Rear Admiral Raizo Tanaka in cruiser *Jintsu*; the main body under Admiral Yamamoto's personal command in the super-battleship *Yamato*; and a northern area force under Vice Admiral Boshiro Hosogaya, with two carriers and three heavy cruisers and transports to land troops at Attu and Kiska in the Aleutian Islands.

It was the largest assemblage of warships since Jutland. In all, the Japanese had sixteen flag officers in various commands at sea. In retrospect, the Japanese forces were badly split and unable to reinforce one another quickly. The United States had only four flag officers at sea: Rear Admirals Fletcher, Spruance, Kinkaid, and Smith.

Admiral Yamamoto was counting on surprise and expecting no opposition, since the U.S. Pacific Fleet had no battleships and he thought two carriers had been sunk in the Coral Sea fight. He expected to occupy Midway Island and then wait for Nimitz to respond with what was left of his fleet.

Yamamoto was unaware that Nimitz learned of Japanese dispositions from the top-secret Ultra intercepts resulting from breaking the Japanese code. Nimitz had set up a special intelligence center at his Pearl Harbor headquarters, headed by two brilliant officers: Commanders Edwin T. Layton and Joseph Rochefort, both trained Japanese language experts. Among their enlisted personnel were the bandsmen of the sunken battleship *California*, whose sense of rhythm proved helpful in working out the chords and syncopations of the ciphers. The intelligence team at Fleet Radio Unit, Pacific, (FRUPAC) succeeded in a partial break of the Japanese JN-25 naval cipher.

In his basement office at CinCPac headquarters, Joe Rochefort and his relatively small group of cryptologists worked tirelessly with intercepted Japanese radio messages. The code tended to be broken in bits and pieces—a word here, a sentence there. Since the Japanese used letter groups to refer to Pacific target islands, the code-breakers patiently tried to put the jigsaw together, without ever getting a perfect read on an enemy signal. Sometimes the thrust of the deciphering indicated that something big was up. The question was where and when. Then there was the difficult task of evaluation of incomplete radio intelligence, which was subject to different interpretations. Commander Layton credited Commander Rochefort with an uncanny ability to piece together fragments of decrypted intercepts into a coherent picture of enemy plans and intentions. This ability earned the trust of Admiral Nimitz, even when Washington placed a different interpretation on the same intelligence.

The main radio intelligence receiving centers were at Pearl Harbor and in Washington, and sometimes their evaluations did not match. Still, given the intricacies of the Japanese language, it was a magnificent achievement and a priceless asset in wartime. The decoded Ultra messages and their existence fact was one of the most closely held secrets of the war. Recipients of Ultra intelligence—task force and submarine commanders—were never told the source of such information.

In May 1942, a sharp split developed between the Washington naval intelligence establishment and Commanders Layton and Rochefort in Pearl Harbor. Rochefort deduced through bits of decryption Admiral Yamamoto's grand design to attack Midway Island. But the Washington people convinced Admiral King that the Japanese assault would be directed toward the South Pacific, along the lifeline to Australia. On May 14, Rochefort got the break Nimitz was waiting for. Rochefort burst into Layton's office and said, "I've got something so hot here it's burning my desk." Rochefort showed Layton a partially decrypted message. It contained the words "*koryaku butai*," which was a code word for "invasion force." The geographic designator "AF" followed it. Rochefort believed AF stood for Midway Island.

Washington continued to disagree, further suggesting the Japanese planned to hit the Panama Canal or California, and tried to bring the Pearl Harbor intelligence staff to heel. The exchanges became nasty. Nimitz stood by his intelligence staff. Joe Rochefort concocted a clever ruse to prove his case. The U.S. Midway Island commander was instructed by secure undersea cable to send a radio message in plain language complaining that his water distillation equipment had broken down, and he needed a water barge sent from Hawaii. The next day, the Japanese radio at captured Wake Island reported that AF was short of water, thus confirming the identity of AF as Midway.

Defying Washington, which still believed that the Japanese fleet was aimed at the South Pacific, Admiral Nimitz went out on a limb and ordered all his carriers, including *Yorktown* from the South Pacific, to speed back to Pearl Harbor to repulse the expected attack on Midway. He messaged Washington: "Considerable differences in estimates probably on the same data is noted." The message infuriated the Washington intelligence gurus, even more so when King did a rare about-face and messaged Nimitz that he now agreed with the Pearl Harbor findings. This waiting period for *Yorktown* to return to Pearl was described as the most anxious that the Nimitz staff underwent during the entire Pacific war.

Nimitz was desperately short of carriers. *Saratoga's* torpedo damage had been repaired, but the carrier was training its air group in San Diego and was unable to depart until June 1. The new *Wasp* was still crossing the Atlantic from Gibraltar. *Lexington* was 2,400 fathoms underwater in the Coral Sea. *Yorktown* was heading back to Pearl with serious damage from the Coral Sea action. *Yorktown*, flagship of Admiral Fletcher's task force, made it to the Pearl Harbor dry dock on May 27, and 1,400 shipyard personnel worked round the clock in a Herculean effort to patch her up. In record time, the big carrier was made battle worthy, the dry dock was flooded, and *Yorktown* moved into the harbor, taking on replacement planes.

Enterprise and *Hornet* of Admiral Halsey's Task Force 16, which had missed the Coral Sea action because of the Tokyo raid, had also rushed to Pearl Harbor, arriving on May 26. In Pearl now, there were three cruiser divisions under Rear Admirals Spruance, Kinkaid, and Smith. When Bill Halsey turned up in *Enterprise*, he had a nasty case of dermatitis— a painful skin disease that left his whole body in a rash. He had lost 20 pounds. Doctors confined him to a hospital; he was crushed that he would miss the forthcoming battle.

Spruance thought Nimitz would select an aviator admiral to command Halsey's task force. But Nimitz consulted Halsey, who recommended that Raymond Spruance, an old and trusted friend, be given command of the *Enterprise* task force, taking over his flagship. It was a choice that surprised many—but a fortunate one. Though not an aviator and without direct carrier experience, Spruance had a brilliant mind and cool judgment. He had commanded the cruiser screen that operated with carrier forces from the outbreak of war. Admiral King said that, next to himself, Spruance was the smartest officer in the navy. (Kelly Turner might have disagreed.)

Spruance was the direct opposite of Halsey, self-effacing, clear thinking, publicity hating. Halsey's illness may have been a blessing in disguise. Halsey's impulsiveness could have invited disaster with U.S. strength so limited. What was needed in a commander, Nimitz thought, was the ability to calculate coolly under stress, while at the same time showing a fighter's instincts. Nimitz believed Spruance had those qualities. Spruance inherited Halsey's experienced staff, headed by the irascible but knowledgeable aviator, Captain Miles Browning. However, Spruance brought along his flag lieutenant, Robert Oliver, who served as a personal aide.

Miles Browning was one of the most difficult officers in the U.S. Navy. He would be Admiral Spruance's principal aviation advisor and was considered an expert in the subject. He had received an early promotion to captain and a Distinguished Service Medal for his role with Halsey in the early carrier strikes. He had a hawk-like visage and an unpredictable manner, often excitable, angry, and given to emotional outbursts. He drank a lot on the beach and was unruly and insulting when he drank.

But Halsey always stood by Browning. The irony was that Halsey was not an administrator and hated planning, but Browning was worse. Hence, the staff files were a mess and Browning's overbearing manner demoralized the staff. Still, Spruance, on coming aboard, told his inherited staff officers, "Gentlemen, I want you to know that I do not have the slightest concern about any of you. If you were not good, Bill Halsey would not have you." When a staff officer wandered into the flag mess and tried to retreat when he found Spruance sitting in an easy chair reading the mimeographed radio news, Spruance waved him down. "Come in and relax," the admiral said. "This is our home. We have nowhere else to go."

The question facing Nimitz and his staff was whether to defend both Midway and the Aleutian Islands with carriers, or concentrate the flattops against the attack on the former. Nimitz decided to form a North Pacific force under Rear Admiral Fuzzy Theobald, who had been ComDesPac, with cruisers *Indianapolis*, *Louisville*, *Honolulu*, *St. Louis*, and *Nashville*, and ten destroyers. The old battleships, too slow to keep up with the fast carriers and still weak on air defense, were left swinging around their anchors in San Francisco Bay. In preparing for battle, Nimitz had the advantage of using Midway Island for land-based planes, an unsinkable carrier, and his warships had radar.

Because Rear Admiral Fletcher was senior to Spruance, Nimitz made him OTC when the two task forces joined up. Admiral King was disappointed with Fletcher's performance in the South Pacific, believing him to be indecisive, slow reacting, and not aggressive enough. But Nimitz supported Fletcher. During the coming action, however, Spruance would exercise what amounted to an independent command from the tiny flag bridge atop *Enterprise*.

The gung-ho King, who always wanted action, nevertheless instructed Nimitz "to employ strong attrition tactics and not—repeat—allow our forces to accept such decisive action as would be likely to incur heavy losses in our carriers and cruisers." As usual, the top brass wanted it both ways: aggressive tactics without heavy losses.

To his fighting admirals, Nimitz ordered, "You will be governed by the principle of calculated risk, which you will interpret to mean the avoidance of exposure of your force to attack by superior enemy forces without good prospect of inflicting, as a result of such exposure, greater damage on the enemy." In other words, get in there and fight. It was a sweeping order, since the U.S. task forces faced a vastly superior fleet.

During the last week of May, the various, disparate forces were moving into action. Admiral Nagumo's carrier striking force departed Japan's Seto Inland Sea on May 26. Yamamoto with the main body followed on May 28. The Japanese transports left Saipan in the Mariana Islands in late May 27. Kurita's cruisers sailed from Guam at the same time. Ultra predicted where the Japanese carriers were heading. And Joe Rochefort's staff was painstakingly putting together bits of decrypted messages to get a reading on Admiral Yamamoto's carrier disposition.

Rear Admiral Robert H. English, ComSubPac, who had been captain of the *Helena* in Pearl Harbor, positioned U.S. submarines around Midway, but they proved somewhat ineffectual. Admiral Spruance with *Enterprise*, captained by George Murray, and *Hornet*, under Pete Mitscher, steamed from Pearl on May 28. Admiral Fletcher's *Yorktown*, with Captain Elliott Buckmaster in command, left on May 31 after emergency repairs. Spruance sent a low-keyed visual signal to his force outlining his plans, ending: "The successful conclusion of the operation now commencing will be of great value to our country. Should carriers become separated during attacks by enemy aircraft, they will endeavor to remain within visual touch." The key to success was surprise, to get the jump on the Japanese with a first strike.

On June 3, Catalina flying boats searching 700 miles northwest of Midway Island spotted Japanese warships, elements of the Midway Occupation Force. B-17s from Midway Island bombed the transports that afternoon and reported striking battleships or cruisers, though they actually made zero hits. The Catalinas dropped three torpedoes, one striking the oiler *Akebono Maru*, killing or wounding twenty-three Japanese sailors.

The Battle of Midway was on. A CinCPac analyst declared, "The whole course of the war in the Pacific may hinge on the developments of the next two or three days."

Ten

TRIUMPH
AT MIDWAY

June 1942

Admiral Nimitz suggested positioning the carriers about 200 miles
northeast of Midway Island to outflank the incoming Japanese. Spruance
and Fletcher agreed. Aboard *Yorktown* northeast of Midway, Admiral
Fletcher received the first reports of the U.S. aircraft sightings and correctly deduced that the ships were not the main body but a transport
group. He relied on his intelligence report that the Japanese carriers
would approach Midway Island from the northwest and launch at dawn
on June 4. At 1950 on June 3, Fletcher changed the course of his joint
task force to the southwest in order to gain position for a dawn launch,
hoping to catch the Japanese carriers off-guard. By sunrise on June 4,
there was a gentle breeze from the east, forcing the carriers to turn away
from the enemy to launch planes. *Yorktown* and *Hornet* initiated a search
effort by dive-bombers. At that time, Nagumo was 215 miles to the west,
sending off his first strike against Midway Island.

At 0534 on June 4 came an intercepted message from a Catalina
search plane: "Enemy carriers." Next the message: "Many enemy planes
heading Midway bearing 320 degrees distant 150." Then: "Two carriers
and battleships bearing 320 degrees distant 180 [miles from Midway]."
This position was about 200 miles west southwest of Task Force 16.

The report turned out to be inaccurate by about 40 miles, but
Fletcher and Spruance now knew the rough position of the enemy carriers. Fletcher needed to recover his search planes aboard *Yorktown*. He

instructed Spruance to proceed ahead to attack with *Enterprise* and *Hornet*. Fletcher would follow after *Yorktown's* planes were back onboard. Tom Kinkaid, with the cruiser screen, wisely signaled Captain Mitscher aboard *Hornet*: "Screen will conform to your movements. Operate without reference to me." This allowed the junior Mitscher to have effective tactical command of this group. Mitscher had been selected for rear admiral a few days earlier but remained as captain of *Hornet*.

The first Japanese carrier strike against Midway Island seriously damaged the powerhouse, the marines' command post, seaplane hangers, and oil storage tanks. Many planes on both sides were shot down in aerial combat or by anti-aircraft gunners. Six new U.S. Marine Avenger torpedo planes were dispatched without fighter protection against the Japanese force. Five were shot down before they could reach launch position. One U.S. plane crashed into the flagship *Akagi's* flight deck and bounced into the water.

Admiral Nagumo kept ninety-three planes with torpedoes and bombs armed and on deck to handle American carriers if they were sighted. His cruiser floatplanes on search missions found nothing. At 0700, he received a message from his commander of the Midway strike that a second attack was needed. At 0715, Admiral Nagumo made a critical decision: he ordered the waiting planes to be stowed below in the hanger deck to clear decks for the returning Midway strike. And he ordered torpedoes changed to bombs for the second attack on Midway, which took a precious hour.

At 0728 Nagumo received a message from a floatplane of a sighting of ten enemy ships. But the report was vague, with no mention of carriers. Nagumo didn't cancel a second Midway attack. Fifteen minutes later, he changed his mind. He signaled his force: "Prepare to carry out attacks on enemy fleet units. Leave torpedoes on those attack planes which have not as yet been changed to bombs." Finally, Nagumo radioed the search plane for further details and received the message: "Enemy is composed of five cruisers and five destroyers," which was followed by "Enemy is accompanied by what appears to be a carrier."

Luck was not kind to Admiral Nagumo. Learning that he might have to deal with a U.S. aircraft carrier, he was stuck with empty decks he had to keep clear for the returning Midway strike planes. Then sixteen Marine Corps dive-bombers from Midway aimed at the carrier

Hiryu but missed. Only eight returned to the island, six of them with major damage. Fifteen B-17s left Midway to hit the Occupation Force ships, but were diverted to the carriers and found them at 0810. They dropped bombs from 10,000 feet claiming several hits on two carriers. But all the bombs missed. Another Marine Corps strike also dropped bombs but again all failed to hit their targets.

While Admiral Nagumo was directing his force, Admiral Spruance was equally busy. In carrier warfare more than most, the side that strikes first gains great advantage. Hit the enemy before he can get off his planes to attack you. Spruance had originally planned to launch a strike at 0900, about 100 miles from the enemy. But Miles Browning, his caustic chief of staff, suggested attacking two hours earlier to catch the Japanese refueling their planes. It was a difficult decision for Spruance. The greater distance meant losing planes, which could run out of fuel. But Spruance took the calculated risk. He separated his force into two groups. *Enterprise* took cruisers *Northampton*, *Vincennes*, and *Pensacola* and destroyers *Balch*, *Benham*, *Aylyn*, *Monaghan*, and *Phelps*. *Hornet* led cruisers *Minneapolis*, *New Orleans*, and *Atlanta*, and destroyers *Ellet*, *Worden*, and *Conyngham*. It was current doctrine to keep the aircraft carriers operating separately, though experience would soon change this flawed procedure.

At 0702, after again checking the ranges and bearings to the suspected Japanese force, Spruance gave the fateful order: "Launch the attack!"

Planes began taking off from *Enterprise* and *Hornet*.

Spruance's second major decision was to launch an all-out attack, a "full load." This meant planes had to be lifted from the hanger deck, which slowed the launch. Spruance wanted a coordinated attack: torpedo planes going in flat and low; dive-bombers screaming in from directly overhead; and fighters provided protection against Zeroes. Because of delays in launching, Spruance realized he needed to get some planes in the air toward the Japanese, rather than waiting for a formal coordinated attack.

At 0745, he ordered Lieutenant Commander C. Wade McClusky, *Enterprise* air group commander, to attack with his dive-bombers without waiting for the torpedo planes or fighter escorts.

After the planes were away, Spruance instructed the force to resume its base course—240 degrees, or west-southwest—at 25 knots. Fletcher delayed launching *Yorktown's* air group because he thought he might get information on additional carriers that he could more profitably attack. He still remembered wasting a full-scale attack on the little carrier *Shoho* in the Coral Sea. At 0838, with no further information, Fletcher launched *Yorktown's* torpedo planes and half his dive-bombers with fighter escort.

Admiral Nagumo kept his four carriers—flagship *Akagi*, *Kaga*, *Hiryu*, and *Soryu*—headed toward Midway Island, grouped in a boxlike formation in the center of a screen with two battleships, three cruisers, and eleven destroyers. They had come through the attack from Midway planes without a scratch. But Nagumo was worried. At 0837 he began recovering planes from the Midway strike. At 0917 the planes were onboard, and refueling and re-arming began. Nagumo changed course away from Midway to 70 degrees, east northeast.

High in the clear, blue sky punctuated with billowing white clouds, Commander Stanhope C. "Stan" Ring, *Hornet's* air group commander, led his dive-bombers with fighter cover. He failed to spot the Japanese after Nagumo's course change. Radio silence prohibited any effective exchange of information with his carrier. Mitscher in *Hornet* received intelligence on the location of the Japanese carriers but did not forward this to his planes because of the iron rule of radio silence. This blind acceptance of the rule of radio silence, common at the time, was a grave mistake. Thirteen of his bombers and all of his Wildcat fighters had to land at Midway for fuel, or ditched in the sea and missed the events to come.

Lieutenant Commander John C. "Jack" Waldron, heading *Hornet's* unblooded Torpedo Squadron 8, sensed the weakness of his old Devastator "torpeckers." The slow Devastators were ill named, as Commander Jimmy Thach put it, "they were more devastating to the crews in them." Jack Waldron, at forty-one the oldest squadron commander, had written presciently the evening before, "I want each of us to do his utmost to destroy our enemies. If there is only one plane left to make a final run-in, I want that man to go in and get a hit. May God be with us all."

Waldron's torpedo planes became separated in the clouds from Stan Ring's dive-bombers, and when he found no Japanese at the expected location, he turned them northward. At 0920 he sighted smoke on the horizon. In reporting the contact, Commander Waldron requested permission to withdraw and refuel before hitting the enemy.

Spruance replied: "Attack at once."

Waldron led his squadron down to the deck, and without fighter escort, he bore in—straight, low, and excruciatingly slow—through the deadly enemy warship flak screen. Worse was Torpedo Squadron 8's exposure to the fast, dangerous Zero carrier fighters screaming down from overhead. Between the dense anti-aircraft fire and the murderous Zeros, Torpedo Squadron 8 fell, plane after plane, out of the sky.

Fifteen Torpedo Squadron 8 aircraft and thirty pilots and crewmen crashed into the sea. The sole survivor was Ensign George H. Gay, who launched his torpedo and pulled out just over a carrier's deck. His plane, holed by an explosive bullet, hit the water. Slightly wounded, Ensign Gay, a twenty-five-year-old from Waco, Texas, reached the surface from the sinking plane, and hid under a rubber seat cushion. He watched the ensuing battle, inflated his life raft at sunset, and was rescued by a Catalina seaplane the next day.

Torpedo Squadron 6 from *Enterprise*, headed by Lieutenant Commander Eugene E. Lindsey, found the carrier *Kaga* and led his slow, cumbersome planes in the attack. Ten of his fourteen planes, including his own, were shot down. No torpedoes hit. Hardly had this attack been thwarted when *Yorktown's* Torpedo Squadron 5, under Lieutenant Commander Lance E. Massey, bore in against carrier *Soryu*. It was another wipeout. Seven creaky Devastators, including Massey's, were shot out of the sky. Again, no torpedo hits. Only six torpedo planes of forty-one from three carriers returned safely. However, the torpedo pilots' sacrifice was not in vain. Their low-level approach brought the Japanese Zeroes down to sea level and in no position to protect the carriers for the onslaught to come.

At 0830, *Enterprise's* Lieutenant Commander Wade McClusky reached the estimated contact point with the enemy, finding only an empty ocean. He was low on fuel and would have been justified to return to his carrier or to Midway. He made one of the critical decisions in the battle—actually in the whole Pacific war—by turning northward to search farther, and from 15,000 feet he sighted a Japanese destroyer speeding northeasterly. Wade McClusky assumed the tin can was heading for a major force, wisely followed the broad wake of the ship, and spotted the carriers. McClusky heard Miles Browning's voice shouting, "Attack! Attack!" "Wilco," replied McClusky, "as soon as I find the bastards!" A few minutes later McClusky sighted the Japanese carrier force, maneuvering to escape the torpedo plane attacks.

McClusky had with him two squadrons of dive-bombers. He ordered his own group to attack *Kaga* and Lieutenant Richard H. Best's to go for *Akagi*. Both squadrons made 70-degree dives at about 280 knots avoiding the enemy air patrol, which was still trying to regain altitude from their slaughter of the U.S. torpedo planes. Three bombs hit *Akagi*, which was fueling planes on deck. The second exploded in the hanger deck among a stack of torpedoes, which set off raging fires. Nagumo, a hot-tempered officer, refused to leave *Akagi*'s bridge, though the captain informed him the flagship was out of control. His chief of staff argued that the lack of communications meant he had to abandon his flagship. He finally dragged Nagumo down to the flight deck and abandoned the ship. Nagumo, holding Emperor Hirohito's portrait, was taken off by a destroyer and transferred to the light cruiser *Nagara* of the screen. The stricken *Akagi* was ultimately sunk by a Japanese destroyer's torpedo.

McClusky and his planes worked over *Kaga*, scoring four hits, with one bomb blowing up the island, killing the captain. *Kaga* was soon a mass of flames, a floating wreck. After an enormous explosion, *Kaga* sank in 2,600 fathoms of water. *Yorktown*'s dive-bombers, led by Lieutenant Commander Maxwell F. Leslie, aimed for *Soryu*. He began his attack from 14,500 feet. *Soryu*'s flight deck was filled with planes waiting to take off. Leslie's squadron attacked in three waves, scoring three hits with 1,000-pound bombs. *Soryu*'s flight and hanger decks were turned into a furnace. Within twenty minutes, Captain Yanagimoto gave the order to Abandon Ship and went down with *Soryu*.

Admiral Spruance's staff under Miles Browning miscalculated "point option," the place where a pilot can expect to find his carrier on his return from a mission. Inexplicably, no one on Spruance's staff let the pilots know that *Enterprise* and *Hornet* were not traveling as fast and far as had been estimated, and the location of point option was therefore revised. Spruance's confidence in Miles Browning was shaken.

The various maneuvers had left the two carriers 10 to 15 miles apart. Wade McClusky's squadron reached point option and found no carriers. He finally located the Big E, with only 2 gallons of fuel left. Others, out of gas, splashed in the sea. As planes ran short of gasoline, they landed on the nearest carrier—if they could find one.

The morning's battle had left three enemy carriers sinking, with no damage to U.S. ships. However, the brave pilots paid a steep price. *Enterprise* lost fourteen of thirty-seven dive-bombers; ten out of fourteen torpedo planes; and one Wildcat fighter. *Hornet* lost all her torpedo planes and a dozen Wildcats. *Yorktown* lost all but one of her torpedo planes, two dive-bombers, and three fighters. It was a severe blow to the U.S. carrier air groups.

Admiral Nagumo transferred tactical command to Rear Admiral Hiroaki Abe, commander of the cruiser and battleship screen. His remaining carrier *Hiryu* was in good shape. Admiral Abe ordered Rear Admiral Tamon Yamaguchi aboard *Hiryu* to mount a full-scale attack on the American carriers. Around noon, *Yorktown* was refueling planes when word came in that thirty to forty enemy planes were approaching.

A combat air patrol was sent to intercept; *Yorktown's* skipper, Captain Elliott Buckmaster, increased speed to almost 31 knots and began maneuvering the ship drastically. Fighter squadron skipper Lieutenant Commander Jimmy Thach, one of the finest pilots in the navy, attacked the incoming Aichi D3A "Val" dive-bombers, and his fighters knocked down most of the enemy aircraft. But a few got through, striking *Yorktown* with three bombs. Two were serious, starting fires, which covered the ship with black smoke. A fire on the island ruined the ship's radar, as well as the flag chartroom.

About 1315 Admiral Fletcher transferred his flag to cruiser *Astoria*. He ordered heavy cruiser *Portland* to take *Yorktown* under tow, but it wasn't needed because *Yorktown's* damage controlmen restored power, got her four boilers back on line, and began making headway. She was refueling fighter planes when a cruiser's radar picked up a second flight of planes from *Hiryu*. *Yorktown* was able to launch eight fighters and some search planes.

Admiral Spruance saw *Yorktown's* plight from the horizon and sent cruisers *Pensacola* and *Vincennes* and destroyers *Benham* and *Balch* to assist the carrier's anti-aircraft screen. Despite valiant efforts at anti-aircraft fire and violent maneuvering, several fast enemy torpedo planes charged in, sending home two fish, knocking out all power, and causing a severe list. *Yorktown's* watertight integrity had been only half restored by the emergency repairs at Pearl Harbor. The carrier was in danger of capsizing. Around 1500, Captain Buckmaster ordered the ship to be abandoned. Four destroyers steered in close to remove the crew.

Admiral Spruance waited until he had confirmed news of the location of the fourth Japanese carrier, *Hiryu*, discovered by *Yorktown's* search planes at 1445. He immediately ordered Browning to launch a second strike from *Enterprise* and *Hornet*. Again Spruance's staff failed him with an unexplained delay in ordering the two carriers to launch their planes against the fourth carrier, some 110 miles away.

Spruance radioed Admiral Fletcher: "Air groups are now striking the carrier which your search planes reported. . . . Have you any instructions for me?" "Negative," the senior admiral replied, "will confirm to your movements."

This left Admiral Spruance in full tactical control of the U.S. naval forces engaged. It was a gallant gesture on the part of Admiral Fletcher, a fighting officer who seemed dogged by bad luck, and Spruance was grateful for Fletcher's message clarifying the command structure.

That afternoon *Enterprise's* dive-bomber squadron, under Lieutenant Wilmer E. Gallaher, delivered four bomb hits against *Hirhyu*, which started raging fires and burned for hours, ultimately causing the carrier to sink. With her went Captain Tameo Kaku and Rear Admiral Yamaguchi, a fine flag officer who was reported to be a successor to Admiral Yamamoto.

As for Yamamoto, he ordered the Aleutian screening group and Admiral Kondo's Second Fleet to link up with his main body the next day, while pulling back the Midway Occupation Force. When an accurate assessment of battle loss was compiled—four carriers and 250 planes—the mood aboard fleet flagship *Yamato* was grim. Yamamoto was unshaven and depressed. His only comment was, "Is Genda all right?" Commander Minoru Genda was the highly esteemed naval air planner assigned to Admiral Nagumo's staff. He had survived *Akagi's* sinking.

But Yamamoto was still offensive minded and was seeking a surface engagement, preferably after dark because his warships were much better trained for night fighting than the Americans. He considered pushing on with his capital ships. Admiral Nagumo was less adventurous. He sent Yamamoto a message warning that his force was outnumbered and desired to retire. Yamamoto promptly relieved Nagumo and replaced him with Admiral Kondo, commander of the Midway Occupation Force. Nagumo was instructed to look after the sinking carriers and their escorts. Yamamoto and Kondo prepared to fight a night battle against the American carrier force. But then Yamamoto changed his mind early on June 5, realizing that instead of winning a night engagement, he might face carrier air attacks after daylight. So he called for an immediate retirement.

June 4 was a glorious day for the American navy, but Spruance, Fletcher, nor Nimitz could be sure what lay in store for their two remaining carriers. Spruance knew that some of the Japanese supporting naval forces, which were still unsighted, contained carriers. Spruance was faced with another major decision: Should he steam westward during the night to be close to the Japanese fleet for air strikes the next morning? Or would that course risk running into the heavy guns of the Japanese battleships and cruisers, which could make mincemeat out of his vulnerable carriers? Spruance chose to back off to the east for the night.

"I did not feel justified in risking a night encounter with possibly superior enemy forces," he said later, "but on the other hand I did not want to be too far away from Midway the next morning. I wished to have a position from which either to follow up retreating enemy forces or to break up a landing attack on Midway."

First withdrawing to the east, Spruance then changed course to the west at midnight. This decision was strongly criticized by the air admirals and their supporters. By steaming to the east, they argued, he gave the Japanese fleet the chance to escape to the west. They claimed it reflected non-aviator Spruance's essential battleship mentality.

Pete Mitscher told his staff that Spruance should have kept all three carriers within visual contact to enhance their anti-aircraft protection. Mitscher was frustrated by the fleet's swing back east. When Spruance's move eastward, rather than a hot pursuit to the west, was reported by his staff to Admiral Nimitz in Pearl, the commander in chief said, "I'm sure Spruance has a better sense of what's going on out there than we have here. We'll learn all about it in the course of time. From here we are not in a position to kibitz a commander in the field of action."

Tom Kinkaid later commented, "Spruance didn't want to head right on west at night and run into surface ships, and so he made a wise decision and headed east. He's been criticized for that. I think Spruance did exactly the right thing."

Intelligence Chief Layton declared, "If Spruance had not exercised the caution he did, our victory could have been shot to pieces before dawn." And historian Samuel Eliot Morison said, "Now that we have ample data of Japanese ship movements, it is clear that Spruance's judgment was sound and his decision correct. . . . If *Enterprise* and *Hornet* had steamed westward instead of eastward after 1900, they would have run smack into a heavy [enemy] concentration shortly after midnight which is exactly what the Japanese wanted."

During the night of June 4, Admiral Kurita's retiring heavy cruisers *Mogami* and *Mikuma* collided. Both were seriously damaged: *Mogami* caught fire and could only make 12 knots, and *Mikuma* trailed oil. That morning a Catalina search plane sighted *Mogami* and *Mikamu*, which were reported as battleships. They were unsuccessfully attacked by B-17s from Midway and maintained their westward course.

Spruance could be faulted because he failed to launch search planes that morning either from the carriers or floatplanes from the cruisers, for reasons never explained. That morning, Captain Browning presented his attack plan. He recommended a 1400 launch with the dive-bombers armed with 1,000-pound bombs. At first, Spruance accepted the plan. Within minutes, however, Wade McClusky barged into the flag plot with a squadron commander and Captain George Murray, *Enterprise's* skipper. They contested Browning's plan, claiming the bombs were too heavy and the range too great; the planes would not have enough fuel to return safely to the carriers. McClusky recommended replacing the 1,000-pound bombs with 500-pounders, for greater range and delaying the launch to shorten the distance. Browning refused to reconsider. Tempers rose and the officers began shouting. McClusky accused Browning of not being familiar with the planes' operating characteristics. Browning told the heroic air group commander to "obey orders."

Spruance intervened. One of the aviators said, "Admiral, we will go if you tell us to. But if we go, we won't be coming back."

Spruance, ignoring Browning and the staff, replied, "I will do what you pilots want." Spruance believed in backing who was right, regardless of rank.

Browning was furious and humiliated. He charged out of the flag plot, raging, and sulked in his cabin. With that performance, Spruance lost all confidence in his chief of staff. It was a sad experience because Spruance, like other fine flag officers, believed that perhaps the most important and difficult task of an admiral was to select his top assistant, his chief of staff, and that much hinged on the right choice.

Later that day, *Hornet*'s dive-bombers found heavy cruiser *Mikuma* and sank her with bombs. That made the score, four Japanese first-line carriers sunk, along with one heavy cruiser. One battleship was damaged as well as one cruiser and three destroyers. This made up for *Hornet* air squadrons' failure to find the enemy carriers on the first day.

The planes returning from this latest strike were low on fuel and night was closing fast. They had little experience at night landings, a dangerous procedure under any circumstance, let alone for inexperienced, battle-weary pilots. Though the task force was under strict orders to keep ships darkened at night, Spruance took the unusual—and life-saving—decision to turn on the lights of the task force, with searchlights illuminating the sky and carrier deck lights switched on, to guide the pilots in. Spruance believed he had to take the risk since he sent the planes out late in the first place. He had to support his pilots. They landed safely, to his deep relief, except for one aircraft, whose pilot was recovered.

Spruance was less than pleased with the performance of *Hornet* and her Captain Pete Mitscher, who disregarded the admiral's order to change his aircraft's ordnance from 1,000-pound to 500-pound bombs. The admiral thought *Hornet*'s planes should have found *Hiryu* earlier and thus saved *Yorktown* from its fatal air attack.

Spruance privately questioned Miles Browning's overall competence. The chief of staff he inherited from Admiral Halsey proved to be testy, disruptive, and a poor organizer—not ideal qualities for his job. He failed to get several important orders to ship captains in time for immediate action. The staff officers, Spruance found, were capable. But Browning provided neither cohesion nor leadership. Samuel Eliot Morison called Browning "one of the most irascible and unstable officers ever to earn a fourth stripe but a man with a slide rule brain." Under Bill Halsey's casual style of command, staff officers were freewheeling—and like him—hasty and impulsive in decisions.

This, Spruance believed, was acceptable in the earlier island strikes, but proved ineffective when trying to cope with a complex fleet battle. The staff's lack of inner discipline pained the meticulous

Spruance. Spruance told Flag Lieutenant Oliver that one must go in with a good plan and stick with it, even when the fog of battle sets in. But one has got to have luck, too. While his opinion of Browning was now low, he did not criticize him publicly. He remembered the damage done to the navy by the Sampson-Schley controversy in the Spanish-American War.

Admiral Spruance surveyed the situation; he had only four destroyers to screen his task force and they had not been seriously refueled since May 31. His pilots were exhausted after three days of constant flying. The enemy maintained its retirement to the west, and Spruance was aware of the naval adage, A stern chase is a long chase. Further he did not want to risk his ships within the 600-mile range of the land-based Japanese planes at Wake Island. Spruance thought he had pushed his luck far enough. He ordered a course turn back to the east, toward Pearl Harbor. The great, decisive Battle of Midway was over. The tide of Japanese advance in the Central Pacific was stemmed.

That evening, freshly shaved and showered, Spruance's staff dined together in *Enterprise's* flag mess. A young officer read aloud radioed news account of a particularly grisly murder in the United States. Another officer wondered how anyone could do such a thing, unless deranged. Overhearing the exchange, Spruance asked quietly, "What do you think I have been doing all afternoon?"

A sad postscript was the struggle to save *Yorktown*. It was clear later that the gallant carrier should not have been abandoned on June 4 when 2,270 survivors boarded nearby destroyers. Even though *Yorktown* took on a list of 25 degrees, the ship reached equilibrium and expert damage control measures might have been employed. Admiral Fletcher detached destroyer *Hughes* to stand by *Yorktown* through the night, sinking her if in danger of capture by the Japanese.

At dawn the destroyer's skipper, Lieutenant Commander Donald J. Ramsey, notified CinCPac that he thought *Yorktown* could be saved. A tiny minesweeper *Vireo* had attached a towline to *Yorktown*, but could make little headway. Captain Buckmaster and Admiral Fletcher should have kept a proper salvage crew aboard, and Fletcher should have ordered a cruiser to take the stricken carrier under tow. Captain Buckmaster selected twenty-nine officers and 141 men, all volunteers, to reboard the *Yorktown* and try to save her. Destroyer *Hammann* tied up alongside *Yorktown* to transfer the salvage party. The salvage crew worked hard, smothered the remaining small fires, jettisoned planes and other loose gear, and counterflooded to correct the list. Things were looking up.

But Admiral Nagumo sent out two cruiser search planes. One of them spotted *Yorktown*, and reported back. Admiral Yamamoto ordered submarine *I-168* to head for the carrier. In the early afternoon of June 6, *I-168* penetrated the escort screen and fired four torpedoes. One missed, two passed under *Hammann's* keel and hit *Yorktown*, and the fourth struck the destroyer amidships. *Hammann* broke in two and sank in four minutes. Captain Buckmaster and the salvage party transferred to destroyer *Benham*. During the night, *Yorktown's* list increased and, by daylight it was clear she was in extremis. At 0600 on June 7, *Yorktown* keeled over and went down in the 2,000-fathom deep.

Admiral Nimitz later issued a pointed comment: "In the event a ship receives such severe battle damage that abandonment may be a possibility, a skeletonized crew to effect rescue of the ship shall be ready either to remain on board or to be placed in an attendant vessel."

Even more than the Coral Sea battle, Midway showed clearly the overriding importance of aircraft carriers and their planes in naval warfare. Despite his heavy preponderance of naval gunfire, Admiral Yamamoto withdrew because he had lost his four first-line carriers in exchange for only *Yorktown*. The Japanese lost 322 aircraft and 2,500 men, including highly trained, valuable pilots. The United States lost 147 aircraft, but many aviators were saved.

The performance of U.S. land-based aircraft at Midway was woeful, despite the wild claims of army pilots, which at the time were accepted as accurate. Better scouting plane reports were clearly necessary. Many reports were, in Admiral Kinkaid's words, "incomplete, inaccurate, and misleading." Midway reflected the courage, if not always the skills, of U.S. carrier pilots who were learning their trade in the caldron. Captain Pete Mitscher was disappointed with *Hornet's* performance and his own in the battle, particularly the failure of his planes to find the Japanese carriers on the morning of June 4. Mitscher also believed the battle showed that carriers should operate together, and *Yorktown* might have been saved had the three carriers closed in with a tighter combat air patrol. Admiral Nagumo proved a ditherer in action. Admiral Fletcher acquitted himself well. But the man of the match was the quiet warrior, Rear Admiral Raymond Ames Spruance.

The Japanese quickly realized what a master Spruance was. Captain Yasuji Watanabe, a staff officer for Yamamoto, described Spruance as having an "air admiral's best character—strong, straight thinker, not impulsive fluctuating thinker; he aims right at the main point and go, not stop. That is good admiral."

"Spruance's performance was superb," commented Samuel Eliot Morison. "Calm, collected, decisive, yet receptive to advice; keeping in his mind the picture of widely disparate forces yet boldly seizing every opening—Raymond Spruance emerged from this battle one of the greatest fighting and thinking admirals in American naval history."

Eleven
LANDINGS AT
GUADALCANAL

June–August 1942

While America celebrated the victory at Midway Island, the Japanese still threatened the South Pacific. Admiral King was determined that the U.S. force should make a stand in the lower Solomon Islands and expel the Japanese from their newly taken positions on the islands of Guadalcanal and Tulagi. King's war plans chief, Rear Admiral Kelly Turner, studied ways to hit the Solomons. King insisted that the operation, code-named "Watchtower," be expedited, though men and materiel were still scarce in the South Pacific. Some officers in the South Pacific dubbed Watchtower "Operation Shoestring." The King-Turner plan involved taking obvious risks and was opposed by General MacArthur and Admiral Robert Ghormley, newly appointed Commander South Pacific, who expressed "gravest doubts" about Watchtower. They recommended postponement. This pessimistic view displeased Nimitz and infuriated King.

In the run-up to Guadalcanal, various staff changes took place. In Pearl Harbor, Admiral Nimitz selected as his new chief of staff Rear Admiral Raymond Spruance, the victor at Midway. Spruance replaced Rear Admiral Milo Draemel, who had served Nimitz well in the first days of his new Pacific command, but increasingly seemed exhausted and out of key with Nimitz's aggressive, forward planning. Draemel moved to the West Coast and eventually to the relative backwater of the Philadelphia Navy Yard.

Captain Soc (for Socrates, so dubbed at the Academy because of his brain) McMorris, Nimitz's war plans officer, was given command of the heavy cruiser *San Francisco*, assigned to the South Pacific. This was a key posting for McMorris—who described himself as the ugliest man in the navy—to qualify for flag rank. Admiral King insisted that a flag officer selectee must have commanded a capital ship—a battleship, carrier, or cruiser. There were only rare exceptions.

Pete Mitscher, now a rear admiral, was given command of Patrol Wing 2 at Pearl Harbor, replacing Pat Bellinger. Newly promoted Rear Admiral George Murray, ex-skipper of *Enterprise*, took over *Hornet's* carrier group. Rear Admiral Tom Kinkaid, perhaps because of his experience escorting carriers in the Coral Sea and Midway battles, was given *Enterprise's* carrier group, though he was a non-aviator. Kinkaid was succeeded as commander of the Cruiser Task Force by another new rear admiral, Frank Lowry, who had commanded *Minneapolis*. Normally a fresh-caught rear admiral was assigned to shore duty to learn the flag officer's ropes. The fast promotion of blooded captains directly to rear admiral billets in charge of combat forces was attributed to the lack of battle-proven flag officers in Pearl in June 1942.

On March 30, 1942, the Joint Chiefs of Staff in Washington divided the Pacific into two overall commands: General Douglas MacArthur was named Supreme Commander of the Southwest Pacific Area. This area was basically west of the 160th meridian (the demarcation line would shift as the war progressed) and south of the equator—which included Australia, the Philippines, New Guinea, the Bismarck Archipelago, and the upper Solomon Islands. The rest of the Pacific Ocean was under Admiral Chester Nimitz in Pearl Harbor. This was Nimitz's second hat, in addition to being CinCPac. The South Pacific was a separate command under Nimitz's jurisdiction and comprised the region from south of the Equator, including the islands of New Zealand, New Caledonia, the New Hebrides (now Vanuatu), Samoa, Fiji, the Tuamotus, the Ellice Islands (now Tuvalu), Phoenix, and lower Solomons. Similarly the North Pacific force came under Nimitz's command.

As Commander South Pacific, Admiral King named Vice Admiral Ghormley, a well-liked and respected officer who, at fifty-nine, seemed in top form. He was a 1906 graduate of Annapolis, a classmate of

Admirals Towers, Fitch, Theobald, Fletcher, Glassford, Kidd, and McCain. He had recently been the senior U.S. naval observer in London. Ghormley was known as a fine administrator, and he was highly regarded by Nimitz, a good friend. But he had a tough job trying to organize his command in the undersupplied South Pacific. His chief of staff was Rear Admiral Daniel J. "Dan" Callaghan, the handsome, former naval aide to President Roosevelt and ex-skipper of the heavy cruiser *San Francisco*. Ghormley raised his flag in Auckland, New Zealand, then shifted to a forward base in Nouméa in French New Caledonia aboard the elderly tender *Argonne*, known as "Agony Maru."

The craggy, rumpled aviator, Rear Admiral Slew McCain (grandfather of Arizona Senator John McCain), who won his wings at the age of fifty-two, was assigned to command all land-based aircraft in the South Pacific area with the title ComAirSoPac. He was based aboard the big, modern seaplane tender *Curtiss* at Nouméa. The major troop strength for the South Pacific was the 1st Marine Division, which was under Major General Alexander A. Vandergrift and arrived in Wellington, New Zealand, in May. The news that the Japanese were building an airfield in Guadalcanal pushed Admiral King to move up the Watchtower invasion of Guadalcanal and Tulagi to August. The plan, as envisaged by Admiral King, was to push up the Solomon Islands and eventually capture the large Japanese base at Rabaul on New Britain, Bismarck Archipelago.

The key appointment for Watchtower was that of Rear Admiral Kelly Turner as Commander Amphibious Force, South Pacific. Turner had been serving in Washington under King as the war plans officer involved in Watchtower planning. But he constantly riled his opposites in the army, forcing General George Marshall to ask Admiral King to replace Turner with a less fractious flag officer. King was aware of Turner's vast capacity for detailed work and a general interest in amphibious operations though without practical experience. Turner seemed a good choice to King. Admiral Nimitz was happy to have Turner in the Pacific, especially since he had been the chief planner for Watchtower. Nimitz thought Turner resembled King in that he was "brilliant, caustic, arrogant, and tactless—just the man for the job." When King informed Turner he was going to the South Pacific, Turner mentioned he knew little about amphibious operations. King said, "Kelly, you will learn."

Kelly Turner passed through Pearl Harbor to consult with Admiral Nimitz, and the Pacific commander recalled that when he was appointed CinCPac, he had asked for Turner as his chief of staff, but was informed that Turner could not be sprung from his job as head of War Plans. When Nimitz was Chief of the Bureau of Naval Personnel, he once met Turner in CNO Admiral Stark's office. He asked Kelly Turner, "Could I look at our war plans?"

Turner replied, "We will tell you what you need to know."

Kelly Turner believed that one of the crucial decisions for a flag officer named to a new command was in selecting a small, first-rate staff. But Turner's first choices in July 1942 were unavailable for such a junior flag officer. Turner accepted what the Bureau of Personnel assigned him, none of whom had amphibious experience. To serve under Turner, officers had to be quick on the uptake and have thick skins.

Another problem plaguing Turner and other "phib" commanders was the shortage of experienced officers to man their ships. The up-and-coming officers in the regular U.S. Navy desired duty in carriers, battleships, cruisers, and destroyers rather than in the auxiliaries—transports, cargo ships, tenders, and the unglamorous, ungainly landing ships that characterized the amphibious forces. By war's end, most amphibious ships were commanded by reserve officers, i.e., non-professionals from civilian strata. Kelly Turner would be forever grateful for the fine commanding officers of his attack transports and cargo ships, mostly regular navy who may have gotten less than "outstanding" ratings in the peacetime navy, but who turned in superb performances in the arduous job of amphibious skippers. In one final irony, as the amphibious groups became more central to fleet strategic operations, it became much more prestigious for a flag officer to command one, rather than simply becoming a battleship division commander of only two or three battlewagons, which were generally part of a larger formation.

In Wellington, Kelly Turner raised his flag in the attack transport McCawley, known as the "Wacky Mac," the former Grace Line passenger ship Santa Barbara. Between Kelly Turner and Admiral Ghormley in the chain of command at sea was now Vice Admiral Frank Jack Fletcher. Though Admiral King was unimpressed with Fletcher's performance at the Coral Sea, and Raymond Spruance won the laurels at Midway,

Nimitz had confidence in Fletcher and recommended him for promotion to Vice Admiral. King and Nimitz were still seeking admirals who would pass the test of command in combat. Most flag officers had yet to be tried.

Fletcher was given command of the overall carrier force in the Watchtower operation with his flag in *Saratoga*, skippered by Captain Duke Ramsey. A newcomer, Rear Admiral Leigh Noyes, the former Director of Naval Communications, was given command of a carrier group under Fletcher, with his flag in Captain Forrest Sherman's *Wasp*, and the group included *Enterprise*, commanded by Captain Arthur Davis, with Rear Admiral Tom Kinkaid aboard. The force boasted the new battleship *North Carolina*, six cruisers, and sixteen destroyers. Another newcomer, Rear Admiral Mahlon S. Tisdale, was carrier screen commander in the heavy cruiser *Portland*.

Turner personally led the invasion force of thirteen transports and five attack cargo ships, carrying the 1st Marine Division. As the invasion force prepared to sail, it picked up an escort force of cruisers (including three Australian) and destroyers, which was commanded by the British Rear Admiral Victor A. C. Crutchley. Rear Admiral Norman Scott commanded a smaller cruiser unit, his flag in *San Juan*, a new "ack-ack" (antiaircraft artillery) cruiser, which only carried dual-purpose 5-inch guns. Turner designated Crutchley as his second in command, despite Crutchley's objections that Admiral Scott, as an American, should be named Turner's number two.

There had been little time to plan or train together, as the various expeditionary force elements assembled at sea in late July. The operation was overshadowed by Frank Jack Fletcher's viewpoint stated during a stormy conference aboard *Saratoga* on July 26 at the training site in Koro, Fiji. Fletcher was cool on the whole operation. He thought it would fail. Further, Admiral Ghormley gave Fletcher no operational instructions nor did Fletcher ask for them or provide his own plan to Ghormley for approval. Ghormley did not attend the crucial meeting. This was a blueprint for trouble.

Fletcher did not seem to have the same concept of his mission as Turner did, who wanted Fletcher to support an amphibious operation and provide air cover until the marines could get the airfield on Guadalcanal working with their own aircraft. Kelly Turner was infuriated when Fletcher announced he would only keep his carriers in the inva-sion area for two days, for he was afraid of Japanese retaliatory air strikes and a submarine threat. His loss of *Lexington* at the Coral Sea and *Yorktown* at Midway seemed to have sapped his fighting spirit.

Fletcher grumbled that Watchtower had been too hurriedly planned, the naval units had not trained together and the logistics were uncertain. He questioned the whole operation, implying it was Kelly Turner's brainchild. Fletcher mentioned that the people who planned Watchtower had no fighting experience. Turner replied angrily, "The decision has been made. It's up to us to make it a success." Turner's chief of staff, Captain Thomas G. Peyton, said too much of the Koro confer-ence was devoted to "fighting the problem, as we used to say at the War College, and too little time to trying to solve the problem." Peyton said he was "amazed and disturbed by the way these two admirals talked to each other. I had never heard anything like it."

Strangely, Ghormley chose to send Rear Admiral Dan Callaghan, his chief of staff, instead of attending himself. Callaghan was dissatisfied with Fletcher's plan for quick withdrawal of the carrier task force. Because of Callaghan's position, Turner assumed that Ghormley would overrule Fletcher's two-day plans for the carrier operations.

As Fletcher recounted, he asked Turner, "Kelly, you are making plans to take that island from the Japs, and the Japs may turn on you and wallop the hell out of you. What are you going to do then? Turner said, 'I am just going to stay there and take my licking.' Kelly was tough, a brain, and a son of a bitch, and that's just what he did."

For his part, Turner said of his failure to appeal Fletcher's decision on carrier support: "Whom to? And who was I to do so? Fletcher was my old boss, and at that moment the most battle experienced commander in our navy. It was his judgment, and it was my job to live with it."

Admiral King expected Admiral Ghormley to command Watchtower personally, at least in the first stage. So did Nimitz. Instead, Ghormley interpreted his ambiguous orders as exercising general com-mand, and he responded by remaining in command at Nouméa. Ghormley did not check Admiral Fletcher's operation orders nor, for that matter, those issued by Turner and Crutchley for the protection of American forces at Guadalcanal.

By now, the razor-sharp Kelly Turner had absorbed many aspects of amphibious operation, which was a complicated process. The phib and troop commanders needed to agree about who was in charge and what sequence needed to be followed. They had to understand command relations; timing and duration of naval gunfire support; air cover; the logistics of combat loading and unloading; ship-to-shore movement; and securing the beachhead. Turner realized what a tremendous effort it was to bring order to the chaos of an amphibious assault. Turner was fortunate in that his marine ground commander, Vandergrift, was steeped in amphibious doctrine, which the marines did so much to develop.

Just after dawn on August 7, the United States engaged in its first amphibious operation since 1898, landing U.S. Marines at Guadalcanal and Tulagi. Turner gave the order: "Land the landing force! Away all boats!" On Tulagi (which lies off the southern coast of Florida Island), the marines found opposition, which they soon overran. On much bigger Guadalcanal on the south side of the sound, the landings near Lunga Point were largely not resisted. It seemed deceptively easy on August 7. The marines soon took over the Japanese airstrip, which they named Henderson Field after a marine pilot killed at Midway. Few suspected that the land battle would slog on for months. Or that Sealark Channel and the waters between Guadalcanal and the Florida Islands could soon earn the grim nickname "Ironbottom Sound," because of the ships sunk in its dark depths. The reputations of admirals, too, would go down in Ironbottom Sound.

The Japanese reacted quickly to the American landings. Vice Admiral Gunichi Mikawa, commander of the Eighth Fleet at Rabaul and a veteran of Pearl Harbor and Midway, ordered a scratch force of cruisers together and boarded *Chokai* to lead them. He also ordered troops in six transports to reinforce the Japanese garrison on Guadalcanal. Mikawa decided to attack the Lunga roadstead after dark, since his crews were trained in night operations and he knew the U.S. forces were not. He planned to approach Guadalcanal early on August 9 and began steaming fast between the various lower Solomon Islands through the narrow, treacherous New Georgia Sound, which became known as "the Slot."

The Allied forces were plagued by the poor performance of long-range search planes. The writ between MacArthur and Ghormley ran through the Solomon Islands, splitting the upper islands at the head of the Slot from the lower islands like Guadalcanal. There was no effective coordination between U.S. Army B-17 search missions, the Australians, the South Pacific land-based planes under Admiral McCain, or scouting aircraft from the three big carriers to the south. If one unit's search was called off because of poor weather, this was not necessarily communicated to Admiral Turner, who would have to assume a particular area had been searched and found clean.

For instance, an Australian pilot in a twin-engine Hudson spotted Mikawa's force but misidentified the heavy cruiser as a seaplane tender. He took his time returning to his base in Townsville, Australia, and had tea before filing his report. Several hours elapsed before news of the sighting—relayed through Australia and then Nouméa—reached Admiral Turner aboard *McCawley* at Guadalcanal. The report of a seaplane tender led Turner and his staff to assume that the ships were planning to establish a seaplane base in at Rekata Bay in Santa Isabel Island along the Slot, well to the north.

In contrast, Admiral Mikawa cleverly used his cruisers' floatplanes to search far ahead and detail the dispositions of the Allied naval forces off Guadalcanal. Furthermore, Mikawa devised a simple battle plan and sent it by blinker light to his captains. His concept was to enter the sound from the south side of western Savo Island and launch torpedoes at the U.S. ships in the invasion anchorage at Guadalcanal. Mikawa would then cross north to the Tulagi anchorage and shell the American forces there, exiting via the north side of Savo Island for a getaway to be out of range of Allied planes the next day.

Admiral Kelly Turner was officer in tactical command (OTC) of the naval forces defending Guadalcanal, while newly promoted Rear Admiral Norman Scott was in charge of a smaller cruiser-destroyer force protecting the Tulagi anchorage, steaming on a north-south patrol on the eastern approaches. Turner had asked Rear Admiral McCain, the theater air commander, to send his patrol planes up the Slot to look for Japanese warships. But McCain reported directly to Admiral Ghormley. So Turner had to request Admiral Fletcher to forward the request through Admiral Ghormley to Admiral McCain. The request got lost in the process, but no one informed Turner that it went missing and there were no search planes up.

Kelly Turner's warship deployment was arguably faulty, though it was no easy task protecting two groups of transports from possible sea, air, and submarine attacks from three directions. Though he was in overall command, he had his hands full in supervising the unloading of troops and supplies from his transports to the roadstead off Lunga Point. Ignoring the principle of keeping forces unified, Turner split the western forces guarding the approach to the waters around Savo Island into two cruiser groups. The southern force comprised Admiral Crutchley's flagship *Australia*, heavy (Australian) cruiser *Canberra*, and heavy cruiser *Chicago*. It patrolled the area between Savo Island and Guadalcanal, a stretch of 7 1/2 miles, back and forth, on a northwest-southeast course.

The northern force of heavy cruisers, the sister ships *Vincennes*, *Astoria*, and *Quincy*, were part of the command of Admiral Crutchley, but under the tactical direction of *Vincennes'* skipper, Captain Frederick L. Riefkohl. The cruisers steamed in a square between Savo Island and Florida Island to the north, a distance of 12 miles. So there were two Allied naval forces that had not trained together and had been issued no joint battle plan by Crutchley or Turner. The northern force captains had never met Crutchley, and there was no flag officer with the northern three cruisers. It is difficult enough for a captain to fight a heavy cruiser, let alone exercise command of three big warships in a night battle.

The eastern force, under Admiral Scott in *San Juan* and with the Australian cruiser *Hobart* and destroyers, patrolled between Guadalcanal and Tulagi and maintained no contact with Crutchley's command. Scott's flagship *San Juan* had the new SG search radar but was far removed from the dangerous northwest approach from the Slot. Some analysts argued that Turner should have placed Admiral Scott with the western cruisers where he would have been most needed. But Turner later pointed out one of the delicacies of senior officer command. Admiral Scott and Captain Riefkohl, acting commodore in *Vincennes*, were Naval Academy classmates. For Scott to supersede Riefkohl in his own ship would be a blow to general morale, not to say naval etiquette. Moreover, Turner said, "a flag officer's effectiveness is always temporarily impaired when suddenly transferred to a strange flagship." But the critical weakness of the overall disposition was to assign only two destroyers to guard the vital approaches west of Savo Island.

Turner ordered destroyers *Blue* and *Ralph Talbot* to patrol north and south from Savo Island and, individually, to cover both western entrances to the sound. But the two destroyer pickets could be as far away as 20 miles from each other at the limits of their patrol stretches.

Additionally, they were too close to the cruisers to give adequate warning. The two cruiser divisions ought not have been separated, but kept under a unified command patrolling as a single force. Crutchley never found time to confer with his cruiser captains and explain how he expected them to fend off an enemy force. He seemed to take the attitude that his cruisers would just pitch in and give any enemy holy hell.

Turner was still bothered by the imminent departure of Fletcher's carriers, while he still desperately needed their air support for a couple more days. Admiral Ghormley in Nouméa did nothing to counter Frank Jack Fletcher's plans, nor did Admiral Nimitz in Pear Harbor. They allowed Admiral Fletcher to call the shots at the scene. Fletcher's air-minded second in command, Leigh Noyes, did not contest the vice admiral's reluctance to supply air cover. The crunch came at 1807 on August 8, when Fletcher messaged Ghormley: "I recommend the immediate withdrawl of my carriers. Require tankers sent forward as fuel running low."

Turner's staff officers intercepted Fletcher's dispatch and were deeply concerned. Most historians agreed with Admiral Turner that lack of fuel was a flimsy excuse. Frank Jack Fletcher, having lost *Lexington* at Coral Sea and *Yorktown* at Midway, was gun-shy of Japanese land-based aircraft and submarines. Fletcher didn't bother to radio Turner directly concerning his critical departure. So Kelly Turner, his ships, and Vandergrift's marines were left on Guadalcanal without air support from the three big U.S. carriers—left, in Turner's phrase, "bare assed." Fletcher's own officers in his task force were dismayed by their admiral's decision to pull out, particularly when the Australian pilot's report finally reached the fleet and indicated that Japanese surface forces were headed southeast down the Slot.

To cap the difficulties on the fatal night of August 8–9, Admiral Turner called a late evening conference to discuss the ramifications of Frank Jack Fletcher's decision to pull out the carriers. He summoned Admiral Crutchley and General Vandergrift to his flagship *McCawley* lying off Guadalcanal's Lunga Point. It is puzzling why Kelly Turner called in Crutchley; the Allied admiral was not in a position to contribute much advice on the tactical situation, and the imperious Kelly Turner was not an officer who often acted on others' advice. However, that morning Crutchley had asked Turner for a "rough outline of the present situation and future intentions." This may have been Turner's response.

Crutchley pulled his flagship *Australia* out of the patrol line to keep the appointment with Turner who was 10 miles away. He signaled Captain Howard D. Bode of *Chicago*: "Take charge of the patrol." Bode was left in command of the southern force and, by extension, the northern force. Admiral Crutchley failed to inform Captain Riefkohl in *Vincennes* of his sudden departure. Crutchley's actions further contributed to the confusion in the Allied command.

At 2230, Crutchley was aboard Turner's flagship *McCawley* off Lunga Point. Vandergrift arrived 45 minutes later. All three senior officers were exhausted. Crutchley asked Turner where he thought the reported Japanese "seaplane tenders" were headed, and Turner replied Rekata Bay in Santa Isabel up the Slot. Turner suggested that an enemy air attack would be launched the next day, rather than a surface action. Turner wondered whether he should pull his transports out, leaving the marines unsupplied, or whether to keep the force unloading supplies and face Japanese air attacks the next day.

It was a dreadful dilemma. Turner proposed to pull out. Vandergrift was aghast at the plight of his 18,000 debarked marines, but hoped to get the most needed supplies ashore during the rest of the night. Turner still thought that the Japanese force coming down the Slot intended to set up a seaplane base, thus the danger would come the next morning from the air, not that very evening from the sea. It was a case of judging enemy intentions rather than capabilities. With no alert from their admirals, the cruiser captains were not really battle minded that fateful night.

The conference broke up at 2355 and Admiral Crutchley returned to his flagship *Australia*. Because of the late hour, he decided not to join up with his force but to remain between his ships and the Guadalcanal beachhead. Crutchley did not inform Captain Bode or Admiral Turner of this decision. Captain Bode had retired for the night aboard *Chicago* and had not taken station at the head of his column—as a flagship customarily did—because he expected *Australia* to return during the night and lead the column. The northern force cruisers were never notified of Crutchley's absence with *Australia*.

So the Allied strong force of cruisers and destroyers off Guadalcanal had subtly shifted from a position of offense to one of defense, not knowing where a threat was coming from and with no clear instructions on how to counter it.

Twelve
DEFEAT AT SAVO

August 8–9, 1942

On came Admiral Mikawa's cruisers on a moonless night marked by occasional rainsqualls, low clouds, and mist. The picket destroyer *Ralph Talbot* between Savo and Florida Island sighted one of two cruiser float-planes overhead, launched earlier by Mikawa. The destroyer signaled: "Warning—warning. Plane over Savo headed east." The warning was received by only a few ships nearest *Ralph Talbot*, including the northern cruisers. But they failed to grasp the significance of the sighting. Commanding officers assumed the planes, which they also picked up, were friendly because they showed running lights. They assumed that Admiral Turner, having received the report, would warn them if the planes were Japanese.

Admiral Gunichi Mikawa steamed on, his ships in a single column: heavy cruisers *Chokai*, *Aoba*, *Kako*, *Kinugasa*, and *Furutaka*; light cruisers *Tenryu* and *Yubari*, and destroyer *Yunagi*. The Japanese ships trained out their torpedo tubes with the deadly long-lance weapons. As the cruisers approached the sound between Savo and Guadalcanal, they spotted the picket destroyer *Blue* heading away toward the far end of her patrol leg. Fifty Japanese guns were trained on the American tin can. But *Blue* steamed on, having not seen the Japanese column to the rear. The disciplined Japanese held fire. Without radar, their keen-eyed lookouts soon spotted the cruisers and destroyers of the southern force and Mikawa gave the order: "All ships attack." Torpedoes leaped from their tubes.

The destroyer *Patterson*, escorting the southern cruisers, sighted the looming Japanese ships in the dark. At 0143 *Patterson* radioed: "Warning—warning: strange ships entering harbor." Just then Japanese floatplanes dropped illuminating flares over the transports, which etched *Chicago* and *Canberra* as choice targets. Shells and torpedoes hit *Canberra* simultaneously, mortally wounding Captain F. E. Getting after he ordered his ship to open fire. But Captain Getting failed to notify Admiral Crutchley or the northern cruisers that he was firing at the enemy. In less than four minutes, *Canberra* herself was out of the war and sinking.

Next came *Chicago's* bloody turn. Torpedoes smacked into the heavy cruiser, slicing off part of her bow. *Chicago* began firing at a trailing Japanese destroyer, as the cruiser headed away from the main battle. Captain Bode, who was still in tactical command, failed to alert the three northern heavy cruisers 7 miles away of the presence of the Japanese invaders, which were now blazing through the sound, having knocked the Allied southern force out of the battle without suffering a single hit.

Mikawa spotted the northern group of American cruisers and changed course to east-northeast. The other ships did not closely follow flagship *Chokai* and divided into two columns. *Chokai* fired four torpedoes at the northern cruisers, which were turning on their patrol track from southwest to northwest, moving quietly at 10 knots. When the Japanese opened up, the rearmost warship, *Astoria*, was hit by a torpedo and shellfire.

Captain William G. Greenman was asleep in his cabin, fully clothed after two days of continuous patrolling. No one had reacted to *Patterson's* warning or to the flares overhead. At last, an alert gunnery officer saw the star shells and ordered General Quarters. At 0150, Japanese searchlights snapped on, followed by salvos of shells. *Astoria's* gunnery officer ordered return firing. A puzzled Captain Greenman arrived on the bridge and thought *Astoria* was shooting at a friendly ship. He ordered, "Cease firing!" The gunnery officer, Lieutenant Commander W. H. Truesdell, replied, "Sir, for God's sake give the word: Commence Firing!" The captain countermanded his order two minutes later, but it was too late for *Astoria*. The Japanese had found the range and turned the heavy cruiser into blazing wreck. She was mortally wounded.

Quincy was next ahead. The heavy cruiser was caught in Japanese searchlights. Captain Samuel N. Moore on the bridge ordered, "Fire at the ships with the searchlights on!" His gunners did so, getting away several salvos. But enemy shells rained down and killed Captain Moore and most of his personnel on the bridge. A surviving signalman tried to steer *Quincy* to Savo Island to beach the cruiser, but the ship was heeling to port, sinking by the bow.

Vincennes was leading the northern column. Captain Riefkohl was in his sea cabin just off the bridge. Duty officers heard *Patterson's* warning message but were unclear as to its significance. Then the aircraft flares started dropping. Riefkohl increased speed to 15 knots and noted searchlights being directed at his following cruisers. The captain thought they came from his southern group and requested by voice radio that they be shut off. With no response, his gunnery officer trained on the nearest light.

Vincennes got off a full 8-inch salvo but was soon hit by enemy shells, which exploded her gasoline-laden floatplanes on the catapults amidships. Then torpedoes from *Chokai* hit *Vincennes*. From his unengaged side, searchlights came on, and Captain Riefkohl thought they were friendly. It was the separated second Japanese column. He ordered the oversized battle flag run up for identification. The Japanese thought the ensign was an admiral's flag and increased efforts to sink *Vincennes*. Her turrets were crushed and twisted, and she was listing heavily. The Japanese moved on, but *Vincennes* was beyond hope and sank about 0250.

The battle had turned into a confusing melee, and the screening destroyers of the northern force, *Wilson* and *Helm*, fired at what they thought were enemy ships, but could never be sure.

At this point, Admiral Mikawa was in a highly advantageous position to continue his slaughter taking on the transports. For undetermined reasons, though, he made two quick course changes that were not followed by his cruisers, and he found his flagship *Chokai* in the wake of cruiser *Kinugasa*. Two shells from *Quincy* hit *Chokai*, one of which blasted the Admiral's chart room, with several staff casualties. At 0220 Mikawa ordered his captains: "All ships withdraw." In two columns, the Japanese force steamed out of the sound between Savo and Florida Island. They ran across *Ralph Talbot* still patrolling the northerly entrance to the sound. The Japanese cruisers fired at the U.S. destroyer, which replied with its smaller 5-inch guns. The plucky *Ralph Talbot* suffered several hits, but its gallant fight may have convinced Admiral

Mikawa that other American warships were moving in, and this rein-forced his intention to retire. He did so at high speed.

The dramatic fight around Savo Island remained a mystery to the other U.S. units in the sound. Admiral Turner, with his transports and escort destroyers, could see the gun flashes and explosions in the squally night from his flag bridge on *McCawley*. But he received no word as to what was going on. Nor did Admiral Crutchley, his flagship alone and out of the action. Admiral Scott in *San Juan* heading the eastern force was well out of it, continuing the patrol and getting no information or orders.

Admiral Fletcher, with carriers *Saratoga*, *Enterprise*, and *Wasp* head-ing south, paused briefly well away from Guadalcanal on his way to retir-ing farther. At 0300 he heard Admiral Turner's rough report of a surface action in the Guadalcanal-Tulagi area. Turner hoped Ghormley would order Fletcher to remain in the area. In addition to his carriers, Fletcher had the new battleship *North Carolina*, six heavy cruisers, and sixteen destroyers—by far the strongest force in his fleet. Forrest Sherman, cap-tain of *Wasp*, three times requested Admiral Leigh Noyes aboard *Wasp* to speed northwestward during the night to launch a dawn strike against the Japanese surface ships and give Turner's ships air cover. Noyes declined even to forward Sherman's request to Admiral Fletcher. At 0330 Ghormley approved Fletcher's earlier request to pull back, before the latest battle reports came in. Fletcher waited no longer nor did he check any further, but simply took off to the south to find his tankers, away from any effective action.

As dawn broke on August 9, the scene in Ironbottom Sound was one of desolation: four Allied heavy cruisers had sunk or were sinking, one heavy cruiser and two destroyers badly damaged. Destroyers picked up survivors from the cruisers in the oil-blackened waters, filled with the debris of once-proud warships. Admiral Turner instructed the unloading of the transports to continue. Around 1600, Turner ordered the amphibious force to depart the beachhead, leaving the U.S. Marines on their own.

Heading back up the Slot, Admiral Mikawa expected an air attack, but none came from Fletcher's departing carriers. Mikawa's ships had escaped almost unscathed, except for damage and casualties to his flag-ship, *Chokai*. On his arrival in Rabaul, Admiral Mikawa was congratulated by Admiral Yamamoto, who expressed private displeasure that Mikawa did not linger to dispose of Turner's transports.

Savo Island was the worst defeat the U.S. Navy ever suffered at sea. The totally one-sided battle pitted forces of roughly equal size. The Japanese performed expertly. The Allies did not. The United States kept the losses secret for two months. Repercussions were felt throughout the navy. Details of the battle were a long time coming. After an investigation, Admirals King and Nimitz agreed that there was a severe failure in the air search intelligence and coordination, the estimate of enemy intentions, communications, radar, and the lack of a flag officer in the southern force. In general, the Allied force was simply not battle minded. The only saving element was the failure of the Japanese to attack the sitting-duck transports at Guadalcanal and Tulagi.

The surviving captains of the heavy cruisers never received another ship command; their expectations of flag rank vanished. Frank Jack Fletcher's decisions left him low in Admiral King's esteem. Fletcher justified his imputed lack of aggressiveness by citing Nimitz's orders not to jeopardize his force without good prospects of inflicting superior damage on the enemy. He believed the danger of Japanese air and submarine attacks justified his decision to retire, and seemed less concerned about the fate of the amphibious force or the landed marines. Admiral Turner never agreed with Fletcher's decision to retire.

The standing of Admiral Noyes, whose role was passive, was not much better, and he was eventually shifted to shore commands. Admiral Ghormley imprinted little control on the battle, nor did he solicit running information of the events. Indeed, he remained in the dark as to what happened for some time afterward. He was faulted for allowing Fletcher to remove his carriers from effective support.

Admiral Crutchley had left his ships without anyone firmly in charge. Perhaps because he was a British officer commanding both Australian and American ships, he escaped censure. Admiral Slew McCain's failure to follow up with land-based searches or warn Turner his planes hadn't completed their mission—actions that Kelly Turner privately deplored—was not held against McCain by higher headquarters.

The most interesting fate was that of Kelly Turner, the self-assured, irascible amphibious commander. As OTC of the ships in the

Guadalcanal vicinity, he was responsible for the dispositions of the forces; he made the estimate of Japanese intentions; and he called a conference aboard his flagship, which took Crutchley and flagship *Australia* out of position. Though doctrine usually advises against dividing one's forces, Turner had tactical reasons (as illustrated earlier) for his decision to split his forces: to cover the three separate approaches to the transport areas.

Turner measured up to his role: "Whatever responsibility for the defeat is mine, I accept.

"For a long time after the 9th of August," Turner added, "I kept trying to fit the pieces together to change our defeat into a victory. It all boiled down to needing better air reconnaissance, better communications, better radar, a more combative reaction, and a greater respect for Jap capabilities."

Admirals King and Nimitz decided the blame for Savo was too evenly divided among U.S. flag officers and captains for any one to be singled out for public censure. King and Nimitz were anxious to find flag officers imbued with fighting spirit in the teeth of adversity among their flag officers. Certainly, Kelly Turner was proving to be a fighter. Although some questioned Turner's tactical judgment, he retained the confidence of King and Nimitz, who were quick to bench rear admirals failing to meet their high standards in combat. That was a lucky break. Terrible Turner would sailor on to become one of the greatest fighting admirals of the war.

Thirteen
ACTION AROUND THE CANAL

August–October 1942

The Japanese did not take the American assault on Guadalcanal lightly. They fought fiercely on land against the U.S. Marines, who called the island battlefield "the Canal." The Japanese high command ordered small groups of fast destroyers, which the marines nicknamed the "Tokyo Express," to run reinforcements down the Slot at night. The Japanese hit the marines with land-based planes during the day and naval shellfire at night, making their lives hell.

On August 24, Admiral Yamamoto planned to land 1,500 troops supported by the Combined Fleet, a flexible force that could add or subtract warships. At Truk, Yamamoto oversaw the main body of the fleet, which had three carriers, three battleships, five cruisers, eight destroyers, and numerous auxiliaries. At Rabaul, Vice Admiral Nishizo Tsukahara had four cruisers and five destroyers with one hundred planes of the Eleventh Air Fleet. The Japanese headed for Guadalcanal, led by Vice Admiral Nobutake Kondo, with the main body of the Second Fleet, the big carriers *Shokaku* and *Zuikaku*, the light carrier *Ryujo*, two battlewagons, and a large screening force.

Vice Admiral Ghormley in Nouméa monitored the Japanese activities with the help of Australian coast watchers and Admiral Slew McCain's land-based search planes. Ghormley assigned his three-carrier force, still under Vice Admiral Frank Jack Fletcher, to protect the convoy routes leading to Guadalcanal in the northeastern quadrant of the Coral Sea. It was a familiar team. Fletcher flew his flag in *Saratoga*, commanded by Captain Duke Ramsey, with a newcomer, Rear Admiral Carleton H. "Bosco" Wright, leading the cruiser screen in *Minneapolis*. The veteran Rear Admiral Tom Kinkaid—an intense chain smoker—rode *Enterprise* with Captain Arthur Davis at the helm, and Rear Admiral Mahlon Tisdale led the screen in *Portland*. Rear Admiral Leigh Noyes was aboard *Wasp*, under Captain Forrest Sherman, with Rear Admiral Norman Scott in charge of screening *Wasp* in light cruiser *San Juan*.

Tom Kinkaid, a fifty-four-year-old non-aviator, did not expect to be chosen for a carrier group command. He was a surface ship sailor who, on his way up, had spent time on various admirals' staffs and invariably received high fitness reports. He was not a brilliant thinker like his classmate Kelly Turner, but he was a dependable, meat-and-potatoes flag officer. He'd been a cruiser screen commander accompanying aircraft carriers in earlier operations, and Nimitz picked him to lead the third carrier group in the Watchtower operation. Kinkaid was the first to admit he was more follow-the-leader in his experience with carriers. He also knew that luck, pure and simple, had played a large role at key points in his career, being in the right place at the right time—such as in the summer of 1942, when there was a dearth of air admirals available for command at Pearl.

On August 23, Admiral Fletcher had no current intelligence on the location and size of the Japanese force, but believed a battle was still days away. He decided he had time to send *Wasp*'s group south to refuel because, he thought, the destroyers were running low. As on previous occasions, Fletcher's concern with refueling seemed unwarranted: the tin cans, while not topped off, had comfortable reserves of black oil to operate.

On the morning of August 24, Fletcher ordered Kinkaid to launch an *Enterprise* search to the north. *Saratoga*, too, sent up planes, and the carrier aircraft found the smaller carrier *Ryujo*, as well as the two bigger carriers farther north. Fletcher was having poor radio communications and was not immediately apprised of the sightings. He found the situation confusing. Fletcher made an unsuccessful effort to divert *Saratoga*'s dive-bombers to attack the big carriers *Shokaku* and *Zuikaku*. As usual in the Pacific, the prevailing winds were easterly, which meant that carriers had to turn eastward to launch and recover planes, a time-consuming operation for the American forces. *Enterprise*'s dive-bombers found *Shokaku* and inflicted minor damage. *Saratoga*'s planes worked over *Ryujo* and, by 2000, the light carrier headed for the bottom. But Admiral Kondo was using *Ryujo* as a decoy and sent strike aircraft from his two big carriers against *Enterprise* and *Saratoga*.

As at the Coral Sea and Midway, the two U.S. carriers operated independently, each the center of a task group, 10 miles apart. *Enterprise* was caught by enemy dive-bombers, which hit the veteran carrier three times, causing fires and major damage. Admiral Kinkaid and his staff were shaken up, but no one on the flag bridge was seriously injured, even though there was death and destruction below. Fast work by the damage control parties saved *Enterprise* from the fate of *Lexington* and *Yorktown*. Captain Arthur Davis was able to build up speed to recover the Big E's returning planes. Again *Enterprise* lost steering control and began careening through the task force, with Captain Davis ordering the No. 5 "breakdown" flag hoisted, and the whistle sounded. Forty minutes later, after almost running down a destroyer, *Enterprise* regained steering control. Admiral Fletcher ordered a general retirement for the night, heading for a southerly fueling rendezvous.

During the evening, Admiral Tanaka aboard cruiser *Jintsu* led his destroyers off Lunga Point to shell U.S. Marines on Guadalcanal. The next day U.S. Marine bombers hit *Jintsu* from Guadalcanal, and Tanaka had to transfer his flag to destroyer *Kagero*. The higher command at Rabaul ordered Rear Admiral Tanaka to return his transports without unloading.

In most ways, this latest engagement—the Battle of the Eastern Solomons and the third big carrier-to-carrier engagement in the Pacific—was a victory for the Americans. They sank a light carrier and prevented the transport force from landing troops, even though it was supported by a huge Japanese fleet. But Frank Jack Fletcher received only limited credit, partly because he was overly concerned about refueling and did not bring to bear the full strength of his carrier force. *Wasp* played no role in the action and *Saratoga* was withdrawn prematurely. Fletcher, with more aggressive tactics, might have inflicted additional damage on *Shokaku* and *Zuikaku*. The battle, too, did not resolve the running debate among air admirals as to whether carriers should operate singly or together.

In the aftermath of the Battle of the Eastern Solomons, the action on and around Guadalcanal developed into a struggle of attrition. The

Japanese controlled the night, the Americans the day. After dark, Japanese destroyer transports under the tenacious Rear Admiral Tanaka steamed down the Slot, landing troops on Guadalcanal or shelling marines. The next day, American planes tried to catch up with the retiring Japanese and bomb their ships. Occasionally, a skirmish would develop in Ironbottom Sound resulting in the loss of a destroyer type.

On August 31, while guarding the Nouméa-Solomons supply route, *Saratoga* was steaming 260 miles southeast of Guadalcanal when she was hit by torpedoes fired by the Japanese submarine *I-26*. Captain Duke Ramsey tried to maneuver the huge ship out of harm's way but couldn't make it. A fish hit near the starboard side below the island, the second time in 1942 she'd been so damaged. But only twelve men were wounded, including Vice Admiral Fletcher, and damage control parties soon had the fires under control. Skipper Ramsey built up speed to allow his planes to take off and head for Espiritu Santo. They then flew to Guadalcanal to fight from Henderson Field, where the marines called the navy pilots "bell-bottom aviators." *Saratoga* made it to Tongatabu, but was out of action for three months while getting extensive repairs at Pearl Harbor.

Admiral Fletcher returned to Pearl Harbor, too. Admiral Ghormley implicitly criticized him for keeping *Saratoga* in a general area where enemy submarines had been previously reported, thereby letting himself be pinned down by the preying Japanese undersea craft. Nimitz planned to give Fletcher a long leave in the United States. In reply to a query by Nimitz about Fletcher, Slew McCain in Nouméa said, "Two or three of these fights are enough for one man. A rest will do him good." After his rest, Fletcher was ordered to report to Washington for two weeks temporary duty.

The personable Frank Jack Fletcher was an unlucky admiral. He had seen more action than any other flag officer, but each battle—Coral Sea, Midway, Solomons—carried a downside for him. Perhaps as a non-aviator he was never comfortable handling carrier groups. His future as far as fighting command at sea would be left to the harsh judgment of Admiral Ernest King, who would look over Fletcher in Washington.

On September 15, carrier *Wasp*, captained by Forrest Sherman, was screening a transport convoy carrying reinforcements for Guadalcanal under the command of Rear Admiral Kelly Turner. Aboard *Wasp* was Rear Admiral Leigh Noyes, heading a task group of four cruisers and six destroyers. Nearby were the carrier *Hornet* and the new battleship *North Carolina*. The Japanese submarine *I-19* was waiting and unleashed a spread of four torpedoes. Captain Sherman ordered right hard rudder, but it was too late. Three powerful fish struck *Wasp*'s starboard side near the center of the ship.

The explosions were withering. Planes on the flight and hanger decks were knocked around, their gasoline igniting. Fires spread to ready ammo boxes and severed all water mains, leaving damage controlmen helpless to fight the fires. Admiral Noyes had been badly injured by the blasts, with burning clothes and a singed face. Captain Sherman soon realized *Wasp*'s wounds were fatal. With Admiral Noyes' approval, Sherman ordered his ship abandoned. A total of 193 men were killed and 366 were wounded.

In *Hornet*'s group, the submarine *I-15* made a big score, too. One torpedo hit the battleship *North Carolina* and another struck the destroyer *O'Brien*. *North Carolina* made it to Tongatabu and thence to Pearl for repairs, while *O'Brien* safely reached Nouméa, but sprung leaks sailing to the West Coast, broke in two, and sank.

The South Pacific Force could not spare the removal from action of the three ships. Only carrier *Hornet* was left operational in the South Pacific. As in the case of Fletcher with *Saratoga*, Admiral Ghormley thought Admiral Noyes erred in crossing his previous tracks several times while standing off from the transports. In defense, Noyes insisted that his track lines had not come close enough to rate a censure. Rear Admiral John Shafroth conducted an inquiry at Admiral Nimitz's orders and concluded that no one should be blamed for the loss of *Wasp*. In the end, Admiral Kelly Turner's transports made it safely to Guadalcanal.

The morale of the marines on Guadalcanal and in the ships fighting around that island was near bottom in early October 1942. It was a desperate time and the issue was in doubt. Admiral Ghormley planned to send in the 164th Regiment of the U.S. Army's America Division to reinforce the hard-pressed marines. To cover Kelly Turner's transports, Ghormley designated Rear Admiral George Murray's *Hornet* group, Rear Admiral Ching Lee's battleship *Washington* group, and Rear Admiral Norman Scott's cruiser screening group.

Admiral Scott was an aggressive, fifty-three-year-old rear admiral and a native of Indianapolis, now flying his flag in the heavy cruiser *San*

Francisco with Captain Soc McMorris commanding. Scott had three weeks to train his force of four cruisers and five destroyers in night sur-face actions. He was a thorough officer, whose destroyer *Jacob Jones* was sunk by a German U-boat in 1917. For the first six months of World War II, he served on Admiral King's staff in Washington pressing for sea duty. He was promoted to rear admiral in May 1942 and assigned to command a cruiser division. In training exercises, Scott kept his ships at battle sta-tions from dusk to dawn, a Spartan procedure but one designed to get the crews battle minded.

For a welcomed change, Scott was a flag officer who devised a plan before going into action. His ships would steam in column with the tin cans ahead and astern of the cruisers. When the enemy was met, the destroyers would illuminate with searchlights, fire torpedoes at large targets, and open fire with their 5-inch guns. The cruisers would fire whenever they saw an enemy ship, without waiting for orders from Scott. Scott's instructions were to interdict the almost nightly missions of the Tokyo Express coming down the Slot to drop off troops on the northwestern coast of Guadalcanal. Unfortunately, Scott had not realized the value of the latest SG search radar, with which both *Helena* and *Boise* were equipped. His flagship *San Francisco*, a poor choice, had an older, much less effective model. Scott's force headed for Ironbottom Sound off Guadalcanal's Cape Esperance on the night of October 11.

Rear Admiral Aritomo Goto was in command of the cruiser-destroyer force approaching Ironbottom Sound in heavy cruiser *Aoba*, with *Kinugasa*, *Furutaka*, and destroyers. The force was making 25 knots on a southeast course. Wisely, Admiral Scott ordered his cruisers to launch their floatplanes. At 2235 Scott instructed his ships to follow his battle plan, forming in a single column. Destroyers *Farenholt*, *Duncan*, and *Laffey* were in the van, followed by cruisers *San Francisco*, *Boise*, *Salt Lake City*, and *Helena*, and bringing up the rear were the tin cans *Buchanan* and *McCalla*.

Admiral Scott led his force steaming northeast about 6 miles west of Savo Island, a column almost 3 miles long. *Helena*, the fourth cruiser in the column, was equipped with the latest SG search radar and, at 2325, picked up a target to the northwest at a distant 16 miles. The target's blob split in three on the radar. *Helena*'s skipper, Captain Gilbert C. "Gib" Hoover, did not at first report her find. Since his flagship *San Francisco* had an early-model flawed radar, Admiral Scott was left in the dark.

The *Boise's* floatplane developed engine trouble and landed near Savo Island. A *San Francisco* search plane reported three vessels heading for Guadalcanal. These were the Japanese transport ships, not Admiral Goto's cruiser attack force. At 2332, Scott ordered his force to reverse course, to steam southwesterly covering the gap between Savo Island and Cape Esperance at the western edge of Guadalcanal. The maneuver was complicated and mishandled. The cruisers were to turn in column, followed by the rear destroyers. But the three forward destroyers were forced to turn separately and then race ahead on the exposed side of the cruisers to resume their place at the front of the column.

Cruiser *Helena's* radar still tracked the enemy. Now *Helena's* Captain Gib Hoover was certain his radar contact was legitimate and informed Admiral Scott he had a target 6 miles away. Scott's radar had picked up no contacts, so the admiral feared that *Helena* might be focused on the three destroyers out in front of the cruisers trying to overtake and reach the front of the column. In another typical communications botch, *Boise* reported to Scott that the cruiser detected five "bogeys" to the northwest. *Boise's* captain meant enemy ships, but bogey was then normally applied to enemy aircraft.

Admiral Scott was not certain what *Boise* meant. Were the radars merely tracking the destroyer division racing along parallel to the cruisers in the darkness? Scott radioed the destroyer squadron commodore, Captain Robert G. Tobin, in *Farenholt*, "Are you taking station ahead?"

"Affirmative," Tobin replied. "Coming up on your starboard side."

Unknown to anyone, *Duncan*, the second destroyer in line picked up an enemy on its radar and headed for it, single-handed. The third tin can, *Laffey*, saw *Duncan* veering out of line but followed the leader, *Farenholt*. Admiral Scott's concern for his destroyer flock was justified. *Helena's* Captain Hoover was sure he had a valid enemy contact, and word reached his bridge that lookouts had made visual contact at 5,000 yards.

Yet again, a communications foul-up occurred. Over voice radio, *Helena's* Captain Hoover queried: "Interrogatory roger," which was the standard signal code for, "Request permission to open fire." But "roger" in voice code also meant simply the receipt of a message. Admiral Scott replied "roger," indicating only, "Your message received." Captain Hoover took this to mean "Commence firing." Captain Hoover repeated his interrogatory to make sure . . . and received the same answer. At 2346

Helena opened fire with her fifteen 6-inch main batteries and 5-inch secondary guns.

Admiral Goto had no radar and no warning of the presence of American forces, so intent was he on his own bombardment mission. The other American cruisers followed *Helena's* lead, *Salt Lake City* with her 8-inch shells and *Boise* with 6-inch batteries. The flagship *San Francisco* belatedly opened up, though normally the flagship would fire first, as did the destroyers.

At 2347, Admiral Scott decided his cruisers were firing on American destroyers and ordered, "Cease firing."

Amazingly, Admiral Goto thought the shells were coming from Japanese warships in the area, and he held fire. For Admiral Goto, this was fatal. An American shell hit his flag bridge, mortally wounding him.

Without realizing it, Admiral Scott had crossed the Japanese T, his ships broadside to the oncoming enemy, pouring in enfilading fire. Goto had ordered a column turn, but this exposed each of his ships in succession to U.S. fire, which continued despite Scott's order to cease shooting. Scott raised Commodore Tobin on voice radio and was finally convinced the cruisers were not shooting at the destroyers. Four minutes after his earlier command at 2351, Admiral Scott ordered his ships to "Resume fire." Precious time was lost. Admiral Scott worried that his captains were firing at their own ships; the cruiser captains with better radar and fire control knew they were hitting the enemy.

Finally, under the command of Admiral Goto's senior staff officer, Captain Kikunori Kajima, the Japanese began striking back with severe hits on *Duncan* that inflicted mortal damage, but not before the plucky tin can got off a torpedo at the cruiser *Furutaka*, sending it to the bottom. The firing continued until midnight when the forces seemed to pull apart and Admiral Scott ordered a temporary ceasefire to regroup. The Japanese continued to fire shells and torpedoes at American ships, which had turned on searchlights. As the Japanese withdrew, they badly damaged *Boise* and wounded *Salt Lake City*. But the Battle of Cape Esperance was over.

In the aftermath of the fierce, intense fight off of Cape Esperance, Norman Scott was the man of the hour, hailed as a fighting admiral— cool, courageous, determined. U.S. naval heroes were in short supply. As usual, both sides overestimated the damage inflicted on the enemy. Still,

Admiral Scott's force sank the heavy cruiser *Furutaka* and three destroyers, with the loss of only one destroyer, USS *Duncan*. But the Japanese landed troops on Guadalcanal as the cruisers and destroyers were battling.

There were hard lessons to be learned from the victory. Scott was not the first admiral to be unfamiliar with the capabilities of the different types of radar. His failure to choose a flagship with the latest radar, like *Helena*, resulted in a near-fatal delay in giving his ships the order to fire. Later, commanders would learn to use their radars and forgo searchlights and recognition lights, which drew instant enemy fire. Also, in this battle, the communications were garbled. There was no code word for enemy ships, "bogeys" meant aircraft. Soon, "skunks" would be adopted to refer to enemy ships. Scott believed his long, single column formation was best for night fighting. But it was dangerously unwieldy to maneuver in formation, and it kept the destroyers from using their most powerful weapon, the torpedo, to best advantage. U.S. faulty tactical dispositions were continued in future engagements, to the navy's loss.

The Japanese were determined to hold on to Guadalcanal. To keep them from doing this, Admiral Nimitz believed that the time had come to relieve his close friend, Vice Admiral Ghormley as Commander South Pacific. Ghormley had been assigned a difficult thankless task, without the troops or ships to bring off the Watchtower operation swiftly. But Ghormley lacked the drive and determination to inspire the depleted forces of the South Pacific command. He was overworked, exhausted, and negative minded about prospects in the area. He was a fine planner but no operator—no leader.

In mid-October, Vice Admiral Bill Halsey had recovered from his severe dermatitis and was on an inspection trip to the South Pacific prior to taking over a new carrier command. When he arrived in Nouméa aboard a seaplane on October 18, a whaleboat picked him up, and Ghormley's flag lieutenant handed him a sealed message. Halsey opened the envelope, and then a second one inside marked "Secret." It was a dispatch from CinCPac reading, "Immediately upon your arrival in Nouméa, you will relieve Vice Admiral Robert L. Ghormley of the duties of Commander South Pacific and South Pacific Force."

Halsey read the message a second time and remarked, "Jesus Christ and General Jackson, this is the hottest potato they ever handed me."

Aboard Ghormley's flagship *Argonne*, Ghormley said, "This is a tough job they've handed you, Bill."

"I damn well know it," Halsey replied.

The appointment of Bill Halsey was immediately welcomed by the sailors and marines in the South Pacific, like an overnight shot in the arm for the morale of one and all. Now they had a leader who would fight with and for them.

An air intelligence officer on Guadalcanal said, "I'll never forget it! One minute we were too limp with malaria to crawl out of our foxholes; the next we were running around whooping like kids."

Halsey took an immediate, personal interest in his ships and captains. As destroyer skipper William Smedberg said, "He made each one of us feel that he knew we were right there, and he knew what we were doing, and he was grateful for what we were doing. He was backing us up."

In late October, Admiral Yamamoto at Truk ordered still another large naval force to press an attack on the U.S. Navy and Marines. This time Vice Admiral Nobutake Kondo deployed a fleet that included carrier *Junyo*, battleships *Kongo* and *Haruna*, four heavy cruisers, one light cruiser, and fourteen destroyers. Vice Admiral Chuichi Nagumo led a striking force consisting of carriers *Zuikaku* and *Shokaku*, light carrier *Zuiho*, battleships *Hiei* and *Kirishima*, five cruisers, and fifteen destroyers.

The American forces in the area now consisted of the *Enterprise* task group under Rear Admiral Kinkaid, supported by Rear Admiral Tisdale's cruisers and the new battleship *South Dakota*. The *Hornet* task group was headed by Rear Admiral Murray and screened by Rear Admiral Howard H. Good's cruisers and destroyers. The two carrier groups operated about 10 miles apart, with Kinkaid in tactical command. To the rear, backing up the carriers was a surface combat force under Rear Admiral Ching Lee in battleship *Washington*, with three cruisers and six destroyers. The two carrier groups were set to rendezvous near the Santa Cruz archipelago, east of the Solomon Islands, with orders to intercept the advancing Japanese forces.

During the night of October 25–26, Admiral Kinkaid headed his carriers northward to close the Japanese. About 0100, a night-flying Catalina search plane reported a Japanese force some 300 miles northwest of *Enterprise*. Admiral Halsey, who normally refrained from offering advice to his commander on the spot, radioed Kinkaid a general message: "Attack, repeat, attack!"

But the Catalina report did not contain the critical data: composition, course, and speed. Admiral Kinkaid faced the dilemma that was often presented to a carrier task force commander: Should he launch loaded dive-bombers at dawn toward this last-reported sighting? Or should he send out search planes across a wide arc to find the enemy and, only then, send out the attack bombers? Kinkaid and his staff chose the latter. Some time after the planes were launched, a message arrived—two hours delayed—from another Catalina patrol craft. It had a better fix on the enemy task force. Kinkaid was again faced with a tough decision. Should he launch the deckload of *Hornet's* strike aircraft toward the new estimated position of Japanese carriers? Or break radio silence and order the planes already in the air to head for the new estimated location of enemy flattops? Kinkaid chose the more conservative solution, to wait until the scout planes verified the position of the enemy, then launch *Hornet's* planes.

At about 0800, *Enterprise* search planes sighted two carriers, and Kinkaid ordered Admiral Murray to launch *Hornet's* planes, leaving some *Hornet* and *Enterprise* Wildcat fighters for defense of the carriers. Unfortunately, *Enterprise* fighter-director officers aboard, controlling both carriers' combat air patrol, were inexperienced. Additionally, Admirals Kinkaid and Murray, as well as Captains Charles Mason of *Hornet* (Naval Aviator No. 52) and Osborne B. Hardison of *Enterprise*, had no clear idea of the composition of the Japanese forces. Still, *Enterprise* dive-bombers found the carrier *Zuiho* and scored two hits, which started fires and shut down flight operations. Both sides launched additional strikes, resulting in opposing planes passing each other en route to targets.

Shortly after 0900 *Hornet's* planes found *Shokaku* and struck with bombs, disabling the big carrier. The cruiser *Chikuma* was also damaged. Japanese planes headed in toward *Enterprise* and *Hornet*. Kinkaid signaled by flashing light and flag hoist: "Prepare to repel air attack." He also ordered Admiral Murray to close up sea room with *Enterprise*. Then he sent up a fighter cap under control of the fighter director in *Enterprise*. But the Japanese broke through and struck *Hornet* with bombers and torpedo planes. Captain Mason got fires under control and arranged for cruiser *Northampton* to rig a towline.

Another Japanese strike located *Enterprise* and scored three bomb hits. An enemy bomb hit battleship *South Dakota*'s forward turret. Fragments sprayed her bridge, wounding Captain Gatch in the neck, as well as injuring several other personnel. For a moment, *South Dakota* temporarily out of control headed for *Enterprise*, but the carrier stepped swiftly out of the battlewagon's erratic path. The ack-ack cruiser *San Juan* was struck by a bomb, which temporarily caused her to lose steering control.

In the afternoon, Japanese planes launched a torpedo strike against *Hornet*, planting a couple of fish in her side. *Hornet* was done for, though she refused to sink. Admiral Murray transferred his flag to heavy cruiser *Pensacola*, while Captain Mason tried to save *Hornet*. He ordered off all the wounded and unessential sailors, who clambered down lines to destroyers *Russell* and *Hughes*. At 1650, Captain Mason gave up the struggle and left his bridge as Japanese planes began another bomb run on the helpless derelict. American destroyers tried to torpedo *Hornet*, but could not finish the job, though the carrier was a blazing wreck. Japanese destroyers later attempted to take *Hornet* in tow but were unsuccessful, so they sent her down with long-lance torpedoes.

So ended the Battle of Santa Cruz Islands. It was a tactical victory for the Japanese, leaving the United States temporarily without an operational carrier in the South Pacific, but Admiral Kondo's move to recapture Guadalcanal was thwarted. The Japanese lost about one hundred planes and nearly as many valuable pilots.

The U.S. carriers' fighter director system was poor. The tactic of keeping the carriers separated, each in the center of a group, became a controversial issue. Admiral Murray and Captain Mason, both veteran aviators, implicitly criticized Tom Kinkaid for the loss of *Hornet*. They argued that the two carrier forces should have been under independent command, coordinated by the senior officer ashore. They also recommended against a single officer controlling the fighter direction. Admiral Murray advised, "Two carrier task forces could not be operated with maximum battle efficiency and remain in visual touch under one OTC when contact with the enemy is sought. Each task force commander must exercise direct control of combat air patrols and carrier air group of own task force."

But Tom Kinkaid disagreed, noting in his after-action report, "By having two carriers together, one carrier can take care of all routine flying while the other maintains her full striking group spotted and ready to launch on short notice. If the carriers are separated, then each must fly its own inner air patrol and combat air patrol and make its own search. . . . Separate control of combat air patrols and carrier air groups of carriers in close proximity would fail to achieve the maximum of effectiveness that results from coordination by one command."

Though Kinkaid was not an aviator, his view would be adopted in the months to come as more fast carriers became available for group operations. Vice Admiral Jack Towers, now ComAirPac at Nimitz's headquarters, blamed Kinkaid for the loss of *Hornet* at Santa Cruz, and he pressed his case that carrier task forces should not be commanded by a non-aviator. Towers argued that Kinkaid held *Hornet*'s planes too long on deck before the launch.

However, Nimitz commended Kinkaid for his actions as commander of the *Enterprise* task group. But even as Kinkaid's career went upward during the war, the loss of *Hornet* dogged him, and he was sensitive to any criticism of his handling the task force at Santa Cruz. Whatever Admiral Towers' doubts, Admirals Nimitz and King respected Kinkaid as a fighting admiral who delivered the goods. Where Frank Jack Fletcher's star was waning, Tom Kinkaid's was rising.

Fourteen
DEATH OF
ADMIRALS

October–November 1942

Despite the constant naval activity in the Solomon Islands, the decisive sea battles there were yet to be fought.

As the naval action continued, many changes were underway elsewhere in the assignment of flag officers in the Pacific. Vice Admiral William Calhoun was named Commander Service Force, Pacific, the fleet logistics and underway replenishment command. Vice Admiral Leary was shifted back from Australia to become Commander Battleships Pacific, replacing Vice Admiral William Pye, whose talents as a strategist were employed as president of the Naval War College. Leary, who had run afoul of General MacArthur, was replaced by Vice Admiral Arthur S. "Chips" Carpender, from the Atlantic. Nimitz combined the administrative carrier and patrol wing commands into one: ComAirPac. Nimitz named Vice Admiral Jake Fitch to fill this billet.

But moves in Washington were to overtake this last appointment. Rear Admiral Jack Towers, as chief of BuAer, was the navy's leading proponent of aviation. Though smooth spoken and mannerly, Towers had—by his advocacy of aviators and his critical comments in the press—offended his superiors, including Secretary of the Navy Frank Knox and Admiral Ernest King. Towers had earlier antagonized Rear Admiral Chester Nimitz when he insisted that his BuAer have the last word in senior aviation appointments, rather than Nimitz's personnel department. Admiral King complained that Towers constantly pushed the "Towers Gang" (longtime aviators) for flag officer appointments, ignoring other considerations.

Towers had been vocal in his criticism of Frank Jack Fletcher's handling of carriers at the Coral Sea and Guadalcanal, declaring dismissively, "he ran away." Additionally, Towers blamed Admiral Kinkaid for losing *Hornet* at Santa Cruz. Towers argued vociferously that carrier task forces must be commanded by aviators, preferably those who weren't Johnny-come-latelies (JCLs), like Halsey, Fitch, and Ted Sherman. In September 1942, he was instrumental in getting seven aviator captains promoted, with King's approval, to rear admirals: Putty Read (ex-*Saratoga*), Elliott Buckmaster (ex-*Yorktown*), Duke Ramsey (ex-*Saratoga*), Charley Mason (ex-*Hornet*), Monty Montgomery (ex-*Ranger*), Arthur Davis (ex-*Enterprise*), and Frank Wagner. With Towers' constant carping, Knox and King wanted to get Naval Aviator No. 3 out of their hair, and out of Washington. They decided to promote him to vice admiral, making him the first pioneer aviator to make three stars, and move him to Pearl Harbor as ComAirPac, thus Admiral Nimitz's top air adviser.

Jack Towers arrived in Pearl in October 1942 and began an uneasy relationship with his boss, Chester Nimitz. Jake Fitch left Pearl to take over from Slew McCain as ComAirSoPac in Nouméa. McCain was approaching burnout stage, and he was assigned to take over Towers' job as chief of BuAer in Washington. The profane, impulsive McCain was known to be an Admiral King favorite, though he was hardly suited to run BuAer. The appointment was not popular with Towers or the Towers Gang, who regarded McCain as a JCL who, while a brave fighter, was a poor administrator without a thorough grounding in carriers or even naval aviation.

In the South Pacific, Halsey's appointment was turning out to be an inspired choice. Halsey was an indifferent administrator with a staff, still under the irascible Captain Miles Browning, that was less than first-rate. But Halsey's gung-ho style of leadership—"Kill Japs, kill Japs, kill more Japs"—was just what was needed to pump up the tired, dispirited sailors, marines, and soldiers in the South Pacific.

Bill Halsey's role in the South Pacific was a diplomatic one, too, since he had to deal with the lofty Douglas MacArthur next door in the Southwest Pacific theater, in areas like the Solomons, where their commands overlapped. At the same time, Halsey's boss (Admiral Nimitz) and Nimitz's boss (Admiral King) did not want their naval commander to get too cozy with the imperious general. MacArthur had a way of "borrowing" U.S. Navy assets for his various operations, which were rarely returned.

Kelly Turner was in Nouméa building up another task force to resupply Guadalcanal. Rear Admiral Good, the cruiser screen commander, came down with a severe case of influenza and had to be evacuated to Australia. Halsey wanted to replace Good with Soc McMorris and give him a spot promotion to rear admiral. But Admiral Nimitz had other plans for McMorris, so Halsey picked Rear Admiral Dan Callaghan, Ghormley's chief of staff, for the cruiser command, partly because it enabled him to make Captain Miles Browning his own chief of staff.

Austere, modest, and religious, Dan Callaghan was silver haired and Hollywood-handsome, and had been a naval aide to President Roosevelt. He pondered where to fly his flag and decided on heavy cruiser *San Francisco*, of which he had been skipper in the first months of the war. Callaghan was also a native of San Francisco. Veteran combat officers worried that *San Francisco* was still not equipped with the latest SG radar, and would have preferred that Callaghan pick a cruiser, like *Juneau*, *Atlanta*, and in particular *Helena*, with SG radar. Furthermore, *Helena* had the most experienced battle skipper, Captain Gib Hoover, and was armed with a main battery of fifteen 6-inch guns. But Dan Callaghan had been serving in a staff job and was not fully aware of radar's importance at sea. Indeed, Callaghan placed the ships with the latest SG radar toward the rear of his column rather than up front, thus indicating he and his staff, largely taken from Ghormley's people, had given little forethought to the critical value of the SG radar. *San Francisco*'s skipper was also new, Captain Cassin Young, who won the Medal of Honor at Pearl Harbor as executive office of repair ship *Vestal*.

The battle-experienced flag officer who logically ought to have been in command was Rear Admiral Norman Scott, victor at Cape Esperance. But Callaghan was fifteen days senior, so Scott was relegated to second in command. Norman Scott raised his flag aboard the anti-aircraft cruiser *Atlanta*, carrying the class' sixteen 5-inch dual-purpose guns, rather than heavier main batteries. *Atlanta* and her sister ship, *Juneau*, were designed to provide anti-aircraft fire for task forces. They displaced only 6,000 tons and were lightly armored; their thin skins made them vulnerable to gunfire and torpedo attacks.

On November 9, CinCPac intelligence picked up word that enemy forces were gathering for another major attempt to regain Guadalcanal, and relayed the message to Admiral Halsey in Nouméa. He and Browning looked at their disposition chart; their forces were widely scattered. Kelly Turner, Commander Amphibious Forces, South Pacific, was at sea in transport *McCawley* en route from Nouméa to Guadalcanal with several transports loaded with troops, food, ammunition, and supplies and a cruiser-destroyer escort. Norman Scott was departing Espiritu Santo in the New Hebrides with his cruisers and destroyers, as well as transports with additional troops. Dan Callaghan, Scott's senior, was at sea with his cruisers to escort Turner's transports into the Guadalcanal anchorage. Admiral Turner's reinforcements were to arrive off Lunga Point on November 12.

Coming up from behind was the carrier group with Rear Admiral Kinkaid in *Enterprise*, accompanied by Rear Admiral Ching Lee in battleship *Washington*, with battlewagon *South Dakota* and four destroyers. The plan was that if *Enterprise*—still limping from the Santa Cruz battle— could not get into the area in time, Lee's battleships would forge ahead to protect the transports in the anchorage. In a letter of instruction to Admiral Callaghan, Kelly Turner said, "You have under your control your own tactical operations. If we can *really* strike the enemy hard, it will be more important for you to do so than to protect my transports. Good luck to you, Dan. God bless all of you and give you strength."

On the Japanese side, Admiral Kondo at Truk had two light carriers, four battleships, eleven cruisers, and some thirty destroyers to cover eleven transports that would unload more troops. Kondo planned to bombard Guadalcanal's marines, and the Japanese admiral expected heavy opposition from the U.S. Navy.

On November 11, Admiral Scott's transports *Zeilin*, *Libra*, and *Betelgeuse* began unloading in the face of Japanese attacking aircraft. On November 12, Admiral Turner's transports anchored and debarked troops. He was protected by both Admirals Callaghan and Scott's forces in Ironbottom Sound. Admiral Fitch's land-based air-relayed enemy sighting reports to the various U.S. flag bridges during the day, indicating a heavy Japanese presence that night.

*

Turner made a critical decision. He ordered Callaghan to escort the recently unloaded transports clear of Ironbottom Sound, then return with his force at night and strike whatever enemy ships appeared. Turner left Callaghan to devise his own tactics with his five cruisers and eight destroyers. Norman Scott, the experienced junior admiral, would play no tactical role in the coming fight.

Callaghan ordered his ships to maneuver in a single column with destroyers in the van and rear. The formation consisted of destroyers *Cushing, Laffey, Sterett,* and *O'Bannon*; cruisers *Atlanta, San Francisco, Portland, Helena,* and *Juneau*; destroyers *Aaron Ward, Barton, Monssen,* and *Fletcher.* The first three destroyers had no SG radar, while the blooded *Fletcher,* which had SG, was at the rear of the column. The thirteen-ship column formation allowed the admiral to maneuver more easily in restricted waters, but the rear destroyers were in no position to join the van tin cans in a torpedo attack. The ships had not operated together before. Callaghan issued no battle plan. This was not a good sign.

The leading element of the Japanese bombardment group steaming toward Savo Island to give the marines a pasting was Vice Admiral Hiroaki Abe's battleships *Hiei* and *Kirishima,* cruiser *Nagara,* and six destroyers. As the Japanese approached Savo Island, midnight slipped by. It was Friday the 13th of November.

At 0124, an alert radar operator aboard *Helena,* eighth ship in Admiral Callaghan's long column, detected a suspicious blip on his screen, which developed into an unfriendly contact. *Helena* had also been first to spot the enemy at Cape Esperance. Her captain, Gib Hoover, had commanded destroyer squadrons at the Coral Sea and Midway, and was one of the most heads-up skippers in the fleet. *Helena* sent out the message: "Contacts bearing 312 and 310 [northwest], distant 27,000 yards [about 16 miles] and 32,000 yards." That suggested a screening group followed by another force. Three minutes later, Admiral Callaghan ordered a slight course change to meet the enemy head-on, rather than maneuver for a flank attack. As the range quickly decreased, so did the initial American radar advantage. As the forces closed at 40 miles an hour, gunners and torpedomen wondered why the order to open fire did not come. They wondered for ten long minutes.

On *San Francisco's* flag bridge, Admiral Callaghan upped speed to 20 knots and ordered another course change to due north, before the rear ships had managed to follow the leader in the last turn. Since *San Francisco* lacked the latest radar, he called on *Helena* and destroyer *O'Bannon* for composition, ranges, and bearings of the enemy force over voice radio—called talk between ships (TBS). This network was also used for urgent tactical orders from the flag to the ships, leading to a confusion of voices on the single-channel circuit. Sometimes high-priority messages were drowned out by lesser chatter, sometimes by repeats for earlier orders. It was going to be hard to maintain tactical discipline over the TBS.

The Japanese weren't listening in; Admiral Abe, without radar, thought his ships were alone around Savo Island.

The range was closing fast, with the U.S. ships locking on to the enemy with their fire control radar, but still no orders came from Admiral Callaghan. Commodore Thomas M. Stokes of Destroyer Division 10, in the leading van destroyer *Cushing*, sighted Japanese tin cans crossing ahead from port to starboard. He flashed the word, as *Cushing*'s skipper, Lieutenant Commander Edward N. Parker, swung the ship to the left to unmask torpedo tubes. Stokes' destroyers tried to keep up with their commodore's turn to port. Immediately behind, *Atlanta* had to swing sharply left to avoid a collision. Tactical discipline was disintegrating.

"What are you doing?" Callaghan demanded over voice radio.

"Avoiding our own destroyers," replied Atlanta's Captain Samuel P. Jenkins, who carried Rear Admiral Norman Scott aboard.

By now, the Japanese force became aware of an enemy contact. An invaluable eight minutes were lost—as well as surprise.

Commodore Stokes asked, "Shall I let them have a couple of fish?"

Callaghan finally granted permission. By then the Japanese had sped past into the darkness. The van of Callaghan's formation was in some confusion. At 0145, Callaghan gave the semi-order: "Stand by to open fire."

Japanese searchlights snapped on, picking out the high bridge of *Atlanta*, which rose above the tin cans in front, a fine target. *Atlanta*'s gunnery officer ordered: "Commence firing! Counterilluminate!" The range was down to 1,600 yards, less than a mile. The cruiser's 5-inch batteries opened up, but not soon enough. Enemy ships concentrated on the lit-up *Atlanta*. A 14-inch shell slammed into the bridge, killing

Admiral Scott, who was standing outside the chart house, and all but one of his staff.

Finally, the order came from Admiral Callaghan's flagship *San Francisco*: "Odd ships commence fire to starboard, even ships to port." This was a confusing order since some ships could not see enemy ships on their designated side. Others had targets on their undesignated side. Then Japanese destroyers exploited their superior weapon, the long-lance torpedoes. At least one, possibly two, hit the thin-skinned cruiser *Atlanta*.

The night action quickly disintegrated into a wild melee. The tin can *Cushing* fired at destroyers and was hit herself. Skipper Parker sighted battleship *Hiei*, swung sharply, and fired six torpedoes, forcing the big wagon to turn away. But *Cushing* suffered several more incoming blasts and was soon a wreck. Astern, *Laffey* almost rammed *Hiei*. *Laffey* fired torpedoes at the battleship, but the distance was too short for the fish to arm. Machine gunners sprayed the Japanese battleship's tall pagoda bridge structure. Then *Laffey* was mortally damaged by more shell and torpedo hits. The next two tin cans, *Sterett* and *O'Bannon*, fired at any enemy they could see, which turned out to be *Hiei*.

O'Bannon's skipper, Lieutenant Commander Edwin R. Wilkinson, ordered check fire. But then, spotting the huge *Hiei*, *O'Bannon* launched two torpedoes. The battleship was so close that it could not depress its 14-inch guns to blow *O'Bannon* out of the water. The admiral on the bridge of *Hiei* was perhaps blinded by all the American fire directed at him and ordered a course change to clear the immediate area. The American ships had penetrated his formation, between his two battleships and his destroyers.

Then came a strange order from the flagship: "Cease firing own ships!" A seeming repeat of Cape Esperance.

Flagship *San Francisco* was the sixth ship in the column. Captain Cassin Young's heavy cruiser had delivered several salvos at *Hiei*, and then shifted and fired more salvos at what was described as a "small cruiser or a large destroyer." *Atlanta* was now ahead of *San Francisco* and dead in the water. *Atlanta* crewmembers believe their small cruiser was hit by *San Francisco* shells, and cite the presence of green dye on her decks, the color used by *San Francisco* ammo to mark salvos. *San Francisco* sailors think the flagship was firing across *Atlanta* at a Japanese ship beyond, but may have hit the American ship. Perhaps that's why Admiral Callaghan gave his unexpected cease-fire order.

Cruiser *Portland's* Captain Lawrence "Larry" DuBose queried the flagship's order: "What's the dope, did you want to cease fire?"

Callaghan answered, "Affirmative."

Callaghan's cease-fire order led to *San Francisco's* undoing. The flagship was caught in enemy searchlights, and battleship *Kirishima* and others blanketed *San Francisco* with shells. Admiral Callaghan was killed instantly on the flag bridge and Captain Young on the navigating bridge. Nearly everyone else on the bridges was killed or maimed.

Portland reopened fire but was hit in the stern by an enemy torpedo, affecting her steering gear. Still, *Portland*, known as "Sweet Pea," directed by Captain DuBose, was able to land salvos on *Hiei*. The two following cruisers, *Helena* and *Juneau*, fired at enemy targets during the furious fifteen minutes, though they too were confused by Callaghan's cease-fire order. A Japanese torpedo smacked into *Juneau's* forward fireroom, which took the small sister ship of *Atlanta* out of action. The four rear destroyers were in the dark through lack of orders and effective radar.

Destroyer *Barton*, commissioned only in May, had a short life. She opened fire with 5-inch guns and torpedoes, but was in turn struck by two long-lance torpedoes in her fireroom and engine room, which broke the tin can in half. She sank almost immediately with most of her crew lost. Behind her, *Monssen* launched torpedoes but was highlighted by star shells and soon found herself an enemy target. Shells rained down and, within minutes, *Monssen* was a blazing hulk.

Once the Japanese battleships pulled out to the northwest, fighting between the destroyers continued, but the melee was so confused that gradually the forces retired away from one another. *Atlanta* was doomed, as were *Cushing*, *Laffey*, *Barton*, and *Monssen*. *San Francisco* was shattered, steered by the communications officer, Lieutenant Commander Bruce McCandless. The senior officers were all dead. *Portland's* stern damage forced her to steer in circles through the night. *Helena's* Captain Gib Hoover, unable to contact Callaghan or Scott and believing he was senior captain afloat, ordered the ships to rendezvous near Guadalcanal and exit eastward via Sealark Channel.

On the Japanese side at dawn, battleship *Hiei* limped away with severe damage to communications and steering gear, receiving some fifty hits. She would be destroyed that day by planes from carrier *Enterprise* taking off from Guadalcanal. Destroyers *Akatsuki* and *Yudachi* were badly damaged and three others suffered lighter damage, *Ikazuchi*, *Murasame*, and *Amatsukaze*. Vice Admiral Abe was sent back to Tokyo in disgrace. The United States was left without an admiral alive with night surface battle experience.

On the morning of Friday the 13th, *Helena*—with Captain Hoover acting as tactical commander—led *San Francisco, Portland, Juneau, O'Bannon, Sterett,* and *Fletcher* out of Ironbottom Sound, zigzagging at 18 knots and heading for the New Hebrides. About 1100, *Juneau* was 1,000 yards off *San Francisco's* starboard side, when she was spotted by the submarine *I-26*, which fired a spread at the cruisers. Two missed *San Francisco* but a third hit *Juneau* under her bridge. The light cruiser detonated and sank at once, sending up only a plume of smoke. Captain Hoover, who had been decorated for heroism as skipper of *Helena*, had a most painful decision: whether to leave behind a destroyer to search for *Juneau* survivors in Japanese torpedo water, making the destroyer an easy target. An army Flying Fortress appeared overhead, attracted by the explosion.

Helena sent a message to the pilot to be relayed to Admiral Halsey: "*Juneau* torpedoed and disappeared latitude 10 degrees 32' S, longitude 161 degrees 2' at 1109. Survivors in water. Report ComSoPac."

The message was never relayed through the complex channels to Halsey. No one knew *Juneau* had left survivors still in the sea. About 140 men were in the water. All but ten sailors ultimately perished. Of the crew of *Juneau*, almost seven hundred died in the explosion or in the water. They included the five Sullivan brothers from Waterloo, Iowa, and the news of their deaths caused national mourning.

In the subsequent inquiry, Admiral Halsey ordered Captain Hoover deprived of a sea command; he had left no life rafts or boats behind, nor did he break radio silence to report the loss and possible survivors. *Helena's* crew was shocked that its popular and admired captain was ordered ashore. Later, Halsey decided he had treated Hoover, a splendid ship commander, too harshly. Some attributed Halsey's snap decision to the negative influence of Captain Miles Browning, his chief of staff.

Nimitz was sympathetic, writing that the action of *Helena*'s skipper "was the result of a decision made by him when confronted by a difficult situation . . . the necessity for getting his damaged ships back to a base was balanced against the natural instinct of every naval officer to go to the rescue of officers and men in distress and danger. . . . Whatever may be the opinion of Captain Hoover's decision, he was the responsible officer on the spot and from his war record his courage may not be questioned. . . . It is recommended that he be given a suitable command at sea after he has had a reasonable rest period in the United States."

It was not to be. Captain Gib Hoover, despite his courage and skills as a skipper—he won three Navy Crosses—was not given a command at sea again. So sadly the U.S. Navy lost the fighting talents of one of the most accomplished warship captains in the Pacific.

Fifteen
DUEL OF THE BATTLEWAGONS

November 1942

The Japanese were still determined to regain "Cactus," the code name for Guadalcanal, and Henderson Field from the U.S. Marines. Vice Admiral Gunichi Mikawa, Eighth Fleet commander, in heavy cruiser *Chokai*, departed the Shortland Islands of the Solomons with four heavy cruisers, two light cruisers, and six destroyers to head down the Slot and bombard Henderson Field. The redoubtable Rear Admiral Raizo Tanaka led eleven destroyers escorting eleven transports with troops, planning to unload the soldiers on the night of November 14. To back them up, Vice Admiral Nobutake Kondo, in heavy cruiser *Atago*, pulled together battleships *Kirishima* and *Nagara*, and four destroyers with air cover provided by two carriers, which maintained their position at long range.

Admiral Halsey in Nouméa ordered Admiral Ching Lee's gunfire group—new battleships *Washington* and *South Dakota* and four destroyers—to intercept the Japanese force bound for Guadalcanal. But Halsey's staff was laggardly in getting Lee's battlewagons heading north, and they were unable to reach Guadalcanal by the night of November 13. Consequently, Admiral Mikawa's force, with Rear Admiral Shoji Nishimura heading the bombardment unit, gave the U.S. Marines a shellacking.

The morning of November 14, U.S. search planes spotted Tanaka's transports, the Tokyo Express, heading down the Slot. Admiral Tom Kinkaid in *Enterprise* launched planes to attack the Japanese transport force. The tenacious Tanaka watched grimly in the afternoon as

American planes chewed up his transport force. But rather than withdraw, Tanaka transferred soldiers from the blazing transports to his destroyers and pressed on toward Guadalcanal. Tanaka lost seven transports but boldly steamed on with the Tokyo Express: four transports and eleven loaded-down destroyers.

Ching Lee—a fifty-four-year-old Kentuckian with a nickname, originally "Chink," given him at the Naval Academy for an obscure reason—was the foremost heavy gunnery expert in the fleet. He won gold medals in the 1920 Summer Olympics in rifle team shooting and was a bright student at the War College. With an easygoing manner that disguised a mind like a computer, Lee served as fleet readiness assistant to Admiral King in the first months of the war. A cheerful, understated officer with a dry wit, he wore wire-rimmed glasses, which made him look like a professor, not unlike Kelly Turner. Lee raised his flag in the battleship *Washington*, whose crew was proud to have him aboard from September 1942 for two and a half years.

Once a bridge "talker," who transmitted the admiral's instructions, he drank several cups of coffee during an extended watch and needed to relieve himself. He chose the admiral's head just off the bridge. An unpopular staff officer spotted the talker and chewed him out so loudly that Admiral Lee's attention was drawn.

"Sir, this man was urinating in your head."

Pulling on his ever-present cigarette, Admiral Lee, in exasperation, replied, "Well, what the hell did you expect him to do, piss over the side?"

The fast battleship *Washington* was one of the newly commissioned capital ships now reaching the Pacific. She first served a short period in convoy operations in the North Atlantic. On her first operational mission, *Washington* lost an admiral in a mystifying episode in the North Atlantic.

Rear Admiral John Wilcox, a stern, distant officer who once crossed swords with Raymond Spruance at the War College and was Commander Battleships Atlantic, raised his flag in *Washington*. He was leading a U.S. force across the Atlantic to the British base in Scapa Flow in the Orkneys to operate with the British fleet. The force included heavy cruiser *Wichita*, flying the flag of Rear Admiral Robert C. "Ike"

Giffen; the new carrier *Wasp*; the heavy cruiser *Tuscaloosa*; and eight ships of Destroyer Squadron 8, whose commodore was Captain Don P. Moon. Little more than twenty-four hours out of Casco Bay, Maine, the weather turned nasty and rough. Around 1030 on May 27, *Washington* was formation guide, her decks cleared to weather the pounding seas. The formation was making 18 knots with rain and snow reducing visibility from the windswept decks. Wilcox's chief of staff, Captain John L. "Jimmy" Hall Jr., suggested a slight change of course to allow the battleship's aircraft and catapults to be secured at the stern. Wilcox approved. Hall was on the flag bridge, Wilcox in his cabin.

A few minutes later, the admiral was seen briefly on the main deck chatting with an officer in the ship's aircraft division at the stern. Two other crewmen saw the admiral making his way forward, unaccompanied by his marine orderly, normally always present as a bodyguard. He asked directions to a ladder leading to an upper deck. Moments later, a seaman happened to look at the ocean and saw a baldheaded man in the water. He gave the man overboard alert. Buoys and life rafts were dropped and destroyers dispatched to search in the heaving seas. It was quickly learned that the admiral was missing. *Wasp* launched search planes, and one crashed with the loss of two airmen. Admiral Giffen, who now had tactical command, ordered the force to continue on base course. The admiral was lost to the sea.

An inquiry was held aboard *Washington*. The few crewmen who saw him said he looked distracted and quite pale. It was never ascertained why the admiral was walking around the open decks without his orderly, who normally would have been stationed outside the admiral's cabin door to accompany him everywhere. The board of inquiry decided Wilcox died as the result of an accident. Captain Harry W. Hill, commanding officer of *Wichita*, said Admiral Giffen thought Wilcox seemed nervous in the preceding weeks and might have cracked under pressure. Gunnery officer Edwin Hooper later remarked, "There were all sorts of conjectures as to whether he jumped, was pushed, or was washed over. A man was seen struggling in the water by *Tuscaloosa*, astern of us, and a destroyer saw his body face down in the water. That's all we'll ever know."

Steaming north at high speed, Ching Lee's force was unable to prevent Admiral Nishimura's cruiser bombardment of the marines on Guadalcanal. He received a report that a heavy force—it turned out to be Kondo's—was making the run of the Tokyo Express heading for Ironbottom Sound. Lee ordered armor-piercing shells readied and the radar double-checked. On the evening of November 14, Lee reached the western edge of Guadalcanal. He placed his four tin cans at the head of his six-ship column, with *Washington* and *South Dakota* following.

Unfortunately, like Admiral Callaghan, Lee had no chance to practice with his force. The battleships hadn't operated together. *South Dakota*'s turret two had been damaged at Santa Cruz, and two of the 16-inch guns were not working. *South Dakota*'s skipper, Captain Thomas Gatch, was still nursing wounds from the Santa Cruz battle. The four destroyers all came from different divisions, with no commodore on board. They were of different classes with different characteristics, and were picked by Admiral Kinkaid to join Lee because they had the most fuel aboard. None of them had the latest SG radar gear. *Walke*'s skipper was selected to command the destroyers because he was the senior officer. It was the first time the U.S. Navy risked battleships in the constricted waters around Savo Island, and some staff officers in Nouméa questioned committing two new battleships, expensive and prestigious as they were, to such confined waters. Savo Island, in the middle of the navigating area, could interfere with the battleships' radar. But Admiral Halsey was determined to interdict the Japanese warships, at any price. Ching Lee thoroughly briefed Captain Davis, who closely studied the charts of Ironbottom Sound and adjacent reef-strewn areas with his navigator.

Admiral Lee led his force north, passing to the west of Savo Island, where he could see the fires of Admiral Tanaka's transports burning in the far distance. Lee then turned east into Ironbottom Sound, passing the north side of Savo. The area seemed clear of Japanese ships, and Lee turned his column south, and then westward, having circled Savo Island. Lee needed hard intelligence on the whereabouts of the Tokyo Express. In the rush to pull his force together, Admiral Lee was not given a call sign. He radioed Guadalcanal asking for the latest information and signing his last name to the query.

He received the curt reply: "We do not recognize you."

Lee shot back: Cactus, this is Lee. Tell your big boss [General Vandergrift, who knew Lee's nickname] Ching Lee is here and wants the latest information."

Before Vandergrift could answer, the battleships picked up voice radio conversation among PT boats patrolling from Tulagi: "There go two big ones but I don't know whose they are!"

The last thing Ching Lee wanted was to be attacked by his own forces. He again voice-radioed Guadalcanal: "Refer your big boss about Ching Lee. Chinese, catchee? Call off your boys!" Another version recalled by a bridge officer went: "This is Ching Chong China Lee. Refer your big boss about Ching Lee. Call off your boys!" The exchange, in one form or another, went into battleship lore. A later version had Lee barking to the PTs: "This is Ching Lee—you musn't fire fish at me!"

The PTs immediately acknowledged that they knew who Lee was and were not after his force. Cactus messaged back to Lee. "The boss has no additional information."

At this point, Admiral Kondo had split his force into three, with two screens and the main bombardment group: Kondo's flagship heavy cruiser *Atago*, her sister cruiser *Takao*, and battleship *Kirishima*. Cruiser *Sendai*, with Rear Admiral Shintaro Hashimoto aboard, led the screen approaching Savo Island to the northeast.

Hardly had Lee turned his ships to the west when *Washington*'s radar picked up *Sendai* at 9 miles distance. Lee, dragging on a cigarette, warned Captain Davis: "Stand by, Glenn. Here they come!"

At 2316, Admiral Lee ordered his captains: "Open fire when you are ready!"

Moments later, 16-inch shells splashed around *Sendai*, which released a smoke screen and headed back northward to get out of range. A second Japanese screening force under Rear Admiral Susumu Kimura approached Ironbottom Sound from south of Savo, and was picked up by the lead U.S. destroyers *Walke*, *Benham*, and *Preston*, which opened fire. U.S. destroyer *Gwin* sighted Kimura's flagship cruiser *Nagara* leading four destroyers and blazed away with her 5-inch guns. Destroyers *Ayanami* and *Uranami* fired their long-lance torpedoes at 2330. The American destroyers came under heavy attack but fired back at the two leading enemy tin cans. The Japanese fish blew off the bows of both *Walke* and *Benham*, and left *Walke* and *Preston* sinking. The U.S. tin can attack was led by *Walke*'s Commander Thomas Fraser, who, in Admiral Lee's words, "was beyond admiration and probably saved our bacon." Commander Fraser died in the sinking of *Walke*.

Washington and *South Dakota* were sorting out targets on their radar when *South Dakota's* suffered a loss of electrical power, which left the battlewagon temporarily helpless. But once again, with the Japanese split into three forces, the action around Savo Island was turning into a wild melee.

By 2348, Admiral Lee realized his four destroyers were either sinking or badly damaged, and he ordered them to retire. *South Dakota* had regained electric power but had lost track of *Washington* and closed on Admiral Kondo's main bombardment force. The Japanese caught *South Dakota* in their searchlights, and although their destroyers' torpedoes missed, shells began hitting the American battlewagon.

Admiral Lee was tracking a large target, at first fearful that it was *South Dakota*. When the Japanese illuminated, Lee saw the enemy and opened fire with *Washington's* 16-inch main battery at the battleship *Kirishima*. This was a rare World War II action in which battleships engaged one another directly. An estimated nine out of seventy-five of the 16-inch shells from *Washington* hit *Kirishima*, as well as forty of the 5-inch shells. The Japanese battlewagon was soon reduced to a mass of flames, steerless and out of action. *Washington* and *South Dakota* struck cruisers *Atago* and *Takao*, which had revealed themselves with their own searchlights. But *South Dakota* suffered hit after hit: her communications were out, one main turret was inoperable, and the radar plot was destroyed. Captain Thomas Gatch, his ship crippled, set a southerly course for retirement.

The Japanese withdrew to the northwest, as Admiral Kondo ordered a general retirement, with *Washington* and Lee in pursuit, a one-ship task force. Alone northwest of Savo Island, Admiral Lee decided the battle was over, and he ordered *Washington* to withdraw but along a westerly course to draw any following Japanese stragglers from pursuing the wounded *South Dakota* and destroyers *Gwin* and *Benham*. As *Washington* retired, Japanese destroyers fired torpedoes at her, but Captain Glenn B. Davis expertly maneuvered out of their way as he speeded up to 26 knots to lose the enemy tin cans. In *Washington's* wake, Admiral Kondo ordered the dying battleship *Kirishima* scuttled, so as not to fall into American hands at daybreak. It was the first enemy capital ship sunk by a U.S. battleship since the Battle of Santiago de Cuba in 1898. In a postscript, the redoubtable Tanaka resumed his advance to Cape Esperance with four remaining transports and eleven troop-carrying destroyers, and landed them on the beaches of Tassafaronga. Raizo Tanaka truly was one of the finest fighting admirals of the Pacific war.

On the way to Espiritu Santo, the badly damaged *Benham* began sinking and was dispatched by her escort *Gwin's* gunfire. *Washington* was almost undamaged, but forty-two big shells struck *South Dakota*, with thirty-eight men killed or missing and sixty wounded. She returned for repairs—and publicity—to the United States, where, *Washington* blue-jackets complained, she got the credit for winning the naval Battle of Guadalcanal.

Ching Lee had fought an aggressive, intelligent battle, losing three destroyers while sinking an enemy battleship and destroyer. Once again, the United States had to go into action with a scratch force that hadn't trained together, and one that was exposed to the lethal long-lance torpedoes expertly handled by the Japanese navy.

Captains Glenn Davis of *Washington* and Thomas Gatch of *South Dakota* proved to be brave, accomplished ship-handlers. They would both soon be promoted to flag rank. Ching Lee would become the premier battleship commander in the Pacific. More importantly, the naval Battle of Guadalcanal marked the ascendancy of the United States in those bloody waters. Though over the three days it lost more ships and two fighting admirals, Admiral Turner got his marine replacements ashore, and the United States sank two enemy battleships.

The Japanese hung on in Guadalcanal for another ten weeks, but it was a last-ditch struggle. The battle also marked a shift for the Americans from the defensive to the offensive. At sea, on the ground, and in the air, the U.S. forces were in the ascendancy, and President Roosevelt in mourning the loss of his friend, Admiral Dan Callaghan, could declare, "It would seem that the turning point in this war has at last been reached."

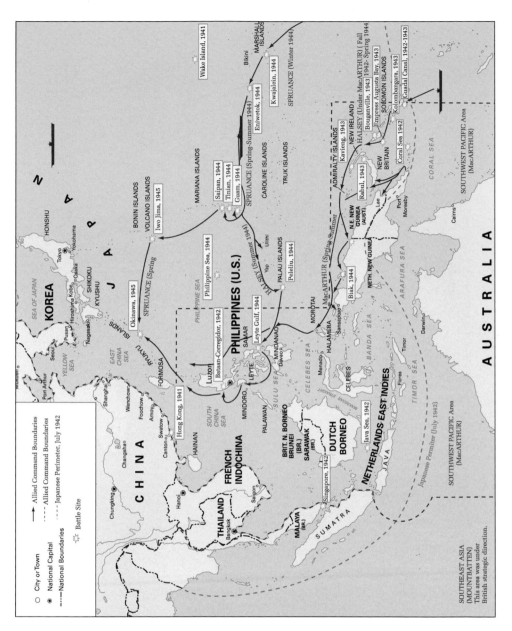

THE SECOND WORLD WAR
THE PACIFIC THEATER,
1941 - 1945

←—N—

SCALE OF MILES

0   300   600   900

Courtesy U.S. Military Academy

Marc A. "Pete" Mitscher, left, and Willis A. "Ching" Lee, right

Holland M. "Howlin' Mad" Smith with Chester W. Nimitz in the back seat of the jeep and King in the front seat, Saipan, 1944

Mitscher and his chief of staff, Arleigh A. "31-Knot" Burke

Left to right: Raymond A. Spruance, Mitscher, Nimitz, Lee

"The Big Three" *left to right:* Nimitz, Ernest J. King, Spruance

Foreground, left to right: Smith, Kelly Turner, Harry W. Hill

Left to right: Russell S. Berkey, Douglas MacArthur, Thomas C. "Tom" Kinkaid aboard the USS *Phoenix,* 27 February 1944

William F. "Bull" Halsey

John S. "Slew" McCain

Left to right: Theodore S. "Ping" Wilkinson, Kinkaid, Daniel E. "Uncle Dan" Barbey

Mitscher, commander, Fast Carrier Task Force, during a pensive moment on his flag bridge while observing flight operations of Task Force 58

Mitscher sitting with his charts and pencils in his flag plot aboard the USS *Randolph*

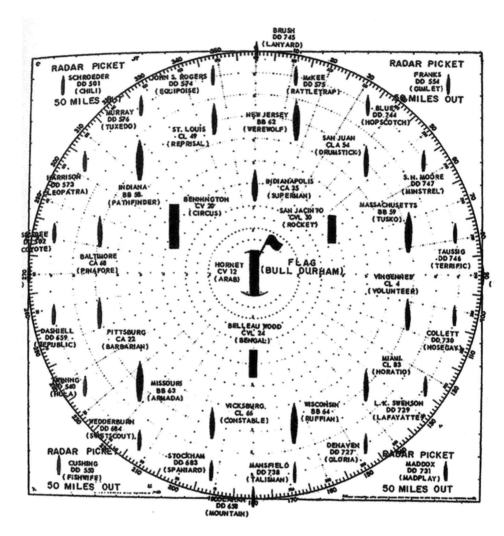

Task Group 58.1 Flag Plot Maneuvering Board on 24 March 1945. This was the largest assemblage of naval power ever in a single formation. The formation allowed the carriers to turn quickly into position to launch planes.

Sixteen
LONG-LANCE MENACE

November 1942–February 1943

Admiral Halsey's battered South Pacific Force was finally augmented by replacements: the repaired *Saratoga* heading south as the center of a carrier group under newly promoted Rear Admiral Duke Ramsey, former skipper of big, old Sara. New Rear Admiral Ted Sherman, who survived the loss of his *Lexington* at the Coral Sea, was named commander of another carrier force, hoisting his flag in *Enterprise*, relieving non-aviator Tom Kinkaid of that assignment. *North Carolina's* torpedo damage was repaired and she, *Washington*, and *Indiana* formed a fast battleship force under Rear Admiral Ching Lee. In the Fijis, two old, refurbished battleships, *Maryland* and *Colorado*, were under the command of Rear Admiral Harry Hill, a rising, young planning expert who had commanded heavy cruiser *Wichita* in dangerous Murmansk convoys. Taking over the South Pacific cruiser command, Tom Kinkaid raised his flag in *Pensacola*, with heavies *New Orleans* and *Northampton*, and the light cruisers *Helena* and *Honolulu*.

On November 26, Bill Halsey was promoted to full, four-star admiral rank for revitalizing the South Pacific sea and land forces. Jake Fitch was now Commander Air South Pacific (ComAirSoPac) at Nouméa. A separate air command was set up at Guadalcanal called Commander Air Forces Solomons, (ComAirSols), or "Comaircactus," commanded by marine Brigadier General Roy S. Geiger.

If the Japanese had given up sending in their battleships into the Guadalcanal area, they still were intent on re-supplying their troops with soldiers and supplies aboard the destroyers of Rear Admiral Tanaka. In Espiritu Santo, Tom Kinkaid received orders from Halsey to ready his cruiser force to intercept Japanese troop landings on Guadalcanal. Halsey wanted Kinkaid to train the cruisers to fight properly together, particularly at night—a technique not yet mastered through lack of time to train. Halsey also ordered Kinkaid to write an operational fighting plan for cruiser-destroyer action. Tom Kinkaid never got the chance to lead his cruisers into action, because *Washington* transferred him to Pearl Harbor for a major reassignment. But he did leave behind a plan for cruiser operations.

One critical element of the Japanese arsenal that was not taken into consideration by Admiral Kinkaid, nor any other U.S. naval commander, was the long-lance torpedo carried by Japanese destroyers and cruisers. This was a lethal weapon, 24 inches in diameter (versus the U.S. 21-inch torpedo) with a 1,100-pound warhead, almost twice the American model, and a range of nearly 11 miles at 49 knots. The oxygen-fueled long-lance—which reduced the torpedo's wake—had been invented in 1933. The mystery was why U.S. tacticians weren't more aware of the torpedo and its deadly capabilities. Japanese destroyermen trained for years in night maneuvers with the long-lance. It caused more damage to U.S. warships than the big guns of Japanese battlewagons.

The veteran Admiral Kinkaid was replaced by a relative newcomer to the South Pacific, Rear Admiral Carleton "Bosco" Wright, age fifty, who arrived with heavy cruiser *Minneapolis*. It was poor timing, the worst sort of luck. Tom Kinkaid should have kept his command until it was shaped up and tried in battle. Bosco Wright, a fine officer, was put in charge of unfamiliar ships and captains a couple of days before a major combat mission.

Because he was senior to Rear Admiral Mahlon Tisdale, who had more experience in these waters, Wright was designated officer in tactical command. Once again, seniority decided the commander. Wright and Tisdale went over Kinkaid's plan, which involved dividing the force into two cruiser elements, with at least one ship in each group equipped with the latest SG search radar. Also, in communications, there would be no misunderstandings with the use of the word "roger." The captains would not use searchlights in night action, creating bright targets. The destroyers in the van would fire their torpedoes first, and then clear out of the way of the cruisers, which opened up with their big guns. The plan was agreed on.

On November 29, Halsey ordered Wright to intercept a reported force of eight enemy destroyers and six transports heading down the Slot. Wright led his cruiser-destroyer force out of Espiritu for Cactus, 580 miles north. Japanese Admiral Tanaka, meanwhile, was preparing to make a night run and dump supplies off the slight outcropping of northwestern Guadalcanal known as Tassafaronga, where they would be picked up by troops in landing craft. By the evening of November 30, Tanaka was heading for Tassafaronga from the west, while Wright was approaching from the east through Ironbottom Sound.

The American ships entered the sound with four destroyers ahead in the van: *Fletcher*, *Drayton*, *Maury*, and *Perkins*. They were followed by Admiral Wright in *Minneapolis*, *New Orleans*, and *Pensacola*; then by Admiral Tisdale in *Honolulu* and *Northampton*. Two destroyers, *Lamson* and *Lardner*, which were picked up at the last minute from an outgoing convoy, followed behind. But no destroyers, as had been planned, were stationed far enough ahead to act as picket scouts. The eight Japanese destroyers, with Tanaka in *Naganami* leading, traveled in a single-column formation moving south on the west side of Savo Island to make the turn east toward Tassafaronga. The stage was readied.

At 2306, flagship *Minneapolis* picked up blips on the radar screen at 23,000 yards. Admiral Wright radioed his ships and steamed toward the Japanese past Henderson Field. Pre-positioned cruiser scout planes at Tulagi weren't able to assist because, with no wind, they couldn't lift their planes off the glassy surface of the sound.

At 2316, Commander William M. Cole aboard *Fletcher* picked up the enemy and requested Admiral Wright for permission to fire torpedoes, as according to plan. Instead of turning loose the van destroyers to make a torpedo run, Wright held up permission to fire, believing the range was too great. After wasting four valuable minutes, Wright called Cole on the TBS and was informed the range was satisfactory. Wright then said, "Go ahead and fire torpedoes." The four van tin cans fired. But the delay was injurious, for the unsuspecting enemy was fast steaming past the destroyer's point of aim. The U.S. torpedoes were in the water, traveling on an ineffective "following" run.

Next Admiral Wright gave his cruisers the order to open fire over voice radio: "Roger, and I do mean roger!" The cruisers opened up with 8-, 6-, and 5-inch fusillades.

The U.S. fire and the sight of torpedoes in the water was the first intimation that Tanaka had of the American naval force close at hand. But Tanaka's well-trained and disciplined Destroyer Squadron 2 coolly went into action. No gunfire. Torpedoes only. Use enemy gun flashes for the point of aim. Steaming at 24 knots, Destroyer Squadron 2 shifted course slightly to bring torpedo tubes to bear, and let go. They were the deadly, long-lance fish, each with 1,100 pounds of high explosive.

American fire struck first and set the Japanese destroyer *Takanami* ablaze. But before American sailors could congratulate themselves, two torpedoes hit flagship *Minneapolis*, one impacting on the port bow, the other in the after fireroom. Captain Charles E. Rosendahl, the navy's foremost lighter-than-air expert serving a sea tour to qualify for flag rank, struggled to save his ship. He managed to head for the impromptu harbor at Tulagi, and Admiral Wright turned over tactical command to Admiral Tisdale aboard *Honolulu*. Tisdale was a competent, no-nonsense flag officer, who would have been in command of the force had not seniority rules prevailed.

Next in column, *New Orleans'* Captain Clifford H. Roper shifted the helm quickly to avoid colliding with *Minneapolis*. This action put the heavy cruiser in the path of a torpedo, which exploded in the forward magazine, blowing off the bow along with the No. 1 8-inch gun turret. The turret dragged alongside of *New Orleans*, punching holes in her side and grappling briefly with the screws. *New Orleans* had lost a fifth of her ship's length.

Pensacola, the third cruiser in line, was next to suffer from a long-lance, which struck below the mainmast on the port side, flooding the after engine room, knocking out three turrets, and rupturing oil tanks. Captain Frank L. Lowe headed his ship limping toward Tulagi harbor.

Honolulu, known to her crew as the "Blue Goose," sheared to the right of the preceding cruisers, and Captain Robert W. "Bob" Hayler managed to shield his ship from the long-lance torpedoes, firing her 6-inch guns and getting through without a single torpedo hit.

The lucky Blue Goose had Admiral Tisdale aboard who wanted to sweep around Savo Island. Heading toward that landmark, Captain Hayler was advised by his navigator, Commander Kenneth Ringle, that he should turn left. The captain suggested 10 degrees. Commander Ringle replied, "Captain, you'll turn 25 degrees or you'll have to take her over the mountain!"

Northampton, last in the cruiser column, was not as lucky as *Honolulu*. Captain Willard A. Kitts followed behind *Honolulu*, avoiding the three damaged cruisers, and fired eighteen salvos at the Japanese destroyers. But then he mistakenly turned west and ran into a spread of eight torpedoes fired by the destroyer *Oyashio*. Two deadly fish slammed into *Northampton's* side plates, opening the engine room to the sea. Flames consumed the after part of the ship. Captain Kitt's crew fought hard to stabilize the heavy cruiser and get her into the safety of Tulagi harbor, but to no avail. The elegant cruiser slipped beneath the dark waters of Ironbottom Sound at 0240. Heads-up work by destroyers *Fletcher* and *Drayton* succeeded in rescuing 773 of her crew before dawn; fifty-eight went down with *Northampton*.

In Tulagi, *Minneapolis* and *New Orleans* were given coconut log false bows by repair parties on *Vestal*. The snub-nosed heavy cruisers were able to reach friendly ports to the south for further repairs before sailing to the West Coast navy yards in Bremerton, Washington, and Mare Island, California, for permanent new bows.

The Battle of Tassafaronga was a bitter blow to the American navy. Coming after the victories of the November battles around Guadalcanal, it was difficult for Halsey and Nimitz to accept. An alert U.S. heavy cruiser force surprised a lighter Japanese destroyer force. Wright thought he had engaged seventeen ships and sunk nine of them. He actually met eight ships and sank one destroyer, which had been hit by the salvos of five cruisers. The Japanese—at the loss of one destroyer—managed to sink one U.S. heavy cruiser and cause serious damage to three others, which kept them out of the war for months.

Once again, the leading destroyers were tied too closely to the cruisers thus limiting their scope of action, particularly in firing torpedoes. The cruisers might have opened fire when they spotted the enemy and then maneuvered to avoid the torpedo attack they knew must come from the aggressive Japanese tin cans. As in previous night battles in the Solomons, the American column was too long and thus unwieldy, and the importance of radar was again underrated. The admiral's flagship was set too far back in the column, rather than up forward where the admiral could exert better control. Admiral Wright took responsibility for the torpedo damage.

After each battle, flag officers and ship commanding officers filed their action reports. These were meant to be the definitive story of the engagement, as least from the U.S. officers' points of view at the time. These action reports moved up the chain of command, gathering senior flag officers' comments, their "endorsements," which weren't necessarily favorable and, in fact, were often critical. They were circulated to senior officers in the fleet and were read avidly. The reports and endorsements served as a rough guide to the expected conduct of U.S. naval forces in combat. In the action reports on Tassafaronga, the lethalness of the long-lance torpedo fired by Japanese destroyers and cruisers was still not fully appreciated.

If there was any consolation at Tassafaronga, it was the superb work by the damage control parties that saved the three surviving cruisers, which would undoubtedly have been lost earlier in the war. Moveover, the U.S. forces were up against one of the most effective flag officers on any side in World War II—Raizo Tanaka, who performed with his usual brilliance, always leading from the front of his force. Admiral Nimitz paid tribute to Japanese gunfire and torpedo technique as well as their "energy, persistence, and courage." It showed the difference between ships that were highly trained and worked together under a tough leader over long periods, and the American practice of the South Pacific Force of going into battle with a scratch team.

Rear Admiral Wright, his command shattered, was sent back to Pearl Harbor. Admiral Nimitz thought he was the victim of bad luck, having taken command a few days before the fatal action. Nimitz wished to keep him at Pearl, but Admiral King indicated there were already too many rear admirals on his staff and Wright should be sent back to the Navy Department. Unlucky Admiral Bosco Wright did not go to sea again. After serving in Washington, he eventually became commander of the 12th Naval District in San Francisco. Nimitz realized that he and Halsey had to make hard judgments of their flag officers. Nimitz wrote Halsey in December, "Please be utterly frank with me regarding flag officers. We are out to win a war, and not to please individuals. Those not in line for the first team must be sent ashore."

The grim year 1942 passed for the South Pacific Force with the Japanese position on Guadalcanal increasingly precarious, though that was not readily apparent to the Americans. The Japanese emperor, in a year-end message, declared, "The darkness is very deep but dawn is about to break in the Eastern sky. Today the finest of the Japanese army, navy, and air units are gathering. Sooner or later they will head toward the Solomon Islands where a decisive battle is being fought between Japan and America."

The exhausted marines on Cactus were being replaced by army troops under Major General Alexander M. Patch. Admiral Halsey was making plans to break up the missions of the Tokyo Express. For their part, the Japanese began building an airfield at Munda on the island of New Georgia, 100 miles up the Slot from Guadalcanal, thus presenting a new challenge. Admiral Halsey decided on a night bombardment of the Munda airstrip. For this reversal of the Tokyo Express, Halsey chose the newly arrived Rear Admiral Pug Ainsworth—the hefty, outgoing former administrative commander of Pacific Fleet destroyers—to take over Bosco Wright's beaten-down cruiser force. Minnesota-born Pug Ainsworth was an affable officer with a drink in his hand ashore, but a hard-driver and disciplinarian at sea.

Ainsworth's formation was another scratch team: flagship light cruiser *Nashville*, with *St. Louis* and *Helena*, and destroyers *Fletcher* and *O'Bannon*. He was backed up by a distant support group under Rear Admiral Tisdale, with four cruisers and three destroyers. Ainsworth barreled into the Munda waters at 26 knots at 0050 on January 5 and, for an hour with spotting floatplanes overhead, poured 6-inch fire into the island. It was a beautifully executed night mission by an expert ship-handler, Pug Ainsworth, who maneuvered his cruisers like destroyers.

During January, Halsey set up a Cactus Striking Force, comprising the destroyers *Nicholas*, *O'Bannon*, *Radford*, and *DeHaven* under the able Commodore Robert P. Briscoe, to bombard Japanese army positions on Guadalcanal, a sharp reversal of the early months of night fighting.

"Keep pushing the Japs around," Halsey ordered.

In late January, Halsey decided to send in Pug Ainsworth and his cruisers for a second night bombardment in New Georgia, this time in the Kula Gulf against the town of Vila, a Japanese supply point for the Munda airfield. In his flagship *Nashville*, Ainsworth led the veteran light cruiser *Helena* and Commodore Briscoe's tin cans, *Nicholas*, *DeHaven*, *Radford*, and *O'Bannon*.

Under the dangerous light of a full moon, Ainsworth's force charged into Kula Gulf at 0100 on January 24. The cruisers opened up first, expending their 6-inch projectile allotment, some two thousand rounds; then Briscoe's destroyers unloaded their 5-inch guns, with 1,500 shells. Ainsworth steered for home as a Japanese night air attack sought him out, but he retired into a convenient rainsquall and lost his attackers. U.S. planes arrived from Henderson Field after dawn and escorted the fast-moving bombardment force out of the danger zone. Halsey was pleased by the Ainsworth and Briscoe performance.

Halsey's South Pacific Force welcomed new replacements. Rear Admiral Ike Giffen arrived aboard heavy cruiser *Wichita* with escort carriers *Chenango* and *Suwannee* after a voyage from North Africa through the Panama Canal. Giffen had participated in North Atlantic convoy duty and the North African landings and was more concerned with the submarine than the air threat. In the New Hebrides, Halsey assigned Giffen to lead a strong force to protect transports bringing more army troops into Guadalcanal.

In *Wichita*, Rear Admiral Giffen commanded the heavy cruisers *Chicago* and *Louisville*. He was also senior to a second column of new light cruisers under the promising new Rear Admiral Aaron Stanton "Tip" Merrill, leading *Montpelier*, *Cleveland*, and *Columbia*. These three ships comprised Cruiser Division 12—with the absent *Denver*—of the new *Cleveland*-class light cruisers, one of the most effective cruiser divisions of the war. Two destroyer divisions formed their screen. Two escort carriers accompanied the force to provide air support. Ike Giffen was ordered to rendezvous with Commodore Briscoe's Cactus Striking Force at a point 15 miles off Guadalcanal, north of Rennell Island, at 2100 hours on January 30. Giffen was then to lead a daylight sweep up the Slot with the augmented force, while the transport squadron entered Ironbottom Sound to discharge troops and cargo. Air defense was left to Giffen's own judgment.

Admiral Giffen mishandled the deployment of his small carriers. They should have been dispatched well ahead of the cruiser-destroyer forces, and outside of Japanese land-plane range. Instead, they were part of the main force, thus the formation had to slow down every time the carriers turned away into the wind to launch or recover planes. Giffen referred to them as his "ball-and-chain." And so they were, because of the way he positioned them.

Giffen was intent on making the rendezvous with Briscoe on time. He dropped off the carriers and proceeded ahead at 24 knots. As Giffen headed north without air cover, blips indicating strange aircraft appeared on the cruisers' radar screens. Proper communications might have established quickly whether they were friend or foe. But Ike Giffen insisted on strict radio silence, so the fighter-director team in *Chicago* had no way of vectoring out an air patrol to clarify the situation. The sun was setting with mysterious blips still on the radar screens.

The blips were enemy planes from the new Munda airfield and airstrips further up the Slot. Giffen's force was nearing Rennell Island to the south of Guadalcanal. The two cruiser columns were led by the destroyers in a V formation, which was fine for possible shifting into battle disposition for a surface fight; but it left the cruisers' sterns unprotected against air attack.

Just before sunset, the radars indicated bogies 60 miles away to the northwest. However, Giffen did not alter his formation, change course or speed, or issue instructions to his captains on repelling an air attack. Among others, *Chicago* secured from General Quarters and was not fully prepared for an air assault.

The shrewd Japanese air commander circled to the south to come up on Giffen's force from behind and make his attack from east to west. Torpedo planes dropped their fish, one of which was avoided by *Louisville* by a last-minute, sharp turn. With no damage, Admiral Giffen apparently decided the worst was over and continued on the same course in the same formation, and even ceased zigzagging. He seemed obsessed with making the rendezvous with Briscoe's destroyers to the north.

The Japanese dropped floating flares, which indicated the U.S. formation's course. These served as beacons for their spotting planes to lead bomber and torpedo aircraft for a second attack in the dusk. One plane bored in and launched a torpedo, which just missed *Chicago*. Another exploded against *Louisville* but was a dud. A plane hit by anti-aircraft fire crashed close aboard *Chicago*, spraying her deck with flaming gasoline that lit up the cruiser as a target. At 1945, a torpedo struck *Chicago*, flooding after compartments and the fire room, knocking out three of the four screw shafts.

A dud torpedo hit flagship *Wichita*. The admiral's staff was confused by all the images on radar, which Giffen thought looked like a "disturbed hornet's nest." He did not order a protective smoke screen, but he finally changed course to the southeast. *Chicago*'s crew struggled to right the 11-degree list to starboard, but the heavy cruiser needed to clear the danger zone. At 2030 *Louisville* managed the difficult task of connecting a steel towing cable to *Chicago's* anchor chain and began hauling the stricken cruiser away from Rennell Island, a fine example of seamanship by *Louisville's* skipper, Captain C. Turner Joy.

When Admiral Halsey in Nouméa learned of *Chicago's* plight, he ordered the two escort carriers to send up a dawn combat air patrol, as well as Rear Admiral Ted Sherman's *Enterprise* task group to move up with protective aircraft. The fleet tug *Navajo* took over towing duties from *Louisville*. Halsey also called off the intended cruiser mission in the Slot and ordered the ships to return to the New Hebrides. The tin cans circled *Chicago* at daylight, but no one aboard the cruiser thought to vector out a combat air patrol from its fighter-director center. A Japanese torpedo plane force headed for *Enterprise* but, seeing its protective force of fighters, changed targets to *Chicago*.

Nine Japanese torpedo planes bore in. *Navajo* tried to turn *Chicago's* bow toward the incoming planes. Anti-aircraft fire and *Enterprise* aircraft, led by Lieutenant Commander James "Jimmy" Flatley, shot down several planes. But four torpedoes slammed into *Chicago's* starboard side, dooming the veteran cruiser, which the U.S. carrier force was unable to save. Captain Ralph Davis ordered Abandon Ship, and *Navajo*, with a cutting torch, severed the metal towline and turned to pick up survivors. *Navajo* and three destroyers rescued a total of 1,049 crewmembers. *Chicago* sank in the afternoon with colors flying, so ending the Battle of Rennell Island.

Admiral Halsey was angered at what he considered Ike Giffen's shortcomings and mistakes in judgment: his inexperience, his determination to make the rendezvous with Briscoe, his failure to set up a proper protective anti-aircraft screen, his failure to utilize the escort carrier planes, and his inability to handle *Chicago's* fighter-director facilities. Admiral Nimitz and his staff also wondered how a force of six cruisers could absorb a night attack, have one ship crippled, and then on the next afternoon leave *Chicago* behind to go it alone and be sunk by a similar attack; meanwhile three aircraft carriers were in the vicinity capable of giving air support. Ike Giffen's replied that he was just following Halsey's orders to clear the area with his remaining cruisers. Rear Admiral Giffen, though a favorite of Admiral King while in the Atlantic, never led a task force in the South Pacific again.

Over three nights in early February, despite an American PT boat, a Catalina Black Cat, and surface ship surveillance, the Japanese evacuated 11,706 soldiers from Guadalcanal unbeknown to the U.S. command. Tanaka's destroyers took them off under American noses. Admiral Nimitz was deeply impressed by this brilliant operation and declared, "Only skill in keeping their plans disguised and bold celerity in carrying them out enabled the Japanese to withdraw the remnants of the Guadalcanal garrison."

But evacuation doesn't win wars. Though the loss of warships was roughly even, the overall Battle for Guadalcanal was won by the United States, which was now ready to advance up the Solomons. The U.S. Navy's admirals had learned many painful lessons on fighting in the grim struggle in and around Ironbottom Sound. They would heed those lessons well. And the fighting admirals, Kelly Turner, Ching Lee, Tom Kinkaid, Duke Ramsey, Ted Sherman, Tip Merrill, and Pug Ainsworth were names the Japanese admirals would come to respect.

Seventeen

FIGHTING FLAGS: PUG, TIP, ARLEIGH

February–July 1943

In the Solomons, Admiral Halsey's South Pacific command—under pressure from Admiral King to keep moving—occupied the small Russell Islands between Guadalcanal and New Georgia, which had been evacuated by the Japanese. Rear Admiral Turner was in charge, even though he had just suffered a bout with malaria and a suspected mild coronary, which sent him to the hospital ship *Solace*. Ever the fighter, Kelly Turner downplayed his illness; he still worried that he was blamed by some senior officials for the Savo Island defeat, and that enemies would use his illness as a pretext to get him relieved. And there were some politicians who lost relatives—or whose constituents did—who blamed Turner.

Turner was not paranoid. Though flag officers and senior captains maintained stiff upper lips when disappointed over appointments, they were an ambitious lot and were often resentful of what they considered unfair promotions of their peers, or just being passed over. In June 1942, Congress suspended the selection boards because senior officers could not be spared from the fleet to staff the boards. They were replaced with a panel of officers scattered around the navy who would recommend officers up to the rank of captain. Promotions to rear admiral were handled differently, and possibly unfairly. The Bureau of Naval Personnel sent lists of eligible senior captains to various flag officers in the fleet and asked for their recommendations.

But the flag officer might not personally know some of the captains on the list, while having served with, and been favorably disposed toward, others. These recommendations were sent to a board comprising Admiral King, his senior staffers—Admirals Frederick Horne, Richard Edwards, Randall Jacobs, who was the chief of personnel—and the secretary of the navy. Invariably, Ernie King had the final say.

King restored the rank of commodore, a one-star flag officer, as a way of creating "spot" promotions. This was an official rank, as opposed to the honorary title of commodore used for division and squadron commanders, who were normally commanders or captains. King tried to sideline rear admirals who didn't make the grade at sea in combat. But he found himself with more flag officers than he wanted or needed. During wartime, senior officers insisted on remaining on duty until mandatory retirement, often the age of sixty-four. Once an officer was promoted to vice admiral, he stayed there. He could not be shifted to a lower rank, as was the case in the army and the peacetime navy. King was responsible for the vice admirals since he and the secretary of the navy alone chose the three-stars. Promotion to flag rank sometimes seemed capricious or unfair, depending on who was doing the selecting. Similar to the outside world, friends in high places played a role in the selection of flag officers.

In the Solomons, the need was to keep up the momentum of the newly re-designated Third Fleet, though Halsey preferred the title, Commander South Pacific. Admiral King acted as blowtorch from Washington, pushing for the advance up the Solomons; otherwise, scarce men and materiel would be assigned to other areas of operation. While Admiral King admired Halsey's fighting qualities, he thought correctly that Halsey was weak on staff work and advance planning. Like Spruance, King believed that although the erratic Miles Browning—still Halsey's chief of staff—was brilliant in aviation matters, he was a poor organizer and administrator, the essential qualities of his position.

Halsey relied on his two new aggressive cruiser division commanders, Rear Admirals Pug Ainsworth, age fifty-six, and Tip Merrill, age fifty-two, to keep the pressure on the Japanese in New Georgia, the next sizable set of islands up the Solomons chain. Pug Ainsworth—who had been Commander Destroyers Pacific before his assignment to the South Pacific—was big, broad, and affable, while Mississippian Tip Merrill was trim, soft-spoken, and shy. But he also was determined, energetic, and a master ship-handler. As one of his captains remarked, "Tip Merrill was one of those men who thought best under stress." Merrill commissioned the new battleship *Indiana* and sailed her to the South Pacific before taking over Cruiser Division 12, winning his admiral's stars in February 1943.

Merrill believed in Nimitz's dictum "training, training, training," and he honed the crews of his new light cruisers, *Montpelier*, *Denver*, and *Cleveland*, after which the class was named. Merrill was immediately popular. Seaman James J. Fahey, whose battle station aboard *Montpelier* was a 40-mm gun platform near the bridge, said, "Everyone took to him the first time they saw him. They don't come any better than Admiral Merrill."

The skipper of *Denver* was Captain Robert B. "Mick" Carney, a bright and capable ship-handler who molded *Denver* into one of the best ships in the fleet. He knew Tip Merrill as someone who had a magnetic personality, was short of stature, and a crack shot with an infectious laugh, and whose idea of an officers club was finding a palm tree and breaking out a bottle of bourbon. Merrill's chief of staff, Commander Bill Smedberg, said, "He loves people and he'll drink with anybody who wants to drink with him. He'll never leave the club until he has to, when there isn't anybody left. One problem is getting him to back to the ship because he's having such a good time."

On March 6, 1943, Merrill led his cruisers and three destroyers, *Waller*, *Conway*, and *Cony*, on a high-speed run into Kula Gulf to bombard the airstrip at Vila, on Kolombangara Island, near Munda. Commander Arleigh Burke was commodore in command of the tin cans, flying his pennant in *Waller*. In the darkness, Merrill's force picked up two skunks on radar, which turned out to be Japanese destroyers, *Minegumo* and *Murasame*, heading outbound after delivering supplies. *Waller's* radarman also picked up the contacts.

"Are you sure," Burke asked. "Not just a rock?"

"I'm sure, sir. It's a ship all right."

Burke hesitated, then gave the order for *Waller* to fire a spread of five torpedoes.

Just then, Tip Merrill ordered the light cruisers to open up with their quick-firing 6-inch guns. Gunfire and torpedoes quickly sank the two destroyers. Not content, Merrill continued his bombardment plan on schedule hitting runways, living quarters, supply dumps, and parked aircraft. Enemy shore batteries, which answered back, were soon silenced. Merrill led his force back down the Slot at 30 knots. It was a gem of an operation.

In assessing his own performance, Commander Burke was harsh. He believed he had been remiss in not accepting the radarman's judgment immediately. He almost repeated the mistake of Admiral Wright at Tassafaronga of delaying too long. Had he released his torpedoes a bit sooner and reported this, Tip Merrill might have delayed his cruiser fire, which could have prematurely alerted the enemy. Months later, in a conversation with a young ensign on his bridge, Burke asked, "Son, can you tell me the difference between a good officer and a poor one?" The junior officer began a long explanation about dedication, leadership, and tactical skills. Burke listened, then said quietly, "The difference between a good officer and a poor one is about ten seconds."

In May and June, Tip and Pug alternated with their cruisers on bombardment missions in the lower Solomons. While these missions little affected the Japanese airfields, they demonstrated that U.S. admirals could aggressively lead their ships into Japanese waters and inflict damage. Tip Merrill drilled his team in tactics for the night cruiser-destroyer battles he expected to fight. First, he trained in daytime off Espiritu Santo, simulating night conditions with his old battleships serving as targets in these maneuvers. Then Burke's Destroyer Division 43 participated in bombardment missions in the Slot. During one attack, Burke in flagship Conway was hit by enemy shellfire, and he was wounded in the back by shrapnel. He was awarded the Purple Heart but remained on his flag bridge, bandaged.

After the exercises, in the officers club Tip would gather his ship captains to talk cruiser-destroyer tactics. The tin can skippers and division commanders, like Burke, invariably complained about being tied to the cruisers' apron strings, instead of being deployed independently, thus making offensive use of torpedoes. Arleigh Burke went out on a limb. Why should the van destroyers up front have to wait for their release by the task force commander once they have spotted the enemy? If the destroyer division commodore knew his business, he should strike at the enemy at once, firing torpedoes, and then pulling clear of the cruisers. Burke, who had studied dozens of action reports, argued that after dark, all the destroyers should be deployed forward of the cruisers so that they could fire their torpedoes without explicit orders and get the hell out of the way.

This was strong medicine for task force commanders. Destroyers were always linked to the heavier ships. Arleigh Burke formulated his thinking in a memo, which pointed out: "The delegation of authority is always hard and under such circumstances as these, when such delegation of authority may result in disastrous consequences if a subordinate commander makes an error, it requires more than is usually meant by confidence—it requires faith."

Tip Merrill was impressed. But before Merrill and Burke could put their tactics into action, Arleigh Burke was transferred to command another destroyer division, this one mainly engaged in local convoy duties, which annoyed the fighting tin can commodore to no end. At one point, Arleigh Burke's tin cans were running down, in need of serious maintenance. Burke requested that his exhausted crews and ships be sent to Sydney for upkeep and repairs. Halsey radioed back: "Keep them in the Solomons."

Finally, a boiler of the destroyer *Saufley* was in such bad shape that Burke sent her to Australia without informing Halsey's headquarters. The other ships in the division anted up all the cash they could find and, while *Saufley* was undergoing repairs, her officers purchased as much beer and whiskey as they could in Australia. When *Saufley* was returning, Burke notified headquarters of his action. He received a message instructing him to call on Halsey the next time he was in Nouméa. Burke did so, expecting the worst.

In his office, Halsey waited before addressing the destroyerman. "Oh, Burke." Halsey looked at notes on his desk. "*Saufley?*" Halsey sat upright. "Why in God's name did you take it in your own hands to send *Saufley* to Sydney?"

"Sir," Burke began, "My boys haven't had any beer or whiskey for months . . ."

Halsey interrupted, shaking his head, "You mean you sent that ship down there for *booze?*"

"Yes, sir, the captain did pick up a lot of liquor. But . . ." Burke was about to explain the urgent need for boiler repairs.

Halsey smiled. "All right, Burke. You win. Your boys have been doing a great job, and I can't condemn you for going out on a limb for them. But don't do it again." Halsey pointed his finger at Burke who was ready with a fuller explanation. "If you had told me you sent *Saufley* for *repairs*, I'd have had your hide."

*

On Guadalcanal, Rear Admiral Charles Mason, ex-skipper of downed carrier *Hornet*, was ComAirSols, at Guadalcanal as head of the Cactus Air Force. Mason contracted serious malaria and pneumonia in March 1943 and was succeeded by Rear Admiral Pete Mitscher. Pete Mitscher received, after the Battle of Midway, his stars and was assigned commander, Patrol Wing Two, which was command of the PBY Catalina patrol planes, in the Hawaiian Islands. Mitscher thought he was being sidetracked in that job, possibly as a result of *Hornet*'s disappointing performance at Midway. Maybe he would not command at sea again. But he kept pressing Admiral Towers, ComAirPac, to move the patrol wing from Hawaii to the South Pacific, closer to real action. On December 1942, Mitscher received orders to become Commander Fleet Air Nouméa in New Caledonia.

In Mitscher's first week in Nouméa, a marine orderly, told by the duty officer to wake a junior officer for a midnight phone call, got into the wrong tent and woke up the grizzled rear admiral.

"You're wanted on the phone, sir," said the young marine.

Blinking, Mitscher replied, "Be damned if I'm going to answer the phone, private."

The private reported back to the duty officer that he couldn't find the junior officer but did wake up "a grouchy old chief."

When the marine pointed out the tent in question, the duty officer paled. But Mitscher took it lightly the next morning, pointing out that being mistaken for a chief petty officer was honorable, and besides the South Pacific was no place for stuffy admirals.

Mitscher was quickly shifted north as ComAirSols, commanding navy, marine, army, and New Zealand planes in the Solomons area. Above him was Vice Admiral Jake Fitch, ComAirSoPac, at Nouméa, and Admiral Halsey.

"I knew we'd probably catch hell from the Japs in the air," Halsey said. "That's why I sent Pete Mitscher up there. Pete was a fighting fool and I knew it."

Mitscher quickly set up a staff and began operations to intercept the almost nightly Japanese air raids on Guadalcanal and initiate air strikes against their bases. Living conditions were dirty and dangerous, but they suited Pete Mitscher. As one of his first actions, he was happy to recommend marine First Lieutenant James E. Swett for a Medal of Honor for shooting down seven Japanese bombers before being forced down with engine trouble.

In mid-April, Commander Layton's fleet radio intelligence unit at Pearl Harbor pieced together snatches of coded radio intercepts indicating that Japanese Admiral Isoroku Yamamoto, commander in chief of the fleet, would arrive at Kahili—a Japanese airfield on the island of Bougainville, New Guinea, north of the Solomons on an inspection visit on April 18. The visit was discussed by Admirals King and Nimitz, and by their superiors, Secretary of the Navy Knox and the president. Would a successor to Yamamoto be more effective? The answer was no. The order was relayed to Halsey and then Mitscher: "Nail Yamamoto."

Mitscher summoned his staff to work out a plan. The job was assigned to eighteen army P-38 Lightnings, twin engined, twin tailed with long range, to cover the one-way distance of 300 miles. Six of the best pilots were selected as the triggermen, the other twelve planes to fly cover. Mitscher took a jeep to watch the takeoff on a Sunday morning. One of the shooters blew a tire on takeoff and aborted; another had fueling problems, which left only four planes in the trigger group under Captain Thomas Lanphier. The P-38s arrived over Kahili right on schedule, spotted two twin-engined Misubishi G4Ms, and promptly shot them down. One plane carried Yamamoto, who was killed along with key staff members; the other carried his chief of staff, Vice Admiral Ugaki, who was badly injured.

In a postscript to his official report to Halsey, Mitscher noting that the date was the same as the raid on Tokyo a year earlier, wrote, "April 18 seems to be our day." Halsey replied, "Looks like one of the ducks in their bag was a peacock."

Pete Mitscher did a splendid job of uniting ComAirSols into a fighting force of marine, army, and navy airmen. He soon fired officers who did not want to fight. He shipped home those who tried but couldn't take it. He insisted on enthusiasm, dedication, and performance, and got the best out of everyone.

In June, the Japanese launched their last air bolt against Guadalcanal and Henderson Field. More than 120 enemy planes from Kahili and Munda airfields approached, but Mitscher was ready with his fighters—Lightnings, Wildcats, and Corsairs. The air erupted in dogfights and it became the largest air battle of the war in the Solomons, and the biggest victory for the United States. A total of 107 Japanese planes were destroyed. Pete Mitscher ordered a case of whiskey for the participating squadrons and made sure the appropriate medals were recommended for the pilots. During his four months as ComAirSols, Mitscher's planes shot down nearly five hundred Japanese and dropped 2,000 pounds of bombs on the enemy.

But Pete Mitscher was running on empty. A visitor, Rear Admiral Putty Read, of NC-4 trans-Atlantic flying boat fame, remarked, "Pete doesn't look a day over eighty." Mitscher picked up a case of malaria and ran a high fever for two weeks. His health was failing, his voice a whisper. In July, it was time to rotate the command to an Army Air Forces officer, Major General Nathan F. Twining, since the Cactus Air Force had been commanded by a marine and naval officer. When debilitated Pete Mitscher headed back to the States for reassignment, many believed that despite his fighting spirit, his frail health would keep him from being given a sea command again.

Kelly Turner was still in charge of South Pacific amphibious operations, now renamed III Amphibious Force, or "III Phib." He was planning the landing on New Georgia, the next major step up the Solomons. Turner set up shop at a Guadalcanal camp dubbed "USS Crocodile—Flagship—Amphibious Forces South Pacific." During the planning, Major General Millard Harmon, the top army officer in the South Pacific, presented Admiral Turner with a first draft of the New Georgia military plan. Turner absorbed it quickly.

"What do you think of the plan?" Harmon asked.

"It stinks," Turner replied. "Who wrote it?"

"Admiral, I did."

"It still stinks." But Kelly Turner flashed Harmon a rare smile.

Turner preached the newly learned amphibious tactics to the officers in his mixed command: Army Air Forces, marine aviators, destroyer captains, transport skippers, and the hell-for-leather PT boat sailors. The owlish Turner pushed the message: "The fellow we are working for is the fellow who walks on the ground. Whatever we are doing, we are doing it solely to get that man on the beach." Turner, though an autocrat, encouraged cooperation among his heterogeneous forces that made up a phib command.

Amphibious doctrine was still developing in the Pacific. The amphibious force commander remained in overall control until the ground commander established supremacy ashore. But this was not a clearly defined point, and Kelly Turner tended to exert control as long as possible. This led infantry generals to complain. Howlin' Mad Smith grumbled that Kelly Turner was an admiral who wanted to be a general. "Lightning Joe" Collins, who commanded the 25th Division on Guadalcanal and New Georgia, complained that Turner tried to control military operations ashore. Another declared that Turner "studied everything, remembered everything, interfered in everything." And *Time* correspondent, Robert Sherrod, noted that Turner could not travel from ship to shore without lecturing the coxswain on how to land his boat.

On D-day, Turner approached New Georgia in his veteran flagship, the attack transport *McCawley*, where he picked out Rendova Island across from Munda airfield for his landings on June 30. Rear Admiral George H. Fort, Turner's number two, led a group attacking Viru and Segi Point at the southern tip of New Georgia. As a backup fighting force, if needed, Admiral Turner had Duke Ramsey's two carriers, Pug Ainsworth's and Tip Merrill's cruisers, and battleship divisions under newly promoted Glenn Davis, late of battleship *Washington* command, and Harry Hill.

On his approach to the Rendova landing, Turner led his ships in two columns flanked by seven destroyers. The Japanese launched an air attack, and Turner ordered his ships to present a broadside target to the oncoming planes until his ships began their final attack. Then he called for a hard-right turn, which exposed only his ships' sterns, leaving a minimum target to the enemy. Some ten torpedo planes managed to launch fish. Skipper Robert H. Rodgers of *McCawley* saw one approaching on his port quarter and tried to dodge it, but it hit his engine room, killing fifteen and wounding eight. It was the only hit scored on Turner's force, but Solomon Islands veteran "Wacky Mac" soon began to sink, and Turner shifted his flag and staff to the destroyer *Farenholt*. He conducted the rest of the landings from the tin can's bridge.

That night *McCawley* was hit by torpedoes from U.S. PT boats in mistaken identity, which sealed her doom. The next morning, back in Guadalcanal, Turner gave Captain Rodgers a bottle of Old Grandad bourbon and promised to get him another ship command. Later Captain Rodgers recalled, "Turner shared the bridge with me countless hours. The long vigils—in which Turner talked to me about every subject under the sun, and he knew about them all—were a part of my life I can never forget."

The army troops that landed on Rendova were successful in securing the island. Then they were ferried over to New Georgia to take the troublesome Munda airfield. They found it slow going and were reinforced by a marine detachment. Eventually, army Major General J. H. Hester was relieved by army Major General Oscar W. Griswold to energize the Munda operation, take the airfield, and secure the island.

On the evening of the Fourth of July, Pug Ainsworth's cruiser-destroyer force was supporting the landings on New Georgia by bombarding Vila. Two surprised Japanese destroyers raced north to escape from Kula Gulf. As they left at emergency speed for the Slot, they fired a brace of long-lance torpedoes. One hit destroyer *Strong* in Ainsworth's force at the incredible distance of 22,000 yards (about 12 miles), probably the longest torpedo hit in the history of naval warfare. *Strong* sank quickly.

Ainsworth returned down the Slot to refuel and rearm at Tulagi. But at midafternoon on July 5, Admiral Halsey informed Pug that the Tokyo Express had ginned up another run from Bougainville down the Slot. Derail it! Flying his flag in *Honolulu*, Pug Ainsworth quickly led light cruisers *Helena* and *St. Louis* and destroyers *Nicholas*, *O'Bannon*, *Radford*, and *Jenkins*. By midnight, Ainsworth, traveling at 29 knots, had skirted New Georgia to port and went to General Quarters without sighting the enemy. Ainsworth slowed down near the entrance to Kula Gulf. But three groups of ten Japanese destroyers, under Rear Admiral Teruo Akiyama, were roaring down the Slot with troops to unload at Vila for the defense of Munda airfield. The Japanese were packing the powerful long-lance torpedoes, the impact of which the U.S. admirals were still unaware; they had seen the damage but didn't realize the speed at which the torpedoes could travel, nor the heavy load of TNT.

At 0140, the American radarmen picked up targets at 24,700 yards. The U.S. force shifted into battle formation, a single column: destroyers *Nichols* and *O'Bannon*, cruisers *Honolulu*, *Helena*, and *St. Louis*, and the two rear tin cans, *Jenkins* and *Radford*. The American officers were puzzled by the unusual Japanese formation and the looming mountain of Kolombangara in the background interfered with their radar signals.

Pug Ainsworth decided to open up with all his ships firing by radar, but he waited too long. He let the enemy get in too close where its torpedoes would be most effective. Still, American shells rained down on the oversize destroyer *Niizuki*, Admiral Akiyama's flagship, killing the flag officer. But *Suzukaze* and *Tanikaze* fired sixteen long-lance torpedoes, cutting through the water at 49 knots. *Helena*'s rapid-firing guns without flashless powder lit her up, making her a choice target.

Three long-lancers struck *Helena* inflicting fatal damage, as she quickly flooded. The U.S. destroyers belatedly fired their own torpedoes, which vainly chased the enemy ships. Some Japanese destroyers landed supplies at Vila. *Nagatsuki* ran aground on a reef and was a dead loss. Commodore Francis X. McInerney remained with his flagship *Nicholas*, which with *Radford* picked up *Helena* survivors and fired occasional rounds and torpedoes at retiring enemy tin cans. At 0617, McInerney had 745 *Helena* survivors aboard and, leaving four boats with volunteers to pick up remaining *Helena* men in the water, headed back for Tulagi. The Battle of Kula Gulf ended with valiant *Helena* sunk and two Japanese destroyers lost, though Pug Ainsworth at the time thought, understandably, that he had done much more damage to the enemy. In a postscript, when Pug Ainsworth reported in person to Admiral Nimitz that he had sunk two Japanese cruisers in the Kula Gulf, Nimitz referred to his radio intelligence chief, Commander Edwin Layton, who reported that only two destroyers were lost.

"How can you sit here on your fat ass, thousands of miles from the action and make such a statement?" Ainsworth demanded. "How can you say this; it's absolutely preposterous!"

"All I can report is what we get from radio intelligence," Layton replied. Ainsworth continued to berate Layton, but two weeks later a Japanese survivor of another sinking ship carried the classified report of the Kula Gulf action, which showed that Layton's version was correct.

On the night of July 11–12, both Pug Ainsworth and Tip Merrill's cruisers were on the prowl to provide gunfire support for the army and marine troops around Munda and to stop the Tokyo Express. As they left the Tulagi anchorage, the big, blustery Ainsworth signaled Merrill: "Give 'em hell, Tip. I'll try to drive 'em through so you can take the forward pass! Pug." Merrill replied: "Admiral Ainsworth, I'm afraid you spoiled the hunting by taking too much game on your last hunt. Good luck! Merrill."

The Tokyo Express was heading for Kula Gulf again, this time led by Rear Admiral Shunji Izaki in light cruiser *Jintsu*, and Destroyer Squadron 2 with five tin cans. They were covering for four destroyer-transports, which played no role in the battle. The famous Admiral Tanaka, whose flagship was *Jintsu*, had been beached in Tokyo for speaking too bluntly to superior officers, thus depriving the Japanese of perhaps their most talented combat flag officer.

Pug Ainsworth was in *Honolulu*, with *St. Louis* and the New Zealand light cruiser *Leander*, and Commodore McInerney's Destroyer Squadron 21. Ainsworth was assigned a second destroyer squadron under Captain Thomas J. Ryan. Unfortunately the two squadrons hadn't trained together and were selected from different units and of different classes. Shades of Tassafaronga! Ainsworth's battle plan was based on learning from earlier actions in the Solomons: single column; when contact is made, the van destroyers fire torpedoes and cruisers bear in and open up with rapid-fire gunnery before the enemy is aware, then turn away from the long-lance torpedoes before regrouping for a further attack.

Just after midnight July 13, a Catalina Black Cat radioed an enemy cruiser and destroyers heading down the Slot. Crossing the mouth of Kula Gulf toward Kolombangara—which means "king of waters"—Ainsworth formed battle disposition and increased speed to 26 knots. At 0100, *Honolulu*'s radar made contact, and the flagship radioed: "I smell a skunk." At 0109 Ainsworth ordered his van destroyers under Commodore McInerney: "Attack with torpedoes."

Japanese Admiral Izaki had no radar, but he had a new device to detect American radar pulses and did so. He knew Pug Ainsworth was coming his way. *Jintsu* switched on her searchlight and opened fire. Ainsworth waited until the range closed to 10,000 yards and then gave the order to commence rapid firing. The Battle of Kolombangara was on. Several salvos from *Honolulu* ranged in on *Jintsu*, causing a devastating explosion midships.

"You got the big one," *Honolulu*'s Captain Bob Hayler announced from his bridge. "We got the cruiser."

As tended to be the case at this stage of the war, all the U.S. ships concentrated on the illuminated, sinking *Jintsu*. Admiral Izaki, the captain, and 482 sailors went down with the flagship.

Ainsworth ordered a turn to the south over voice radio, but not all his captains heard him. This brought him into torpedo water and soon

Leander was hit by a tin fish, which left her with twenty-eight dead. In his flag plot, Ainsworth was trying to sort out what was happening. A Catalina reported Japanese destroyers were heading north.

Ainsworth radioed McInerney: "Go get 'em. Go get 'em!" McInerney pursued but warned the admiral, "Don't throw anything at us!"

Ainsworth responded: "Wouldn't do it for the world—go get the bastards—good luck!"

U.S. lookouts estimated anywhere from three to six enemy ships were burning, possibly because the *Jintsu* split in two, and some ships were simply still firing. At this point, the fighting *Jintsu* was down at the cost of damage to *Leander*. The Allies were ahead.

But Ainsworth thought there were Japanese cripples in the area and he began to search for them. This was an unfortunate decision, since it was hard to separate the enemy from the U.S. destroyers in the vicinity. *Honolulu* spotted Japanese destroyers, which had reloaded torpedoes and returned to the scene. Ainsworth turned to unmask the main batteries of *Honolulu*, *St. Louis*, and destroyer *Gwin*. At that moment, long-lance torpedoes from the Japanese destroyers arrived.

At 0208, *St. Louis* was hit by a long-lance in the bow. Captain Hayler of *Honolulu* maneuvered to avoid other fish, but one caught the lucky Blue Goose in the bow, too. *Gwin* was not so lucky. She received a torpedo in her engine room, which fatally wounded the destroyer.

So sank the only tin can to survive the battleship action that concluded the Battle of Guadalcanal. "She was a great ship," a crewman said, "but we knew she'd been living on borrowed time. I guess all of us lived on that kind of time in the Solomons."

The Allies had suffered three cruisers damaged and out of action. As Pug Ainsworth headed his force to Tulagi, he radioed Admiral Turner for air cover the next morning, and got it.

The ships of the dead Admiral Izaki, the second flag officer to die in seven days, had lived up to the aggressive, tenacious tradition of Admiral Tanaka.

Pug Ainsworth recognized his mistake at the Battle of Kolombangara. He should have used his longer-range guns to advantage at 12,000 to 16,000 yards, instead of closing and entering long-lance torpedo water. He messaged Admiral Nimitz: "One can always see how we should have done it differently and no one knows the fallacy of chasing Jap destroyers with cruisers better than I."

Nimitz replied: "You have fought two hard actions featured by aggressiveness and tactical skill."

At first, Pug Ainsworth and the American command thought that the United States had scored tremendous victory over the Japanese in the Battles of Kula Gulf and Kolombangara, and only later did intelligence prove what the actual score was. An assessment of the two similar battles indicated that American flag officers and captains were still overconfident in the accuracy of their rapid-firing 6-inch guns; in their ability of radar to spot the Japanese before being sighted, since the Japanese had fine optical equipment and well-trained lookouts; and in their dismal ignorance of the stunning impact of the long-lance torpedoes and the Japanese skippers' ability to reload torpedoes speedily. In short, the United States still needed to become aware of the power of enemy torpedoes, to develop night battle tactics, to avoid the rapid turnover of flag tactical combat officers, and use the full potential of radar.

Despite these drawbacks, Pug Ainsworth and Tip Merrill were fighting admirals who, in general, handled their cruisers with skill and aggressiveness. They were learning, as Arleigh Burke urged, to detach their forward destroyers to attack independently. It was now U.S. warships carrying the fight to the Japanese. The Tokyo Express was finally stopped by Admirals Ainsworth and Merrill and was about to be reversed.

The indomitable Kelly Turner, a man of iron determination in the face of adversity, had come to the end of the line in the South Pacific. By July, the fifty-eight-year-old flag officer seemed worn down from his illnesses, his eighteen-hour working days, planning and executing operations, and all the attendant problems of running an amphibious force on a tight budget. His owlish expression was gaunt, his face leathery. He chain-smoked. He was more snappish than ever. At anchorage when in Nouméa, he and a few staffers repaired to the small, raffish, Cercle de Nouméa run by a Frenchwoman, where they knocked back cocktails after a day's work, usually about five o'clock in a back room. (U.S. warships were legally and theoretically dry.)

Unlike Raymond Spruance, Kelly Turner took no exercise. He relaxed over drinks then went back to his flagship for several more hours of paperwork. In recent weeks, he sometimes took a swig out of his private bottle for a lift to keep going, though always fresh the next morning. He had developed many ideas about amphibious warfare: the importance of

logistics, the need to isolate the target, the emphasis on expert small-craft handlers, a distaste for the confusion of night phib operations, and the desirability of bypassing enemy strongholds. Now Admiral Nimitz wanted Admiral Turner with his amphibious expertise for the coming Central Pacific offensive.

On July 15, 1943, Kelly Turner was relieved as commander of III Phib by Admiral Halsey's deputy, Rear Admiral Ping Wilkinson, head of his Annapolis class who'd been Director of Naval Intelligence in late 1941. Kelly Turner left his South Pacific command in excellent hands as he headed for the biggest job of his career. Bill Halsey reflected on Kelly's departure from his command: "If you want something tough done, call Turner."

Eighteen
MACARTHUR'S ADMIRALS

January–June 1943

During 1942, the war in the Southwest Pacific theater went slowly as General Douglas MacArthur—from his headquarters in Brisbane, Australia, some 400 miles north of Sydney—commanded forces struggling on New Guinea. The Japanese quickly established bases on the northern side of the island, the world's second largest. The western half was part of the Dutch East Indies; the eastern, or Papua, was under Australian control. The Battle of the Coral Sea had thwarted a Japanese invasion of Port Moresby, the main city of Papua in southern New Guinea, across the Coral Sea from the northern tip of Australia. The Japanese then began an advance overland across the 13,000-foot Owen Stanley Range to attack Port Moresby from the landside. The advance was stopped by Australian troops, and during the summer the Allies landed a small, unopposed force and established a base at Milne Bay in easternmost New Guinea. In October 1942, MacArthur flew U.S. troops to an airstrip near Buna to expel the Japanese from Papua.

The general was assisted by the U.S. naval forces in the Southwest Pacific area, sometimes called "MacArthur's Navy" (a term the Navy Department disliked). It wasn't much of a navy by Pacific Fleet standards. It had only a few ships and a couple of admirals who sometimes disagreed. MacArthur himself deeply resented the navy's high command in Pearl Harbor and Washington for not allocating him more warships.

That antagonism carried through the war and soured his relations with Admirals Nimitz and King.

But the truth was that Douglas MacArthur wasn't in a position to make use of a fleet. To his many visitors, the four-star general came up with vast ideas for moving up the north coast of New Guinea, taking Rabaul and Kavieng in the Bismarck Islands, then island hopping to the southern Philippines. However, his staff was short on specific plans with specific targets, troop numbers, dates, and tonnages. As Admiral King put it, he wanted MacArthur to "state what his plans—not views—are." Aiming for Japan via the Philippines was the heart of MacArthur's strategy, and the general insisted, often and loudly, that he had made a promise to liberate the Philippines. That MacArthur's personal commitment should be the keystone of the U.S. strategy in the Pacific was sharply questioned by Admiral King, who was influential in such matters with the Joint Chiefs of Staff in Washington.

General MacArthur desired large carriers under his command, but there were none to spare. In any case, Admiral Nimitz did not wish to expose precious carriers to the many Japanese air bases in New Guinea and the Bismarcks. Admirals King and Nimitz believed the fast carriers were the most potent weapons in the naval arsenal, as long as they had sea room to maneuver. They did not want to risk the valuable flattops in supporting secondary operations with high-risk potential from enemy air bases.

MacArthur also requested old battleships that were unengaged in the eastern Pacific. But Nimitz believed they were unsuitable for use around New Guinea. So MacArthur's Navy consisted of a half dozen cruisers supported by Australian and New Zealand ships, some destroyers, U.S. submarines based in Brisbane and Fremantle, and PT boats. MacArthur's command comprised two American submarine bases at Brisbane and Fremantle, which was the port for Perth in the state of Western Australia. After a shaky start, the sub force played a major role, under two flag officers, in sinking Japanese ships. MacArthur directed some submarines to supply guerrillas in the Philippines and other special operations, but the U.S. boats operated mostly independently of the general's command.

General MacArthur didn't see eye-to-eye with Vice Admiral Leary, commander of naval forces in the Southwest Pacific area. At MacArthur's insistence, he was replaced in September 1942. His successor was Rear Admiral Arthur "Chips" Carpender, who served in the Atlantic and whose relationship with his boss was to become as rocky as Leary's, partly because Carpender was loath to commit his few ships in the uncharted, confining waters around New Guinea. In some ways, MacArthur's complaints were justified; it happened that the Southwest Pacific was at the bottom of Washington's list of priorities for soldiers, ships, and amphibious craft. For all his regal trappings and rhetoric, General MacArthur's command was a low-priority backwater, when viewed from Washington.

The Buna campaign in New Guinea was a hard-fought series of skirmishes, with the Americans and Australians pitted against hardened Japanese infantrymen. The Allied advance was bogged down through poor leadership, malaria, and dengue fever. The senior generals rarely visited the fighting front. MacArthur oversaw the campaign from Brisbane and was highly critical of the lack of progress. Finally, he sent the competent, low-keyed Major General Robert L. Eichelberger to assume command with the instruction: "Take Buna or don't come back alive." Eichelberger sorted out the incompetents and provided morale-enhancing leadership. Eventually, in late January, Buna was secured. MacArthur's forces paused to regroup, replenish, and recover from the hard jungle fighting. They needed some months to mount the men and equipment for another push. General Eichelberger was rewarded for his success by being assigned to train troops in Australia for a year in near obscurity. There wasn't room in the Southwest Pacific command for two army heroes.

MacArthur's dim naval prospects improved with the assignment in January 1943 of newly promoted Rear Admiral Daniel E. "Uncle Dan" Barbey as commander of Southwest Pacific amphibious forces, a new formation that, at the time, consisted mainly of Uncle Dan Barbey and his tiny staff.

Dan Barbey was a natural for the job, though he was short of everything except enthusiasm, willpower, and expertise. As a captain, Barbey developed an interest in amphibious warfare, studying Japanese activities in China. In 1941, as chief of staff to the Atlantic Fleet Service Force, he organized an amphibious force with primitive landing vessels in maneuvers with the 1st Marine Division along the North Carolina coast.

In May 1942, Barbey was appointed head of the Navy Department's amphibious warfare section. He helped develop new landing craft: landing ship tank (LST), landing craft tank (LCT), landing craft infantry (LCI), landing ship dock (LSD), and the smaller beaching craft. At age fifty-two, he was promoted to rear admiral in December 1942 and sent to the Southwest Pacific to become MacArthur's phib commander. In March 1943, Admiral King changed the name of the Southwest Pacific naval forces to Seventh Fleet, under now Vice Admiral Carpender, and Uncle Dan Barbey became head of the "VII phib" force.

Barbey was aware that MacArthur, "the General," had fired one navy commander, and that Carpender was on thin ice. He wondered: How long will I last? MacArthur thought the navy conspired against his interests in the Southwest Pacific, and that paranoia was fostered by MacArthur's inner circle, "the Bataan gang." One correspondent noted, "The war between the Yanks and the Japs is only exceeded by the war between the army and the navy."

Barbey called on MacArthur and found him "friendly but deadly serious," and there was no casual banter and camaraderie that pervaded the Pacific headquarters of Admiral Nimitz. Though operating on a shoestring, Barbey gathered some amphibious ships and began to meld a proper force, while troops from the now-named Sixth Army recuperated from the Buna operation. He managed to cadge a flagship, the repair ship *Rigel*, as well as some LSTs, which were the workhorses of amphibious warfare.

In addition to the problem of obtaining ships, Admiral Barbey found that training bases in the United States often regarded the amphibious force as the dumping ground for fresh ensigns coming from civilian life and officers schools—so called 90-day wonders. In San Diego, the idea arose that the phibs were a one-way ticket to the battle zone, that any ship beginning with the letter "L" (for landing) was as expendable as the PT boats in the Philippine campaign. The phibs had green officers and green crews, most of whom had never been out of sight of land. Yet they would soon be entrusted with a variety of difficult seagoing tasks: navigating through reef-strewn, uncharted waters; storing aboard soldiers and supplies in the proper order for unloading; beaching their ships through surf; getting the troops ashore; and then pulling their ungainly, flat-bottomed craft off the beach and fighting off enemy air attacks to get the LSTs safely home. No wonder they were named "large slow targets."

Admiral Barbey interviewed one young ensign, skipper of an LCT in Brisbane, whose experience seemed to be typical. The young man told the admiral that his only hand at leadership was chairman of his fraternity dance at the University of Texas. His only seagoing experience in the navy, during his midshipman course at Columbia University, was three afternoon trips aboard a small sub chaser in the Hudson River.

The first operation Admiral Barbey planned was taking Woodlark and Kiriwina islands, located off the eastern tip of New Guinea, as the initial step to isolate the Japanese stronghold of Rabaul. Barbey moved his own headquarters aboard *Rigel* to Milne Bay in eastern New Guinea to be close to the army commander, General Walter Kruger. The landings were timed to coincide with Admiral Turner's invasion of New Georgia in the Solomons, and took place in late June 1943. To mount the unopposed landings on Woodlark and Kiriwina—the Trobriand Islands famously investigated by anthropologist Bronislaw Malinowski—Barbey commandeered every available landing craft in the Southwest Pacific. The inexperienced crews made their landings at night—sixteen thousand troops and their supplies—on coral-strewn beaches. There was no enemy air or surface action. "As a military feat," Barbey said, "the landings on Kiriwina and Woodlark were of no great moment, but it was an essential first step—or so we thought at the time—in the capture of Rabaul."

But it would take a few months before Uncle Dan Barbey would be able to mount his first real invasion, leading MacArthur's Navy along the north coast of New Guinea.

Nineteen
WAR IN THE
COLD AND MIST

June 1942–May 1943

The North Pacific campaign was a long, hard slog in freezing weather, dense fog, snow, and mists, as well as through poorly charted waters at sea and miring, mushy tundra on the ground. The campaign lasted from June 1942 to May 1943 and did scarcely any American admiral proud. The action centered on the Aleutians, an island chain that reached from the Alaska mainland to Attu, 1,200 miles westward. In mid-1940, the U.S. Army established an Alaskan defense command under Brigadier General Simon Boliver Buckner. The navy did roughly the same, creating an Alaskan sector under the command of the 13th Naval District in Seattle. Navy patrol plane bases were established at Dutch Harbor and Kodiak. Other units were based at Cold Bay and Umnak.

In May 1942, word reached Admiral Nimitz in Pearl Harbor that the Japanese—as part of their attack on Midway in June—intended to land forces in the Aleutians. Nimitz assigned Rear Admiral Fuzzy Theobald, an able but cantankerous flag officer who was ComDesPac, to form a North Pacific Force with five cruisers and four destroyers. The burly Theobald was given command of all the Alaskan defense forces, including the Army Air Forces contingent under Brigadier General William O. Butler.

As part of his command, Theobald had 20 Catalina flying boats, about 85 army bombers and fighters, 9 destroyers based at Unalaska, and 6 submarines. When the Japanese prepared to strike, Theobald had scant information from Nimitz as to enemy movements or plans.

Because of fears that the Japanese might strike at the U.S. West Coast, hundreds of army planes were held in readiness there, rather than being deployed to Alaska.

The Japanese were aiming for the Aleutians. Vice Admiral Boshiro Hosogaya, commander of the Japanese Fifth Fleet, led the enemy forces in a feint against Dutch Harbor in the eastern Aleutians, while actually landing troops at two of the westernmost islands in the chain: Attu and Kiska. The Japanese never planned to land on Alaska proper, much less Canada or the United States. Basically, the operation was a diversion from the serious attempt to take Midway Island, and to forestall any U.S. attempt to attack Japan from the Aleutians.

Admiral Theobald ignored intelligence, collected by Commanders Layton and Rochefort in Pearl Harbor, that suggested the Japanese were heading for Kiska and Attu. Since he believed it was a feint, Theobald instead followed his own hunch that the enemy was heading for Alaska proper and concentrated his warships about 400 miles south of Kodiak near Dutch Harbor, thus placing him about 1,000 miles east of Kiska and Attu. Since Theobald insisted on maintaining radio silence aboard his flagship *Nashville*, he had a poor picture of what was happening and no way to communicate directly with his planes and shore bases. He soon decided to abandon *Nashville* as a flagship in favor of operating ashore from Kodiak, 600 miles east of Dutch Harbor.

Vice Admiral Hosogaya, in the heavy cruiser *Nachi*, led two amphibious groups with a carrier escort, which broke off to launch diversionary air raids on Dutch Harbor. The Japanese force was lucky with the weather and had a clear shot at Dutch Harbor. But the U.S. planes were unable to find the Japanese in the fog-shrouded waters. The Japanese landed unopposed on Kiska and Attu on June 7, 1942, and quickly took over the small U.S. weather stations and their personnel. But the islands never proved to be of strategic value, remaining more of a nuisance than anything else.

Attention quickly shifted to the South Pacific and the struggle for Guadalcanal. Theobald sent the few ships at his disposal for occasional bombardment missions against the Japanese on Kiska and Attu. At Kodiak, Rear Admiral Theobald had under him a cruiser division commander, Rear Admiral Poco Smith, who had accompanied carriers in the South Pacific. The nasty weather, smothered in fog, precluded any serious offensive operation by either side for nearly a year, though the

United States landed troops on Adak Island and built an airfield. The campaign was a stalemate.

The long dark winter did nothing to improve Admiral Theobald's spirits. Bright but temperamental, he quarreled with his army counterparts over the selection of islands on which to land forces and build airstrips. The Alaskan command was a rancorous one. Theobald was not able to work amiably or effectively with army ground or air commanders, nor even with his own officers. Admiral Nimitz, backed by Admiral King in Washington, decided to make changes in the North Pacific. Rear Admiral Tom Kinkaid was moved from the South Pacific to relieve Theobald as Commander North Pacific (ComNorPac), effective January 1943. Admiral Poco Smith was replaced as the cruiser-destroyer force commander by newly flagged Rear Admiral Soc McMorris.

Fuzzy Theobald resented his removal from command and questioned Admiral King about it on his return to Washington. King and Theobald had been old shipmates, but King, finally fed up with Theobald's nagging, let him have it. Theobald's performance was disappointing, substandard. He'd allowed the Japanese land on Kiska and Attu with his task force disposition in the wrong place. He later exacerbated relations with the U.S. Army and Air Corps counterparts in an area that demanded harmony. He was simply the wrong man for the job. He would not be going back to sea. Instead, he was shuffled aside to command the 1st Naval District in Boston, his career dead-ended and his fine peacetime reputation shoaled by wartime demands.

Kinkaid moved quickly to establish smooth relations with his army generals and airmen. He tried to work out a modus vivendi with Vice Admiral Frank Jack Fletcher, who was named commander of the 13th Naval District and the Northwestern Sea frontier in Seattle. Soc McMorris took easily to his new command, hoisting his flag in the ancient light cruiser *Richmond*. After a bombardment mission against the Japanese on Attu, Soc McMorris fought the unusual Battle of the Komandorski Islands. This action pitted an outnumbered U.S. force against a heavy Japanese formation under Vice Admiral Boshiro Hosogaya for three and a half hours near the Russian Komandorski Islands, west of the Aleutians.

Soc McMorris in *Richmond*, with the heavy cruiser *Salt Lake City* and four destroyers, *Bailey*, *Coghlan*, *Dale*, and *Monaghan* under Captain

Ralph S. Riggs, were patrolling on a north-south line 180 miles west of Attu. The crew of *Salt Lake City*, badly damaged at Cape Esperance, called her "Swayback Maru" because of her well-deck. Shortly before sunrise on March 26, 1943, in near-freezing weather, the van destroyer *Coghlan* and flagship *Richmond* picked up a radar contact to the north. They soon discovered it was Admiral Hosogaya's force running reinforcements to the Japanese garrison on Attu. The force comprised two heavy cruisers, two light cruisers, four destroyers, and two supply ships. The latter two were operating separately from the main Japanese force.

Admiral McMorris realized he was outnumbered by two to one. Should he fight or retire? In which direction? The bold McMorris decided to head for the two transports and sink them while holding off the enemy cruisers at long range, and then move back for the Aleutians and the safety of American air cover. McMorris notified Captain Bertram J. Rodgers of *Salt Lake City* that he would conform to the movements of the much heavier ship, though giving overall orders.

At 0840, the Japanese opened fire from 20,000 yards on *Richmond* and then shifted to *Salt Lake City*. Admiral Hosogaya concentrated on the heavy cruiser because her 8-inch guns were by far the longest range in the U.S. force. *Salt Lake City* opened up at 20,000 yards and scored hits on *Nachi* with her third and fourth salvos. Hosogaya steered a course that would preclude McMorris attacking the transports. Reluctantly, Soc McMorris turned away to the west, while still firing. *Nachi* launched torpedoes at extreme range, but they were ineffective. Soon *Salt Lake City's* 8-inch shells were at the 9-mile range and hit *Nachi*. For his part, Captain Rodgers was "chasing the salvos," that is, conning his ship toward the enemy's last splash on the assumption that gunners would not aim twice at the same place.

It was a long-range, seesaw duel between the heavy cruisers: the light cruisers and the destroyers did not waste ammo because they were outranged. The Japanese admiral maneuvered to get between McMorris and the Aleutians, but the wily McMorris headed north and then west before going south. Then the Japanese destroyers fired their fish, but from too great distances. To protect the cruisers, McMorris ordered his tin cans to make a smoke screen.

At 1103, *Salt Lake City* received an 8-inch hit that disabled her engine room. Her boilers lost power. Seawater contaminated her fuel lines. The veteran cruiser went dead in the water.

By now McMorris recognized he had little hope of reaching the transports. Additionally, he was gradually moving westward and could come under range of Japanese land-based planes from Paramushiro in the Kuril Islands. When *Salt Lake City* was hit again, McMorris ordered his destroyers to launch a torpedo attack. Commodore Riggs' tin can *Bailey* led the valiant charge to protect the cruisers. But chances looked slim. *Salt Lake City*'s engine room was in bad shape and she was low on ammunition.

However, expecting a torpedo attack, Admiral Hosogaya turned away. *Salt Lake City*'s plight had been hidden from the Japanese flag officer by the effective smoke screen. When things looked darkest, Hosogaya mistook enemy shell splashes for bombs. He thought he was under U.S. air attack and decided to break off the action. By noon, *Salt Lake City* had restored power. With the Japanese headed for home, Soc McMorris set a course for Dutch Harbor.

The mission of the Japanese transports was thwarted; they returned to base with supplies. Admiral Hosogaya's actions displeased his superiors and he was relieved for not pressing home the attack. The well-directed, well-executed, against-odds performance of Soc McMorris, Captain Rodgers, and Commodore Riggs' gallant destroyers was much admired in the fleet.

In the spring of 1943, the United States decided to regain Attu and then Kiska, respectively. A North Pacific amphibious force was created under Rear Admiral Francis Rockwell, who had been evacuated during the fall of the Philippines. He was based in San Diego with the title Commander Pacific Amphibious Training Command. He would conduct the landing in the two Japanese-held Aleutian Islands with the 7th Infantry Division serving as the main army troop force. Admiral Nimitz assigned three old battleships, *Pennsylvania*, *Idaho*, and *Nevada*, to lead the gunfire support group. Rear Admiral Tom Kinkaid commanded three battleships, six cruisers, an escort carrier, nineteen destroyers, and a variety of supply and amphibious craft.

Kinkaid, as commander of North Pacific Force, found himself in an unusual situation. Although he was under Admiral Nimitz, commander of the Pacific Ocean Areas, the army command in Alaska—with 72,000 troops in the Alaska Defense Command—served under Major General Simon Boliver Buckner, who in turn answered to Lieutenant

General John L. DeWitt, Commander Western Defense Command, with headquarters in San Francisco. Buckner commanded the army forces in the North Pacific area, when they were not directly involved in operations under Kinkaid. Thus, about 14,000 army airmen under Brigadier General Butler reported to Kinkaid for operations. The naval bases and their attached sea commands came under the Alaskan sector of Rear Admiral Charles S. Freeman's 13th Naval District in Seattle, which itself came under the jurisdiction of the new Northwestern Sea frontier headed by Vice Admiral Frank Jack Fletcher.

The command channels seemed to Kinkaid confusing at best. First, he moved his headquarters from Kodiak to some 1,000 miles westward to Adak, which was closer to the scene of the action. The shift was likened to moving from civilization to the frontier. General Buckner was already there, and soon Kinkaid shared a dinner table with the army general and a firm bond established.

Kinkaid's command problems were further heightened by the fact that Rockwell, a classmate of Kinkaid's, was senior to him by three and a half months and seven numbers on the rear admirals' signal list. Rockwell thought the difference important, and Kinkaid got the impression that Rockwell expected to be in command of the Attu-Kiska operation in its entirety. Rockwell introduced Kinkaid to marine Major General Howlin' Mad Smith, who had helped train the army troops in California in amphibious techniques and was to be an observer in the coming invasion.

The invasion force for Attu was beginning to assemble. The three old battleships were under division commander Rear Admiral Howard F. Kingman. Rear Admiral Ike Giffen came up from the South Pacific (and from his lackluster performance at Rennell Island) with his heavy cruisers, his flagship Wichita, San Francisco, and Louisville plus four destroyers. Rear Admiral Soc McMorris now led Richmond, Detroit, and the new Santa Fe, with six destroyers.

As the plans progressed, Kinkaid was disturbed that Rockwell behaved as though they were equals—simply coordinating their operations for the coming invasion—even though both Nimitz and General DeWitt had earlier designated Kinkaid as the supreme command. This was aggravated by the fact that the joint planning was being done at Rockwell's headquarters in San Diego. Kinkaid believed Rockwell was reluctant to forward plans to him for review. Kinkaid also believed

Rockwell should command the assault phase from a transport flagship, as Kelly Turner had done in the Solomons, rather than from the battleship *Pennsylvania*. If *Pennsylvania* needed to be used to repel a Japanese surface force, this would take the amphibious force commander away from his center of operations. Kinkaid got the impression that Rockwell, after the landings at Attu, intended to take the three battleships in his support force back to San Diego without any reference to the ongoing Aleutian operations. Kinkaid advised Rockwell to move his battleships much closer to Attu for bombardment than the 14,000 to 18,000 yards that was stated in the plan.

"The gun power you have available in the battleships and destroyers should be ample to blow the hell out of the Jap installations if the ships can get in close enough to hit their targets," he suggested. Kinkaid was speaking from experience of his cruisers' earlier bombardments in the Pacific. Rockwell ignored the advice.

The invasion took place on May 11, 1943. The ship-to-shore movements were unopposed on Attu, 35 miles long and 15 miles wide. The Japanese decided to fight from prepared, inland positions rather than at the beach. The troops of the 7th Infantry Division were commanded by Major General Albert E. Brown and went ashore at Massacre Bay. They quickly got bogged down in the muskeg terrain and low-lying fog, which they were unused to, and received heavy fire. They dug in, and General Brown called for reinforcements to jolt his stalled advance.

Admiral Kinkaid remained in Adak, following his precept that the overall commander should remain close to a stable base of communications and allow the commanders in the field to get on with the job. Kinkaid desired to complete the operation as soon as possible. There was always the chance that a major Japanese fleet would sortie from Paramushiro in the Kuril Islands and overpower the North Pacific Force. In forty-eight hours, General Brown had moved only 4,000 yards. He complained about the unexpected number of enemy soldiers and the muddy terrain.

General Brown requested heavy road-building equipment, which suggested to Kinkaid that Brown had stopped fighting and intended to consolidate his position for an indefinite period. A naval officer from the flagship *Pennsylvania* visited Brown's headquarters ashore and heard the general complain that it would take six months to secure Attu. That was enough for Admiral Kinkaid; Brown would have to be replaced. Kinkaid asked Rockwell whether Brown had the necessary "stamina and aggressive spirit" to press the attack. Otherwise, Kinkaid planned to replace Brown with Major General Eugene M. Landrum, then at Adak. Rockwell suggested waiting, but Generals Buckner and DeWitt concurred with Kinkaid. Thus, Kinkaid informed Nimitz that he was relieving Brown, who returned to Adak to question his relief. The admiral reported: "After carefully studying the dispatches Brown said if he had been in my place, he would have taken exactly the same action I did take."

By this time on Attu, the thrust of battle had changed, and the army troops under General Landrum moved smartly ahead. The creepy fog that had slowed the Americans had also prevented Japanese search planes from providing intelligence for the Japanese fleet to attack the landing force. Organized resistance on Attu ended on May 29, 1943. Some 600 of the 11,000 soldiers from a landing force were killed and 1,200 were wounded. The Japanese lost 2,351 and 28 had been captured. The operation had been messy; the unloading of the transports was clumsy; the bombardment was from overly long ranges; and the 7th Infantry Division trained for desert fighting was not well led at the top. The troops were not properly equipped for the Aleutians. Rockwell had not solicited advice.

After Attu, planning for the invasion of Kiska began. Francis Rockwell was again in charge of the invasion force. But in June, Tom Kinkaid was promoted to vice admiral, which now clearly defined his seniority over Rockwell. Admirals King and Nimitz weren't pleased with Rockwell's apparent reluctance to work under Kinkaid. Nevertheless, they allowed Rockwell to keep *Pennsylvania* as his flagship for the coming attack on Kiska. At General DeWitt's suggestion, Major General Charles H. Corlett, who oversaw the training of troops at Fort Ord on Monterey Bay, would command them. Given the problems on Attu, Rockwell allotted 34,000 troops for Kiska, including a Canadian brigade of 4,800.

With fog and clouds affecting air reconnaissance, intelligence on Kiska was sketchy. Bombardment groups under Ike Giffin and a new force under Rear Admiral Robert M. Griffin intermittently shelled Kiska with battleships *New Mexico* and *Mississippi* and heavy cruiser *Portland*.

A battleship-destroyer group under Rear Admiral Kingman and a cruiser-destroyer force led by Rear Admiral Wilder D. Baker shelled the island early in August. Finally, on August 15, the invasion force was landed, but by then the Japanese were gone. In another brilliant retirement, reminiscent of Guadalcanal, the Japanese had secretly evacuated five thousand troops without the Americans catching the faintest whiff. Only a few dogs were left behind by the Japanese. This led a U.S. pilot to remark: "We dropped a hundred thousand propaganda leaflets on Kiska. But those dogs couldn't read."

Tom Kinkaid was bitter about the Japanese's escape at Kiska and he probably should have listened to some warnings about the unusual lack of activity on the island. But his stock had risen with Admiral Nimitz, while Admiral Rockwell's less so. King said privately, "I am not satisfied in that they were allowed to evacuate without being 'hampered.'" Rockwell never commanded an amphibious group in the Pacific again. He was assigned, for the rest of the war, to Washington and to head the training command of the Atlantic Fleet Amphibious Force.

After Attu and Kiska, the Aleutians became a Pacific war backwater, but bigger things were in store for Tom Kinkaid.

Twenty

U.S. INTO THE MED

June 1942–January 1944

In the first months of 1942, the United States and the British debated, often heatedly, about committing forces to the European theater. American military strategists held that the invasion of the continent should be through France in 1942. But the British insisted that neither they nor the Americans, not even their combined forces, were strong enough to land successfully in France. Both Washington and London recognized that the Russians were fighting for their very existence against the Germans and needed and deserved help, while Field Marshal Rommel's Afrika Korps threatened Egypt and the Suez Canal lifeline to India and the Far East.

President Roosevelt favored strong action in the Mediterranean, which could be mounted with existing forces and would secure a supply line through the vital inland sea. The problem was that North Africa was controlled by the Vichy French, who had taken a neutral position. Generally, the Vichy French were anti-British, and this influenced the decision to employ as many American troops as possible, in what was named Operation Torch. The overall command of the operation was given to Lieutenant General Eisenhower with Admiral Sir Andrew Cunningham as his deputy in command of all naval forces.

Three amphibious landings were planned: in French Morocco on the Atlantic, and in French Algeria at Oran and Algiers, from which Allied troops would move eastward to attack Rommel's rear. The invasion was fraught with political and diplomatic pitfalls. The Americans and British wanted the Vichy French as allies, despite the fact that they were preparing to invade their territory. The Allies considered Operation Torch as liberation not conquest. But the French themselves were divided in sentiments between the Vichy regime under Marshal Philippe Pétain and the Free French headed by General Charles de Gaulle. Generally, the French National Navy supported the Vichy regime, and it controlled the Moroccan ports and big gun defensive emplacements.

For the United States, the buildup for Operation Torch was a huge undertaking, though some American army officers gave it only a 50 percent chance of success because of the enormous distances involved. Captain Dick Conolly, fresh from a Pacific destroyer squadron command, was one of Admiral King's planners for Operation Torch. The head of the planning staff, Rear Admiral Charles M. "Savvy" Cooke, asked Conolly what he thought of the plan. "I think it will succeed," Conolly said. Savvy Cooke replied, "You and I and Admiral King are the only ones who think it will. Everybody in the Army is against it—the whole General Staff!"

By September 1942, the planning in Washington and London was shaping up. Three task forces would land separately: the western task force embarked in the United States would hit the Casablanca area under American command; the center force at Oran with American and British troops loaded in the United Kingdom; and the eastern force at Algiers with British and American troops also embarked in the United Kingdom.

The western task force was under the command of Rear Admiral Kent Hewitt, who had been appointed Commander Amphibious Forces Atlantic Fleet in April 1942. New Jersey–born Kent Hewitt was a fortunate choice. A large, easygoing, fifty-five-year-old officer with a sharp brain, he was a fine organizer, with a knack for picking a top-notch staff. He was also a meticulous planner with the tact to handle complex and variegated forces in his command, based at Norfolk, Virginia. His style of leadership generated confidence, loyalty, and affection.

Hewitt's task was tough. The landings had to take place before mid-November, before winter sea and surf conditions would necessitate a postponement until the spring. Amphibious techniques, as to Kelly Turner in the Pacific, were new and untried in the Atlantic Fleet. Hewitt trained his crew in the new landing craft in Chesapeake Bay, but everyone was aware that the training was imperfect because of the need for speed. In October, Hewitt called a meeting of some 150 naval and military officers in Norfolk to go over the features of the ambitious attack plan, managing to maintain secrecy.

The plan called for Admiral Hewitt, aboard heavy cruiser *Augusta*, to land thirty-five thousand soldiers at three beaches in northern Morocco, all under the military command of Major General George S. Patton early on November 8, 1942. The forces were broken down so that Rear Admiral Monroe Kelly would land the northern force under Brigadier General Lucien K. Truscott, Jr., near Port Lyautey (now known as Kenitra) with its valuable airport. In the center force attack group, Captain Robert Emmett would land Major General J. W. Anderson's force of twenty thousand at Fedhala, 15 miles north of Casablanca. Rear Admiral Lyal A. Davidson in Philadelphia would disembark General Ernest N. Harmon's smaller force of sixty-five hundred soldiers near Safi, 140 miles south of Casablanca.

The transport landing force had strong backup. The naval covering force consisted of battleship *Massachusetts*, flying the flag of Rear Admiral Ike Giffen, and the heavy cruisers *Wichita* and *Tuscaloosa* with a destroyer squadron. To the rear of the phib force was a carrier group: the *Ranger*, skippered by Captain Calvin T. Durgin, with Rear Admiral Ernest D. McWhorter in command, along with four "jeep" carriers, converted from tankers. These were *Suwannee*, under the command of pugnacious Captain Jocko Clark, who had pressured the Newport News shipyard to rush completion of the ship to make the Operation Torch sailing deadline, *Sangamon*, *Chenango*, and *Santee*.

On October 24, the expeditionary force departed Norfolk with the covering force leaving Casco Bay, Maine. They were joined in mid-Atlantic by the carrier group, which assembled in Bermuda. The trans-Atlantic track took the force, covering an expanse of ocean 30 by 20 miles, south of the Azores and west of the Madeira Islands. There were no breakdowns, straggling, or German U-boat attacks. During the two-week crossing, sailors chipped paint from interior living spaces, mindful of the damage from fire suffered by the cruisers sunk at the Battle of Savo Island. The task force arrived off Morocco with 102 transports and warships on time, just after midnight on November 7. The 4,500-mile voyage was a brilliant feat of navigation and coordination by Admiral Kent Hewitt.

Weather forecasts from Washington suggested high surf and tides, which would cause the landings to be delayed or cancelled. But Admiral Hewitt consulted his staff meteorologist who predicted the storm would abate. Hewitt made the critical decision to go ahead on the landings, with the signal "play ball."

The central force transports loaded their troops into landing craft before dawn. Hewitt didn't order preliminary shelling of the landing on the beaches, mainly because the army was hoping for surprise and didn't trust the accuracy of naval gunfire. Everyone was also uncertain what the French military response would be: Would it fight? Control destroyers that were to lead the landing craft took their places offshore. Gunfire support warships patrolled back and forth. Off-loading in the dark caused plenty of foul-ups in getting troops and equipment into landing craft and then hitting the proper beaches. But surprise was maintained and the landings were successful, though there were many lessons regarding amphibious warfare to be absorbed. Mainly, the U.S. Navy had to learn how to disembark more quickly and master the difficulties of conning landing craft to the proper beaches. The army needed to cope with emergencies and adapt to the limitations of ship-borne transport to shore.

Diplomatic efforts to keep the French forces neutral were not fully successful, and some French guns opened up on the American vessels after dawn broke on November 8. Fire was returned by inshore destroyers and by flagship *Augusta* and cruiser *Brooklyn*. The uncompleted French battleship *Jean Bart*, immobilized at dockside in Casablanca, fired with its one serviceable four-gun turrets at battleship *Massachusetts* but was quickly silenced by her. *Ranger's* planes bombed and strafed French installations.

French destroyers and submarines initiated a brave but futile attack against the American invasion fleet. A light cruiser and a destroyer squadron, along with submarines, sortied from Casablanca harbor and fired guns and torpedoes at *Massachusetts*, *Augusta*, *Brooklyn*, and U.S. tin cans. Four French destroyers were sunk or beached, three others were badly damaged, and Rear Admiral Gervais de Lafond was seriously wounded aboard his flagship *Milan*. Several submarines sallied forth and fired torpedoes, and three were listed as missing. Five U.S. warships suffered minor damage in this Battle of Casablanca.

Farther south at Safi, the landing itself was unopposed, but French guns opened fire at the U.S. warships, as destroyers *Cole* and *Bernadou* landed U.S. Rangers in the harbor area to seize installations. The battleship *New York* and cruiser *Philadelphia* returned fire.

To the north, near Port Lyautey, heavy surf interfered with the landings, which ran into scattered French fire. But the battleship *Texas* and cruiser *Savannah* opened up and soon silenced French artillery resistance. Admiral Kelly sent the French defenders a message: "Join with us. Stop this useless waste of lives and use them later in the fight against your real enemy—Germany."

Later Admiral Hewitt and General Patton had lunch at a brasserie in Fedhala with French Admiral F. Michelier, commanding the Casablanca sector. Hewitt said, "Admiral, we are very sorry to have had to fire on the French flag in order to carry out our operation. We always considered the French our friends and we still want them as our friends." Michelier smiled and replied, "Admiral, you carried out your orders, and I carried out mine. Now I'm ready to cooperate with you in every possible way."

The landing forces at Oran and Algiers that came from the United Kingdom met almost no resistance and a cease fire was soon arranged at Algiers. Sporadic fighting continued at Oran until November 10, when the French capitulated. Admiral François Darlan, a powerful figure in the Vichy regime, in exchange for Allied recognition of his political authority, ordered an end to French resistance on November 11. The American and British forces achieved all their objectives in Operation Torch with a firm foothold in western North Africa. In retaliation, the Nazis occupied all of France and tried to take over the French fleet at Toulon. But the Toulon admiral ordered his ships scuttled.

Anglo-American divisions soon began racing eastward toward Tunisia and Rommel's rear. They hoped to reach the ports of northern Tunisia before the Axis powers could ship in reinforcements. But German troops from Sicily landed by sea and air along the northern and eastern coast of Tunisia, taking the ports of Tunis and Bizerte. They rushed these units to Tunisian's border with Algeria. The Germans had the advantage of short interior supply lines, while the Allies were strung out along the muddy roads of Algeria. In December 1942, Axis counterattacks pushed the Allies back westward and, in February, dealt the Americans a severe defeat at the Kasserine Pass in western Tunisia.

That defeat, however, was the highwater mark of the German defense. The British and American armies regrouped under Generals Harold Alexander and Omar N. Bradley and continued the advance, with General Bernard L. Montgomery entering southern Tunisia and driving north. In May, the Axis forces in Tunisia surrendered, and 275,000 German and Italian soldiers marched into captivity. This cleared the entire northern coast of Africa and, in Admiral Hewitt's words, "the severed life line of the Empire was spliced."

After the seizure of Tunisia, the running argument between military planners in Washington and London continued. The Americans insisted on a full frontal assault in Northern Europe to open a "second front," with Berlin the ultimate goal. The British favored operations in the Mediterranean, "the sea of destiny," partly for historical reasons and partly because they feared the high casualties of attacking the German army in France. The high brass of both nations had learned to compromise—as they had with Operation Torch.

In January 1943, a conference was called in Casablanca attended by the highest American and British command, headed by President Roosevelt and Prime Minister Churchill and including the Combined Chiefs of Staff of the United States and United Kindgom. Consisting of the U.S. Army, Navy, and Air Force chiefs and with British counterparts, the Combined Chiefs of Staff, with President Roosevelt and Prime Minister Churchill, was the top wartime policy board choosing targets, timing, and priorities on all Anglo-American strategic matters. Its decisions were relayed to planning staffs for implementation and would then be carried out by the fighting forces on the land, in the air, and at sea.

The British—Field Marshal Sir Alan Brooke, Admiral of the Fleet Sir Dudley Pound, and Marshal of the Air Force Sir Charles Portal— were united in calling for a holding action in the Pacific against Japan, and concentrating Allied resources on the war in Europe. For their part, General Marshall and Admiral King insisted on keeping up the momentum against the Japanese. As for North Africa, the Americans intended to keep only token forces there and, instead, wanted to build up forces in the United Kingdom for the cross–(English) Channel assault on the continent in 1943. The British believed they wouldn't have the necessary strength until 1944 and pressed for a Mediterranean action. With the troops and equipment already there for use, against Sicily or Sardinia, the British had the goal of knocking Italy out of the war. The conquest of Sicily would also clear the Med of Axis shipping and take some of the pressure off the Russian front.

After hours of bargaining, the decision was finally made to maintain the pressure in the Pacific, to delay the cross-Channel invasion until 1944, and to invade Sicily in 1943 with a joint U.S.-U.K. military and naval force. Dwight Eisenhower was promoted to full general and named Supreme Commander of the North African Theater of Operations with General Harold Alexander as his deputy. Admiral of the Fleet Cunningham was to be the overall naval commander with Air Chief Marshal Arthur W. Tedder as the air commander. However, the United States' decision to go along with the British wish to move in the Mediterranean left Admiral King with a virtually free hand to shape strategic policy in the Pacific war.

General Eisenhower had his hands full in dealing with the ground action in Tunisia and turned over the Operation Husky (Sicily) planning to his subordinates. The plan called for Kent Hewitt, now a vice admiral in command of the newly designated Eighth Fleet, to land General Patton's Seventh Army on the south shore of the Sicilian triangle. Admiral Cunningham would disembark General Montgomery's British Eighth Army on the southeast beaches. The ultimate goal was Messina at the northeast corner, only 3 miles from the Italian mainland.

The joint planners worked together in harmony, with an important exception. The odd man out was the U.S. Army Air Forces, because it rejected a role in the interdiction of enemy beaches, and insisted its mission was to strike inland at German and Italian airfields. That is, air force brass favored "strategic" rather than "tactical" bombing to achieve victory. To do this, Lieutenant General Carl "Tooey" Spaatz, commanding the Northwest African Air Force, formed a strategic bombing force within his command headed by now Major General Jimmy Doolittle, who led the Tokyo raid. Air Vice Marshal Sir Arthur Coningham commanded the tactical air elements with four hundred planes. But the air generals would not commit themselves in advance to direct air support of the troops hitting the beach. The U.S. Navy sailed with the U.S. Army without any guarantee of what kind of air support they could count on.

This led General Patton, who remembered the first-rate help from U.S. Navy escort carriers off Morocco, to plead with Admiral Hewitt to provide some carrier air. "You can get your navy planes to do anything you want," he told Hewitt. "But we can't get the air force to do a goddamn thing!" Hewitt thought this bizarre since the Army Air Forces was part of the U.S. Army.

The navy's escort carriers, however, were tied up fighting the Battle of the Atlantic against German U-boats, and none were assigned to Operation Husky.

The U.S. Western Naval Task Force was divided into three main groups with code names. The "Joss" Force was under Rear Admiral Dick Conolly, the destroyer squadron commander in the Pacific who had caught Admiral King's eye and was assigned by him as a flag officer to the Mediterranean. Conolly was to land the 3rd Infantry Division under Major General Lucien Truscott at Licata.

In training, Conolly consulted with young Ensign Phil H. Bucklew, who commanded the beach reconnaissance force, and the ensign suggested that since he had the most experience he should lead the advance party to Green Beach, because it had the most difficult approach. Conolly said he preferred Bucklew to head the force into Red Beach, where the largest landings were to take place. When the young officer remonstrated, Conolly snapped, "Now let's get something straight. You know I ask a lot of questions, but don't ever forget I still make the decisions here. I concede you are the most experienced person, but where the most troops are is where the most experienced person will be."

Conolly also had the new landing craft, vehicles, personnel (LCVP) he intended to use for Operation Husky, though the army commanders argued for rubber boats, which both Hewitt and Conolly thought absurd. In a pre-invasion meeting to thrash out such issues, General Patton finally turned to his generals and declared, "Once and for all, the navy is responsible for getting you ashore and they can put you ashore in any damned thing they want to."

General Lucien Truscott, aboard Dick Conolly's flagship, worried about the navigation difficulties in reaching the beaches. Conolly told him, "General, don't let that worry you. That's my problem. Set your mind at rest. I'm qualified for this job. There's no guarantee you'll hit everything right on the button, but if anybody can do it, I think I can, because I served fifteen months as navigator of a battleship. I know my vessels."

The "Dime" Force commanded by Rear Admiral Jimmy Hall, who had been chief of staff to the late Admiral Wilcox on *Washington*, would set down the 1st Infantry Division under Major General Terry Allen at Gela. The "Cent" Force was led by Rear Admiral Alan Kirk, former Commander Amphibious Force, Atlantic Fleet, and a brilliant officer who clashed with Kelly Turner over prewar intelligence distribution. He would debark the 45th Infantry Division under Major General Troy Middleton at Scoglitti. Admiral Kirk made sure that all his ship captains and military commanders knew the landing plan and conveyed it to their own underlings. His idea was the rank and file in an amphibious force should have some idea of what was going on to function more effectively. Rear Admiral Davidson led a six-ship cruiser covering force to supply seaborne fire support. In all, Admiral Hewitt had 580 ships and beaching craft in his command.

On the right flank, the Eastern Naval Task Force was commanded by Vice Admiral Sir Bertram Ramsey, and it landed five divisions of General Montgomery's Eighth Army at five beaches south of Syracuse. Ramsey's total shipping reached 795 including backup convoys. American and British troop strength was about equally divided, and the whole force, in terms of the initial assault, constituted the largest amphibious landing in history.

At the army's insistence, Operation Husky landings were launched at night, after midnight on July 10, 1943, though the navy disliked conducting complex amphibious undertakings in the dark. After a rough crossing from North Africa, the night landings turned out to be relatively smooth and successful. Cooperation between the navy and army was exemplary. On shore at the three landing zones, soldiers captured their initial objectives ahead of schedule. The seaborne soldiers were assisted by 3,400 paratroopers of Major General Matthew B. Ridgway's 82nd Division, who jumped behind Gela. But a second drop the next day was a near disaster. General Spaatz in Tunisia decided to send 144 C-47 transports with paratroopers to reinforce the 82nd Division's positions behind Gela. Only belatedly did he inform Admiral Hewitt, who hadn't time to alert all his ships. As usual, from the navy point of view, the air force seemed reluctant for any close cooperation.

The transports, flying at low level, arrived over the drop zone at dusk just as a German air raid was taking place. In the confusion, twenty-two C-47 transports were shot down by friendly fire. "That whole air drop was a botched-up mess," Admiral Conolly declared. "It was a damned disgrace. A scandal."

During the landings, the U.S. army at last appreciated the benefits of naval gunfire. Before the army artillery was in place, the Germans and Italians made sporadic attacks on U.S. positions. But the task forces under Admirals Hall, Conolly, and Kirk were quick to respond with directed fire from cruisers and destroyers, and their attack knocked out approaching German tanks. At one point, General Patton, from a forward command post north of Gela, watched a group of German tanks trundle toward the bridgehead. His units hadn't yet received their anti-tank guns. There was a naval fire control party nearby. He summoned a young ensign, who had a walkie-talkie.

"If you can connect with your goddamn navy," Patton ordered, "tell them for God's sake to drop some shellfire on the road."

Within minutes, the cruiser *Boise* opened up with its 6-inch guns and broke up the tank advance. Patton became a quick convert to the efficacy of naval gunfire support. So did General Eisenhower, who declared, "So devastating in its effectiveness as to dispose finally of any doubts that naval guns are suitable for shore bombardment. The firepower of vessels assigned to gunfire support exceeded that of the artillery landed in the assaults, and the mobility of ships permitted a greater concentration of fire than artillery could achieve in the initial stages."

The Germans launched attacks by planes based at the many airfields in Sicily and Italy and sank the destroyer *Maddox*, the *LST-313*, and the Liberty ship *Robert Rowan* laden with ammunition. Army Air Corps fighter planes were rarely to be seen, since the air command was still concerned with "strategic" targets well behind the front lines.

After a series of skirmishes, the British forces that landed south of Syracuse moved north against increasingly tough German opposition. General Montgomery insisted on commandeering a road to the west to protect his flank, which General Patton had chosen for his advance. So Patton's Seventh Army wheeled farther west and headed for the capital of Palermo instead. After capturing Palermo, Patton moved his army eastward along Sicily's northern coast in a series of naval-assisted leapfrogs. This offshore force was headed by Rear Admiral Davidson, the cool gunnery specialist in *Philadelphia*, and Captain Charles Wellborn's Destroyer Squadron 8. Montgomery's Eighth Army slogged up the eastern flank of the island, but rarely called on the British Royal Navy for support or devised tactics to leapfrog behind the retreating Germans. In a competitive drive for Messina, Patton narrowly beat Montgomery—creating a fractious rivalry that was to extend across Europe.

The capture of Messina on August 17 after a thirty-eight-day campaign—and after news that Benito Mussolini had been deposed—was badly marred by the failure of air and naval forces (mostly British) to block the Strait of Messina. General Montgomery's overall plan had failed to provide for an Axis seaborne retreat to the Italian boot. Though the British had available a battleship force, apparently the memories of the losses at the Dardanelles in World War I and Crete earlier in World War II weighed against moving too closely to the enemy-held coast to break up the retreat.

A hundred thousand Axis troops and their equipment managed to escape Sicily, mostly by night in ferries and other small craft. It was brilliantly conducted by the Germans and Italians, "a glorious retreat," in the words of German Commanding General Fridolin von Senger, himself a master tactician. General Heinrich von Vietinghoff said the evacuation was "of decisive significance for the entire later course of the campaign in Italy." The three escaping German divisions played a vital role in the fighting in southern Italy.

Among the lessons the U.S. Navy learned during Operation Husky was the need for special beach parties to unload the incoming landing craft and to get the equipment forward to avoid chaos on the landing beaches. Furthermore, there was a need for specially equipped amphibious command ships like Admiral Kirk's *Ancon*. Transports like Admiral Hewitt's *Monrovia* or Admiral Conolly's *Biscayne*—a converted seaplane tender—were simply not commodious enough to accommodate admirals, commanding general's staffs, and the complex communications equipment needed to supervise vast amphibious landings.

The navy admirals learned to their sorrow that they couldn't depend on the Army Air Forces for consistent close-in ground support, which was essential to the troops, and that escort carriers needed to accompany naval forces for such backup. The navy considered the air forces' unwillingness or inability to provided support for U.S. ground forces almost criminal. "It was a damned disgrace," Dick Conolly commented.

At one level, the ensigns and coxswains of small landing craft, most reservists in action for the first time, did their difficult jobs at night in heavy surf as real professionals. The performance of the navy admirals in the planning and execution of Operation Husky was superb. Cool under fire and effective were Kent Hewitt, Dick Conolly, Jimmy Hall, Alan Kirk, and Lyal Davidson. For his work in supporting Patton's dash from Palermo to Messina, Davidson was called "a real fighting so-and-so" by George Patton, a high commendation. He added, "On all occasions, the navy has given generous and gallant support."

Even while the fighting was continuing in Sicily, Allied senior planners argued about the next step. A top-level meeting called Trident was held in Washington in late July to settle the matter. Churchill and the British were keen to invade Italy, seeking to take it out of the war. The United States continued to insist that the main focus of energy, troops, and material be directed toward a cross-Channel invasion. On July 25, Italy's dictator, Benito Mussolini, was deposed, and a day later, the United States accepted the British argument that more men and time were needed before invading France. To keep the momentum going, the Americans agreed the Allies should land in southern Italy, codenamed "Avalanche."

The question was where? Most American naval strategists favored a landing north of Naples, a major port that was heavily mined. However, the air forces complained that anywhere north of Naples was unsuitable for the short range of their fighters.

Admiral Dick Conolly, who favored an attack north of Naples at Gaeta, grumbled that since the air force hadn't been supplying close air support anyway, the lack of it wouldn't make much difference. But Conolly deferred to the army's wishes on the grounds that it was the navy's job to take the army where it wanted to go.

Therefore, General Montgomery would land his Eighth Army in Calabria, the toe of the Italian boot, across the Strait of Messina. The ideal plan would have been to cross the strait as soon as Messina was taken. As was his habit, General Montgomery insisted on a delay—until September—to prepare his forces for the invasion. The delay, according to Field Marshal Albert Kesselring, commander of German forces in Italy, was "a gift to the Axis." Montgomery finally crossed the strait on September 3 against slight opposition near Reggio Calabria in Calabria.

On the same day, British warships landed an infantry division near the big harbor of Taranto on the boot's heel.

Six days later, the U.S. force prepared to land in the Gulf of Salerno, south of the scenic Sorrento Peninsula and Amalfi Coast. Vice Admiral Kent Hewitt led the American invasion force in the flagship *Ancon* with General Mark W. Clark, commanding general of the U.S. Fifth Army. Rear Admiral Jimmy Hall headed the southern attack force in the transport *Samuel Chase* with the U.S. VI Corps commanders.

Again, the cruiser-destroyer fire support group was under the command of Rear Admiral Davidson, with four cruisers and a flock of tin cans. En route to Salerno, Admiral Cunningham requested the loan of a cruiser from Admiral Davidson to ship troops to Taranto. Davidson ordered *Boise*'s Captain L. Hewlett Thebaud: "Return at once to Bizerte, report to CinCMed [Commander in Chief, Mediterranean]." Thebaud thought this was some sort of reproof and inquired: "Please repeat." Realizing this, Admiral Davidson provided the reason, adding: "Hope this makes you an admiral!" Later, Thebaud did indeed make flag rank.

The British commanded the northern attack force under Commodore G. N. Oliver with the X Corps, Lieutenant General Sir Richard M. McCreery commanding. Rear Admiral Dick Conolly in *Biscayne* was in charge of an amphibious group in this command. To get into the Avalanche operation, Conolly volunteered to serve under a Royal Navy officer who was his junior in rank, just as Admiral of the Fleet Cunningham agreed to serve under General Eisenhower. Conolly insisted that his flagship must be the closest ship to the beach. The covering force was led by Vice Admiral Sir A. V. Willis with four battleships. A separate British carrier force was headed by Rear Admiral Philip L. Vian.

Once again, despite the objection of Admiral Hewitt, the U.S. Army opposed daylight landings and preliminary naval gun bombardment to obtain tactical surprise, no matter how unrealistic it was to think that such a fleet could approach the German-dominated shore without detection. The Gulf of Salerno was the logical objective because it was the most northerly location reached by air force fighters from North Africa. The Germans were prepared to contest the Allied landings in the Gulf of Salerno with von Vietinghoff's well-trained Tenth Army.

The first waves hit the beach before dawn and continued through the morning against tough but scattered resistance from German dug-in gun positions. The troops were supported by accurate gunfire called in from the offshore cruisers and destroyers. During the day, the Italian govern-ment announced an armistice. But that did not impede the tough German defenders; if anything it reinforced their determination to resist.

On September 11, cruiser *Savannah* was hit by a new German bomb—which was guided by radio from a high-flying plane—knocked out of action, and retired to Malta. On September 13–14, the Germans mounted a strong counterattack against Allied lines making a deep advance and leaving the success of the landings in doubt. General Clark held an emer-gency meeting with General Alexander and Admirals Hewitt and Conolly aboard the latter's flagship *Biscayne*. Clark said he might need the navy to re-embark the northern X Corps to support the southern VI Corps, or vice versa, if necessary. Hewitt and Conolly did not like the idea at all. Alexander heard both views and ordered: "There will be no evacuation."

Not long after, *Biscayne* was the target of a German air attack, which left Captain George C. Dyer, shot through the leg, a bad wound that took him out of action. He had been a valuable chief of staff to Dick Conolly, who left the details to his staff while he made all the major decisions. Aided by massive gunfire from Allied warships, the ground forces drove back the Germans, thus securing the Salerno beachhead. As Marshal Kesselring put it, "On 16 September, in order to evade the effective shelling from warships, I authorized a disengagement on the coastal front."

On September 16, General Montgomery's forces moving north from Calabria linked up with General Clark's Fifth Army units, leading Clark to report to Eisenhower: "We are in good shape now. We are here to stay. . . . I am prepared to attack Naples."

Avalanche concluded with the loss of fewer ships than expected: destroyers *Rowan*, *Buck*, *Bristol*, a minesweeper, a tug, and six LCTs. Three Liberty ships were also sunk. Naples did not fall until October 1. The Allies thought that the Germans would retire to northern Italy before making a strong stand. But Marshal Kesselring decided to defend the Italian peninsula almost ridgeline by ridgeline, and the mountainous terrain favored the defenders. Eventually, the defenders stalled the Fifth Army in the grim, cold winter of 1943–1944 around Monte Cassino along the heavily defended German Gustav Line.

When Mark Clark's Fifth Army grounded to a halt around Monte Cassino in late 1943, Eisenhower and Clark sought a way to resolve the stalemate. Their plan was to seize a beachhead behind German lines at

Anzio and Nettuno about 20 miles south of Rome, the operation code-named Shingle. Prime Minister Churchill eagerly pressed for Shingle. Some senior officers had doubts about the wisdom of the operation. As the buildup for Normandy increased, this meant the landing and back-up forces would be undermanned with men and equipment stretched thin in the Mediterranean theater. They worried about a second Dunkirk.

However, U.S. Fifth Army and Eighth Fleet planners worked out the approach to Shingle, which was completed only ten days before the invasion. Major General John P. Lucas would head the army's VI Corps with the 3rd Infantry Division under Major General Lucien Truscott, as well as the British 1st Infantry Division and airborne and ranger outfits. General Patton was not optimistic about Shingle. In a farewell conversation with General Lucas at Naples, Patton said, "John, there is no one in the army I hate to see killed as much as you, but you can't get out of this alive. Of course you might be badly wounded. No one ever blames a 'wounded' general!"

The naval force would be led by Rear Admiral Frank Lowry, former captain of *Minneapolis* in the Pacific and now amphibious commander of the Eighth Fleet. Admirals Conolly, Hall, and Kirk had been reassigned to new posts in the Pacific or in England.

When Alan Kirk left his flagship, in a typical grace note, he told the ship's company: "Together we have sailed many thousands of miles. I know that the burden of an admiral's flag and an admiral's staff often bears hard on the company of the ship that carries them. You have borne it well, and for myself and men, I thank you. As we go to our separate duties I think we may justly take pride, together, in a task well done. Good luck to you all."

Lowry flew his flag in Admiral Conolly's old flagship, *Biscayne*. Just after midnight on January 22, 1944, Lowry sighted the Anzio lighthouse and dropped anchor 4 miles offshore.

The Allies landed two divisions unopposed. The landings went smoothly and the land forces managed to clear a beachhead 7 miles deep and 15 miles long. In the next three days, however, the navy underwent severe German air raids usually around twilight. They suffered the worst series of invasion losses yet in the Mediterranean. The British destroyer *Janus* was sunk; the *Jervis* was struck by a radio-guided bomb. The U.S. tin can *Plunkett* was hit by a bomb, killing fifty-three crewmen. British hospital ships were targeted and *St. David* sunk. The U.S. destroyer *Mayo* struck a mine and was badly damaged. The minesweeper USS *Portent* was sunk. On January 29, the British light cruiser *Spartan* was hit by a radio-guided bomb and swiftly capsized. The next day the U.S. Liberty ship *Samuel Huntington* sank after severe damage from a German bomb.

But by the end of January, the fleet of LSTs managed to unload men and cargoes and clear the dangerous waters around Naples. U.S. cruisers *Philadelphia* and *Brooklyn* and escorting destroyers served as gunfire support ships. But when Lowry requested of Admiral Hewitt heavy cruisers for longer-range fire support, he was informed none were available. Once again, the U.S. Air Force was unable or unwilling to provide close air support for the ground troops.

With what he thought were insufficient forces, General Lucas was slow in consolidating his gains ashore and lost the opportunity for a quick strike ahead toward the Alban Hills—the objective designated by General Alexander. This delay allowed the Germans to marshal an effective defense surrounding the beachhead. Lucas was not an aggressive commander, and even with this knowledge, Generals Alexander and Clark inexplicably put him in charge of what was designed as a high-speed operation: to take the Alban Hills and cut the German supply line to its Tenth Army on the Gustav Line. In Lucas' defense, he was aware of the German's ability to pinch off fast-moving columns, and decided to concentrate on building up the beachhead, which was always in jeopardy from counterattack.

After eleven days leading the most harassed U.S. naval landing in the Mediterranean, Admiral Lowry was ordered to retire, turning over to Royal Navy Rear Admiral John A. V. Morse. "The work of the navy under his direction," Admiral Hewitt said of Lowry, "has been one of the outstanding achievements of this operation." The assault phase of Shingle was over. But the struggle on the ground continued, with the Allies losing some ground to the tough German troops rapidly deployed.

Soon the Allied troops became bogged down in the winter mud and cold, and the purpose of Shingle seemed blunted. Similarly, the Fifth Army was stalled at the Gustav Line. Finally, General Lucas carried the can for the lack of Shingle's success, and was replaced by General Lucian Truscott. But it was a long, grim struggle; the invasion had turned into a siege. Units from the Anzio beachhead did not link up with advancing Fifth Army troops until May 25, and only then it was on to Rome.

Twenty-one
CENTRAL PACIFIC CRANKS UP

June–November 1943

After Guadalcanal was secured and Admiral Halsey's forces moved up the Solomons, Admirals King and Nimitz turned their attention to the long-awaited drive across the Central Pacific. With the British insisting on putting off a continental landing until mid-1944, Admiral King had the green light to organize a drive straight across the Pacific, island hopping to Japan. This put him in direct conflict with General MacArthur, who argued that the Pacific strategy should concentrate on moving up New Guinea and then arcing across to regain his beloved Philippines, before moving northward to the Japanese home islands through Formosa or China's coast. However, the Joint Chiefs of Staff decided against MacArthur's southwest Pacific advance-only strategy, believing a two-pronged drive would be more effective and keep the Japanese off-guard and guessing.

Nimitz knew that in the early summer of 1943, the Pacific Fleet was weak, but building rapidly. The new fast carriers were about to arrive at Pearl Harbor, and most of his other ships were busy in the South Pacific or winding up in the Aleutians. On the amphibious side, the 2nd Marine Division was not yet fully trained, and the three army divisions were earmarked for defensive duties in the Hawaiian Islands. In mid-June, the Joint Chiefs of Staff in Washington gave Nimitz the go-ahead for planning to take the Gilbert Islands, Situated 2,000 miles southwest of Pearl Harbor, the Gilbert Islands were seen as the steppingstone to the more strategic Marshall Islands on the "Road to Tokyo."

As he awaited the troops and ships, Chester Nimitz's main task was to pick the leaders for the Gilbert Islands invasion, known as Operation Galvanic, and resolve problems involving conflicts between surface and air admirals. The choices could be critical. He had his eye on his trusted, proven chief of staff, Raymond Spruance, and considered allowing him to go to sea again as commander of the newly created Central Pacific Force. Nimitz and Spruance shared quarters, along with the fleet medical officer, Captain Elphege A. M. Gendreau.

Nimitz was deeply concerned about the morale of his sailors. Knowing this, Spruance revealed that aviators had told him after the Battle of Midway of their concern that their future was hopeless. They had to keep flying, mission after mission, until their number was up. Spruance persuaded Nimitz to institute a rotation policy for aviators, when after a certain amount of combat time, they would return stateside for duty as instructors, before going to sea again. This policy was continued through the war and extended to submariners.

Spruance was a businesslike administrator, preferring a stand-up desk and no chairs so visitors didn't tarry. Nimitz recognized in Spruance an experienced strategist and tactician proven in combat, as well as a sound thinker, a good listener, and someone with a clear analytical mind. One day, Nimitz's intelligence chief, Edwin Layton, brought Spruance the news that captured Japanese documents showed that had Spruance continued west during the night of June 4 at Midway, he would have steamed directly into Admiral Yamamoto's battleships.

Spruance sighed in relief: "The weight of a score of years has been lifted from my shoulders."

In Pearl, Nimitz was under pressure from the air admirals for senior posts on the CinCPac staff and seagoing appointments. The most persistent of the air advocates was Vice Admiral Towers, ComAirPac, who complained that Nimitz had no high-ranking air advisers. Nimitz and Towers had not hit it off in Washington; when Nimitz was head of the Bureau of Navy Personnel, Towers, as chief of BuAer, argued that he, rather than Nimitz, should be instrumental in making the key aviation appointments in the fleet. Towers also irritated Ernie King with his insistence that naval aviation should have a more independent status, similar to the Army Air Forces. He openly sneered at what he called the battleship gang. So neither Nimitz nor King was keen about giving Towers a top command at sea. Nimitz preferred to use Towers' administrative skills, which were enhanced by his savvy chief of staff, Captain Forrest Sherman, late skipper of *Wasp*. Furthermore, choosing both Spruance and Towers for commands in the same fleet would lead to problems because Towers was senior in rank to Spruance.

The Pacific waters were further roiled in the summer of 1943 by a study by retired Admiral Harry Yarnell, a longtime proponent of naval aviation. It was not clear who commissioned the study, but it consisted of a poll of naval aviators to sound out their views of their role in the Pacific war, though Vice Admiral Frederick Horne, Vice CNO, approved it. Yarnell sent a questionnaire to fleet commanders and directly to aviators, and the results kicked up a storm.

Generally, the consensus was that the carrier was the primary weapon of the naval war, and that carrier forces should be commanded by aviators, who knew best how to use them. They pointed out that the fleet commanders had only one or two airmen on their staffs, usually junior in rank and influence. They recommended that either the force commander or chief of staff at all echelons be an aviator. It was one thing for Yarnell privately to sound out senior aviators, but when his form letter reached Nimitz's desk in Pearl Harbor, CinCPac hit the roof. He disqualified himself from taking part in the exercise but criticized Yarnell for bypassing the chain of command to contact officers directly on such a sensitive topic. Nimitz asked his top officers for their comment on Yarnell's form letter. Resentments were stirred up. Ted Sherman wrote that naval aviators should have a dominant voice in all naval policy, not just aviation matters. He further recommended that naval aviators hold all the highest positions, including Nimitz's. Admiral Towers seemed to support the Yarnell findings, which did nothing to further his rocky relations with his boss, Chester Nimitz.

But Towers was instrumental in getting new air admirals to Pearl Harbor for consideration as carrier task force commanders. The senior aviator was Charles "Baldy" Pownall, who had been Commander Fleet Air in San Diego until he was relieved by the home-coming, exhausted Pete Mitscher. Rear Admiral John H. Hoover also arrived in Pearl. He was widely known as "Genial John" because of his sour demeanor. Neither Nimitz nor Towers warmed up to Hoover, though Spruance admired him; the short, pugnacious Hoover was an Academy classmate of Spruance, appointed from Montana.

Hoover was assigned to command all the land-based air in the Central Pacific and, later, the forward bases and areas. Ted Sherman showed up from the South Pacific, but his often overbearing, bombastic style failed to impress Nimitz or Towers, and he was soon shifted back to the South Pacific, where Admiral Halsey welcomed him as his senior carrier commander. Raddy Radford, who had done a brilliant job as director of naval air training in Washington, was promoted to rear admiral, one of the few officers to reach flag rank without ever having commanded a ship.

One May morning, Nimitz and Spruance were walking to headquarters from their living quarters when Nimitz suddenly said, "There are going to be some changes in the high command of the fleet. I would like to let you go, but unfortunately for you, I need you more here."

"Well," Spruance replied, "the war is the important thing. I personally would like another crack at the Japs, but if you need me here, this is where I should be."

The next morning, during a similar walk, Nimitz said, "I have been thinking this over during the night. Spruance, you are lucky. I decided I am going to let you go after all."

The precise assignment had to wait for Admiral King's approval. On May 30, Spruance was promoted to vice admiral. Spruance knew that the Gilbert or the Marshall Islands would be the next objective, and he decided on having his old shipmate, Captain Carl Moore, as his chief of staff. Carl Moore was a brilliant planner, whom King refused to promote to flag rank because he had grounded the cruiser *Philadelphia* in December 1941 outside Maine's Portland harbor. King was unforgiving in such matters. Still, he had need of Moore's planning talents on the staff of the Joint Chiefs. Moore, age fifty-three, was a master at clarifying in simple language an operation plan laden with intricate detail. Spruance functioned best when discussing plans with a small staff, supervising, making the decisions, but leaving the writing of plans to others. Moore quickly accepted Spruance's offer.

On August 5, Spruance was named Commander Central Pacific Force in charge of the next Pacific operation. As one staff officer at Nimitz's CinCPac headquarters observed: "The admiral thinks it's all right to send Raymond out now. He's got him to the point where they think and talk just alike."

For his part, Spruance said of Nimitz, "He is a marvelous combination of tolerance of the opinions of others, wise judgment after he has listened, and determination to carry things through." Galvanic would be the biggest amphibious landing yet in the Pacific war, and Spruance needed one man to command the amphibious phase and another to lead the troops ashore. Spruance picked Kelly Turner, most recently involved in the New Georgia landings, as amphibious commander.

Nimitz pondered on the selection of an appropriate troop commander. On an inspection trip to the South Pacific, Nimitz took along Major General Howlin' Mad Smith, who was chief of marine training on the West Coast. He had been an observer at Attu, and yearned to get a combat command. In Nimitz's plane, flying back to Pearl Harbor, Smith was depressed because he believed that fate had decreed that when he returned to the West Coast, he would remain stuck in training commands. Nimitz called the marine general into his compartment and said, "Holland, I am going to bring you out to the Pacific this fall. You will command all marines in the Central Pacific area. I think you will find your new job very interesting."

Smith and Kelly Turner were delighted to join Raymond Spruance, although they frequently quarrelled with each other over tactics and command responsibilities. What they had in common was a fierce determination to fight. Spruance was aware there would be sharp differences between the two strong-willed senior officers, but he believed he could reconcile their views.

Spruance had no particular preference for an air admiral to lead the carrier force and left the choice to Admiral Nimitz, who picked Rear Admiral Baldy Pownall, the senior air rear admiral in Pearl Harbor. Pownall was an affable, experienced aviator who had not commanded in combat. Spruance's lack of interest in the choice of his air commander baffled Jack Towers, who kept up his running criticism of Spruance—and by extension Nimitz—for not relying on senior aviation advisers. But King and Nimitz viewed the role of ComAirPac as building and maintaining an air force while giving advice, but not to command it at sea. A brilliant officer whose knowledge of naval aviation was unparalleled, Jack Towers nevertheless had a way of showing his scorn for black-shoe flag officers, which left him high and dry on the beach, when what he desperately wanted was to command carriers at sea.

Vice Admiral Towers was against invading the Gilberts, believing the United States should attack the Marshalls directly. But Spruance, and eventually Nimitz, argued that it was wiser to get a flanking position in the Gilberts before moving forward. Spruance agreed that the Tarawa Atoll should be the primary target, but objected to seizing the atoll of Nauru and suggested Makin Atoll (now Butaritari) instead. Nimitz agreed; Admiral King got the Joint Chiefs of Staff to redraft the operational order; and the planners in Pearl got down to work.

Meanwhile, Admiral Soc McMorris replaced Spruance as CinCPac chief of staff. With Carl Moore's help, Spruance began knitting together the complex plan of Operation Galvanic. In modern warfare, plans had to be made well in advance, with targets selected and resources assigned. Generally, the choicest targets were those with usable airfields and harbors.

Kelly Turner sorted out the amphibious side of the operation with his usual rigorous attention to detail, still insisting he should control the entire landing operation until the island was secure. Turner and Howlin' Mad Smith argued endlessly about command responsibility of troops on ships and ashore. Spruance turned the matter over to Carl Moore, who insisted that command responsibility had to be clear, particularly in the first stages of an invasion when the outcome might be in doubt and quick decisions were needed. Finally, Carl Moore devised a compromise: Turner would be in command of everything until the marine general had established a headquarters on land, then Smith would take over command of troops.

Moore knew the running fight between Turner and Smith could be potentially disastrous. Smith had a visceral suspicion approaching paranoia of the navy; he imagined countless affronts against him and his Marine Corps. The army resented being under the command of a marine general. But in the end, Carl Moore wrote operations orders for Spruance, which were models of clarity: every commander knew to whom he reported and who reported to him. Like Admiral Nelson, Raymond Spruance made it plain what he expected everyone to do.

The tireless Turner had the enormous task of coordinating disparate navy, marine, and army units from Hawaii, San Diego, New Zealand, and Alaska. The Central Pacific Force would in the future be designated Fifth Fleet, and was now virtually the entire Pacific Fleet—with the exception of Halsey's South Pacific Force, or Third Fleet. The battleships were under Rear Admiral Ching Lee of the Guadalcanal victory.

Admiral Raymond Spruance devised a fleet command system whereby Kelly Turner was in tactical command of the amphibious forces while they were underway. The carrier commander was similarly in tactical command of the flattops during air operations. In the event of a major enemy fleet action, Spruance would take control of the battle line, possibly leaving Ching Lee in tactical command if desired. In that way, Spruance allowed the specialists to control their own formations, but he retained overall authority and issued the overall orders.

Spruance and Turner insisted that the carrier force provide overhead cover to protect the marines as they stormed ashore. Jack Towers disagreed, arguing that the fast carriers should be detached to operate independently, hitting Japanese air bases in the Marshall Islands and elsewhere. It was reminiscent of the Army Air Forces' insistence on strategic rather than tactical bombing. Towers' carrier commanders, many of whom had been selected by him, agreed.

In October, Towers went even further, complaining that too much force was being assigned to the Gilbert Islands and that Spruance was using a sledgehammer to drive in a tack, to which Spruance replied, "That's the way to win wars." Towers also complained that Spruance had no senior aviator on his staff. When Towers continued to write letters to Nimitz suggesting that he should be made the task force commander, Nimitz asked Towers whether he would like to trade jobs with Vice Admiral Jake Fitch as ComAirSoPac. "Please let me hear from you at an early date," Nimitz said. Towers knew he had overstepped and dropped the matter. He realized his current job was more important than the South Pacific assignment.

But Spruance compromised to the degree that, in the Galvanic plan, he would let the fast carriers roam widely but insisted they must return to cover the amphibious force during the actual landings. The difference in the use of the fast carriers would remain a stormy issue between the surface and air admirals. Spruance always worried that he might face the main Japanese fleet steaming from the Truk bastion, which was considerably closer to the Gilbert Islands than Pearl Harbor.

By now, the new *Essex*-class, 27,000-ton carriers were steaming into Pearl. They could operate at 33 knots and carry three thousand men aboard, including the big air group. First was *Essex*, commanded by the brainy Wu Duncan, followed by *Yorktown*, skippered by Jocko Clark. They were two of the "Young Turks" airmen who were also splendid ship-handlers.

Essex, Yorktown, and the other large carriers of the class were equipped with flag bridges on the island, one deck below the navigation bridge from which the captain directed the ship. The flag bridge was about 315 feet from the bow and 545 feet from the stern and some 80 feet above the sea. The open bridge itself wrapped around the flag plot and behind steel bulkheads with six portholes. On the bridge were signal lights, telescopes, and gyrocompasses, as well as speed, course, and rudder indicators. The admiral customarily had a chair mounted on the open flag bridge, where he observed air operations and debriefed returning pilots from air strikes. Inside, the flag plot was the nerve center of the admiral's force. It was equipped with a chart table; radio TBS communications gear; sea and air radars; compasses; speed indicators; rudder angle dials; anemometer (for measuring wind); a position plan indicator, which located all the ships in the force in relation to the flagship; and a blackboard with the call signs of those ships. Immediately aft of flag plot was the admiral's sea cabin, a spartan cubical where the flag officer could nap.

Arriving with the two *Essex*-class carriers was *Independence*, the first of nine light carriers converted from cruiser hulls, known as light aircraft carriers (CVLs). The CVLs were smaller than the *Essex*-class carriers, with only thirty-three planes, but they could make more than 30 knots and were able to operate with the fast carrier force. Additionally, the older Wildcat fighters were being replaced by the new Hellcats, more than a match for Zeros.

In late August, Admiral Baldy Pownall took a three-carrier force out for a warm-up operation in a raid on isolated Marcus Island, his first combat action. Pownall hoisted his flag aboard Jocko Clark's *Yorktown*. New Rear Admiral Monty Montgomery rode as a makee-learn observer in *Essex*.

As Jocko Clark's *Yorktown* sallied forth, the signal tower on Ford Island blinked farewell: "You look good out there, honey." The three carriers launched five attacks against installations and aircraft on Marcus Island. Although Wu Duncan and Jocko wanted to strike again, Admiral Pownall decided the pilots were getting tired and called it a day.

At one point, Admiral Pownall came up to Jocko Clark's navigation bridge and moaned to Clark and navigator Commander George

Anderson: "Why did I ever come to carriers?" The two *Yorktown* officers were shocked and pretended not to hear. When Pownall took the ladder down to the flag bridge, Clark said, "Did you hear what I heard? We don't need an admiral in the navy with that *attitude*. We're here to *fight!*"

Clark's opinion of Pownall further plummeted when Clark urged the admiral to search for two downed pilots from *Yorktown*, and Pownall turned down Clark on the grounds that it was time to depart. Clark exchanged furious messages with the admiral only one deck down, until Pownall finally came up again.

"We'll go back and get them in the morning."

"No," replied Pownall, "I'm afraid they're expendable."

The volatile Jocko Clark exploded. "You've got the widest yellow streak up your back of any admiral I've ever seen in my life. Goddamit. I don't care if when I return to Pearl I don't have a ship and I don't have a command. You can make me a seaman second [class] tomorrow, but this is my ship and I'm going to send out a search for them! Do I have permission?"

"All right. Send them out now, 75 miles."

"They're going out 125 miles, all the way back to Marcus."

Clark launched search planes, but the five downed airmen were not found. However, Clark's action showed the aviators of *Yorktown*'s air group that the captain really cared about them.

Clark thought that Pownall was a fine peacetime officer who was prone to anxiety, and that the admiral behaved like a cautious old woman. The colorful Jocko, part Cherokee and a youthful Oklahoma cowboy, believed carriers should be handled aggressively, and Pownall was not the man for the job. Nor was Captain George Fairlamb, commanding officer of *Independence*. Shaken by the stress of combat command, Fairlamb lost his composure on the bridge and was relieved as soon as his ship reached Pearl.

Despite Pownall's timidity, the Marcus strike was considered a success. On returning to Pearl, Pownall recommended to Nimitz that "a naval aviator of sufficient rank with the necessary carrier experience under wartime conditions" command the new fast carrier forces. About this time, Pete Mitscher was making rapid strides recuperating in San Diego, and wrote Admiral Towers: "Dear Jack: I am feeling great now. When do I get out of here?"

*

In 1943, Captain Truman J. Hedding, a crack pilot, was appointed to a special board of experienced aviators to work out tactical instructions for larger groups of carriers. In 1942, many lessons were learned, but carriers usually operated alone with their escorts. Now, there was a need for a doctrine that spelled out how to maneuver twelve to sixteen carriers in the same overall formation. It was developing into a war of vastly new dimensions.

Furthermore, Hedding pointed out that never again would the carriers operate in support of battleships; rather the battlewagons and cruisers would maneuver primarily for protection of the carriers. Hedding and his associates developed the concept of the circular formation with one, two, or more carriers in the center. They would be surrounded by battleships and cruisers to provide anti-aircraft fire, and a farther concentric ring of destroyers to supply anti-aircraft, anti-submarine watch, and act as plane guards. Then, a single carrier task group of two or three flattops would be joined by two or three other groups in a massive fast carrier task force. But maneuvering this force was dependent on wind direction. Carriers invariably had to launch and recover planes into the wind, which often came from the opposite direction of the basic fleet course. "It was quite a job tactically handling the many task groups," Hedding said.

In another pre-Gilberts raid, the carrier forces experimented with formations in a strike against Wake Island. Monty Montgomery, who was in command, planned to operate the six new carriers assigned him in a single formation, which would be the largest carrier group since the Japanese attack on Pearl Harbor. Monty, a fine and steady fighter but irritable from migrane attacks, would vary his task force disposition between a group of six flattops, two groups of three carriers, and three groups of two carriers each. The junior rear admirals were Raddy Radford in *Lexington* and Hubert Van Ragsdale in *Independence*. The submarine *Skate* was assigned lifeguard duty off Wake Island. The raid and tactics were viewed as highly successful, though twelve U.S. planes were downed from anti-aircraft fire and defensive fighters. *Skate* picked up six airmen survivors, including the air group commander, and when the submarine returned them to *Lexington*, a grateful Captain Felix B. Stump signaled *Skate*: "Anything on Lexington is yours for the asking. If it is too big to carry away, we will cut it up in small parts"

*

As Operation Galvanic shook down, Kelly Turner was in command of what was designated V Amphibious Corps, or V Phib. He chose as his second in command the bright, upbeat Rear Admiral Harry Hill, who had served under Turner in Washington and commanded old battleships in the Pacific. Hill combined gallantry, determination, expertise, and good cheer in equal measure. Kelly Turner liked and trusted Harry Hill.

When Hill reported to Turner for duty, Turner said, "Welcome aboard, Harry. I'm glad to see you."

Hill replied, "Glad to be here. What job do you have for me?"

"All you have to do is capture Tarawa, target date November 1."

The task was complex: Admiral Spruance's overall operation plan ran to 324 pages, while Kelly Turner's amphibious operation plan was 140 pages long.

The 2nd Marine Division in New Zealand under Major General Julian C. Smith was picked to assault the Tarawa Atoll; a regimental combat team of the U.S. 27th Infantry Division in Hawaii, led by Major General Ralph Smith, would take Makin Island, which had a seaplane base. Betio Island of Tarawa Atoll, with its airstrip as the target, was only 300 acres of low-lying coral rock and coconut palms. One problem that faced the planners was getting troops ashore over a fringing coral reef washed by unknown but suspected high and erratic tides—in yet untested landing craft with inexperienced coxswains.

Kelly Turner, in battleship *Pennsylvania* with Marine General Howlin' Mad Smith, chose to command the northern force hitting Makin Island, since it was closest to any likely Japanese opposition from sea or air. A fire support group was headed by Rear Admiral Ike Giffen in cruiser *Minneapolis*, and another by Rear Admiral Robert M. Griffen in battleship *New Mexico*. Rear Admiral Henry M. Mullinnix commanded escort carriers in *Liscombe Bay*, which would provide close-in air support.

Harry Hill led the southern force in battleship *Maryland* attacking Tarawa Atoll, with Major General Julian Smith, (the third general named Smith involved). Hill's fire support group was headed by Rear Admiral Kingman in battleship *Tennessee*, with newly promoted Rear Admiral Lawrence DuBose commanding the bombardment cruisers in *Santa Fe*. Rear Admiral Van Ragsdale was in charge of the escort carriers in *Sangamon*.

Vice Admiral Spruance decided to fly his three-star flag in the heavy cruiser *Indianapolis*, because it was fast and could move around quickly. Unlike a battleship or carrier, *Indianapolis* was not essential to any particular fire support mission, so he felt free to shift easily from one formation to another. Lastly, the flag quarters were limited and this met another of Spruance's requirements: room for only a small, effective staff.

The Central Pacific Force comprised 6 fast carriers, 5 light carriers, 7 escort carriers, twelve battleships, fifteen cruisers, 65 destroyers, 33 large amphibious transports, 29 LSTs, 28 support ships of various sorts, 90 army bombers, 66 navy land-based bombers, and some 200 marine aircraft.

Under the new doctrine, a carrier group would be under the tactical control of the senior air admiral, even if a more senior admiral commanded escorting surface warships.

The fast carriers, augmented by several new 27,000-tonners, were now designated Task Force 50 under Baldy Pownall and split into three task groups (TGs), his own TG 50.1, with his flagship *Yorktown*, *Lexington*, and the CVL *Cowpens*. As now arranged, the fast battleships were tied into the carriers providing anti-aircraft support. In TG 50.1, these were under Rear Admiral E. W. Hanson in *South Dakota*, with *Washington*.

The Northern Carrier Group, designated TG 50.2, was under Rear Admiral Raddy Radford in *Enterprise*, with the CVLs *Belleau Wood* and *Monterey*. The battleships were led by Rear Admiral Glenn Davis, who had commanded *Washington* at Guadalcanal, flying his two stars in *Massachusetts* with *North Carolina* and *Indiana*.

The Southern Carrier Group, named TG 50.3, was under Rear Admiral Monty Montgomery in *Essex*, with *Bunker Hill* and *Independence*. The cruiser escort was commanded by Rear Admiral E. G. Small in *Chester*. The Relief Carrier Group, designated TG 50.4, was led by Rear Admiral Ted Sherman in *Saratoga* with CVL *Princeton*, and a cruiser screen under Rear Admiral L. J. Wiltsie in *San Diego*. At Jack Towers' recommendation, Nimitz designated Rear Admiral Genial John Hoover as Commander Defense Forces and Land-Based Air, thus commander of all the search aircraft in the area, on seaplane tender *Curtiss*.

Finally, the massive Central Pacific Force began converging on the Gilbert Islands from the far-flung bases: troop ships, supply vessels, carriers, battleships, cruisers, destroyers, minesweepers, and landing craft.

Fleet Commander Spruance accompanied the northern force, but turned tactical control over to Kelly Turner, who thus controlled the courses, speeds, drills, exercises, and dispositions of the immediate force from Pearl, and *Indianapolis* conformed to his movements. Spruance rarely acted as OTC of his own fleet. His staff supervised the overall progress, but the minute-by-minute movements within the fleet were the responsibility of the task force and task group commanders junior to Spruance.

Admiral Spruance relaxed aboard *Indianapolis*. He had created a plan that all could follow. He placed trust in subordinate commanders whom he had selected to do their jobs well. Execution of the plan was the job of those commanders. For the time being, his job was that of an observer until a command decision was necessary—either coping with a disaster or a chance to take on the Japanese fleet. And when that time came, he wanted his mind fresh. That was Spruance's way.

On Makin Island, D-day, November 19, the naval bombardment opened up. Kelly Turner noticed one of his cruisers firing at a Japanese cargo ship in the lagoon without success and without closing the range. Angrily, he signaled the cruiser skipper: "Close the range and sink her, or cease fire!"

Landing units of the 27th Army Division was easy, but once ashore the soldiers made slow going against a small force of Japanese of three hundred combat troops and five hundred labor forces. The 27th Division had an able commander in Ralph Smith, but he was hobbled by the fact that the division was U.S. National Guard, and therefore politicised with aging officers of limited ability. Having spent two years in the Hawaiian Islands, the troops had lost any edge they once had. Aboard flagship *Pennsylvania*, Marine General Holland Smith was furious with the slow-moving army. He went ashore and was shot at by nervous U.S. soldiers. His anger at the 27th Division's lack of verve created deep ill will between marine Smith and army Smith that would have searing consequences. It took four days to secure Makin Island in what Spruance thought should have taken a day and a half at most. Spruance shared Howlin' Mad Smith's view of the poor performance of the 27th Army Division's senior officers.

Offshore, a Japanese submarine caught up with the escort carrier *Liscombe Bay*, flagship of Rear Admiral Henry Mullinnix—the popular, young commander of three escort carriers. *I-175* torpedoed the thin-skinned jeep carrier, which exploded in a mass of orange flame, showering debris on battleship *New Mexico*, 1,500 yards away. *Liscombe Bay* sank quickly, taking down Admiral Mullinnix—apparently fatally wounded in the flag plot—and the skipper, Captain I. D. Wiltsie, with 642 of the ship's crew. Henry Mullinnix, an Indiana native, graduated first in his Class of 1916 at the Naval Academy, studied aeronautical engineering at the Massachusetts Institute of Technology, and was among the brightest of the new air admirals. After captaining *Saratoga*, he was promoted to flag rank at the age of fifty-one and assigned to command an escort carrier division in the Gilbert Islands operation. He was the fourth U.S. admiral to die in action. Spruance believed that if the army had moved more quickly on Makin, *Liscombe Bay* could have been withdrawn earlier and spared its fate.

Japanese patrol planes from the Marshalls and Truk lit up the U.S. fleet at night for the incoming bombers to strike. But Kelly Turner, with his experience in the Solomons, expertly maneuvered the force he had trained to avoid incoming dive- and torpedo bombers. No hits were scored. Farther north, Radford's new night fighters successfully staved off a Japanese air attack, but at the cost of one of the best pilots in the navy, Commander Butch O'Hare. O'Hare, Commander of *Enterprise*'s Air Group, was pioneering night tactics against the incoming enemy when he was shot down.

The assault on Tarawa Atoll proved to be altogether more difficult. Spruance in *Indianapolis* linked up with Harry Hill's southern force. Hill, who impressed Spruance as a natural leader with vigor and initiative, messaged his boss: "My dear Raymond, we had a fine training period in Éfaté [New Hebrides] and I think the boys are all prepared to do their job in good fashion, providing we get a break in the weather and tidal conditions on the beach. I have had a little trouble in convincing some of my fire support boys that when I say I want close fire support I mean *close*."

The landings were launched against tiny Betio Island at the southwest corner of the Tarawa Atoll, and its airstrip. Admiral Harry Hill and General Julian Smith rode the old battleship *Maryland*, whose fragile communications tended to freak out whenever the wagon fired her big guns. Betio was pounded by carrier air strikes and the guns of battleships and cruisers for two and a half days, which was then thought to be sufficient to wipe out defensive emplacements. Nobody realized how much gunfire the well-constructed Japanese bunkers could endure. The marines had to go ashore over tricky reefs surrounding the beaches, and the low, unpredictable tides didn't leave enough clearance for landing craft. The islanders called it a "dodging tide," which ebbed and flowed several times a day at unpredictable intervals.

On D-day, the tide was low. Marines had to jump out in water up to their necks with full packs and to struggle 500 yards ashore in the face of fierce Japanese crossfire. Bullets peppered the water. Landing craft burst into flame. Once the marines were ashore under heavy fire, the pall of smoke prevented Harry Hill's spotter from providing accurate support ship fire. *Maryland's* communications broke down, so neither Harry Hill nor Raymond Spruance could get an accurate appraisal of what was happening on the island. About five thousand marines landed on D-day and one-third became casualties.

So stiff was the Japanese defense of some 4,500 first-line troops that the situation was critical halfway through the first day, November 20. In early afternoon, General Julian Smith messaged General Holland Smith in Pennsylvania: "Issue in doubt." Spruance's staff pressed him to send advisory messages to Hill or those ashore. But in the Nimitz tradition, Spruance said, "I pick men who I believe are competent to do the job, and I am going to let them to it." Spruance would adhere to this principle through the war. Spruance calmly watched and waited.

Howlin' Mad Smith released the marine reserves to help save the situation. The next day, with a higher tide, the landing craft could get directly to the beach, and the battle began turning against the defenders. After seventy-six hours of savage combat, the Japanese were forced into smaller pockets and the airstrip was taken. Finally, the island was secured and a U.S. plane landed. The cost was high: of the nearly 19,000 marines landed on Tarawa; 984 were dead and 2,072 wounded. The navy suffered grievously, too, with 746 men killed in action in the Gilbert Islands, mostly on *Liscombe Bay*. The enemy left only seventeen wounded prisoners and 129 Korean laborers on Tarawa.

When the casualties became known, many American politicians, and some military men, objected to the high cost. "Bloody Tarawa" became the editorial shibboleth to criticize the marines and navy for supposedly needless loss of life. But most senior officers and historians believed that the Gilbert Islands had to be taken, and that the navy and marines had learned valuable lessons. These lessons from the first Central Pacific assault, recognized by the high command to the boat coxswains and platoon commanders, would save many lives in future operations.

While the dodgy tides were bad luck, Spruance emphasized that Tarawa showed that pre-landing bombardments required days not hours. Spruance also recommended many improvements: enhanced landing craft to get over reefs with troops aboard; probe and destroy underwater obstacles; provide intelligence on beach gradients, which led to the development of underwater demolition teams (UDTs); train night fighters for carriers; provide safer bomb stowage compartments on escort carriers; and have special amphibious command ships with improved communications equipment for the various commanding officers and staffs.

In retrospect, Samuel Eliot Morison called the Gilbert Islands the "seedbed for victory." Admiral Nimitz concurred, flashing a signal to *Indianapolis* when Spruance entered Pearl Harbor: "CinCPac is very proud of the way your task force completed its recent mission. For you and your flapship, a special welcome. Well done. Nimitz."

Twenty-two

MARSHALLS BREAKTHROUGH

November 1943–February 1944

The senior flag officers of the Central Pacific Force, now known as the Fifth Fleet, sailed back to Pearl and began planning for the assault on the Marshall Islands, northwest of the Gilberts. The Marshalls were the next step to the Carolines, the Marianas, and Tokyo. The centerpiece of the Marshalls was Kwajalein Atoll, with the lesser atolls of Wotje, Majuro, Maloelap, and Jaluit to the east, and Eniwetok (now Enewetak) to the northwest. Admiral Kelly Turner, commanding the amphibious phase, insisted that the lessons of Tarawa showed that much longer pre-invasion bombardment would be needed and more supporting destroyers.

The Gilberts invasion resulted in backbiting at Pacific Fleet headquarters. General Howlin' Mad Smith gave an interview questioning the need for Tarawa, though he had made no pre-invasion complaints. Army Lieutenant General Richardson complained the land-based planes under Admiral Hoover were mishandled and accomplished little. He also objected to army units coming under marine and navy command. Admiral Hoover blamed General Hale's air force bombers for flying too high and bombing too inaccurately. Towers blamed Spruance for having little experience in overseeing shore-based aircraft and, for that matter, carriers at sea. Towers' constant criticism of Spruance at headquarters caused the normally placid Spruance to come to despise him, at least professionally, and to see him as being guided by self-serving and ambitious motives.

*

It could be argued that the criticism of the naval command was self-inflicted by the U.S. Navy. Perhaps influenced by the famous Sampson-Schley argument that roiled high navy professional circles for years, the top admirals developed a loathing for publicity and sharing information with the press to explain their points of view and reasons for actions. Admiral King believed that the less information given to the press, the better. He and Nimitz saw no reason why correspondents should be given accommodation on warships going into combat.

In some ways King's myopic view was justified. A correspondent for the *Chicago Tribune*, Stanley Johnston, learned at the time of the Battle of Midway from a high-placed officer that the United States was aware of the Japanese navy's order of battle before Midway. Irresponsibly, the *Chicago Tribune* printed Johnston's story, which logically suggested the United States had broken the Japanese code. Columnist Walter Winchell repeated the story in two broadcasts. The navy was aghast. President Roosevelt and Secretary of the Navy Frank Knox, a Chicago publisher, wished to prosecute archconservative *Chicago Tribune* publisher Robert McCormick, for felony violation of U.S. security laws. Top navy brass argued against prosecution, knowing that a public trial would only draw more attention to the code-breaking success.

This argument persuaded nearly everyone, with one notable exception. A misguided Congressman and Roosevelt ally, Elmer J. Holland of Pennsylvania, castigated McCormick in the House of Representatives, declaring, "Somehow our navy had secured and broken the secret code of the Japanese navy." The code breakers at Pearl Harbor and the high brass viewed the incident as treachery compounded by idiocy. Fortunately, neither speech sank in with the Japanese and they did not change the code.

Another example of too much information leaked out, and a major breach of security, occurred when Congressman Andrew Jackson May, a sixty-eight-year-old member of the House Military Affairs Committee, returned from a fact-finding trip to the Pacific and held a news conference. He revealed that he learned that the Japanese claims of U.S. subs sunk were overstated because their depth charges were not powerful and were not set deep enough. This catastrophic blunder was relayed through the press to the Japanese, who immediately set their heavier depth charges to explode deeper. Vice Admiral Charles Lockwood,

ComSubPac, declared privately, "I hear Congressman May said the depth charges are not set deep enough. He would be pleased to know [they] set them deeper now." Lockwood believed May's statement cost the Pacific Submarine Force ten submarines and eight hundred officers and men.

Admiral King's restrictive view of the press was shared by Admiral Nimitz, Admiral Spruance, and others. It was the traditional navy way to keep a low profile. This led to widespread complaints among the correspondents who were gathering in Honolulu. And these complaints were shared by junior naval officers who believed their combat achievements were overlooked by the American people. The navy, in effect, was getting bad press. Navy officer Joe Bryan, a peacetime journalist, said that the anti-press attitude of Annapolis types was "suicidal." He pointed out that "some refuse to give correspondents a scrap of information and then they complain that the goddamn army is getting credit for winning the war."

Certainly, General MacArthur was a master at spinning the correspondents assigned to his headquarters in Brisbane, and every communiqué issued by him suggested that he personally commanded the operation at hand. The communiqués gave the impression that MacArthur and his forces were winning the war single-handedly. This served to deteriorate relations between the army and navy in the Southwest Pacific. Similarly, the Army Air Forces was quick to get its version of events to the press, and for months after, the public believed that air force bombers had sunk a number of enemy ships at Midway. In reality, they sank none, and they hit none.

As the war progressed, the pressure by the correspondents and their reading public led King and Nimitz to loosen restrictions on reporters and give them more access. While they believed that looking after reporters and getting their copy to the United States for them was tedious, it began to sink in that the public's view of the navy's role in winning the war could only be enhanced by getting out the appropriate information, supplied by professional reporters and writers. They were assisted by the influence of the Secretary of the Navy Frank Knox, a newspaper publisher who kept up steady pressure to keep the flow of stories coming.

In Pearl, attention focused on the Marshall Islands. The question that troubled planners for the code-named "Flintlock" was: which of the atolls to hit first? Kwajalein was the obvious target, since aerial photos showed an airstrip 70 percent completed. But Kelly Turner pointed out that it was likely to be the most heavily defended, thus U.S. casualties could be severe, which was undesirable particularly after the loss of the Gilberts. So Admirals Spruance and Turner and General Howlin' Mad Smith opted for a two-step campaign, first securing Wotje and Maloelap, closer to Pearl Harbor, before taking on Kwajalein, the Japanese headquarters for the Marshalls. However, Nimitz was backed up by his chief of staff, Rear Admiral Soc McMorris, and his chief war planner, Rear Admiral Forrest Sherman, both of whom favored a direct attack on Kwajalein with its two airfields and deep harbor.

At a decisive meeting on December 14, Nimitz polled his warrior chieftains: Kwajalein or the outer islands first?

"Raymond, what do you think now?"

"Outer islands," Spruance said.

"Kelly?"

"Outer islands," Turner replied.

"Holland?"

"Outer islands."

So it went around the room, except for Forrest Sherman. When Nimitz had taken his poll, he said quietly, "Well, gentlemen, our next objective will be Kwajalein."

After the meeting, Spruance and Turner continued to argue with Nimitz that it was too dangerous to hit Kwajalein first. CinCPac showed his steel.

"This is it. If you don't want to do it, the Navy Department will find someone else to do it. Do you want to do it or not?"

Kelly Turner frowned, his heavy brows bristling. Then he said, "Sure I want to do it." That settled, planning went ahead, with Nimitz taking his usual command position that he would prescribe the "what, where, and when," and leave the "how" to his subordinate commanders.

Earlier in the month, Rear Admiral Baldy Pownall led a six-carrier task force in a strike against the Marshalls. He was assisted by carrier task groups under Admirals Montgomery in *Enterprise* and Ted Sherman in the new *Bunker Hill*. Pownall's aircraft sank four Japanese merchant vessels and fifty-five planes, twenty-eight of them in the air, at Kwajalein Island. But returning pilots noticed additional Japanese long-range torpedo planes, called "Bettys," parked on the airstrip at Roi Island in the atoll. The aviators expected to hit these choice targets in a second strike. But Pownall did not wish to hang around for an additional attack. Jocko Clark, skipper of flagship *Yorktown*, and his squadron commanders pleaded with Pownall to launch another strike. Pownall refused, though Clark pointed out that the planes from Roi would undoubtedly attack the American force later in the day.

Jocko Clark pleaded with Baldy Pownall, "You'd better get back there and knock out those Bettys or they'll come and get you!" In his frustration, Skipper Clark pounded the table in his charthouse, and complained to his officers, "Goddamn it. You can't run away from airplanes with ships."

Just as Jocko predicted, Japanese torpedo planes bored in on Pownall's force heading back to Pearl. One fish hit *Lexington* in the stern. When *Yorktown* got into Pearl, Jocko Clark went directly to CinCPac headquarters, taking the aerial photos of the Japanese sitting duck planes at Roi to Forrest Sherman. Sherman immediately strode into Soc McMorris' office and said, "You want to see the fish that got away?" Clark and other air officers were vocal in their complaints that Baldy Pownall was not aggressive enough to lead the fast carriers into battle. Clark circulated an unsigned critique of Pownall's performance.

Admiral Jack Towers agreed with Clark and others. Admiral Nimitz asked Towers for his personal and private assessment of the top air admirals. Towers quickly complied with a highly personal view:

Vice Admiral Jake Fitch: "All-around experience. Physically tough. Aggressive. Popular. Fine qualities of leadership."

Rear Admiral Genial John Hoover: "An enigma. Physically fit. A positive character. Not popular. Standoffish. Lack of close relationship between him and his staff. Ability as a commander carrier task force untried."

Rear Admiral Ted Sherman: "Self-interest. Very unpopular with aviators because of intolerance. Able but not for high command because of personality absolutely precludes establishment of wholehearted loyalty."

Rear Admiral Black Jack Reeves: "Efficient, determined."

Rear Admiral Monty Montgomery: "Energetic, courageous and determined."

Rear Admiral Baldy Pownall: "Overcautious in plans and operations. He worries intensely before and during operations. Lack of aggressiveness resented by subordinates."

Rear Admiral Pete Mitscher: ""Tops for carrier force command."

Towers' view of air admirals qualified for combat carrier command was increasingly sought by Nimitz. The best brains among new air admirals, Towers told Nimitz, were Forrest Sherman, Raddy Radford, Ralph Davison, and Slats Sallada. All four would become fine combat commanders and efficient administrators. Towers recommended that Pownall, who "worries intensely before and during operations," be replaced by a more aggressive admiral. But Towers added he would be pleased to have Pownall in any administrative capacity.

Towers further suggested to Nimitz that Pownall be replaced by Rear Admiral Mitscher, currently in San Diego as Commander Fleet Air, West Coast, as senior carrier group commander. Forrest Sherman concurred, noting that Mitscher's aviation experience went back to the ancient USS *Langley*, and he was available.

At Nimitz's suggestion, Soc McMorris sounded out Spruance on the suggested change of command. Spruance had developed a liking for the mild-mannered Pownall. He was against replacing him, though Spruance had no expert knowledge of the finer points of carrier group command. Also, Spruance still remembered unfavourably Mitscher's uneven performance with *Hornet* at Midway. Nonetheless, Nimitz, though he respected Spruance's judgment more than Towers', went ahead without Spruance's approval to order Mitscher to Pearl Harbor as senior carrier commander.

Nimitz found it difficult to explain to Pownall in a meeting on December 27 why he was being replaced, since the action took Pownall by surprise. Nimitz said that some of the senior aviator officers believed he was too cautious, that risk was involved in success, though he admitted that Admiral Spruance had approved of Pownall's conduct. Pownall attempted to defend his premature departure after the Kwajalein strike, but he was unconvincing. However, Nimitz found away to help Pownall save face.

Under pressure from the air admirals and Undersecretary of the Navy James Forrestal, who was a naval pilot in World War I, Admiral King decided to make Jack Towers Nimitz's deputy. A shuffle of the top jobs got underway. Nimitz's deputy had been Vice Admiral John Newton, who was transferred to the South Pacific to become Admiral Halsey's deputy commander. Towers became Deputy CinCPac and Commander in Chief, Pacific Ocean Area (CinCPOA). Pownall was shifted to replace

Towers as ComAirPac, though the job was downgraded to become mostly administrative and logistical. Nimitz also allowed Spruance to take Pownall along on Flintlock as a special aviation advisor.

Mitscher's new command was only temporary and, if his performance in the upcoming Marshalls was disappointing, Nimitz could always replace him. No naval aviator disagreed with the appointment of Mitscher, who was highly regarded in the aviation community as a fine flier, ship-handler, and carrier tactician, and who, while soft-spoken, was a forceful leader. Best of all, Pete Mitscher was a fighter, a warrior, and he had a dedicated following among rising junior officers that was rare in the fleet.

Towers would have much preferred commanding the carriers, but he could hardly turn down the number-two job in the Pacific, particularly when he had been pressing Nimitz to choose an air admiral as deputy. Towers suspected, too, that Ernie King was not going to let him get a sea command. Others wanted the top carrier command, among them Ted Sherman, who by now was perhaps the most combat-experienced carrier flag officer. But the blustery Sherman had a way of rubbing his superiors the wrong way. Sherman concluded, "I apparently am left out on a limb as usual."

Nimitz instead sent Sherman temporarily to the South Pacific to head Halsey's carriers and was welcomed there by the South Pacific commander. Slew McCain desired the job, too, but Admiral King wanted to keep him in Washington in the new job of Deputy CNO for Air.

Towers' judgment undoubtedly swayed Nimitz when he recommended Mitscher: "A quiet, hard-working officer, of great strength of character. He is tough and aggressive. Has always turned in a splendid job. Particular attention is invited to his recent performance of duty as ComAirSols. I regard him as tops for carrier task force command."

As planning progressed, Mitscher would command the fast carriers, designated Task Force 58, aboard Jocko Clark's *Yorktown*. Under him were four carrier task groups: TG 58.1 commanded by Rear Admiral Black Jack Reeves in *Enterprise* with *Yorktown* and *Belleau Wood*; TG 58.2 headed by Monty Montgomery in *Essex* with *Intrepid* and *Cabot*; TG 58.3 led by Ted Sherman in *Bunker Hill* with *Monterey* and *Cowpens*; and TG 58.4 commanded by newcomer Rear Admiral Samuel P. "Si" Ginder in *Saratoga* with *Princeton* and *Langley*.

Mitscher had command of all the carriers and battleships in Task Force 58, but in the event of a surface engagement, Spruance would detach the battleships under Ching Lee in *Washington*, who would command, unless Spruance chose to exercise personal control. Ching Lee took the subordination of his battleships to the carriers with good grace, unlike some other disgruntled battleship admirals. For Mitscher, the command was an enormous responsibility for a rear admiral: the four task groups of fast carriers and battleships, capable of 30-plus knots, with cruisers and destroyers. As his signature headgear, Pete Mitscher adopted a long-billed, khaki fisherman's cap, which other air admirals emulated with marine fatigue or engineer caps, but never had quite the cachet as Mitscher's. Without his distinctive headgear, Pete Mitscher's head looked like that of a wizened bald eagle.

After the Gilberts, Spruance worked out some principles of Pacific warfare that he would follow in the battles to come. Unlike the aviators who argued that their carriers alone would defeat the Japanese fleet, Spruance believed the war would be won primarily through amphibious operations. Toward that end, he insisted his planning staff swiftly apply violent, overwhelming force. A corollary was that the invasion area would be isolated, which meant not only sea and air superiority but also secure communications to support invasion forces.

In terms of his flag officers performance, Spruance noted:

> Things move so fast in naval actions, and the consequences that hang on the results of these actions are often so momentous, that fast teamwork is essential. Teamwork is something that comes best from association, training and indoctrination. There are too many variables possible in war for everything to be foreseen and planned for ahead of time. Our plans can be made out in great detail up to the time we hit the enemy. After that, they have to be flexible, ready to counter what the enemy may try to do to us, and ready to take advantage of the breaks that may come to us. To do that, the man on the spot must know where he fits into the operation, and he must be able to act on his own initiative either without any orders at all, because radio

silence may be in effect, or on very brief orders because
there is no time for long instructions.

Spruance's bold plan, Operation Flintlock, called for three attack
forces and was similar to the Gilberts. Spruance, while commanding
the Fifth Fleet, was in the heavy cruiser *Indianapolis* but would exercise tactical control only if the Japanese fleet sortied from Truk. Rear
Admiral Kelly Turner led the Joint Expeditionary Force, Task Force
51, from a new amphibious command ship, *Rocky Mount*. Aboard
Rocky Mount was Major General Howlin' Mad Smith, again leading
the U.S. Marine and Army landing force. The northern attack force
was under the command of Rear Admiral Dick Conolly, newly arrived
from the Mediterranean in another new command ship, *Appalachian*.
He was assigned the capture of Roi and Namur Islands on the north
side of Kwajalein Atoll. Kelly Turner took tactical control of the
southern attack force, which would hit Kwajalein Island on the south
side of the lagoon, where the airstrip was being constructed. Rear
Admiral Genial John Hoover remained in command of all land-based
aircraft, some 350 combat planes. Hoover ordered his planes to bomb
the various outlying atolls in the Marshalls: Mili, Wotje, Maloelap,
and Roi-Namur.

Pete Mitscher had the chance to show what his properly deployed
fast carriers could do to support an amphibious operation. In the
Gilberts, they had been basically used defensively. His plan was to wipe
out enemy aircraft in the Marshalls before Japanese planes could get into
action to disrupt the invasion. Mitscher believed that tactical air support
at the beachheads could best be provided by the escort carriers with the
phib groups, while the bigger flattops independently roamed the ocean.
The carrier air strikes would destroy Japanese air opposition, either by
attacks on ground installations, or in the air.

As D-day for Flintlock neared, the Japanese made no effort to mount
a naval attack against the incoming invasion fleet, perhaps distracted by
Allied operations against Rabaul in the Bismarcks. Unknown to the
United States, the Japanese high command decided to concentrate its
Pacific defenses on a line running from the Marianas, to Truk, through
western New Guinea, and all the way to Timor. The garrisons in the
Marshalls were left to fend for themselves.

The invasion of Kwajalein, the world's largest coral atoll, was set for January 31, 1944. Most of the atoll's islands were tiny, but the Japanese had built coral-runway airstrips on Roi Island in the north and Kwajalein Island in the south. Dick Conolly was slated to hit Roi and its sister island Namur with the 4th Marine Division, while Kelly Turner would land the army's 7th Infantry Division on Kwajalein Island.

When Dick Conolly turned up in Pearl Harbor as an amphibious group commander after his successes in Sicily and Salerno, he consulted with Kelly Turner and cited some techniques used by the Sixth Fleet in the Mediterranean. Conolly had trained his amphibious group in San Diego while Turner was engaged in the Gilberts.

"If you stay around here," Turner growled, "you and I are going to fight!" But Turner mellowed slightly toward Conolly. In one Kwajalein pre-invasion conference at Pearl, Turner told Conolly, "As a result of the experience we've had at Tarawa, I want to make sure that we use enough gunfire on getting this island ready." Conolly replied testily, "Admiral, I'm going to sink that goddamn island. There won't be any place for the marines to land!" The other brass looked aghast, but Turner smiled and said, "That's the way to talk, boy."

On January 27, Raymond Spruance's staff witnessed a rare outburst of displeasure from the admiral. *Indianapolis* had joined the task group headed by Monty Montgomery. To Carl Moore's surprise, Spruance began reading Montgomery's operation plan, a detail with which he was rarely concerned. Spruance was suspicious of an aviator's ability to follow his plans, after his run-ins with Towers at Pearl. Spruance had asked for a battleship bombardment of Roi, but it was not included in the plan. A furious Spruance grabbed a pencil and scribbled a dispatch to Montgomery: "It was my expressed desire that Roi be made inoperative by surface ship bombardment at the earliest possible time." Then, he ordered Montgomery precisely what to do and how to do it. A badly chastened Montgomery hastily complied.

Rear Admiral Oley Oldendorf, who commanded the fire support units of the northern force, peeled off from Conolly's ships to bombard the island of Wotje and quickly rejoined the fleet. That set the stage for the invasion of the northern end of Kwajalein at Roi-Namur by Conolly's amphibious force. The plan called for securing nearby, uninhabited, tiny islets to serve as artillery bases on D-day, February 1, while the main transport force entered the lagoon and landed the 4th Marine Division on the south beaches. During the preliminary bombardment, Dick Conolly insisted that his bombardment battleships, cruisers, and destroyers move close to the beaches for accuracy—in fact, much nearer than prewar doctrine called for. He picked up his voice radio and instructed bombardment captains, "When I say close-in, I mean *close-in*, under two thousand yards!" For this, the marines were grateful and gave him the nickname, "Close-In" Conolly.

Despite some glitches caused by unexpectedly rough weather in the lagoon and malfunctioning landing craft, the marines got ashore on D-day and quickly took the airfield on Roi. Then they joined in their comrades to seize adjacent Namur Island, which was connected by a landfill. Moving quickly, the marines fought hard and successfully and, by the next day, had secured Namur. Conolly sorted out initial confusion among small landing craft. Altogether, it was a fine performance by Dick Conolly's sailors and Harry Schmidt's marines. Watching the operation from his flagship *Indianapolis*, Admiral Spruance remarked, "Seeing this proves you can put complete faith in the men you have selected to do a job."

And Captain Charles Wellborn, who commanded destroyers in Sicily and replaced Captain George Dyer as Conolly's chief of staff, said this of his boss:

> I've served with a lot of fine officers but he seemed to have the best perception of all as to what the role of a commander was, what the role of his chief of staff was, and what the role of each one of his staff officers was. He seemed to know better than most how you fired up a team, to have them at the peak on the day of the operation. He didn't have the brightest mind of all the people I worked with—but he had an understanding of leadership that I thought was outstanding, getting the staff at breakfast, then personally circulating around various people who comprised the force. He had personal contact with them. He had great enthusiasm and transferred this to the people in his force. He was outgoing and a scrapper. As a wartime leader he had the right natural equipment and knew how to use it.

*

Kelly Turner's southern force headed for Kwajalein Island on the southern tip of the atoll. The 7th Infantry Division had fought at Attu and reorganized in Hawaii under Major General Charles Corlett. As at Roi-Namur, the plan was to secure several small adjacent islets first, to set up artillery before the main assault on Kwajalein, which was launched on February 1. During the initial bombardment, Kelly Turner, like Dick Conolly, ordered his ships to close the range. One battleship captain objected, "I can't take my ship in that close."

Turner fired back, "What's your armor for? Get in there!"

The army troops were landed without incident at the western tip of Kwajalein and began to move forward. Unlike marine doctrine, which was to attack quickly, take your losses, and seize the objective as soon as possible, the army preferred to bring all possible fire to bear ahead of the troops before they attacked. The troopers of two army regiments moved slowly but surely and secured Kwajalein Island late February 4. Howlin' Mad Smith, as usual, was dissatisfied with the army's slow pace. But General Corlett reportedly threatened to put General Smith under arrest if he came ashore in 7th Division territory.

In the next few days, the army managed to clear the Japanese from several nearby islets. By February 7, the whole of Kwajalein Atoll was in American hands and Admiral Turner's Joint Expeditionary Force had completed its mission. The complex landings on some thirty islets, with fights on ten of them, had ended within a week with remarkably limited American casualties. A total of 372 soldiers and marines were killed in action, and no navy ships were sunk. The Japanese lost almost eight thousand soldiers. The difficult lessons of Tarawa were put to good use at Kwajalein. The battle also set a high watermark in cooperation among the army, navy, and marines.

On February 1, a task group under Rear Admiral Harry Hill was assigned to take Majuro Atoll, some 250 miles southeast of Kwajalein. The few Japanese on the island of Majuro had left, and Hill steamed into the lagoon in *Cambria*, an attack transport with special communications facilities, and landed army troops, which took over the island and atoll. The bloodless capture of Majuro proved to be a major plus for the Pacific Fleet, which used its deep, protected harbor as a major naval and air base in forthcoming operations. The only casualties were to two battleships,

Washington and *Indiana*, which collided during night maneuvering. The skipper of *Indiana*, Captain J. M. Steele, lately [an unpopular member] of Nimitz's staff, was court-martialed and relieved of command, effectively ending his career.

The fast capture of Kwajalein enabled Admiral Spruance to recommend to Admiral Nimitz that the Fifth Fleet seize Eniwetok Atoll quickly, rather than after an extended preparation. The atoll lies 325 miles northwest of Roi-Namur and only 1,000 miles from the Mariana Islands farther to the west. Like other atolls, Eniwetok consists of a necklace of islets around a large lagoon. Its name suggests its strategic position, for it means "land between west and east." In the north, the key islet was Engebi with a 4,000-foot bomber strip. In the south, the twin islets of Eniwetok and Parry were the targets with radar stations and artillery and military barracks.

Harry Hill in *Cambria* commanded the operation called "Catchpole," with marine units under Brigadier General Thomas E. Watson; these units had not been used at Kwajalein. There was also a regimental combat team of the 27th Infantry Division, which had fought at Makin Island. Eniwetok was softened up by attacks by Ted Sherman and Si Ginder's fast carrier groups. On February 15 the Eniwetok Expeditionary Group, 51.11, sortied from Kwajalein with the 22nd Marine Regiment and the 7th Division's 106th Regimental Combat Team (RCT). There were about eight thousand men in the landing force. Harry Hill and General Watson's plan called for taking adjacent islets to Engebi, and then Engebi itself, which had the only airstrip. Then the force would hit Eniwetok and Parry Islands in the south. The landings would take place from the lagoon side. The bombardment group was commanded by Rear Admiral Oley Oldendorf with battleships *Pennsylvania*, *Colorado*, and *Tennessee*, along with cruisers *Indianapolis*, *Portland*, and *Louisville* (the flagship).

There was some confusion in the initial landings. A subchaser, *SC-1066*, was designated as convoy guide, though it hadn't participated in rehearsals. The subchaser led the transports to a position off the wrong beach. Admiral Hill relieved the young skipper of *SC-1066* on the spot. General Watson fired the commander of his artillery for underperformance. Hill also sent a sharp message to the transports' commander, ordering him to shape up by the following day or ship out. But there was no opposition and the adjacent islets were easily taken. The next day Engebi fell with one thousand Japanese dead.

Next came Eniwetok, but the fighting was much harder. Watson decided to hit the atoll with his main force, army and marines, and take Parry later. The landings met only light resistance, but General Watson was displeased with the slow advance of the army's 106th RCT. He complained it "did not move forward rapidly from the beaches (thereby causing a serious congestion), did not operate in close cooperation with tanks and failed to realize the capabilities of and to use to the fullest extent naval gunfire and close support aviation."

Once again, the army versus marines tactics were evident on Eniwetok. The marines believed in overrunning defenses as quickly as possible. At night, they dug in and observed strict fire discipline. The army preferred to take full advantage of artillery and mechanized equipment, pounding down the front before advancing. At night, the army troops shot at everything they thought was moving. General Watson and Harry Hill believed the army troops were as slow as their 27th Division comrades on Makin Island. But on February 21, Admiral Hill declared Eniwetok secured. The next day, after a hard fight, the marines took Parry Island and, except for mopping up, Eniwetok was in American hands.

As Harry Hill's expeditionary force approached Eniwetok, Vice Admiral Raymond Spruance led a bold assault on the Japanese bastion of Truk, centerpiece of the Caroline Islands and anchor of the outer defense system. Truk served as the headquarters for the Japanese Combined Fleet, and Admiral Yamamoto's successor, Admiral Mineichi Koga, usually kept his flagship—the super-battleship *Musashi*—anchored there. Truk was thought to be the toughest Japanese nut in the Central Pacific, and strategic planners frequently debated as to whether to take Truk head-on or to bypass it. Topographically, Truk was unique. It had the usual large ringlet of small islets and a central lagoon. But inside the lagoon were several large volcanic cones rising to 1,500 feet. It constituted the best fleet anchorage in the Central Pacific.

Raymond Spruance decided on a combined air and sea attack on the same day, February 17, Eniwetok was being invaded. Spruance shifted his own flag from cruiser *Indianapolis* to the new battleship *New Jersey*, with 16-inch guns and a 32-knot speed, as Commander Fifth Fleet. Under Spruance, Pete Mitscher commanded Task Force 58, with three carrier groups: TG 58.1 under Black Jack Reeves in *Enterprise*, with *Yorktown* and *Belleau Wood*; TG 58.2 with Monty Montgomery in *Essex*, with *Intrepid* and *Cabot*; and TG 58.3 led by Ted Sherman in *Bunker Hill*, with *Monterey* and *Cowpens*.

Spruance had six battleships under Ching Lee in *North Carolina*: *New Jersey, Iowa, Massachusetts, South Dakota*, and *Alabama*. Spruance had the option of commanding the battle line himself (as well as the fleet), or to turn over tactical command to Ching Lee, as Pete Mitscher had direct command of the carriers. The carrier task groups all had cruiser and destroyer screens, with Rear Admiral Larry DuBose in *Santa Fe*, Rear Admiral L. J. Wiltse in *San Diego*, and Rear Admiral Ike Giffen in *Minneapolis*.

Approaching Truk, Spruance first unleashed his carrier aircraft under Mitscher's direction. Mitscher launched fighters at sunrise on February 17 from five different fast carriers to knock out enemy aircraft in the air and on the ground. The fighters strafed three airfields and they were followed by dive-bombers loaded with fragmentation and incendiary weapons, which hit the installations at the airbases. Fewer than one hundred of the 365 planes at Truk remained undamaged. Next, the light carriers in the force launched a mix of fighters and bombers to hit the ships in the lagoon. Most of the larger warships had shifted westward from Truk to the Palaus. But the carrier planes found naval auxiliaries and merchantmen and did considerable damage. That evening, the Japanese mounted their only counterattack and sent a torpedo into *Intrepid*, forcing her out of the action.

Between midnight and sunrise, Mitscher ordered the first night carrier strike on shipping in Truk lagoon with a dozen Avenger bombers. The Avenger was designed as a torpedo plane, but with the unreliability of U.S. torpedoes, carrier air group commanders configured the plane to carry bombs when wanted. The blacked-out planes using radar sank about a third of the shipping destroyed at Truk in the two-day attack. Altogether, the planes sank three auxiliary cruisers, one destroyer, two submarine tenders, an aircraft ferry, six tankers, and seventeen freighters, amounting to some 200,000 tons.

In conjunction with the air strikes, Spruance conducted a surface sweep around Truk to catch departing Japanese ships. With his flagship *New Jersey*, he exercised direct command, selecting *Iowa* and cruisers *Minneapolis* and *New Orleans*, with four destroyers and a combat air

patrol from the light carrier *Cowpens*. In detaching the two biggest bat-
tlewagons with only two heavy cruisers and four tin cans, it seems that
Raymond Spruance was embarking on a personal attack as a fighting
admiral. As Spruance's surface force moved counterclockwise around
Truk, his ships sank a light cruiser, a destroyer, a subchaser, and a trawler.
The Japanese fleet did not contest this adventurous sortie. The attack on
Truk rattled Japanese morale, and never again was it used as a fleet flag-
ship anchorage. It also ceased to be a prime U.S. target for invasion.

The conquest of the Marshall Islands opened the way for the massive Central Pacific advance and moved up the Pacific Fleet's timetable.
As Dick Conolly noted, "The Marshalls really cracked the Japanese
shell. It broke the crust of defenses on a scale that could be exploited at
once. It gave them no time adequately to fortify their inner defense line
that ran through the Marianas." The capture of the Mariana Islands was
next on the Fifth Fleet schedule. The fleet's admirals had been blooded
and would form a close-knit fighting team: Spruance, Mitscher, Turner,
Conolly, Hill, Lee, Oldendorf, (Ted) Sherman, Montgomery. It was a
team of warrior leaders shaping up to win the naval war.

Twenty-three

SOUTH PACIFIC ROLL-UP

August 1943–April 1944

As the Central Pacific forces mounted a grand sweep westward, the South Pacific ships and troops under Admiral Halsey and General MacArthur leapfrogged up the Solomon Islands and along New Guinea. General MacArthur had become unsettled by the navy's move across the Central Pacific, through the Gilberts and the Marshalls. He was opposed to the cross-Pacific strategy, believing it diverted resources from his theater and his drive up New Guinea to the Philippines. If he didn't get moving, he saw the Southwest Pacific could be reduced to a sideshow while the Central Pacific drive would hold center stage. The argument continued as to whether the two Pacific drives were mutually supporting or competitive.

Bill Halsey had a bad scare in August. His son, William Frederick Halsey III, was an aviation supply officer aboard *Saratoga*. (The sons of Admirals Nimitz and Spruance were officers in Pacific submarines.) When *Saratoga* put into the New Hebrides, young Halsey decided to fly to Nouméa to spend a night with his father. On his return trip in a TBF Avenger with two other planes in the flight, a navigational mistake led to the three planes ditching in the sea. The next day, Halsey was informed and asked if he wished any special measures to be taken.

"No," Halsey said, "my son is the same as every other son in the combat zone. Look for him just as you'd look for anybody else."

Search planes found the crews of the three planes on an island two days later.

*

Officers from Washington turned up at Halsey's headquarters in the new gray uniform, which was a pet project of Admiral King, who thought the tan uniforms looked too much like the army's. Everyone loathed the grays. Halsey called them bus driver suits. When King heard of the objections to his new uniform, particularly in the Pacific, he issued a reminder that grays were authorized as an alternative uniform for the entire navy. Halsey read King's message at the next staff meeting. Then he added, "Gentlemen, you have heard the edict. There will be no more derogatory remarks about that damned gray uniform. Officers and chiefs in my command are at liberty to wear the damned things—if, that is, they are so lacking in naval courtesy and have such limited intelligence as to prefer dressing differently from the commander of the force." No gray uniforms were seen in the Pacific, except by visiting brass from Washington.

In Nouméa in July, Rear Admiral Mick Carney, ex-skipper of the cruiser *Denver*, took over as Halsey's chief of staff. Admiral King was finally able to get rid of the irritating Miles Browning as Halsey's chief aide—over the vehement protests of Bill Halsey who wanted to give him a spot promotion to rear admiral. Instead, King gave him command of the new fast carrier *Hornet*. The appointment would turn out badly.

Though several senior officers—in MacArthur's command and elsewhere—claimed credit for the leapfrog strategy, it had been around for some time and had not put to actual use. The concept was followed when Admiral Ping Wilkinson, with Halsey's approval, decided to bypass Kolombangara Island in favor of landing at Vella Lavella Island to the northwest. The move was pulled off without opposition; a group of fast destroyer transports landed troops on August 15, 1943, with Admiral Wilkinson flying his flag aboard the destroyer *Cony*—which was quite unusual for a commanding admiral to fly a flag in a lowly tin can.

As the campaign advanced, a series of sharp destroyer actions were fought in the Slot. In a notable one, Commander Frederick Moosbrugger, who had taken over from Arleigh Burke as commodore of two destroyer divisions, sank three Japanese destroyers with no U.S. loss in the brilliantly conducted Battle of Vella Gulf on August 6. Moosbrugger had followed a night action plan devised by Burke and left him chagrined that he missed the battle, though he applauded his successor's achievement. "Dear Moose," Burke wrote, "Your battle the other night will go down in history as one of the most successful actions ever fought. It was splendidly conceived and brilliantly executed . . ." Moosbrugger showed that U.S. destroyers' torpedoes were a force to be reckoned with, perhaps more than the cruisers' quick-firing guns. Moosbrugger went on to become a successful commodore of destroyer squadrons.

The next big jump in the Solomons was to the large, mountainous island of Bougainville. In preparation, Rear Admiral Tip Merrill's cruiser-destroyer force bombarded Japanese positions, and Rear Admiral Ted Sherman's carrier task group pounded Japanese airfields around the Buka Passage between Bougainville and Buka. On November 1, the affable Ping Wilkinson, who was turning out to be a first-class amphibious commander—as befitted an officer who graduated first in his Annapolis class—ordered his III Phib to land the 3rd Marine Division at Empress Augusta Bay on the western side of Bougainville—only 210 miles from the Japanese bastion of Rabaul.

The landings were successful, but the American command waited anxiously for the expected Japanese counterattack. Japanese Admiral Koga, Yamamoto's successor, preferred to keep the main body of his fleet in Truk. He ordered Rear Admiral Sentaro Omori to intercept Tip Merrill with two heavy cruisers, two light cruisers, and six destroyers. Although Tip Merrill was protecting the anchorage, he was now headed toward Omori's ships.

Rear Admiral Merrill's four light cruisers were accompanied by Arleigh Burke's new command, Commander DesRon 23, which he nicknamed the "Little Beavers," with Commander Bernard L. "Count" Austin as his subordinate division commander. Count was the nickname hung on Austin at the Naval Academy by an upperclassman. As commander of the destroyer screen, Arleigh Burke was known as the "dog boss," dog for destroyer.

Admiral Omori deployed his force in the usual short columns, three of them.

Tip Merrill arranged his force for a night action: Burke's four van destroyers, then his cruisers led by flagship *Montpelier*, followed by Count Austin's four tin cans bringing up the rear. But for the first time, Tip Merrill did not tie the destroyers to the cruisers, giving them instead the flexibility to maneuver independently, depending on circumstances. Merrill's battle plan was to place the cruisers across the entrance to Empress Augusta Bay to prevent any enemy ships from getting in and shelling the beachhead. He also planned to open fire with his cruisers just outside the maximum range of Japanese torpedoes. Additionally, he intended to hold cruiser gunfire until his tin cans had launched their own fish.

At 0227 on November 2, pips showed up on flagship *Montpelier's* radar screen, showing the Japanese force in three columns. At 0231, Arleigh Burke's four destroyers cut loose for a torpedo attack. "My guppies are swimming," Burke reported on voice radio.

Merrill reversed course with the rest of his ships. With a simultaneous 180-degree turn, the rear destroyers were now becoming the van. Merrill ordered Count Austin's tin cans to attack independently. Merrill waited for Burke's torpedoes to hit and then ordered his cruisers to open fire with their 6-inch guns. Shells hit the cruiser *Sendai*, flagship of Rear Admiral Matsuji Ijuin, and jammed her rudder. Destroyers *Shiratsuyu* and *Samidare* collided when maneuvering to avoid shellfire, and the damage took them out of the night action.

Japanese star shells lit the scene and the American cruisers. Merrill ordered his ships to make smoke and avoid getting hit by enemy fire. The two Japanese heavy cruisers, *Myoko* and *Haguro*, made a 360-degree circle in an effort to locate the U.S. warships. The destroyer *Hatsukaze*, in the Japanese third and southernmost column, attempted to dodge American shells but cut between the two Japanese heavy cruisers, colliding with Admiral Omori's flagship *Myoko* at 0307.

Merrill executed another about-face, keeping his cruisers out of enemy torpedo range while pumping out constant fire from his ship's 6-inch guns. Despite the funnel and chemical smoke, Merrill's captains maintained a tight formation during complex maneuvering. Finally, Admiral Omori's flagship got the range and landed on USS *Denver* three 8-inch shells, which failed to explode.

Burke was busy reforming his Little Beavers and led them back into action at 32 knots, shelling the sinking *Sendai* and then helping destroyer *Spence* finish off *Hatsukaze* with his tin can flagship *Charles Ausburne*. Meanwhile, a stray enemy torpedo meant for the cruisers hit destroyer *Foote*, which disabled the ship.

In the melee, Burke's destroyer *Charles Ausburne* straddled Count Austin's *Spence*. Austin shouted over the TBS: "Cease firing! Cease firing!

Goddammit that's me!"

"Were you hit?" queried Burke.

"Negative," Austin said. "But they aren't all here yet."

"Sorry," Burke said. "I won't shoot any more but you'll have to excuse the next four salvos. They're already on their way."

Finally, Tip Merrill, seeing he had run out of targets as the Japanese retired at high speed, ordered his destroyers to form up with the cruisers and proceed for home while undergoing daylight enemy air attacks. He picked up a force of unloaded U.S. transports and escorted them back to Guadalcanal. On coming into Purvis Bay, in Florida Island across Ironbottom Sound from Guadalcanal, the base routinely signaled: "What do you require?"

"Sleep," Admiral Merrill replied.

Merrill directed his force expertly through complicated maneuvers. Once Burke's tin cans fired their fish, they pulled away without a clear follow-up plan. And Count Austin's destroyer division, which had never trained together, had difficulty following Merrill's commands and was late getting into action. Burke emphasized the value of surprise, allowed the destroyers to operate independently, and stressed the need to waste no time in opening fire. "It is necessary that [commanders] realize the value of time," he said. "It is the only commodity you can never regain." He added of his ships: "Their action was not the passive acceptance of finding themselves in a fight and then conducting a good battle. They went out looking for trouble, they found it, they sank it, and they then looked for more."

All in all, it was an outstanding performance, which protected the vulnerable transports and beachhead on Bougainville. The battle ended with a Japanese cruiser and destroyer sunk, and two heavy cruisers and two destroyers banged up, with severe damage to only one U.S. tin can. Of his ships and men, Merrill reported, "It functioned as a well-drilled team. Each officer and each man did his job as he had been trained to do it . . . officers and men alike were brave and confident. They were confident in their superiors, in their subordinates, and in themselves."

Admiral Halsey decided to keep the pressure on the key Japanese base of Rabaul, the sheltered harbor on the island of New Britain in the Bismarcks. He ordered a carrier force under Rear Admiral Ted Sherman in *Saratoga* with *Princeton*, the cruisers *San Diego* and *San Juan*, and nine destroyers, to hit heavily defended Rabaul and the warships in port. It was a high-risk operation, but Halsey was determined to take it.

Aboard *Princeton* was Air Group 23 led by Commander Hank Miller, who had taught the army pilots to take off from the old *Hornet* in the Tokyo raid. On the morning of November 5, the carriers launched all their planes. Flying through heavy flak, the planes found many warships and proceeded to drop bombs and torpedoes. While the carrier planes sank no ships, they seriously damaged four heavy cruisers, two light cruisers, and several destroyers. The United States lost ten planes out of the ninety-seven in the strike. Ted Sherman made a quick getaway, and Bill Halsey was delighted with the results. Halsey ordered a follow-up strike by Ted Sherman's carriers and a second force commanded by Monty Montgomery in *Essex* with *Bunker Hill* and *Independence*. He was escorted by a cruiser division under the command of capable Rear Admiral Larry DuBose. The additional damage convinced the Japanese that Rabaul was no longer defensible against American air attack, and they ceased using it as a major cruiser base.

Despite his self-concern and chip on his shoulder against Nimitz and Towers, Ted Sherman was a notable and aggressive carrier force commander with his own quirks. Aboard *Saratoga*, a young quartermaster, Roger Bond, was dashing up a ladder to the bridge, while Admiral Sherman was descending to the flight deck. They met at a tiny landing, with the sailor blocking the way, and almost collided. The taller quartermaster was startled to see the two stars on Sherman's fatigue cap. He tried to move aside.

"Son," the admiral said, "how long have you been in the navy?"

"About a year, sir."

"Well, I've been in for forty years, and now people get out of my way when I'm coming. And when you're in forty years, they'll get out of your way. Do you understand me?"

Commodore Burke's Little Beaver squadron ran constant missions in the Slot, usually at a top speed of 33 or 34 knots. On one operation, *Spence* had powerplant trouble and was capable of only 31 knots. Burke decided to take the tin can along and the squadron moved at a slightly lesser speed. Captain Ray Thurber, Halsey's operations officer, radioed Commodore Burke to report his position and speed. Burke complied and ended: "Proceeding at 31 knots." The phrase struck Thurber's fancy. When Halsey learned the Japanese planned to land ground forces on Buka Island, immediately north of Bougainville, he sent Arleigh Burke to intercept. Halsey's message was written by Captain Thurber: "Thirty-one-knot Burke, get this. Put your squadron athwart the Buka-Rabaul evacuation line about 35 miles west of Buka. If no enemy contacts by early morning, come south to refuel same place. If enemy contacted you know what to do. Halsey."

Correspondents learned of the dispatch, which had ironic overtones because a destroyer in top shape could make 35 knots. They used "31-Knot Burke" in their stories, which pictured a hell-for-leather destroyerman, creating a famous naval nickname in the war. It suited the blue-eyed, fair-haired Burke, of Swedish extraction from Colorado, who was always on his tin can's bridge, flying his commodore's pennant from the mast. A pennant is a flag with a notch in it: a blue stripe for a squadron commander; a red stripe for a division commander.

Burke had five tin cans with him in DesRon 23: his flagship *Charles Ausburne*, *Claxton*, and *Dyson*, and Count Austin's depleted division with *Converse* and *Spence*. At 0141 on November 25, *Dyson* made a radar contact 11 miles to the northeast, off Cape St. George on New Ireland Island. *Dyson* notified Burke who told his squadron: "Hello DS [DesRon] 23. Hang on to your hats, boys. Here we go." The contact turned out to be five destroyer-transports in two columns, steaming at 25 knots on a westerly course. Arleigh Burke headed directly for the enemy. Burke's plan called for his division to launch torpedoes first, while Austin covered. Then, Burke was to pull away and provide cover for Austin's tin cans to give a crack with torpedoes. At 0156, Burke's destroyers reached their firing position, launched a fifteen-torpedo spread, and turned 90 degrees away. The Japanese were taken by surprise and Burke's fish hit two new destroyers, *Onami* and *Makinami*, disintegrating the former, while *Makinami* remained afloat somehow, while slowly sinking.

The Japanese retreated to the north. Burke left Austin to finish off any other ships as he pursued the enemy. He radioed Nouméa headquarters: "Making 31 knots to intercept the enemy."

Ray Thurber, who was familiar with Japanese tin can capabilities, replied. "Thirty-one-knot Burke, you've got to get off your ass and make 33 knots if you're going to catch those boys."

Thus encouraged and unencumbered by the limping *Spence*, Burke increased speed to 33 knots and slowly closed range. It was a straight chase and Burke ordered the forward gun mounts on his ships to open fire at the fleeting Japanese. Several 5-inch shells hit *Yogiri*, and the warship sank just after 0300.

Austin's destroyers ran across the sinking *Makinami* and poured gunfire into the Japanese destroyer, putting her under. Dawn was approaching. Count Austin was low on fuel, heading toward Rabaul, and voice-messaged Burke: "Arleigh, I hope the Japanese fuel tanks fit our hoses because I'm going to be out of fuel by the time we get there."

"I get it," Burke replied, and ordered the Little Beavers home.

The Battle of Cape St. George on Thanksgiving Day was a jewel of an action: three enemy ships sunk with nary a nick to the U.S. destroyers. Tip Merrill awarded Arleigh Burke the Navy Cross for the battle. Admiral Pye, president of the Naval War College, called it "an almost perfect action, that may be considered a classic."

As the marines and army troops were fighting to secure Bougainville and the northern Solomons, General MacArthur—with the aid of Rear Admiral Uncle Dan Barbey's VII Phib—was jumping up the northeast coast of New Guinea. In a series of small but effective steps, Barbey landed American and Australian army troops at Nassau Bay in June, followed by Lae and Salamaua in September, and Finschhafen in October.

In November, McArthur's Navy had another drastic shakeup. For months, MacArthur had been expressing dissatisfaction with his navy commander, Vice Admiral Chips Carpender. MacArthur believed Carpender lacked the necessary drive and clout with Washington to get the ships he wanted for the Seventh Fleet. Carpender, like Admiral Leary before him, thought it was an unacceptable risk to deploy warships in the restricted waters around New Guinea in easy reach of the many Japanese air bases. Senior navy officers believed Lieutenant General Kenney, MacArthur's air force chief, failed to provide much air support for naval operations and seemed to think that "damn navy" was one word.

For their part, navy officers were indignant that MacArthur's grandiose communiqués rarely gave the navy credit for its part in operations. The Seventh Fleet commander was always in an awkward position: under the immediate operational command of General MacArthur, but under the authority of Admiral King in Washington and dependent on Admiral Nimitz in Pearl for the assignment of most of the major ships, particularly carriers. It was Admiral King, not MacArthur or Nimitz, who wrote Commander Seventh Fleet's fitness reports, always an important consideration for a flag officer.

So Vice Admiral Carpender was sent home to command the 9th Naval District at the Great Lakes Naval Station in North Chicago, Illinois. Casting for his replacement, both King and Nimitz were impressed by Tom Kinkaid's ability to get along with army and air force counterparts in the Alaska command. They agreed this quiet, thoughtful officer would be the best man to offer MacArthur for the Seventh Fleet job. King, in particular, believed Kinkaid would "not give away the store" to the autocratic MacArthur, and would not be consumed by MacArthur's "Philippines first" strategy. Luckily, Tom Kinkaid was content to let Dan Barbey manage VII Phib operations without interference. The Seventh Fleet submarines based in Brisbane and Fremantle under Rear Admiral Ralph Christie continued their highly effective operations against Japanese shipping. One problem Tom Kinkaid immediately encountered: "MacArthur had gotten word I was a fighting admiral and he immediately expected a large fleet to come in behind me." The Seventh Fleet would remain understrength.

To support the New Guinea amphibious effort and put the pressure on Rabaul, Halsey and MacArthur agreed to land the 1st Marine Division under Major General William H. Rupertus at Cape Gloucester—located on the northwestern tip of New Britain Island, across the Vitiaz Strait from New Guinea's Huon Peninsula. In a meeting with Admiral Barbey and others, General MacArthur complained about the lack of ships and planes for a proper amphibious assault. After the meeting, MacArthur grumbled in Barbey's presence, "There are some people in Washington who would rather see MacArthur lose a battle than America win a war." Not long after, Barbey visited Admiral King in Washington, who complained to him that General MacArthur seemed more interested in making good his promise to return to the Philippines than in winning the war.

Admiral Barbey led the invasion in destroyer *Conyngham*—another example of a commanding admiral riding a destroyer as his flagship. He pointed out one anomaly of being a flag officer during a Japanese air attack: "Everyone else was concentrating on doing his own particular job. The skipper and the bridge personnel were swinging the ship at high speed to avoid the torpedoes and bombs; the lookouts were reporting incoming planes; gun crews were doing what gun crews are supposed to do; ammunition crews were feeding the guns; the firemen and engineers were driving the ship at more than her rated speed; everyone had a job and was busy doing it, but me. I was just a spectator in my seat on the starboard wing of the bridge. It would have been far easier on the nerves if I could have shot a gun or handled a wheel."

The troops were carried by destroyer-transports, LSTs and LCIs. Newly selected Rear Admiral Russell S. Berkey, former skipper of cruiser *Santa Fe*, commanded a cruiser-destroyer covering force in flagship *Nashville*. The marines landed at 0830 on December 26, and immediately struck out to seize a Japanese airfield. It was a tough fight; the marines lost 228 dead and 772 wounded in the tropical rain forests against the Japanese by January 16, 1944. The marines, veterans of Guadalcanal, said Gloucester was worse because of the heavy, persistent rain.

As the marines reinforced their positions on Cape Gloucester, Uncle Dan Barbey moved farther along the New Guinea coast with a landing at Saidor, where he and the marines found no Japanese and took over an airstrip. The success of the VI Phib's leapfrogging operation led MacArthur, Kinkaid, and Barbey to plan a longer jump to the key base of Hollandia (now Jayapura). The great fortress of Rabaul, with some one hundred thousand defenders, was being reduced to near impotence with almost daily U.S. bomber raids. Rabaul, it was now realized, could be bypassed, just like Truk.

On Bougainville, the largest island in the Solomons, the marines were replaced by army troops, which kept the Japanese bottled up in the northern and southern sections of the island. This left U.S. forces to use harbors and airfields in the center, and the Japanese withdrew the bulk of their troops with Bougainville effectively in American hands.

Next on the agenda of Admiral Halsey's South Pacific Force, now the Third Fleet, was Green Island, lying between Bougainville and Rabaul, only 115 miles from the latter. Admiral Ping Wilkinson, commander of III Phib, commanded the invasion forces. He was supported by the veteran cruiser admirals, Tip Merrill in *Montpelier*, and Pug Ainsworth returning from a West Coast overhaul with *Honolulu* and *St. Louis*. With his usual low-keyed efficiency, Ping Wilkinson landed New Zealand troops on February 15, 1944, which quickly dispatched the seventy Japanese soldiers on the island, helping to close the ring around Rabaul.

During their short breaks between missions, Tip Merrill liked to go ashore with Pug Ainsworth and his cruiser captains to hoist a few. Mick Carney, who had been skipper of *Denver*, recalled, Merrill was "one of the most magnetic personalities I've ever known . . . a little fellow with an infectious laugh that started everybody in the vicinity laughing. He was a ruthless slave-driving SOB as far as training was concerned, but when you came into port, he used to say, if we could find a palm tree and a bottle, we'd set up an officers club." When the easygoing Tip Merrill received word that the son of Mick Carney, now Halsey's chief of staff, was going to marry the daughter of General Sutherland, MacArthur's chief of staff, he messaged Carney: "Wedding announcement noted. Paragraph. Jesus Christ! Intertheater solidarity is very much to be desired, but is it necessary to go this far?"

The final effort of the South Pacific Force was directed against Emirau Island, halfway between Kavieng and the Admiralty Islands. Since the Japanese had never occupied the island, Emirau was taken easily on March 20, 1944, and served as a valuable air base from which New Ireland could be kept under watch and bombed.

Admiral Halsey kept his cruisers and destroyers busy, particularly Arleigh Burke's DesRon 23 Little Beavers, in shore bombardments against targets on New Britain and New Ireland, including Rabaul and Kavieng. South Pacific planners thought Rabaul and Kavieng would be eventual targets for invasion, though they would be strongly defended. But a consensus was building in Nouméa, Pearl, and Washington that these tough strongholds might well be bypassed and neutralized by frequent U.S. bomber raids. Such was the U.S. local command of the sea that Rear Admiral Robert Griffen was able to take a group of old battleships—*New Mexico*, *Mississippi*, *Tennessee*, and *Idaho*—with two escort carriers, and fifteen destroyers to bombard Kavieng and its nearby air fields on March 15.

In bypassing Kavieng and Rabaul, the U.S. planners at the Joint Chiefs of Staff decided to take the Admiralty Islands, to the north of

New Guinea and west of New Ireland. The chief objective was Manus Island, the biggest in the group with the excellent Seeadler Harbor, which could accommodate a large U.S. task force. Nearby Los Negros Island could provide the flatland for air bases. The operation was delayed while the command situation between General MacArthur and Admiral Halsey was clarified. MacArthur at first objected to Halsey's forces occupying the Admiralties, for he considered the islands his own turf.

On February 29, Admiral Uncle Dan Barbey ordered his deputy, Rear Admiral William Fechteler, to take charge of landing the U.S. 1st Cavalry Division on Los Negros Island. Vice Admiral Kinkaid was aboard the cruiser *Phoenix* along with General MacArthur, but Kinkaid wisely left the amphibious specialists in tactical command.

The light landing force, one thousand troopers of the 1st Cavalry Division under Brigadier General William C. Chase found more Japanese than it had expected on Los Negros. Reinforcements were summoned and hard fighting ensued until March 8, when a landing force entered Seeadler Harbor on Manus Island. Organized resistance ended on March 15 and mopping up operations continued. On May 18, a U.S. naval and air station base was established on Manus Island, and the encirclement of Rabaul and Kavieng was complete.

Barbey, Fechteler, and Rear Admiral Berkey in command of the cruiser support landed General MacArthur's naval team of amphibians along the north coast of New Guinea, successively at Aitape, Humboldt Bay, and Wakde. With additional operations at Biak and Sansapor in May and July, New Guinea was, for practical purposes, in Allied hands by the summer of 1944.

These 1944 landings effectively put the South Pacific command out of business, in terms of offensive operations, with the ground action shifting to MacArthur's Southwest Pacific Area. Bill Halsey's cruisers and destroyers had fought brilliant night battles as they reclaimed the Slot from the well-trained but faltering Japanese commanders. No one realized that never again in the Pacific would there be the kind of cruiser-destroyer combat that characterized the exploits of Tip Merrill, Pug Ainsworth, Arleigh Burke—and Raizo Tanaka. The gallant cruisers and tin cans would soon be absorbed within much larger fleet formations (spearheaded by carriers) and act as escorts and anti-aircraft support with only the occasional bombardment mission.

Arleigh Burke knew what combat command was like. "Without the stress and strain and limit on time," he commented, "nobody can actually duplicate the strain that a commander is under in making a decision during combat. Consequently it's a brave man, or an incautious one, who criticizes another man for the action which he took in battle unless it is obviously an error caused by lack of character."

Captain Burke had been looking forward to repeated action against the enemy in his beloved tin cans. He was shocked and upset to receive a dispatch from the Bureau of Naval Personnel in late March 1944, detaching him from command of DesRon 23: "You will proceed via first available government transportation including government air to the port in which Commander Carrier Division 3 may be. Upon arrival report to Commander Carrier Division 3 as his Chief of Staff."

Burke was dismayed. He hadn't any recent experience in big ships. He didn't know who Commander Carrier Division (ComCarDiv) 3 was, nor where to find him. His boss radioed a splendid sendoff to "Captain 31-Knot Burke," ending: "All hands in the South Pacific are proud of the workmanlike job you have done. Well done indeed and good luck. Halsey."

Twenty-four

WESTWARD TO THE MARIANAS

March–June 1944

Though the Joint Chiefs of Staff had approved a dual route to Japan—along the New Guinea, and the Mindanao axis, and across the Central Pacific—General MacArthur continued to press for his single approach to the Philippines. MacArthur had not strongly opposed the occupation of the Gilberts and Marshalls because they protected his long supply line to the West Coast. But with the conquest of the Marshalls, and his own gathering advance along the northern New Guinea coast, MacArthur objected to Admiral King's next target in the Pacific: the Mariana Islands—Saipan, Guam, and Tinian. They were 3,000 miles west of Pearl Harbor; 1,000 miles from the advanced base at Eniwetok. MacArthur was unaware that Admiral King was backed by General Hap Arnold, head of the Army Air Forces, because Arnold wanted bases in the Marianas to support the still-secret B-29 long-range bomber, which could hit Japan from them.

The Marine Corps losses at Tarawa gave MacArthur the ammunition he thought he needed to oppose further assaults against Japanese-held Pacific islands. Claiming his victories were at minimum cost, he urged Washington to redirect the Central Pacific offensive to support his own drive in the Southwest Pacific. If he were given the naval forces, he promised, he would be in the Philippines in ten months. But the Joint Chiefs rejected MacArthur's pleas. Admiral Chester Nimitz called a conference in Pearl Harbor in late January 1944 to discuss strategy, and invited senior army, navy, and air force officers to attend.

Curiously, Nimitz himself was leaning toward a single approach strategy, perhaps because of the shock of the losses at Tarawa. The Mariana Islands were big and rugged and far beyond range of land-based Allied air support. Some of Nimitz's staff turned toward this view. Admiral Jack Towers was against the Marianas operation because of the danger of air attack from Japan and enemy airfields on Iwo Jima and Chichi Jima. He recommended bypassing the Marianas and going for Palau in the Western Pacific. Nimitz's chief aides, chief of staff Soc McMorris, and chief planner, Rear Admiral Forrest Sherman, went along, too. Vice Admiral Tom Kinkaid—Commander of the Seventh Fleet—and Lieutenant General Kenney, also supported MacArthur's Southwest Pacific concept. Nimitz forwarded this sharply revised strategic assessment, superseding the Central Pacific drive, to Ernie King in Washington.

Douglas MacArthur, though he did not personally attend the conference, was elated. He wrote General Marshall in Washington urging that the majority of the forces in the Pacific should be placed under his command and that the naval elements should be assigned to Admiral Halsey, who would also come under MacArthur's command. He recommended that his headquarters absorb any available British land and sea forces. MacArthur was clearly seeking to make himself the overall commander in the Pacific in the war against Japan.

Predictably, Admiral King blew his stack. He quickly messaged Nimitz: "I have read your conference notes with much interest, and I must add with indignant dismay." King added that the New Guinea approach to the exclusion of the Central Pacific drive "is absurd." To King, Nimitz's inexplicable about-face on the Central Pacific drive reinforced King's earlier doubts about his Pacific commander's ability to stand up for the U.S. Navy strategy against the blandishments of General MacArthur. King could never quite rid himself of the view that Chester Nimitz was a "fixer," King's word for anyone who served in the Bureau of Personnel or similar high bureaucratic positions.

The Joint Chiefs of Staff soon ended the strategic argument with an overall directive that called for neutralizing Truk, invading the Marianas on June 15—called Operation Forager—and Palau on September 15. Afterwards, Pacific Fleet forces would support the invasion of Mindanao by MacArthur's forces. The decision of whether to invade Luzon or Formosa was left open.

Meanwhile, Raymond Spruance was elevated to full admiral as Commander Fifth Fleet at age fifty-seven. Kelly Turner received a third star as amphibious commander, though a few congressmen who blamed him for the Savo Island disaster temporarily held up his promotion. On a quick visit to Washington, Dick Conolly put in a good word for Turner with key legislators, though he never told him. Pete Mitscher, now confirmed as the Task Force 58 carrier commander, was raised to vice admiral and three stars. Ching Lee was also promoted to vice admiral as Commander Battleships Pacific. Not to be denied, Howlin' Mad Smith received his third star as lieutenant general.

The Pacific Fleet command structure under Admiral Nimitz now had three main elements: Admiral Spruance's Fifth Fleet, Vice Admiral Charles Lockwood's Submarine Force, and Vice Admiral William Calhoun's Service (Supply) Force. The Fifth Fleet in turn comprised the Fast Carrier Forces (TF) 58, under Vice Admiral Mitscher; the Joint Expeditionary Force under Vice Admiral Turner and Lieutenant General Smith; and the Forward Land-Based Aircraft under Vice Admiral Genial John Hoover.

In another administrative move, Admiral King and Admiral Nimitz, at a regular meeting in San Francisco, devised a way to use Bill Halsey's services, now that the South Pacific area was falling behind the war's power curve. Vice Admiral John Newton would become Commander South Pacific. Bill Halsey, as Commander Third Fleet, would alternate in command with Raymond Spruance's Fifth Fleet. The ships would remain the same at sea, but the admirals and their staffs would switch between commanding the fleet and returning to Pearl to plan the next operation. In this way, Spruance would command the Marianas operation, while Halsey and his chief of staff, Mick Carney, would plan the Palau invasion. One team fought while the other team planned the next fight. As Halsey explained the naval two-platoon system, "instead of the stagecoach system of keeping the drivers and changing the horses, we changed drivers and kept the horses."

Yet another change that was to cause anguish among admirals, Admiral King—prodded by new Secretary of the Navy James V. Forrestal—bent to the pressure of Jack Towers and the air admirals. He decreed that all non-aviator commanders of major task forces must have an aviator as chief of staff, and all aviator commanders take a surface ship officer as chief of staff. This stirred up resentments among both black and brown shoes. It meant that Admiral Spruance would have to give up his trusted right-hand man, Captain Carl Moore, a move Spruance tried to resist. Vice Admiral Mitscher would have to find a black-shoe officer to become his chief of staff and replace the expert aviation tactician Truman Hedding. Washington's new dictum was wrenching for senior flag officers who developed personal and professional relations with their trusted and accomplished chiefs of staff.

Pete Mitscher relied heavily on Captain Hedding, who grew up in Pennsylvania and New Mexico and was among the brightest and most capable aviators in the navy. Hedding, a tall, lean, taciturn, forty-one-year-old officer, had helped develop modern carrier tactics, including the circular formation with more than one flattop. He had been air officer and executive officer of the new carrier *Essex* under Captain Wu Duncan. On promotion to captain, Hedding became chief of staff to Rear Admiral Pownall, who was the senior carrier commander aboard Jocko Clark's *Yorktown*.

Hedding explained the planning process:

> Admiral Nimitz . . . would draw up a plan. He would state the objective of the plan, what he would like to have accomplished, and give certain timings, and a broad idea of what the operation would consist of. But he would never say how to do something. He would tell you what he wanted to be done, to the fleet commanders or the operational commander at sea, and he would tell you what forces you would have to do this job. Then you would take that and sit down and broaden your plan, based on that. So then the task force would have a plan.
>
> The planning would be coordinated with the marines, the army, and the amphibious command. All that had to be done under Commander Fifth Fleet, who would draw up the plan. He would have an annex of what the carrier task force should do, and what the amphibious force should do, et cetera. Then we each in turn would write up our own operation orders. At that

time in our operations orders we would designate the task group commanders and what ships they would have. We would outline the basic plan—what would be done and the timing.

The task group commanders would then take the task force operation orders and draw up their own operations orders, in which they would get into the details of the actual missions to be flown from what carrier—how many planes, how many fighters, how many divebombers, how many torpedo bombers, and what their particular targets would be. Once we would issue our order, we would more or less ride along, just like Admiral Spruance was riding along, or Admiral Lee, who had the battleships.

As Admiral Pownall's chief of staff, Captain Hedding was aboard during the controversial Kwajalein strike, which was instrumental in Pownall's relief. Hedding and Jocko Clark, his air group commander, all urged Pownall to launch a follow-up attack. "Pownall knew his business but he just wasn't aggressive enough," Hedding commented.

Recognizing Hedding's many talents, Pete Mitscher kept him on as his own chief of staff when he took over as senior carrier commander of the Fifth Fleet. So Mitscher was upset when King insisted that his order be carried out: Mitscher would get a black-shoe chief of staff, like it or not. Nimitz sent Mitscher the names of four captains to choose from to replace Truman Hedding.

"Admiral," Hedding said on receiving the dispatch, "it looks like you're going to get a new chief of staff."

"What do you mean?" Mitscher replied.

"Well, here," Hedding said, handing over the dispatch.

Mitscher read it and said, "I'm not going to do it."

"Admiral, I don't think you have much choice."

"I guess maybe I don't. Do you know any of these people?"

"Yes," Hedding said, "I know all of them."

"Okay, they're going to relieve you. You pick one. I don't care who he is. You pick him."

"Okay. Pick Arleigh Burke." Hedding had been at the Annapolis Naval Postgraduate School with Burke and was aware of his reputation as a destroyer squadron commander in the South Pacific. Hedding mentioned this to Mitscher.

"All right. If that's the one you think it should be, then answer the dispatch and send it in."

The Fifth Fleet was heading for a strike on Palau in the western Caroline Islands in late March. On March 27, in the process of absorbing South Pacific units transiting Espiritu Santo, the fleet and Burke's DesRon 23 joined up just north of Green Island in the northern Solomons. Burke's flagship *Charles Ausburne* came alongside of Mitscher's flagship *Lexington* and 31-Knot Burke transferred across on a chair hooked to a high line. He carried a sea bag and a briefcase.

Truman Hedding went back to the stern to greet Arleigh Burke, who was still burned up about the new job. They exchanged salutes and handshakes.

"Who is Commander Carrier Division 3 anyway?" He asked Hedding.

"Well, it's Admiral Mitscher. Just relax, Arleigh. You're getting the finest job you could ever get. You'll see. Let's go up and meet the admiral."

On the flag bridge, Mitscher, in his swivel chair facing the ship's stern as usual, said, "Welcome aboard, Burke."

"Glad to be aboard, Admiral."

That was all. Burke was unimpressed with Mitscher's small stature, laconic style, and hushed voice. He assumed the ill feeling was mutual. Burke and Hedding went to his quarters below.

Burke was still fuming, "I don't know anything about carriers. Destroyers are my navy."

"You're about to become knowledgeable about carriers, chum, whether you like it or not. You'll learn."

Hedding hoped to have some time to snap in Burke. A meeting of the chiefs of staff of the task group commanders was being held that day aboard *Lexington*. Burke observed Hedding going over the task force's orders with them, and the individual task group's orders to be sure everyone understood them. However, after the conference, the plane carrying Commander James Averill, chief of staff to Rear Admiral Si Ginder, commander of TG 58.4, crashed on takeoff from *Lexington*, killing Averill.

Mitscher summoned Hedding. "You've got to go over and be Si Ginder's chief of staff for this operation. He can't operate alone.

We've got everything done, our orders are all written, and we've got Burke here."

Hedding was jolted by what he found on *Yorktown's* flag bridge. The staff seemed to go into shock at the news of the death of their chief. Captain Hedding told Admiral Ginder, "Look, we've got to draw up your own op order and get everything squared away here. Let's get going."

"Okay," Ginder said, "You do it."

Hedding rallied the shaken staff and began writing operation orders as the task force steamed toward Palau. Ginder holed up in his emergency cabin and never came out. He showed no interest in the plans Hedding presented him. Instead, he concentrated on his pet project, the ship's newspaper, which he personally edited and most everyone thought extremely corny. Hedding, in effect, ran the task group of four carriers: *Lexington, Yorktown, Princeton,* and *Langley.*

"I took all the day watches," Hedding said. "I had a communicator who was wonderful, and he took the night watches. In the day watches, you had to make sure that the strikes went out on time, the task group was turned into the wind, and all that business—in other words, the tactical command of the task group. Admiral Ginder would come up once in a while and ask how things were going. Normally he wouldn't even budge out of his cabin. He just stayed down there in his skivvies all the time. I don't know whether he was frightened or what happened, but he just went to pieces."

After the mission, Hedding returned to *Lexington.*

"What in the world is the matter with Ginder?" Mitscher asked.

"Admiral, I don't know but there's something badly wrong with him because he doesn't do anything." Hedding had known Ginder for years and thought he was a first-class officer, though lacking combat experience. Hedding didn't think Ginder would crack, but he did.

"Well, we'll have to get rid of him," Mitscher said.

Ginder was quickly detached as task group commander, and Mitscher named the newly flagged Jocko Clark to replace him. Ginder didn't measure up to combat but his administrative skills were valued and Nimitz placed him in charge of aircraft replacement escort carriers.

Mitscher, Hedding said, "could make decisions that were hard to make, that would hurt people. Anyone in command has to do that. Admiral Nimitz did it all the time." Hedding believed that the two flag officers he would put in the top category, which epitomized all that naval officers should aspire to, were Chester Nimitz and Pete Mitscher.

Arleigh Burke was a quick study. Faced with Mitscher's near silence, he plunged into reading everything he could on carrier warfare tactics: manuals, aircraft publications, reports, operation orders, battle plans. He spoke at length to flag staff officers and examined equipment. From the flag bridge, Burke marvelled at the size of the force: four carrier groups with seventy-eight warships spread from horizon to horizon. They waited for Burke's instructions.

Over the weeks, he learned that Mitscher didn't care for personally issuing orders over the voice radio. So Burke began giving the word, using Mitscher's call sign, Bald Eagle. At one point he saw a group of Japanese torpedo planes heading to the force and, without instructions, picked up the radio phone ordering the ships to turn toward the enemy planes.

He wondered whether he had been too impetuous.

"Well," Mitscher said, "it was about time, Captain Burke."

During Task Force 58's support for General MacArthur's Hollandia operation, Burke observed how Mitscher debriefed his pilots on the flag bridge after operations and was impressed by the amount of relevant information Mitscher extracted from his airmen. He noted Mitscher's taut, taciturn command style and cogent advice with no words wasted. Mitscher, he thought, was one of the few officers in the navy who could indicate a command with a glance.

As the weeks wore on, Truman Hedding coached Arleigh Burke in the ways of carrier aviation, and together they planned a method to shorten and simplify operations orders. Burke was intent on decentralizing the operations of carrier groups under Mitscher's command so that there was a standard operating procedure. Therefore, when commanders chose to depart from the norm, they knew what the norm was. Mitscher kept Hedding on as deputy chief of staff, which was convenient because Hedding was junior to Arleigh Burke. But after the Marianas, Hedding was finally detached to CinCPac as a planning expert.

As he left Mitscher's carrier, the admiral said to Hedding, "Well, Truman, it looks like this Burke's going to turn out real good."

*

Mitscher led Task Force 58 in strikes in support of MacArthur and Barbey's Hollandia operation, and the task force also hit Truk, and then headed back to Majuro, the capital of the Marshall Islands, for a breather before the coming Marianas operation. Admiral Spruance and his chief of staff, Captain Moore, were worried that the fast battleships were not getting enough training together. They sought to give Ching Lee the opportunity to move out his battlewagons as a tactical unit: practicing staying closed up in column, making tight simultaneous turns, and concentrating on firing targets. They were concerned about the battleships' ability to fight at night.

One of Mitscher's carriers was the new *Hornet*, with the difficult Miles Browning commanding. Browning proved to be as much of a martinet as a carrier captain as he'd been as Halsey's chief of staff. He was overbearing with all his senior officers, and berated department heads without indicating what he was complaining about. Morale on the three-thousand–man *Hornet* sank accordingly. In the Hollandia-Palau strike, Jocko Clark, Commander TG 58.1, newly promoted to rear admiral at the tender age of fifty, hoisted his flag in *Hornet* as Commander TG 58.1. Normally, a new flag officer would be assigned duty ashore, and Jocko was headed for the Quonset Point Naval Air Station in Rhode Island, when Admiral King changed his orders to keep him in the Pacific. Mitscher was delighted and posted Jocko to his lead carrier group.

Jocko Clark was an expert ship-handler, a fine art in itself. Essential to becoming a good ship-handler was what generations of mariners have called a "seaman's eye." This ability, acquired after many years at sea in conning a ship, involves judgment and understanding of the various forces at work on a ship—wind, sea, current, speed, eccentricities—and the confidence to deal with them. A skipper may have deficiencies in some areas, but if he can handle his ship well at sea and coming into port, he earns the respect of his crew and of others observing his ship's performance. Seamanship is the hallmark of all fine naval officers.

However, some surface ship sailors grumbled that many senior naval aviators were not particularly good ship-handlers. They necessarily spent much of their careers as pilots and squadron commanders, hence they lacked the experience as duty officers on the bridges of warships. Now, they were suddenly appointed executive officers of carriers or fleet auxiliaries and then commanding officers, without the requisite ship-handling skills. There was some truth to this. But Truman Hedding, splendid aviator, made the case for aviator ship-handlers, "We're all ship-handlers if you scratch any naval officer. Under the skin, he's a boat steerer, whether he's an aviator or not."

Aboard *Hornet*, the observant Jocko Clark thought that Miles Browning—a Naval Academy classmate—was a poor, even sloppy ship-handler, particularly in the dangerous confines of a port. Browning frequently misjudged his mooring approaches. Clark reported to Mitscher that the *Hornet* under Browning was "a jittery ship." In Majuro, a slight explosion of a carbon dioxide container on *Hornet* led to a brief panic, with two sailors falling overboard. Browning failed to muster the crew quickly or send out a rescue boat, for he hadn't even realized the men were missing. He was brought before a Board of Inquiry, which found him guilty of negligence. Mitscher recommended Browning's relief. Spruance assented. Browning was fired on May 29 and transferred to the faculty of the army's Command and General Staff College in Leavenworth, Kansas—a long way from the sea or a naval air station—where he spent the rest of the war.

As Arleigh Burke closely observed his boss, Pete Mitscher, he saw that the Admiral believed his task group commanders should be experts in handling their air groups and their surface ships. They must use their initiative to depart from standard procedure when such modifications were deemed necessary and effective. Their most critical quality, Mitscher believed, was that they were courageous and aggressive. A great commander needed to be ruthless in assessing the performance of his subordinates: those not up to the task would be replaced by someone who could deliver. Some admirals were just not capable of performing well when under great stress or responsibility. Only during battle would this be revealed. Burke believed that Mitscher thought that ensuring that subordinates fight with skill, judgment, and courage was the most important—and often most distasteful—duty of a combat commander.

The Mariana Islands plans for Operation Forager were set, though there was a momentary setback when five LSTs blew up in Pearl Harbor after an accident occurred when loading ammunition for Forager. The shortage of LSTs meant that two had to be sent up from the South Pacific to fill the requirements. Forager went ahead.

"The objective is the capture of Saipan, Tinian, and Guam in order to secure control of sea communications through the Central Pacific for the support of further attacks on the Japanese," Kelly Turner instructed in his operations order. Turner would personally lead the Northern Attack Force to hit Saipan with Howlin' Mad Smith, commanding the 2nd and 4th Marine Divisions, mounted in Hawaii and the West Coast. The genial and competent Rear Admiral Dick Conolly, carrying the III Phib Corps under Major General Roy Geiger and assembled in the Guadalcanal area, commanded the Southern Attack Force aimed at Guam. The Floating Reserve was commanded by Rear Admiral William H. "Spike" Blandy, former Chief of the Bureau of Ordnance, with the 27th Army Infantry Division still commanded by Major General Ralph Smith.

Kelly Turner led the amphibious planning for Forager. A U.S. Marine officer who served on his staff, Colonel Robert E. Hogaboom, said, "Admiral Turner had an almost unbelievable capacity for work. He drove himself without mercy, and he expected and demanded the same of those around him. I never saw him relax or take his ease." But Kelly Turner turned to alcohol for sustenance after a hard day's planning. As he put it, "When I came back from the Marshalls, I was dead tired. I stayed dead tired for the rest of the war." Nimitz was concerned but was assured by Spruance that Turner's drinking was under control.

In early June, the massive assault force began assembling in the far reaches of the Pacific, heading for the Marianas. From Majuro Lagoon on June 4, Pete Mitscher's Task Force 58 sallied forth: seventeen fleet carriers, seven fast battleships, twenty-one cruisers, and sixty-nine destroyers. At sea, trailing behind, Kelly Turner's Amphibious Force comprised 535 ships carrying 169,000 assault troops.

The landings were preceded by a series of air strikes by the carriers of Task Force 58 at enemy airfields and harbors. The four carrier task groups were under three veterans—Rear Admirals Jocko Clark (*Hornet, Yorktown, Belleau Wood, Bataan*), Monty Montgomery (*Bunker Hill, Wasp, Monterey, Cabot*), Black Jack Reeves (*Enterprise, Lexington, Princeton, San Jacinto*)—and a newcomer, Rear Admiral William Keen Harrill (*Essex, Langley, Cowpens*). Other air admirals joined the carriers for the coming battle. Vice Admiral Slew McCain, slated to take over the task force under Bill Halsey, rode as an observer in the fleet flagship *Indianapolis*.

The erudite Rear Admiral Ralph Davison, the first of the junior escort carrier group commanders to move up, was attached to *Yorktown* as a makee-learn. Kelly Turner's bombardment force included eight jeep carriers under three new rear admirals: Slats Sallada, Gerry Bogan, and Felix Stump. The fresh admirals had all skippered big carriers.

On the morning of June 14, Admiral Lee's seven fast battleships detached from Task Force 58 to conduct a shore bombardment on Saipan. However, the bombardment was a fizzle. The new battlewagons had spent so much time with carrier formations that they hadn't practiced shore bombardment. Thus they shot from long ranges with poor spotting and results. The next day, the bombardment assignment was taken over by the old battleships under Rear Admiral Oley Oldendorf, and a cruiser division under Pug Ainsworth that had much more experience in the technique. This effort silenced several coastal batteries and damaged Japanese supply lines.

The invasion was launched on the morning of June 15, with Kelly Turner supervising from the flag bridge of the amphibious command ship *Rocky Mount*. The landings went off without major hitches, but hard fighting ensued on the beaches and as the American troops moved inland. The beachhead came under fire from Japanese artillery batteries sheltered in the rugged hills.

At sea, Admiral Spruance began receiving intelligence reports of a major move of the Japanese fleet. Because of the American advance, the Japanese had moved away from Truk and based its warships mainly in the southern Philippines. A major base there was Tawitawi Island, used because of its strategic position covering the approaches to Mindanao and its proximity to the oil supplies of Borneo in the Dutch East Indies. American submarines had devastated oil shipments to Japan and more northerly naval bases.

The reorganized Japanese Mobile Fleet was headed by Vice Admiral Jisaburo Ozawa, a fifty-seven-year-old veteran carrier commander and expert tactician. He was a skilled counterpart to Pete Mitscher. By mid-May the Imperial Japanese naval headquarters recognized its fleet would have to challenge the U.S. Navy in its inexorable advance westward. Admiral Soemu Toyoda, commander in chief, designated the Western Carolines as where a decisive battle would have to be fought if the United States moved toward the Marianas.

On June 13, submarine *Redfin* off Tawitawi spotted a major force of carriers, battleships, cruisers, and destroyers heading north. *Redfin* surfaced after dark and flashed the message to Rear Admiral Ralph Christie, Commander Submarines Southwest Pacific in Brisbane. Soon Admiral Spruance off Saipan was alerted. On June 15, submarine *Flying Fish* spotted another large force exiting the San Bernardino Strait between Leyte and Samar in the eastern Philippines. Because of the Japanese penchant for splitting their naval forces, it was difficult for either Nimitz's staff in Pearl, or Spruance's on *Indianapolis*, to assess enemy intentions. But it appeared major forces were heading for the Marianas. This was backed up by two sightings of an enemy force by the submarine *Cavalla* in the Philippine Sea, the vast body of water that extends hundreds of miles east of the Philippines to the Marianas. Admiral Spruance, expecting battle, postponed the invasion of Guam.

American intelligence estimated that Admiral Ozawa might have as many as nine carriers and fifty to sixty ships, which would easily be outnumbered by the American fleet. Ozawa's key advantage was that his carriers would be travelling east and able to launch and recover planes in the winds coming from the east while continuing on course. The opposite was true for Mitscher's carriers, which had to reverse course to handle aircraft. Furthermore, Ozawa could use the Japanese air bases in the Marianas to shuttle-bomb the American fleet positioned between the U.S. carriers and the islands, while remaining out of range of U.S. aircraft.

Meanwhile, Spruance ordered Mitscher to attack the northerly islands of Iwo Jima and Chichi Jima, used as refuelling bases for aircraft coming south from Japan to attack the U.S. fleet. Mitscher, in turn, dispatched his point man, Jocko Clark's TG 58.1, and Keen Harrill's TG 58.4 for the assignment.

Jocko Clark was eager to get on with the mission and return in time for the expected big battle with the Japanese fleet. By contrast, Keen Harrill dragged his heels, complaining to Clark that heavy weather would sock in the Jimas, meanwhile the Japanese fleet was probably approaching, but his ships were low on fuel. Clark couldn't believe that Harrill would fail to carry out his orders. He was flown in a *Hornet* Avenger to Harrill's flagship *Essex* to discuss the situation. Clark and Harrill's chief of staff, Captain H. E. Regan, spent some time trying to convince Harrill of the need to block the threat of air attacks from the north. Finally, Clark exploded: "If you do not join me in this job, I will do it myself." That shook Admiral Harrill, who agreed to participate.

Possibly anticipating problems with Harrill, Mitscher's orders did not specify either Clark or Harrill as OTC. Harrill was senior to Clark and ordinarily would have assumed command, but Mitscher left them to operate together but independently. The two task groups carried out the strikes. Jocko charged in at 25 knots, shot down twenty-five planes, and sank a troop transport. He speedily returned to Mitscher's Task Force 58. But Clark had lost confidence in Harrill, who he thought was a fine officer but "had lost his zip." Mitscher concurred. On June 29, operating off Guam, Harrill was stricken with appendicitis and transferred to a hospital. Then he was sent back to the United States to a fleet air command at Alameda, California.

Aboard *Indianapolis*, Raymond Spruance anxiously awaited further intelligence on the movements of the Japanese fleet. Generally, an enormous advantage accrues to the carriers that find the other side first. On June 16, Spruance held a conference aboard Admiral Turner's flagship *Rocky Mount* to plan for the coming battle. Kelly Turner's amphibious force would remain in place off the beachhead; Ching Lee's new battleships would form a battle line if a surface fight seemed imminent; and Pete Mitscher's four carrier groups would provide the striking force. While Spruance retained overall command, he delegated tactical control of the force to Pete Mitscher, and to Lee if a surface fight should develop.

On the evening of June 17, the submarine *Cavalla* sighted part of the Japanese fleet still steaming eastward. Both sides were girding for a climatic struggle at sea. The actions in the next few days in the Philippine Sea and on Saipan would spark two of the biggest controversies of the Pacific War. The first concerned the tactics employed by Admiral Raymond Spruance. The second was a bitter argument between the U.S. Marines and U.S. Army command.

Twenty-five

MARIANAS TURKEY SHOOT

June 1944

The U.S. and Japanese main battle fleets appeared to be heading for a climactic showdown battle—a modern Jutland. In *Indianapolis*, Admiral Raymond Spruance ordered some surface elements from Turner's Expeditionary Force to join Task Force 58, thus forming up the Fifth Fleet. On the afternoon of June 17, he issued his battle plan:

"Our air will first knock out enemy carriers, then will attack enemy battleships and cruisers to slow or disable them. Battle Line will destroy enemy fleet either by fleet action if the enemy elects to fight or by sinking slowed or crippled ships if enemy retreats. Action against the enemy must be pushed vigorously by all hands to ensure complete destruction of his fleet. Destroyers running short of fuel may be returned to Saipan if necessary for refueling."

Spruance added an additional message to Admiral Mitscher in the carrier *Lexington* and Admiral Lee in battleship *Washington*:

"Desire you proceed at your discretion selecting dispositions and movements best calculated to meet the enemy under most advantageous conditions. I shall issue general directives when necessary and leave details to you and Admiral Lee."

So Spruance gave Mitscher broad but vague authority to employ Task Force 58 against the enemy. The two ultimate missions of the fleet were somewhat at variance: to seek out and sink the Japanese fleet, and to protect the amphibious force at Saipan beachhead.

*

That evening submarine *Cavalla* made a second sighting of "fifteen or more large combatant ships," with a course heading due east, making 20 knots. This led Spruance to conclude there were at least two Japanese forces at sea. Spruance and Mitscher, with the submarine sighting intelligence, took different tactical views. Spruance, who had responsibility for the Saipan beachhead, was worried that Admiral Ozawa might outflank him to the south and strike the vulnerable transports.

By contrast, Pete Mitscher wished to press on to westward, possibly engaging in a night surface action, followed by air strikes the next morning. Spruance and Mitscher were both aware of the enemy's prevailing-wind advantage; they could steam eastward while launching and recovering planes. And they could use their airfields in the Marianas as shuttle-bombing bases to hit the U.S. fleet. Additionally, Japanese search planes had a range of 500 miles, compared to Mitscher's aircraft's lesser range of 350 miles. The Japanese attack planes' range was 300 miles versus the American planes' 200-mile range.

Mitscher queried Battle Line Commander Lee: "Do you seek night engagement? It may be we can make air contact late this afternoon and attack tonight. Otherwise we should retire eastward tonight."

Pete Mitscher and Arleigh Burke expected Ching Lee to be enthusiastic. But the battleship admiral replied: "Do not, repeat, not believe we should seek night engagement. Possible advantages of radar more than offset by difficulties in communications and lack of training in fleet tactics at night."

Lee, the victor of the Battle of Guadalcanal, believed the risks of night action with a force that had no sustained night training were too great. He was probably right. Task Force 58 reversed course into the eastern night.

On the following morning, Mitscher sent out search planes to the west, but they failed to sight any enemy. An afternoon search also made no sightings, leading Spruance to believe Admiral Ozawa's forces were at least 400 miles away.

But Japanese search planes had spotted elements of the vast Fifth Fleet on June 18. Admiral Ozawa ordered an important course change, from northeast to southwest in order to maintain a 400-mile gap that would give him the range advantage over U.S. carrier planes during the night. He planned then to head for the Americans the following morning.

On the morning of June 18, all four of Mitscher's carrier groups formed up together. Mitscher deployed the three strongest groups on a north-south line, 12 miles apart: Jocko Clark's 58.1, Monty Montgomery's 58.2, and Black Jack Reeves' 58.3. This allowed any one group to conduct flight operations without interfering with another. Mitscher ordered out Ching Lee's battle line, so that it would not be a complicated last-minute maneuver, and placed it to westward on the enemy side. To the north of Lee's battleships, Mitscher stationed Keen Harrill's TG 58.4 to provide cover.

On June 18 after the deployment was complete, Admiral Spruance messaged Admiral Mitscher: "Task Force 58 must cover Saipan and our forces engage in that operation." It would turn out to be a controversial message. Spruance wished to steam westward in daylight to seek the enemy, but reversed course to the east at night to guard against a flank attack directed at the beachhead and amphibious ships. Spruance agreed with Lee that a night battle action was not desirable because tactical uncertainties would neutralize U.S. superiority. Spruance added: "But earliest possible strike on enemy carriers is necessary."

Between 2030 and midnight on June 18, Admiral Spruance received critical intelligence. Admiral Nimitz sent him a message giving him the location of an enemy force obtained by high-frequency direction-finder bearings. Ozawa had broken radio silence to contact Guam, and his transmissions were intercepted. Ozawa was about 300 miles west—southwest of the Fifth Fleet at 2030. If Spruance continued east he would not be in position to strike Ozawa at dawn; the range would be too long.

For his part, Pete Mitscher received the same intelligence. At 2325, Burke recommended to Spruance by voice radio: "Blue Jacket. This is Bald Eagle. Propose coming to course 270 degrees in order to commence treatment [of the enemy] at 0500. Advise."

Spruance and his staff aboard *Indianapolis* mulled over Mitscher's proposal well past midnight. He thought a garbled report by the submarine *Stingray* might suggest the Japanese force was closer than the direction-finder reports indicated. At 2330, he decided against a course reversal. With Admiral Togo's waiting game at Tsushima in mind, Spruance thought he could not leave Saipan unprotected. Not knowing where the Japanese were or if they had split their forces south and north, he could not take the chance of letting them slip in behind him. He decided to continue easterly during the night. It was an agonizing decision, one to be sharply criticized by the air admirals.

Spruance messaged Mitscher: "Change does not appear advisable. Believe indications given by *Stingray* more accurate than that determined by direction finder. If that is so continuation as at present seems preferable. End run by other carrier groups remains possibility and must not be overlooked. (The term "end run" was to become familiar in later battle analyses, stemming from the American football phrase to run around end, or outflank, rather than striking straight on.)

Spruance was familiar with the standard Japanese naval tactics of splitting their forces to attack from different directions, as they had in the great Battle of Midway two years earlier. And he viewed his primary mission was protecting the beachhead, troops, and shipping. But unlike Midway, Spruance had not yet pinned down the location of the enemy carriers, while the Japanese, with their superior scouting planes, had a good idea of where to find the Fifth Fleet.

Admiral Pete Mitscher and his chief of staff, Arleigh Burke, along with assistant chief of staff Truman Hedding, were stunned by Spruance's momentous decision. They believed he had placed the fast carriers on the defensive without thoroughly consulting his air admirals. The aviators thought that the old battleships under Rear Admiral Oley Oldendorf and the six escort carriers assigned to protect the beachhead were adequate. Further, the end run concern was outdated by the wide-ranging eyes of carrier and land-based search planes that could detect any secondary pincer movement and quickly attack. Burke and Hedding urged Mitscher to try to convince Spruance to follow his suggestion. Mitscher replied, "No, he's made up his mind, and we'll carry out his orders."

"If carriers are properly utilized," Jocko Clark said, "it is not possible for surface ships to make an end run around them." The airmen believed that battleship sailors like Spruance failed to appreciate the new mobility and power of the fast carrier striking force.

The dawn search at 0530 on June 19 launched from Mitscher's carriers, which were now all due west of the Marianas, failed to find the Japanese. Nor did any shore-based American patrol planes discover the enemy fleet. Spruance messaged Admiral Harry Hill off Saipan: "Get additional patrol planes as soon as you can handle them and increase night search to 700 miles." That morning, an American fighter from a carrier patrol shot down a Japanese snooper, indicating the enemy was in the area and aware of the U.S. presence.

As a perfect tropical day unfolded, nearly one hundred thousand sailors in the Fifth Fleet were ready for action. Mitscher's problem was that he could not steam quickly west toward the Japanese because he had to reverse course to launch and recover aircraft. Spruance messaged Mitscher that if the morning search planes found no enemy, they might strike targets on Guam and Rota. Hearing this, Rear Admiral Montgomery voice-messaged Mitscher, which was really intended for Spruance's ears: "I consider that maximum effort of this force should be directed toward enemy force at sea; minor strikes should not be diverted to support the Guam-Saipan area. If necessary to continue divided effort, recommend detachment of sufficient force for this purpose."

Admiral Ozawa was hoping to use Guam as a base for shuttle-bombing the American fleet, so an effort there would not actually have been a "diversion." As it was, earlier morning attacks on Guam had disrupted Ozawa's shuttle plan. It was going to be a busy day in the carriers for the young reserve fighter directors, who supervised interception of enemy planes. Lieutenant Joseph R. Eggert was the task force director in *Lexington*, as each carrier had its own director for its aircraft, coordinating with task group and task force, and each task group had a fighter director. These reserve officers played a critical role. They kept track of the intricate process of identifying enemy planes, vectoring out the proper number of fighters to intercept them, giving them orders for altitudes and positions for attack—all by voice radio.

On the morning of June 19, Admiral Ozawa deployed his force into battle formation. Three carriers—*Chitose*, *Zuiho*, and *Chiyoda*—under Admiral Sueo Obayashi led the way, line abreast. They were screened by four battleships, nine heavy cruisers, and eight destroyers. Well behind came Ozawa's own carriers *Taiho*, *Shokaku*, and *Zuikaku*, which were screened by two heavy cruisers, one light cruiser, and seven destroyers. Next to Ozawa was Admiral Takaji Joshima's carrier division—*Junyo*, *Hiyo*, and *Ryuho*—screened by a battleship, a heavy cruiser, and eight destroyers. An hour and a half before sunrise, Ozawa launched search planes. Many ran afoul of Mitscher's own search aircraft and were shot down.

This clash led Mitscher at 1019 to launch every available fighter plane in Task Force 58. He ordered the carrier decks cleared of bombers so that every fighter could get into the air as soon as possible to protect the fleet. He ordered: "Keep fighters available to repel those attacks, landing planes as necessary." The late morning was filled with dozens of dogfights as the carrier fighters, from high-altitude positions, swooped down on incoming Japanese bombers and torpedo planes escorted by fighters.

In the enemy's first massive air raid, forty-two out of sixty-nine were shot down. No enemy planes got through to the carriers, but a bomb hit the veteran battlewagon *South Dakota*, killing twenty-seven men and wounding twenty-three. The carriers *Wasp* and *Bunker Hill* and cruiser *Minneapolis* were damaged by bomb near misses but continued operating.

A second Japanese wave approached. Planes had taken off from the carrier *Taiho*, Admiral Ozawa's flagship, and one dove into the sea, in a failed attempt to explode an incoming torpedo from U.S. submarine *Albacore*, commanded by Lieutenant Commander J. W. Blanchard. The fish hit *Taiho* doing mortal damage, and she sank six hours later. At 1130, *Cavalla* spotted the big carrier *Shokaku*, and Lieutenant Commander Herman Kossler fired a spread of fish into the ship. She sank three and a half hours later, when the bomb magazine exploded.

The second attack wave was met about 60 miles west of Task Force 58 by scrambled Hellcats, led by Commander David McCampbell of *Essex*. The battle line sent up a fierce curtain of anti-aircraft fire. During the late morning and early afternoon, American carriers maneuvered violently to evade Japanese bombs and torpedoes. No carrier was hit, though some were damaged by near misses. Of the 128 Japanese planes launched in the second wave, ninety-seven failed to return to their carriers.

Still another Japanese wave approached the task force, rather half-heartedly. Seven of forty-seven were downed. Task Force 58 took a brief breather and Mitscher sent out search planes to find the Japanese carriers, but they were again unsuccessful. The fourth and last Japanese carrier raid closed on the U.S. fleet. These planes were met by the American Hellcats, which included Commander McCampbell. They shot many down, including several trying to land at the Orote airfield on Guam. Of the eighty-three attacking Japanese aircraft, seventy-three were downed or totally damaged on the ground at Orote. Ozawa's main threat was finished. Half the planes he sent into battle were gone, some by ships' flak fire, but most by U.S. Hellcats. Incoming U.S. pilots personally reported to Mitscher, who was sitting backwards in his swivel chair on his flag bridge. He had a knack of drawing valuable information from the lowliest ensign-aviators, and making prompt decisions based on this intelligence.

During the battle, Admiral Mitscher's flag communicators pulled a fast one on the Japanese. Lieutenant j.g. Charles A. Sims, a Japanese language expert, tuned in on the Japanese air coordinator who was directing enemy planes close to the U.S. fleet. Thus he was able to foresee the direction of many Japanese attacks and vector Hellcats to defend. Someone suggested shooting down this individual, who was now being referred to as "Coordinator Joe." This idea was rejected because he was supplying too much good information to the United States. When Coordinator Joe headed for home, Flag Operations Officer Jimmy Flatley suggested downing him. "No, you can't shoot that man down," Arleigh Burke ordered. "He did us too much good today!"

In the late afternoon, the Japanese mounted scattered attacks and lost even more planes, and the U.S. fleet began to add up the results. They were stunning. At a lost of only twenty-three U.S. planes shot down and six lost operationally, the Japanese casualties were about 315 planes on June 19, the cream of what was left of their carrier air force. One U.S. pilot was heard to exclaim, "Why, hell, it was just like an old-time turkey shoot down home!" It was the greatest carrier battle of the war and, because of the one-sided nature of Japanese aircraft losses, it was soon was dubbed, "The Great Marianas Turkey Shoot."

Throughout the action, Task Force 58 was moving steadily eastward because of the need to dispatch and land planes. At 1500, Admiral Spruance ordered the fleet to turn west to seek out the Japanese. Mitscher ordered a speed of 23 knots, hoping to close the enemy during the night. Admiral Lee was ordered to keep his battle line out ahead of the carrier groups.

On the carriers, pilots told their stories to air combat intelligence officers. Crews refueled and rearmed planes.

But the dawn-launched searches failed yet again to find Ozawa's carriers, turning short of the area where the Japanese admiral was refueling. So, strangely, with all the search assets at his disposal—carrier planes, flying boats, land-based, long-range four-engine army aircraft—Pete

Mitscher still had no hard evidence of the Japanese carriers' location. Inexplicably, Mitscher did not mount a nighttime search—planes with belly tanks—to find an enemy he expected to fight the next day. Historian Samuel Eliot Morison believes this was partly due to Mitscher's reluctance to risk pilots' lives in dangerous searches. In fact, he was strangely unenthusiastic about using night fighters at all.

Whatever the case, Mitscher still did not know where the Japanese main body was. Admiral Ozawa was not about to give up. He transferred his eight-rayed flag to the heavy cruiser *Haguro*, but the warship lacked equipment for instant communication with the carrier divisions. Hence, Ozawa was not apprised of the massive losses to carrier air groups. He ordered his fleet to refuel on June 20 and proceed with the plan to attack the U.S. forces at Saipan. He was also misled by the vastly exaggerated accounts of damage done reported by Japanese pilots. Ozawa's lack of information and communications left his ships in a certain amount of disarray. But, again inexplicably, Mitscher failed to send out a large search effort, which would probably have found the Japanese milling around their refueling rendezvous.

Ozawa transferred his flag to the big carrier *Zuikaku* at 1300 on June 20, and he learned the full extent of Japanese losses. The loss of more than three hundred planes did not deter him, though he delayed his scheduled strikes until the next day. Finally, at about 1540 an *Enterprise* Avenger pilot, Lieutenant Robert S. Nelson, sighted the Japanese force, the first since the action began.

But Nelson's sighting message was garbled when it arrived on Mitscher's bridge at 1542. Mitscher had to make a fast decision; time was running out and the sun would go down by 1900. Mitscher had only three task groups with him.

Much to his disgust, Mitscher had to leave Keen Harrill's group behind near Saipan to refuel, because Harrill insisted his destroyers were low on oil. Mitscher believed Harrill was dragging his heels again. Jocko Clark fueled his destroyers of TG 58.1 from the carriers and notified Mitscher: "Would greatly appreciate remaining with you. We have plenty of fuel." Mitscher replied: "You will remain with us all right until the battle is over."

Mitscher informed Spruance that he intended to mount an all-out strike, though recovery would have to take place after dark. It was a daring measure: Mitscher expected losses but believed it might be the only chance to strike the Japanese fleet.

Lieutenant Nelson sent a clarifying message, indicating the Japanese fleet was split in three groups, heading west and apparently fueling from oilers. Mitscher was well aware of the risks he ran in sending off aviators to attack an enemy and return after dark. Few were trained in night carrier landings.

But Pete Mitscher gave the fateful command, "Man aircraft!" and said, "Give 'em hell boys. Wish I were with you."

At 1621, Mitscher ordered Task Force 58 to turn into the wind and launch planes. Full deckloads of Hellcat fighters and Helldiver dive-bombers and Avenger torpedo planes took off from six big carriers—*Lexington, Yorktown, Hornet, Enterprise, Wasp, Bunker Hill*—and five light carriers—*San Jacinto, Belleau Wood, Cabot, Monterey, Bataan*. All Hellcats and Helldivers carried extra belly tanks of precious fuel.

The incoming American planes had to hit and run in a half hour before tropical sunset, with no time for coordinated attacks. They found the enemy oilers first and mortally damaged *Genyo* and *Seiyo Maru*. Torpedo planes from *Belleau Wood*, led by Lieutenant George B. Brown and Lieutenant Warren R. Ormark (JG), attacked the carrier *Hiyo* and hit the flattop, which, after additional internal explosions, went under. Other carrier planes badly damaged the flagship carrier *Zuikaku* with bombs and strafing fire, but failed to sink the veteran warship. The pilots also damaged carrier *Chiyoda*. The American planes called it a day and headed back to their carriers. The Japanese had lost all but thirty-five planes out of the 430, which had been aboard the carriers early on June 19.

Now came the hard part. All those American planes had to fly back to their carriers as night descended over the Philippine Sea, and a black night it was. Few aviators were trained in night-flying techniques over open water, let alone carrier deck landings. Because of the need to reach enemy carriers before sunset, most pilots had flown at top speed, burning up gasoline. All the U.S. returning planes were low on fuel. Their planes had battle damage. The pilots were exhausted after long flights and fighting. The total darkness was disorienting. For two hours, the two hundred surviving pilots struggled against exhaustion and tension to make it back.

Admiral Mitscher ordered his carrier groups to open out, with 15 miles between them, for added maneuvering room in the night recovery.

At 2045, the first returning planes reached the carrier force, which had to turn away from the west to head into the wind.

Pete Mitscher then made one of the decisions most appreciated by aviators in the entire war. Scorning the blackout in the fleet to protect against enemy submarines and airborne snoopers, Mitscher instructed Burke aboard the flag bridge of *Lexington*: "Turn on the lights."

The fleet lit up. Actually, Jocko Clark in his flagship *Hornet* had anticipated Mitscher's decision, turning on his large searchlight and informing Mitscher. The outlying warships in the screen flicked on their red and green running lights and red masthead lights. They fired star shells into the black night to illuminate the scene. Carriers lit up their decks with glow lights. Each carrier's signal bridge sent a 24-inch (in diameter) searchlight straight up into the pitch-black sky to mark its position for exhausted aviators. One pilot said the scene resembled a "Hollywood premiere, Chinese New Year, and the Fourth of July all rolled into one."

As planes ran out of gas, they splashed in the sea, hoping to be near a destroyer. Others crash-landed on carrier decks. When Mitscher saw a *Hornet* plane land on *Lexington*'s flight deck, he immediately sent a message to incoming aircraft: "All planes from Commander Task Force 58. Land on any base you see."

Incoming planes chose the first carrier available, as their tanks ran dry. Almost half the aircraft landed on the wrong carrier. One flight deck recovered planes from eight other flattops. All in all, it was a hectic two hours. The tin cans performed mightily in picking up crews from the sea. Mitscher summed up the aircraft and aviator losses: twenty planes missing and presumably shot down in combat; eighty planes destroyed in deck crashes or ditching in the sea. That night and the next day, many aviators were rescued from their life rafts. The total loss in personnel was sixteen pilots and thirty-three crewmen. It was a remarkable performance by carrier deck crews and rescue ships.

Pete Mitscher forever endeared himself to his pilots. TURN ON THE LIGHTS! They were not expendable.

To a news correspondent on *Lexington*, Mitscher said, quietly yet firmly, "The way we run the navy we spend millions of dollars designing and building a big carrier. We put three thousand men aboard and a big screen of ships and then send her seven thousand miles from home. Then we launch planes. The whole striking force of this carrier, all we spent in preparation and operation up to this point, finally is spearheaded in a hundred young pilots. Each of these boys is captain of his own ship. What he thinks, his confidence in what he is doing, how hard he presses home the attack, is exactly how effective we are. We got the best goddamned men in the world."

The next morning Spruance and Mitscher gave chase to the fleeing Admiral Ozawa, though not with any real hope of success, since the fleets were more than 300 miles apart. Ozawa had too much of a lead, and the destroyers of Task Force 58 did not have enough fuel to maintain high speed. Mitscher ordered a slower speed of 16 knots to search for American aviators and enemy stragglers. During the day, Ozawa opened the distance beyond the effective range of U.S. dive-bombers. Ozawa had fought a fine tactical battle, striking at the U.S. carriers while keeping his fleet out of their range. He kept his inferior force together and handled the refueling well. But he could not make up for the inexperience of his pilots, who went down like wounded birds.

At 2030 June 21, Spruance ordered the fleet to return to Saipan, leaving some ships to search for downed fliers. This paid off: floatplanes from cruisers Indianapolis, San Francisco, and Minneapolis picked up nine aviators. The Catalina and Mariner patrol boats from Saipan covering wide sectors plucked another fifty-nine aviators from the hostile waters of the Philippine Sea.

On Task Force 58's way back to Eniwetok for replenishment and rest, Jocko Clark requested that his TG 58.1 strike on Iwo and Chichi Jima. Mitscher dubbed it "Operation Jocko," and it was a success, destroying nearly seventy Japanese planes in the air and on the ground, and adding another feather in Jocko's Cherokee headgear. His aviators printed cards announcing membership in the "Jocko Jima Development Corporation," offering locations in the various Jimas, "only 500 miles from downtown Tokyo."

The Great Marianas Turkey Shoot left the U.S. fighting admirals with mixed feelings. The Japanese fleet had got away. There was a widespread feeling among the air admirals—Mitscher, Montgomery, Reeves, Sherman, Towers—of a rare opportunity to destroy the Japanese fleet was muffed. Jocko Clark said, "It was the chance of a century missed." Some compared it to Jutland, with Jellicoe allowing the German fleet to slip away. In his report, Pete Mitscher declared, "The enemy escaped. He had been badly hurt by one aggressive carrier strike, at the one time he was within range. His fleet was not sunk." Ted Sherman said, "There were no end runs in aerial warfare." Monty Montgomery wrote, "Results of the action were extremely disappointing to all hands, in that important units of the enemy fleet, which came out in the open for the first time in over a year and made several air attacks on our superior force, were able to escape without our coming to grips with them."

In Pearl Harbor, Vice Admiral Jack Towers complained the failure to hit the Japanese fleet was the fault of leaving a non-aviator [Spruance] in charge. The fast carrier force should have not been tied down to supporting an amphibious operation. Yet again, Towers angered Admiral Nimitz and surface ship admirals with his blanket indictment of non-aviators. He wanted Spruance fired, naturally, seeing himself as Spruance's replacement. Towers was ignored by Nimitz who supported Spruance's actions, as did Kelly Turner, Ching Lee, and Soc McMorris. They maintained that while Mitscher was responsible only for his Task Force 58, Raymond Spruance had responsibility for the overall success of the Marianas invasion, Operation Forager. The marines were still fighting; the Guam and Tinian forces had yet to be landed. Spruance could not take the chance that Ozawa's force was not simply one arm of the Japanese Mobile Fleet.

None of the air admirals adequately answered an obvious question: Why were the American air searches from land and sea so unsuccessful? Admiral Ozawa generally knew where the American fleet was. Spruance had no hard intelligence on the Japanese whereabouts. Air search intelligence was slow in reaching Spruance. How could he then depend on the carrier planes to find an elusive enemy?

Admiral King supported Spruance's decision. "As the primary mission of the American forces in the area was to capture the Marianas, the Saipan amphibious actions had to be protected from enemy interference at all costs. Spruance was rightly guided by this obligation." When he next met Raymond Spruance on Saipan, King said, "Spruance, you did a damn fine job there. No matter what other people tell you, your decision was correct."

Pete Mitscher had the chance to criticize Raymond Spruance's actions. Arleigh Burke drafted the after-action report and insisted that Mitscher read the last two pages, which were critical of Spruance's decision. Mitscher read the summary.

"Do you know Admiral Spruance very well?" he asked his chief of staff.

"Yes, sir."

"What do you think of him?"

"I think he's a mighty good man, but he made a mistake this time, Admiral. He made a big mistake. This is true."

"Yes, it's all true," Mitscher said. "But what good is it going to do to send in a report like this?"

"It tells the truth."

"You don't think the truth does more harm than good sometimes?"

"No, sir."

"Well, it does."

Mitscher paused and in his low, gentle voice said, "You and I have been in many battles, and we know there are always some mistakes. This time we were right because the enemy did what we expected him to do. Admiral Spruance could have been right. He's one of the finest officers I know of. It was his job to protect the landing force. Don't you think you ought to take it back and rewrite those last two pages?"

"No, sir," Burke replied. "But I will."

The criticism was deleted.

As for Spruance himself, he refused to get into a public conflict over his actions. Years later, he told a visitor, "I'm not a gambler. In an operation as important as the Marianas, you watch out for end runs. My mission was to protect the amphibious landing on Saipan. The enemy knew where I was, and I did not know where it was. The Saipan landings were at a critical stage. So I didn't let Mitscher go west. We accomplished what we set out to do. It was disappointing that we did not do more. Midway was much more satisfying."

There was another serious fallout in Operation Forager, one that reverberated in the highest reaches of the Pentagon. In the drive from the Saipan beachhead to the north of the island, Lieutenant General Howlin' Mad Smith had placed two marine divisions, the 2nd and the 4th, abreast on the flanks with the U.S. Army's 27th Infantry Division in the center of the line. On June 23, the 27th Army Division regiments, in the eyes of H. M. Smith, did not keep up with the marines' flanking divisions, leaving them in a dangerous position. The 27th Division, led by Major General Ralph Smith, failed to improve its position the next day. Howlin' Mad Smith was highly displeased. He had watched the 27th Division on Makin and Eniwetok and believed it to be badly led. It was a former New York National Guard unit, and some of the high officer appointments smacked of state politics, though Ralph Smith himself was highly regarded in the army.

Holland Smith decided to relieve Ralph Smith and replace him with army Major General Sanderford Jarman, who was designated to become island commander. Five other army divisional commanders had been relieved in the Pacific, though none by a marine general. Smith checked with Kelly Turner aboard *Rocky Mount* who concurred, as did Admiral Spruance on *Indianapolis*. Howlin' Mad Smith relieved Ralph Smith on the evening of June 24. In part, the firing was due to their different tactical doctrines: the marines believed in charging ahead and mopping up later; the army moved more slowly, first clearing the way ahead with artillery fire. The abrupt action by General Smith caused a firestorm at army headquarters in Hawaii and raised a rumpus in sections of the American press, even though Nimitz wished to keep it quiet.

Lieutenant General Robert C. Richardson, head of army forces in the Central Pacific who had wanted to be in operational command in the Marianas, ordered an army inquiry. Then he made an unannounced—and uninvited—visit to Saipan on July 12 to award medals to soldiers after the island was secured. Richardson upbraided Holland Smith, saying, according to Smith: "You had no right to relieve Ralph Smith. The 27th is one of the best-trained divisions in the Pacific. I trained it myself. I want you to know you can't push the army around the way you've been doing. We've had more experience in handling troops than you have, and yet you dare removed one of my generals. You marines are nothing but a bunch of beach runners anyway. What do you know about land warfare?"

General Richardson planned to complain to Kelly Turner. Carl Moore visited Kelly Turner on his flagship and advised him to remain cool. Turner's mood was particularly testy, which Moore thought was due to a hangover. Moore and his boss, Raymond Spruance, were aware that Kelly Turner was a heavy drinker after working hours, but also knew he was always fresh in the morning for another sixteen-hour day. In fact, when apprised of Kelly Turner's drinking habits, Nimitz was fond of revising President Lincoln's remarks on General Grant: "Let me know what brand of whiskey Kelly's drinking to so I can feed it to some of my other admirals."

Captain Moore warned Admiral Turner about admonishing General Richardson: "For goodness sake, Kelly, this seems to me an awful thing to do. It isn't going to do a bit of good for the war or the force for you to raise that kind of an issue."

"I'm going to do it anyhow," Turner replied.

When Richardson came aboard, Turner let Richardson have it with a blast of invective, reminding the general about protocol and the chain of command—in front of an embarrassed Carl Moore. Richardson turned white and replied that he was not accountable to any officer in the Marianas. Richardson went to Spruance, who tried to downplay the situation. "That's just Kelly Turner's way." Turner and Howlin' Mad Smith sent a letter of complaint to Nimitz, who was anxious to keep the peace in the services.

The Army Board of Inquiry headed by General Simon Boliver Buckner concluded, as expected, that Ralph Smith's relief was unjustified. Most of the senior army officers believed that Howlin' Mad Smith's behavior was intemperate and untimely. Army Brigadier General Roy Blount, a board member, later called Smith: "A stupid egomaniac. A perfect ass if ever one lived."

The "Smith versus Smith" affair left a lot of bad blood. Many army generals recommended that army troops never again be commanded by Lieutenant General Howlin' Mad Smith, or by any marine general. Howlin' Mad Smith was elevated to a new post, Commander, Fleet Marine Force Pacific, which put him in administrative charge of all aarines in the Pacific, but gave him no operational command in the invasions to come.

Howlin' Mad kept the controversy alive in his memoirs, *Coral and Brass*, which severely criticized Ralph Smith, Robert Richardson, Chester Nimitz, Kelly Turner, Raymond Spruance, Harry Hill, and just about everyone who didn't agree with him. He called Tarawa a tragedy that should have been avoided, neglecting to mention he had signed off on the plans. For his part, Ralph Smith behaved honorably and was reassigned as a valuable military attaché in Paris to the provisional French government.

Reporters asked Kenneth McArdle, in civilian life a first-rate newspaperman who was a Pacific Fleet public relations officer, about Ralph

Smith's relief. He recommended to Soc McMorris that the news be immediately released since Ralph Smith was back in Hawaii and the story was circulating. McMorris said no. Nimitz backed him up because he thought the news might further damage Ralph Smith's career. Nimitz preferred the news to come from Washington. In the running controversy, some U.S. publications chose sides: the Luce magazine tended to back the marines and Howlin' Mad Smith. The Hearst newspaper solidly supported the army and General MacArthur, who Hearst wanted to be supreme commander in the Pacific. But the publicity flap did neither the marines nor the navy any good.

The Marianas campaign drew to a close with the capture of Saipan, Tinian, and Guam. At the end of the Saipan battle, Vice Admiral Chuichi Nagumo, who led the carriers against Pearl Harbor and Midway and was commander of the Central Fleet, died by his own hand.

Kelly Turner had a brief, explosive argument with Harry Hill and the marines over the choice of landing beaches on Tinian. Hill, who was commanding the landing forces, preferred the northern beaches (White Beach Area) where the troops could be supported by artillery from nearby Saipan. Turner thought the White Beach Areas were too narrow, and insisted on beaches well to the south, which were heavily defended. Hill recalled that Turner was in a terrible mood. He was wearing a brace to support a painful back problem but wouldn't talk about it. Hill hoped Turner would listen carefully to his argument for the White Beach Area and was surprised when he "got literally blasted out of the cabin."

Howlin' Mad Smith, too, favored the northern White Beach Area and argued with Turner. "You are not going to the White beaches," Turner declared. "I won't land you there."

Smith replied, "Oh yes you will. You'll land me any goddamned place I tell you to." A serious rupture threatened. Smith thought that, as usual, Kelly Turner was acting like a general.

Harry Hill reluctantly took the matter to Admiral Spruance, who favored the White Beach concept and decided to poll his commanders: Marine Generals H. M. Smith, Harry Schmidt, Thomas Watson, and Admirals Hill and Turner, all of whom were sat around his conference table. Turner was the last to speak; the others favored the White Beach Areas. Spruance hated to overrule his veteran phib commander. But Turner agreed on the northern beaches and the crisis was averted. Harry

Hill landed the 2nd and 4th Marine Divisions, which rolled up Tinian in a week. Despite the temporary acrimony, Harry Hill never lost his admiration for Kelly Turner. "He had a comprehensive grasp of every detail and a ready solution for every problem that develops."

During fire support duty, Rear Admiral Theodore D. Ruddock, a battleship division commander aboard *Maryland*, was wounded when a Japanese torpedo plane hit the old battlewagon.

As a sidelight to Raymond Spruance's understated command style, he was a passenger in the destroyer *Philip* riding with H. M. Smith and other brass to a flag raising on Tinian. The officer of the deck was a young lieutenant named Benjamin C. Bradlee, who would become the storied editor of the *Washington Post*. The commanding officer of *Philip* told Bradlee simply to take the ship to Tinian, while he himself looked after his VIPs.

Impressed with having a four-star admiral aboard, Bradlee ordered the tin can to steam at 30 knots "for a real destroyer spin." En route, the quartermaster suddenly announced: "Attention on the bridge. The Admiral is present." Bradlee saluted Spruance and asked the admiral if there was anything he would like to see. Spruance smiled and shook the lieutenant's hand and said he would just like to look around. Spruance picked up the file of all navy (ALNAV) messages from the commander to the fleet and thumbed through it, stopping at the one he appeared to be looking for. Spruance left the file open at the page. Then he left. Bradlee hastily rushed to see what the message was. It was from the Commander Fifth Fleet that no ship should steam faster than 15 knots, unless ordered otherwise, to conserve fuel. A chastened Bradlee checked with the captain and knot by knot reduced speed to the standard 15 knots to enter Tinian harbor.

The big island of Guam, a prewar American possession, proved a tougher nut. Rear Admiral Dick Conolly, who had an ambivalent relationship with Kelly Turner, led the Guam attack force. Turner admired Conolly's abilities and fighting spirit. But some officers believed Turner regarded Conolly as a possible amphibious force competitor. As Conolly waited and stewed over his post-Kwajalein assignment, Turner told him, "I find you operate independently very well, and I don't want you with me. You and I won't get along. But I'd like to have you do these independent operations, and I'm thinking of asking them to give you the Guam operation."

"I'm delighted to operate independently," Conolly said. "I want the [Guam] job."

"All right," Turner said, "You can have it."

When Vice Admiral Kelly Turner told Conolly he needed a bombardment expert to seek out targets on Guam without harming the local Chamorro population, Conolly replied, "I have the fellow, Kelly. His name is Conolly." In his flagship *Appalachian*, Conolly had under his command battleship-cruiser bombardment units led by Rear Admiral Pug Ainsworth in *Honolulu* and was assisted by Rear Admirals George L. Weyler in *New Mexico*, Turner Joy in *Wichita*, and Bob Hayler in *Montpelier*. They pounded Guam for thirteen days, a new record for sustained invasion bombardment. "Close-In" Conolly measured up to his nickname. "Turner wasn't easy to work with," Conolly reflected. "But after you got to know him, I admired his professional competence, his high intelligence, his drive to get things done, his determination to push through regardless of anything."

An underwater demolition team (UDT) destroyed beach obstacles and left a sign reading: "Welcome marines!" The troops were under the command of Major General Roy Geiger, who was told by Conolly, "My aim is to get the troops ashore standing up. You tell me what you want done to accomplish this and we'll do it."

By the middle of August, the Marianas were secured and Guam was prepared for use as a forward U.S. submarine base, while Saipan and Tinian were turned into airfields for B-29 bombers able to reach Japan. Some five thousand American lives were lost in the campaign, while taking more than sixty thousand Japanese personnel. The Japanese had lost most of their carrier pilots and, while flattops remained afloat, they were impotent vessels. The United States breached the inner Japanese defense line. This resulted in the fall of the Tojo government in Tokyo, which began the war at Pearl Harbor. But the Marianas showed that the Japanese fighting men were still formidable and that future victories would be costly indeed.

Twenty-six
THE INVASION OF FRANCE

January–August, 1944

The invasion of France, one of the most critical operations of the war, was a long time in planning. From America's entry into the conflict, U.S. strategists believed that a massive invasion of the continent was necessary to force Germany to surrender. For over two years, U.S. and U.K. political and military leaders wrangled over when and where the invasion should take place.

The United States insisted on a major cross-Channel drive, heading east to the heart of Germany. The British, who had lost approximately a million men in World War I with another two million wounded, sought to delay such a massive and presumably bloody undertaking as they searched for a less deadly way to attack the Nazi heartland. They preferred to whittle down German strength by bombing, blockade, raids, and peripheral attacks. After arguments and delays—and two years of detouring through North Africa and Italy—the Allies agreed on a cross-Channel landing. In late 1943, General Eisenhower was selected to become Supreme Commander, Allied Expeditionary Force, because it was contemplated that the United States would eventually supply the bulk of the combat troops.

As planning progressed, Ike's three chief deputies were chosen: Field Marshal Bernard Montgomery, land forces; Air Chief Marshal Trafford Leigh-Mallory, air forces; and Admiral Sir Bertram Ramsay, naval forces. "Overlord" was the code name given to the overall operation, "Neptune" to the naval side. Under the utmost secrecy, the beaches of Normandy were selected as the landing sites. One of the toughest logistics nuts to crack was getting enough LSTs committed to the invasion fleet from the Mediterranean and new construction in U.S. shipyards.

"The destinies of two great empires," Winston Churchill commented, "seem to be tied up in some goddamned things called LSTs."

U.S. Rear Admiral Alan Kirk, who had led an amphibious assault group in Sicily, was picked to head the Western Naval Task Force in Overlord. Though Alan Kirk seemed a natural choice, over the weeks Admiral Harold Stark in London developed the impression that Kirk did not like the British, particularly Admiral Ramsay, his naval superior. Stark communicated this apprehension to Admiral King in Washington, who thought Stark was implying that Kirk should be replaced. King told his deputy, Admiral Dick Edwards: "This is no time to change him."

So King left Kirk in place and hoped for the best. Although Alan Kirk was actually a natural diplomat, he was placed in an awkward position. A two-star flag officer, he set up shop in London near four-star Admiral Stark, Commander U.S. Naval Forces Europe. But Ernie King kept Stark outside the immediate chain of command for Overlord. Kirk had the right to report directly to King on Overlord matters. Kirk's status was not helped when he realized that Admiral Ramsay had conceived the role of the American navy as decidedly secondary in the Normandy landings. Naturally, Kirk expected the U.S. Navy and troops to play an equal role, as they did in Sicily.

Admiral Kirk noted that the British and American navies had quite different ways of approaching operational planning. Admiral Ramsay, for instance, devised an operation order some eleven hundred pages in length, vastly detailed. Kirk pointed out that U.S. senior commanders issued broad directives to subordinates, who were encouraged to work out the details. "Our greatest asset," Kirk said, "was the resourcefulness of the American sailor." In this, the American naval style was similar to the German army's vaunted *auftragstaktik*, which loosely means "mission-type orders." This embodies the principle that commanders tell subordinates what to do and when to do it, but the subordinates are left to work out how to do it. This was much the same way that Admiral Spruance operated in the Pacific.

The Americans were upset and confused by the detailed plans drawn up by Admiral Ramsay's staff at Norfolk House in St. James Square, London. Kirk's staff officers would at times make suggestions to the effect that "we could do it better this way or that way," Kirk said. "These were never accepted by Admiral Ramsay's staff. In fact, we got some rather tough little comments back, directed at me for allowing these younger officers to speak out against the voice of the commander in chief. It got to be a little bit touchy, a little bit awkward."

Admiral Kirk was disappointed that the British foresaw Operation Neptune as a set piece. "In other words," he said, "no initiative was possible. It was like a fireworks display. You set off a little wick at a certain point and certain things began to burn, lights go off, and what not, a somewhat formalized affair."

Furthermore, Bertram Ramsay chose to exercise naval command of the invasion from a base near Southampton on the English Channel and expected Alan Kirk to do likewise. But Kirk was determined to command his Western Naval Task Force from the bridge of a flagship, *Augusta*, off the beaches.

With Admiral Kirk in *Augusta* would be Lieutenant General Omar Bradley commanding the U.S. First Army. Rear Admiral Don Moon was assigned to lead the landing force for Utah Beach in the attack transport *Bayfield*, with a fire support group of cruisers, battleship *Nevada*, and destroyers under Rear Admiral Morton Deyo in cruiser *Tuscaloosa*.

The Omaha Beach force to the east was headed by Rear Admiral Jimmy Hall in amphibious force flagship *Ancon*, with a bombardment group under Rear Admiral Carleton F. Bryant in battleship *Texas*. The Utah Beach force would land the 4th Infantry Division and elements of Major General Lightning Joe Collins' VII Corps. Behind the Utah beaches, the U.S. 82nd and 101st Airborne Divisions would drop during the night to secure the rear. At Omaha, elements of the U.S. 1st Infantry Division under Major General Clarence R. Huebner, and units of the 29th Infantry Division, would comprise the assault force.

The outspoken Admiral Jimmy Hall, shortly before the invasion, complained to the visiting Vice Admiral Savvy Cooke—Admiral King's right-hand man—that he needed more destroyers for the initial bombardment. "It's a crime to send me on the biggest amphibious attack in history with such inadequate gunfire support."

"Hall, you've no right to talk that way," Cooke replied.

"Who has a better right to talk that way?" Hall snapped. "If you're threatening to get me detached from my command, I know you could do it. But I don't think you would do that. I don't think you have the right to tell me that I have no right to talk that way. All I'm asking you to do is detach a couple squadrons of destroyers from some convoy, give me a chance to train them in gunfire support for the army."

Hall got the destroyers. "Thank God I did," he said.

For the landings east of Omaha at beaches Gold, Juno, and Sword, five British and Canadian divisions were earmarked. The British 6th Airborne Division would drop behind Sword Beach to secure the eastern flank of the whole Normandy beachhead.

Cooperation of the air forces with the invasion groups was better than that in the Mediterranean. But it was still a matter of bargaining with the U.S. Air Force and the Royal Air Force, rather than coming under a joint command—as was the case in the Pacific. Admiral Hall, for one, was disappointed in the air forces' concept and conduct of supporting troops ashore.

The invasion plan, for U.S. admirals, differed significantly from those in the Pacific. There, the distances were vast, often the invasion fleet sailed more than a thousand miles. At Normandy, though, distances were much shorter and logistics, while enormously complex, were easier to handle. The Pacific islands, with the exception of the Solomons, were isolated and once the attack started, no enemy reinforcements arrived. The Japanese-held Pacific islands could be pounded for days and hours by naval bombardment and air strikes, since surprise was less essential and the defenders had little room for maneuver.

At Normandy, pre-invasion bombardments had to be limited to retain surprise and keep mobile German reinforcements from being deployed against the incoming troops. In the Pacific, invasion forces usually had to suffer enemy air attacks through part of the operation. In the Mediterranean, German airpower was a continuing threat. But at Normandy, Allied control of the air was near absolute. Tides were higher in the English Channel and posed a knotty problem of when to land: at low tide to avoid beach obstacles and let the landing ships clear off more easily, or high tide to debark soldiers closer to beach objectives? The weather was generally much rougher for landing craft in European landings than in the Pacific.

At Normandy, it was necessary to construct artificial harbors to protect incoming shipping, known by the code word "Mulberry." These were buttressed by sunken-ship breakwaters known as Gooseberries. Winston Churchill was keen on the artificial harbors and piqued the interest of President Roosevelt in the concept. But U.S. Navy salvage and other experts, like Admiral Hall, thought they were an expensive waste, predicting that most would be destroyed in the first storm, which is what happened in late June. "It was the greatest waste of manpower and steel and equipment that I had seen planned for any operation in World War II," Hall said. Because of the enormous amount of men and materiel to be funnelled through the bridgeheads to take on the German army, the engineering problems associated with Overlord invasion over the weeks were tremendous.

General Eisenhower set the target date for June 5. Before that, troops began boarding the five-thousand–craft armada in secrecy. Allied intelligence deception efforts had been successful: the German high command expected the invaders to land in Pas de Calais across Dover Strait, the shortest sea route. However, the weather closed in and Eisenhower was forced to set back D-day by twenty-four hours. But that was it: any further delay would have to delay the operation for two weeks because of weather and tides. Ike pondered all the options. At 0415 on June 5, he made the fateful decision.

"O.K. We'll go."

The huge invasion fleet departed from a dozen English, Welsh, and Northern Ireland ports and assembled off the Isle of Wight. Then in convoys, the fleet moved across the choppy English Channel through the night, with the young amphibious skippers doing an amazing job of navigation and station keeping under arduous conditions—maneuvering through high winds, choppy seas, and soupy fog. German electrical, contact, and magnetic mines were a constant danger, and the U.S. minesweeper *Osprey* and U.S. destroyer *Corry* were sunk by them offshore.

At 0550 on June 6, the navy opened up a heavy bombardment against the landing beaches and fortifications. At 0630, U.S. troops began storming ashore at Utah and Omaha Beaches. At Utah Beach, twenty-three thousand soldiers landed during the day with light losses. But 10 miles east at Omaha, the story was dramatically different. Steep bluffs 150 feet high just behind the beach created difficult obstacles. Underwater obstacles at the beaches hampered landing craft and a tough German division, undetected by Allied intelligence, was defending the area with well-placed artillery fire.

The scene along the beach was one of near chaos, as troops struggled across the beach to seek the safety of the seawall. Many junior officers were killed and units left leaderless. At one point, army senior officers aboard Admiral Hall's flagship *Ancon* worried that the outcome could be in doubt. But Jimmy Hall reminded the generals that the early stages of an amphibious operation usually looked hopelessly confused, and that beach masters and army officers ashore usually straightened things out. Still, one young naval officer commanding an LCI said that enemy fire was such on the beach, "It seems a miracle this beach was ever taken."

The battleship *Arkansas* and U.S. destroyers provided call fire to knock out German emplacements throughout D-day. They also hit German panzer tanks moving up to assist the beach defenders. Field Marshal Gerd Von Rundstedt attributed part of the German defeat along the Normandy coast to "the power of Allied naval guns, which reached deep inland . . . making it impossible the bringing up the reserves needed to hurl the Allied invasion forces into the Channel."

The 1st and 29th Divisions managed to get 34,000 men ashore at the cost of 2,400 casualties. Major General Huebner established his 1st Division headquarters at 1900, followed by Major General Leonard T. Gerow setting up V Corps command post. Gerow's first message to General Bradley that first evening was, "Thank God for the United States Navy!"

Farther east, the British and Canadian troops had an easier time because of the lack of bluffs and determined resistance, and military units reached objectives several miles inland. Thus the Overlord foothold was established on the shores of France, in some places precariously, and they were there to stay.

Offshore in flagship *Augusta*, General Bradley and Admiral Kirk watched developments with deep concern. Kirk ordered bombardment ships to keep up fire support for the troops throughout the day. At Utah, battleship *Nevada* and flagship *Tuscaloosa* maintained a high rate of fire with 14-, 8-, and 5-inch guns that ranged far inland in support of the paratroopers. Major General Matthew Ridgway, commander of the 82nd Airborne Division, thanked the gunners of *Nevada* personally for knocking out German positions, which threatened his troops. Admiral Mort Deyo said, "Never before has it been attempted to silence with naval gunfire so extensive and elaborate a system of coast defenses as found here." At Utah, Admiral Moon reported, "The initial action has been won. Next phase will be a race between the buildup of the Allied forces and movement by the enemy reserves."

German mines proved to be the most dangerous weapon against U.S. warships. In addition to destroyer *Corry* and minesweeper *Osprey*, mines sank destroyer *Glennon*, destroyer escort *Rich*, minesweeper *Tide*, and transport *Susan B. Anthony*. A German plane in a night attack sent a glide bomb into destroyer *Meredith*, breaking her back. And in night raids German PT boats, called E-boats, torpedoed and sank two LSTs.

Eventually, the invasion beaches merged into a single broad foothold and moved forward, while the massive resupply effort continued night and day with hundreds of thousands of Allied troops now in position to forge ahead. For instance, at the American beaches by June 18, nearly 315,000 troops and 41,000 vehicles landed. About the same amount of men and vehicles landed at the three British and Canadian beaches. By now it was clear that the German troops could not dislodge the two Allied armies, and it was only a matter of time before General Eisenhower's forces would break out into the open country and race for Paris.

To support the Overlord operation, the Allied planners finally decided on an invasion of Southern France to link up with the major assault in Northern France. For months, however, Winston Churchill opposed the operation, first called Anvil. He believed that troops earmarked for Anvil would necessarily be taken from the Italian campaign. Churchill still harbored his fixation of hitting Europe in its "soft underbelly," through the Balkans to Vienna, though what was soft about the mountainous terrain and tough German defenders he never explained. After months of haggling, President Roosevelt supported by Josef Stalin, convinced Churchill at the eleventh hour that Anvil was a logical concomitant of Overlord. The code name was changed to "Dragoon" because some intelligence officers thought that "Anvil" had been compromised. The perhaps apocryphal story is that Churchill picked the new name because he had been dragooned into accepting the Southern France operation.

The Dragoon force rapidly took shape. The major landing forces would be the U.S. Seventh Army under Lieutenant General Alexander Patch with the U.S. 3rd, 36th, and 45th Infantry Divisions from Italy, and the French II Corps headed by General Jean de Lattre de Tassigny.

As usual, command relationships were tricky. The Allied Supreme Commander in the Mediterranean was British General Sir Henry "Jumbo" Wilson. The Allied Naval Commander in the Mediterranean was Admiral Sir John Cunningham, and under him came U.S. Vice Admiral Kent Hewitt, Commander of the Eighth Fleet. Their relationship was not always comfortable. The Royal Navy was used to being supreme in the inland sea and did not relish being upstaged by the U.S. naval upstarts.

Kent Hewitt would command the Dragoon show aboard his flagship *Catoctin*. Riding as an observer was the new Secretary of the Navy James Forrestal. Hewitt was assigned three attack force commanders, who would each land an army division in the initial invasion. Admiral Hewitt, during the planning stage, managed to convince his army counterparts that daylight landings would be more effective when conducted after a shore bombardment.

On the western flank, Force Alpha was commanded by Rear Admiral Frank J. Lowry, who led the amphibious forces landing at Anzio. A gunfire group, under Rear Admiral J. M. Mansfield of the Royal Navy, led British cruisers and a battleship supported it. In the center, Force Delta was headed by Rear Admiral Bertram Rodgers, who was skipper of *Salt Lake City* at the Battle of the Komandorski Islands in the Aleutians. A bombardment group was led by Rear Admiral C. F. Bryant in the battleship *Texas* and backed up Rodgers, in flagship *Biscayne*. Rear Admiral Don Moon, who recently commanded the amphibious assault at Utah Beach in Overlord, led the eastern flank, Force Camel. A heavy gunfire unit was headed by Rear Admiral Morton Deyo, in the heavy cruiser *Tuscaloosa*, with the battleship *Arkansas* backing up this phib group.

The U.S. landings would take place between St. Tropez and Cannes on the French Riviera. The further objectives were the bustling seaports of Toulon and Marseille. Rear Admiral Lyal Davidson, an experienced Mediterranean hand, was leader of the gunfire support group in heavy cruiser *Augusta*, while Rear Admiral Theodore Chandler, recently arrived from Naples, headed a transport group. The various forces received air support by two carrier groups, one commanded by Rear Admiral Calvin Durgin and the other by British Rear Admiral T. H. Troubridge. The invasion was set for August 15. Preparations were intense.

The intensity took its toll. Admiral Moon, who had a distinguished war record, was a perfectionist. Admiral Jimmy Hall believed Don Moon took on too many details himself and did not delegate authority. "If you try to do everything yourself," Hall said of his observations of Moon, "the human mind and human body just can't stand it." Admiral Moon worried that he hadn't enough time to get his Force Camel into proper shape. After sleepless nights, he suggested on August 4 a delay in D-day to Admiral Hewitt, who tried to reassure Moon that things weren't in bad shape. He would personally observe final rehearsals and recommend postponement to General Wilson if necessary. To Hewitt, Moon seemed satisfied with this assurance. But the following morning, worn down mentally and physically, Moon shot himself dead in his stateroom aboard *Bayfield*. Admiral Hewitt's chief of staff, Rear Admiral Spencer S. Lewis, replaced him.

The Dragoon landings were preceded by the most intense air and sea bombardments in the Mediterranean campaign. Admiral Hewitt knew that an operation the size of Dragoon would not be kept secret, with the ships and troops coming from ports in North Africa, Sicily, Corsica, and Italy. But he hoped that by selecting a number of targets, he could keep German General Johannes von Blaskowitz, Commander of Army Group G, in the dark as to the exact landing beaches. The bombardments were successful and on D-day, August 14, Hewitt's ships landed seventy-seven thousand men and twelve thousand vehicles between St. Tropez and Cannes. Another five thousand American and British paratroops landed inland to seize key junctions and strong points. Allied casualties were fortunately light and troops moved inland quickly. Only one LST and two PT boats were lost. The next day Hewitt's ships landed the French 1st Infantry and 3rd Algerian Divisions, which met no opposition and wheeled west for Toulon and Marseille.

French resistance fighters in the lower Rhône Valley harried the retreating Germans. The Germans launched a few air raids against the Dragoon ships, but they soon evacuated their airfields and retreated north. In fact, the Germans began a strategic withdrawal across the whole of the South of France, going north toward the Vosges Mountains near the German border. Sharp fighting occurred at the ports of Toulon and Marseille, but they were taken on August 28, with a valuable assist from accurate and frequent gunfire support of Admiral Davidson's ships. In four weeks, Allied forces pressed northward some 400 miles and linked up with formations in Northern France. With the Mediterranean now safe and the

French ports open, thousands of tons of supplies began streaming through Marseille to the Allied fighting fronts.

All in all, the skilled Kent Hewitt and his subordinates brilliantly executed Dragoon. At the end of the operation, French Admiral G. Lemonnier, liaison to the Eighth Fleet, praised Admiral Hewitt and "the extraordinary competence of his staff and of his task group commanders, with whom for our squadron and division commanders, cooperation was at once easy, agreeable and effective."

Admirals Hewitt got a more personal sort of praise from the Provençal villagers. On the first day of the landings, Hewitt went ashore with General Patch near St. Raphael. Admiral Lemonnier begged to accompany them, and Hewitt invited the French admiral. Hewitt and Patch graciously let Lemonnier, though junior, step first on French soil. They boarded a jeep. They were heading into town when they passed a girl on a bicycle who, in the excitement, fell off. The jeep stopped to help her. She rushed up and gave the French admiral a large kiss.

"The French there in the South of France," Hewitt said, "when they recognized Admiral Lemonnier as a French admiral, just went wild. They had never been told anything. They didn't know whether France still had a navy. So he got a royal welcome and as soon as he told the crowd who General Patch and I were we got an equally warm welcome. This is another one of the things that the landing in the south of France did. It liberated that part of France immediately and gave a tremendous boost to French morale."

In Europe, Kent Hewitt, Alan Kirk, Dick Conolly, Jimmy Hall, and Frank Lowry proved to be exceptional amphibious force commanders. Hewitt and Kirk would remain in Europe, while Hall and Lowry would follow Conolly to the Pacific.

Twenty-seven
RETURN TO THE PHILIPPINES

July–October 1944

In Washington, Pearl Harbor and Brisbane, the big question after the seizure of the Marianas was: What next? Pacific strategy had been kept fluid, mainly because of the sharp differences between General Douglas MacArthur and Admiral Ernest King. MacArthur had his heart set on advancing up New Guinea and taking the Philippines, south to north. He argued the United States had a moral duty to liberate the Philippines.

Admiral King, on the other hand, believed the re-conquest of all the major Philippine Islands would bog down army and navy forces for purely sentimental reasons. Additionally, it would cause major casualties and not hasten the drive to Japan. King argued that the Central Pacific drive should be split in two, the left flank heading for the big island of Formosa and the Chinese coast from which to bomb Japan. The right flank could move up the Bonin Islands to support B-29 bomber raids from newly captured Saipan.

The strategy remained undecided when President Roosevelt visited Hawaii after the Democratic convention had nominated him for a fourth term. He wished to consult personally with MacArthur and Nimitz. Admiral King and General Marshall weren't invited because Roosevelt saw them frequently in Washington and knew their views by heart.

The president arrived aboard the new heavy cruiser *Baltimore* at Pearl Harbor. Two dozen admirals and generals in dress whites lined up dockside to welcome him. As the *Baltimore* tied up, its superstructure was lined with sailors. Vice Admiral Soc McMorris, in charge of the greeting

Joseph J. "Jocko" Clark

Nimitz with, left, Charles H. "Soc" McMorris, his chief of staff, and
Forrest P. Sherman, his war plans officer

Donald B. "Wu" Duncan

Forrest P. Sherman

Arthur W. "Raddy" Radford, left, and John H. Towers, right

Clark, left, and Radford, right, aboard the *Yorktown,* summer 1943

Thomas L. "Tommy" Sprague

Charles A. "Baldy" Pownall

Rear Admiral Turner, left, with Major General Alexander A. Vandegrift, USMC, on the flag bridge of the *McCawley* during the Guadalcanal operation, July–August 1942

Foreground, left to right: Gerry Bogan, commander, Task Group 38.2, and Robert B. Pirie, his operations officer in flag plot during Philippines operations

Jesse B. "Oley" Oldendorf

McCain wearing his "lucky cap"

Clifton A. F. "Ziggy" Sprague

Left to right: Aaron Stanton "Tip" Merrill, Robert W. "Bob" Hayler, and Walden L. "Pug" Ainsworth relaxing in a South Pacific officers club between engagements in the Slot

Daniel J. "Dan" Callaghan, killed in action aboard *San Francisco* during the night Battle of Guadalcanal, November 1942

Norman Scott, killed in action aboard *Atlanta* during the night Battle of Guadalcanal, November 1942

Richard L. "Dick" Conolly, one of the finest amphibious admirals who commanded in the Mediterranean and the Pacific

Don P. Moon, who died by his own hand
on 5 August 1944

Left to right: Dwight D. Eisenhower and his two chief naval aides, Alan G. Kirk
and Morton Deyo, aboard the USS *Tuscaloosa,* May 1944

party, gave the order: "Right face!" Two of the brass turned the wrong way—to the raucous cheers of the enlisted men aboard *Baltimore*.

At a meeting in Honolulu, MacArthur presented Roosevelt with an impassioned plea for his Philippines strategy, to which neither the president nor Nimitz objected. MacArthur returned to Australia, believing he had won his case. But the decision would be taken at the level of the Joint Chiefs of Staff. In the end, a rough timetable was drawn up: the Central Pacific forces were to take the islands of Palau in the Carolines on September 15 and MacArthur was to land on Mindanao Island in the southern Philippines in November. Meanwhile, MacArthur with his naval commanders, Vice Admiral Kinkaid and Rear Admiral Uncle Dan Barbey, would secure the rest of the New Guinea northwest coast and the island of Morotai.

In the summer of 1944, Admiral King's dictum that carrier force commanders have surface ship chiefs of staff, and vice versa, was fully carried out, as had Arleigh Burke's relief of Truman Hedding. Halsey already had a non-aviator in Mick Carney. Admiral Tom Kinkaid received Commodore Valentine H. Schaeffer, an aviator who had been captain of the light carrier *Bataan*. Ching Lee was assigned fiery Commodore Tom Jeter, recently commanding officer of *Bunker Hill*, though sharp personal differences soon led to a communications breakdown between the two men. Some surface admirals, members of the gun club, resented the rise of the air admirals, but others like Rear Admiral Larry DuBose—a cruiser commander in Jocko Clark's task group—easily accepted that a junior air admiral would be his senior tactical commander. Such was the changing nature of naval warfare that fast battleships tended to serve as anti-aircraft platforms with the carrier groups, rather than as an independent battle line. Vice Admiral Lee rarely had the opportunity to train with his ships in night gunnery, which explained his reluctance in the Marianas to engage the Japanese after dark.

The most wrenching of the moves was Raymond Spruance's loss of Carl Moore, to be replaced by aviator Rear Admiral Arthur Davis, who had captained *Enterprise*. Davis wanted to get a carrier group, but he and Forrest Sherman disliked each other, and Davis thought Sherman would oppose such an assignment for him.

Spruance depended heavily on Moore to handle the immense amount of paperwork and operations orders of the Fifth Fleet. When Admiral King made an inspection trip to the Marianas in July, Spruance made one last attempt to keep Moore and get him promoted to rear admiral. But King was adamant. He still had it in for Moore for running the cruiser *Philadelphia* into a rock off Portland harbor in December 1941, even though Moore had served brilliantly as a staff officer in *Washington* and with Spruance. Moore did himself no favors during King's Marianas visit when he was obviously cool to the commander in chief of the U.S. Fleet aboard *Indianapolis*.

After King left, Spruance indicated to Moore that he could be reassigned as chief of staff to Admiral Slew McCain when he took over command of Task Force 58 from Pete Mitscher. The idea was that Moore could keep the impulsive and inexperienced McCain out of trouble. Would Moore accept the job? Moore blew up. He said he wouldn't think of doing it. First, he was reduced from chief of staff to a fleet commander, to only the task force commander. Second, Moore believed he was being put into an embarrassing position: if he kept McCain out of trouble, McCain would get the credit, but if something went wrong, Moore would get the blame. When asked about accepting the assignment, Moore retorted, "Make me commander of Task Force 38 and I'll take the responsibility for it and that's fine, but don't put me in a position of that sort."

That sealed Moore's fate with King. Rear Admiral Wilder Baker, a surface ship combat veteran, got the Task Force 38 job. Carl Moore was reassigned to a staff job in Washington for the rest of the war. Spruance was heartsick over losing Moore, but he knew that one could only go so far against Ernie King and no further. On parting in Pearl Harbor, Carl Moore said of his old friend and boss: "Admiral Spruance saw me off and he expressed appreciation and affection as best he could without being sentimental or emotional. We spoke of what a good time we'd had together, and how we'd played ball and worked together with such success and such pleasant relations. He spoke of my being free and willing to express my views, and that's what he wanted. We parted in the greatest good spirits, and nothing difficult, either emotionally or sentimentally, nothing unpleasant, a very pleasant affair."

The planned change of command of the Pacific warships from the Fifth Fleet to the Third Fleet took place. The ships remained the same but Bill Halsey took over from Raymond Spruance. The choice of replacement for Pete Mitscher as commander of the carrier task force under Halsey caused much discussion in high navy circles. Jack Towers wanted the job, but King blocked his way. Some proposed Ted Sherman's name. But King decided this was a good time to get Slew McCain out of Washington as he had requested. He pushed Nimitz and Towers into accepting McCain in the post.

It was not a popular choice. The up-and-coming air admirals saw McCain as a Johnny-come-lately. The scheduled carrier force takeover from Pete Mitscher was delayed while the inexperienced McCain snapped in. Instead, Mitscher headed Task Force 38 with Arleigh Burke, newly promoted to one-star commodore, while McCain took command of TG 38.1. It was an awkward situation because McCain was senior in rank to Mitscher. TG 38.2 was commanded by Rear Admiral Gerry Bogan, widely considered a top-flight air commander, in *Bunker Hill*; TG 38.3 led by Rear Admiral Ted Sherman in *Essex*; and TG 38.4 headed by brainy Rear Admiral Ralph Davison in *Franklin*. Now, there was a clear progression in an air admiral's career: command of a fast carrier, followed as a flag officer in command of an escort carrier group, which led to heading a fast carrier group.

Ralph Davison was an interesting case. A brilliant aviator and thinker, on the bridge of his flagship he was quiet, yet forceful and combat minded. Captain James Russell, his chief of staff, remembered Davison as "a very considerate man, a wonderful man, a very learned man, cool in battle. He had one fault. He liked his whiskey. In Ulithi, he'd go ashore and would be mellow most of the time we were in port. But we'd get out to sea and he went back to work, terrific under attack, a wonderful commander."

Davison and Russell revised carrier doctrine to state that carriers must turn to the starboard when hit by enemy planes. That way the ship would heel to port, sloshing burning fuel away from the vital island and control spaces on the right-hand side of the flattop. He also assigned one cruiser escort to aid a stricken carrier and one to tow if necessary. Davison firmly instructed his staff officers to keep their noses out of the ship and the carrier air group's business: that was the province of the skipper.

Slew McCain was not every aviator's favorite air admiral. Though physically he looked like the shrunken Pete Mitscher, the resemblance stopped there. McCain was dishevelled; rolled his own cigarettes with loose tobacco spilling on his uniform; wore a disreputable, crumpled cap; and was basically impulsive. At sea, he had an unimpressed staff. The aviators viewed him as a latecomer who was awarded wings at the

advanced age of fifty-two. He rose to vice admiral through his
Washington connections with Admiral King in the BuAer, and later as
deputy CNO for Air, where Jake Fitch succeeded him. McCain had no
seagoing experience in handling carriers, nor did he like staff work,
which soon showed in his tactical orders to Task Force 38. But Halsey
liked him, respecting the fighting qualities he showed as Commander
South Pacific Air at Nouméa.

In another important development, Admiral Halsey—unlike
Spruance—often assumed tactical command of the Third Fleet carrier
task force at sea almost at a whim. This left the experienced, capable
Pete Mitscher and Arleigh Burke with nothing much to do, never knowing when they would be given tactical command. Carrier operations had
changed dramatically since Bill Halsey took *Hornet* on the Tokyo raid.
Halsey and his chief of staff, Rear Admiral Mick Carney, might have
benefited from a makee-learn period, but it was difficult to assign a four-
star admiral to such status.

On August 28, Halsey led Task Force 38 out of Eniwetok to bomb
Yap, Palau, and Mindanao, as well as execute a side strike at the Bonin
Islands. The aim was to destroy Japanese aircraft that might impede
the coming invasions of Morotai in the Molucca Islands and Peleliu
in Palau. En route, Ralph Davison's carrier group struck the island of
Chichi Jima, and a young naval aviator, Lieutenant j.g. George H. W.
Bush (JG), was shot down on a bombing run on September 2. He was
picked up by the lifeguard submarine *Finback*, which sank two
Japanese cargo ships before returning the future U.S. president to his
carrier, *San Jacinto*.

In the Philippines, Admiral Halsey found much less air opposition
than expected. He made a prescient and valuable suggestion to Nimitz
on September 13. Nimitz passed it along to Admiral King and General
MacArthur. The message suggested that the Palau, Mindoro, and
Mindanao landings be cancelled as unnecessary and that the troops
and ships earmarked for these operations be diverted instead to the
central Philippine island of Leyte.

The suggestions were bucked up to the Joint Chiefs of Staff in
Washington, who approved the accelerated schedule. Admiral Nimitz,
however, insisted that Peleliu be taken to protect the eastern flank, and
that MacArthur continue with plans to invade Morotai to provide air
bases. Leyte was approved for assault in October, followed by the taking

of Luzon, using the combined naval resources of the Seventh and Third Fleets. MacArthur was delighted because it meant his dream of making the Philippines the priority was realized. Admiral King was forced to accept that his idea of taking Formosa and then creating a foothold on China would be too difficult and time-consuming. Instead, the Fifth Fleet would invade Iwo Jima in the Bonins in early 1945 and then assault Okinawa. At long last, a joint strategy all could agree on was formulated.

To take Peleliu, Admiral Nimitz assigned the III Phib Force under now Vice Admiral Ping Wilkinson, landing the 1st Marine Division commanded by Major General William H. Rupertus. D-day was set for September 15. The planners had not realized how rough the terrain was on the small island, or how well the Japanese defenders were dug in. This led to false optimism on the part of the senior commanders. After three days of shelling the island, Rear Admiral Oley Oldendorf—commander of the bombardment group in heavy cruiser *Louisville*—mistakenly commented, "We have run out of targets." And General Rupertus unfortunately predicted to correspondents that Peleliu would be secured in four days.

Instead the fight for Peleliu was long and bloody. The Japanese defended it from underground caves. It took nine weeks to secure the entire island, with the help of the U.S. 81st Infantry Division, and to finish off the last Japanese resistance. The battle was little heralded at the time and cost 1,794 U.S. lives with 8,000 wounded. The entire Japanese garrison was almost wiped out. The taking of Peleliu gave the United States an important airstrip and anchorage. But most historians believe it wasn't worth the cost and should have been bypassed. Insisting on taking Peleliu was perhaps Chester Nimitz's only strategic mistake in the war.

One bonus of the Palau operation was the seizure of Ulithi in the western Carolines. The huge atoll of Ulithi that had a fine anchorage was undefended and proved to be one of the most useful advance bases for the U.S. fleet in the Western Pacific.

On September 15, too, MacArthur's forces invaded the island of Morotai, lying between New Guinea and the Philippines' big southern island of Mindanao. It was located in the middle of the Moluccas group, but was lightly defended and had the potential for building airfields. The assault on Morotai was performed by VII Amphibious Force under the overall command of Uncle Dan Barbey, who led the White Beach invasion in flagship *Wasatch*. Barbey's number two, Rear Admiral William Fechteler, commanded the ships assaulting Red Beach.

A naval gunfire support group—headed by Rear Admiral Russell Berkey, former commanding officer of *Santa Fe*, in light cruiser *Phoenix*—backed up the phibs. Six escort carriers providing close-in air support were commanded by Tommy Sprague. The VII Phib landed about twenty-eight thousand army troops of the XI Corps commanded by Major General Charles P. Hall. During the operation, General MacArthur turned up as an observer aboard the light cruiser *Nashville* with Philippines President Sergio Osmeña. The landings went off unopposed. After a couple of false starts, airfields were built on Morotai, which served as the springboard for land-based air operations to cover the coming assault on the Philippines.

That assault was scheduled for October 22, 1944, against the island of Leyte. For the first time in the war, the Pacific Fleet and the ships of the Seventh Fleet under the Southwest Pacific command would work in concert. The relationship turned out to be complicated and confusing. Overall command of the troops rested with General Douglas MacArthur and under him Lieutenant General Walter Kruger, commander of the U.S. Sixth Army. MacArthur had under his command, too, the Fifth Air Force under General George Kenney and the Seventh Fleet, headed by Vice Admiral Tom Kinkaid. Kinkaid controlled two assault forces: the Northern Attack Force, commanded by veteran Rear Admiral Barbey, that would land on Leyte's eastern shore; and Vice Admiral Ping Wilkinson's Southern Attack Force, which had been detached from Admiral Nimitz's Pacific Fleet command.

There was some awkwardness in the amphibious command structure. Admiral Nimitz assumed that all the amphibious landing forces would come under the command of Ping Wilkinson, who was the most senior and experienced in large-scale operations of the assigned officers. Under Wilkinson would be Barbey and one of the veteran Central Pacific commanders, but Douglas MacArthur had a high regard for Barbey and did not want him under the command of a Central Pacific admiral. However, if Barbey were overall commander, the other amphibious force leaders would have to be junior to him, which ruled out the blooded Central Pacific admirals.

Nimitz believed that while Barbey was perfectly competent, he had not the experience of large-scale landings that his own admirals did. A fudge was arranged where Wilkinson led one force and Barbey the other, each reporting directly to Kinkaid. This setup was unwieldy because Kinkaid had other aspects of the command structure to worry about. Dick Conolly, who would operate under Wilkinson, believed Kinkaid should have appointed a single admiral to command the amphibious operations while he concentrated on the broader aspects of the fighting. This was Admiral Spruance's style of command. At Leyte, it was not to be. As Conolly later said, "The reason for Kinkaid's decision was that MacArthur did not want Barbey superseded, even though Wilkinson was very senior to him. He did not want anyone put over Barbey. We had come into the Southwest Pacific from the Central Pacific and we were considered outsiders."

Tom Kinkaid also had the use of several Pacific Fleet gunfire support groups lent to the Seventh Fleet by Nimitz for the amphibious operation. In addition, seventeen escort carriers in several groups were assigned to provide air cover for the assault landings. The senior air admiral of the baby flattops was Rear Admiral Tommy Sprague.

In the chain of command, Admiral Kinkaid reported to General MacArthur, who reported directly to the Joint Chiefs of Staff in Washington. Admiral Nimitz in Pearl Harbor had no command jurisdiction over the Seventh Fleet.

While the vastly augmented Seventh Fleet handled the invasion of Leyte, landing 130,000 army troops, a massive force patrolled at sea: Admiral Halsey's Third Fleet. This comprised four carrier task groups under Vice Admiral Mitscher, with a total of seventeen fast carriers and six fast battleships along with cruiser and destroyer screens. Bill Halsey reported directly to Admiral Nimitz in Pearl Harbor and his fleet did not come under General MacArthur's authority.

So the two enormous U.S. fleets involved in the Philippines operation came under two separate chains of command, one leading to MacArthur and Washington, the other to Nimitz in Pearl Harbor and Admiral King in Washington. This separation of command was not taught at the Naval War College. It came about because the two strong-willed Pacific commanders, MacArthur and Nimitz, wished to run their own theaters and not take orders from each other. And, for the first time in the Pacific war, their commands met in Leyte Gulf. Nimitz did not wish his valued fast carriers to come under MacArthur's orders because he might misuse and endanger them. MacArthur did not want his army's part in liberating the Philippines to come under naval command. It would be difficult for two such independent officers as MacArthur and Halsey to cooperate or coordinate easily in their efforts at sea. There was no provision for any direct contact between them. The divided structure could lead to confusion and might well be a recipe for disaster.

Halsey's orders from Nimitz were to "cover and support" the Leyte operation by launching air strikes against Japanese airfields in the Western Pacific and to provide "strategic support" by destroying Japanese naval forces threatening the Phillipines area. In addition, Halsey's orders contained the instruction: "In case opportunity for destruction of major portion of the enemy fleet is offered or can be created, such destruction becomes the primary task." This sentence became the controlling factor in Bill Halsey's later controversial actions, for it gave Halsey license to interpret his primary job as destroying the enemy fleet

Halsey welcomed this order because he thought Admiral Spruance had been too cautious at the Marianas in his concern to protect the amphibious forces rather than pursuing the Japanese fleet. Nothing in Nimitz's instructions indicated that Halsey had to clear any of his actions with MacArthur; he alone could determine the priorities in any critical decision. As Captain Carl Moore put it later, Halsey believed "if a situation arises or can be created for the defeat of the Japanese fleet, that will become the major objective. In other words, the hell with everything else."

The Japanese were expecting a landing in the Philippines, but they didn't know where or when. There were more than three thousand islands in the archipelago. Thus the main landings on Leyte met only token opposition. Serious Japanese army forces remained behind the beaches in the hills. And it took the Japanese naval forces four days to deploy to contest the U.S. Seventh and Third Fleets in Leyte Gulf.

Meanwhile, Halsey's Third Fleet stormed around the Western Pacific, launching air strikes off Okinawa, Formosa, and the Philippines. From Formosa, base of the Japanese Commander in Chief Soemu Toyada, the Japanese fought back fiercely. Japanese aircraft flew five hundred missions in three days. Slew McCain's TG 38.1 was hit by torpedo planes and the new heavy cruiser *Canberra* (one of the few U.S. ships to be named after a foreign one, lost at Savo Island) was badly crippled on October 13. Another torpedo plane crash-landed on the deck of Admiral Davison's flagship *Franklin* and slithered across the deck before plunging over the side.

The following evening enemy torpedo planes struck the new light cruiser *Houston*, named for the heavy cruiser sunk in the Java Sea. Two days later, the ship took another fish in her side. In a masterpiece of seamanship, the two stricken cruisers were taken under tow less than 100 miles from Japanese air bases. It was slow and difficult, for both damaged ships had settled low in the water. The cruisers *Santa Fe*, *Birmingham*, and *Mobile*, under the command of Rear Admiral Larry DuBose, were assigned as escorts. The group was named Crippled Division 1 or "CripDiv 1." Finally, the fleet tugs *Munsee* and *Pawnee* took over the tow.

The Japanese planes continued to attack the wounded prey, and another torpedo hit *Houston*. The cruiser's crew feared the ship would have to be abandoned, but the gallant little tug Pawnee signaled: "We'll stand by you!" Admiral DuBose aboard *Santa Fe* closed *Houston* and he roared through a bullhorn to *Houston's* skipper, W. W. Behrens, "Is your case hopeless?" Captain Behrens fired back, "Not hopeless, grave." Slowly CripDiv 1 edged out of the danger zone, eventually reaching Ulithi Lagoon on October 27. During this period, the Japanese thought they had inflicted a major defeat on the U.S. fleet and reported as such over the radio. Halsey replied with his own message that cheered the American people: "Am retiring toward the enemy following the salvage of all the Third Fleet ships recently reported sunk by radio Tokyo."

Now came the Leyte invasion. The Seventh Fleet assembled in Hollandia in New Guinea (which is 1,250 miles from Leyte) and Manus in the Admiralty Islands. This comprised fewer ships than Normandy, some seven hundred. When combined, however, with the eighteen carriers, six fast battleships, seventeen cruisers, and sixty-four destroyers of the Third Fleet, it formed the greatest naval striking force in history.

The first to enter Leyte Gulf were small assault forces to clear out the islands lying in the entrance to the gulf. Then the underwater demolition teams and the minesweepers followed to clear a channel into the gulf and to the Leyte beaches. On October 20 the massive invasion fleet approached. The Northern force—under the Seventh Fleet's Rear Admiral Barbey in *Blue Ridge*, and his subordinate commander Rear Admiral

William Fechteler in *Fremont*—landed the army's X Corps, consisting of the 1st Cavalry and 24th Infantry Divisions.

In all, some 81,000 men and 115,000 tons of supplies and equipment would come across the beaches near the town of Tacloban. The Southern force, commanded by the Third Fleet's Ping Wilkinson in *Mount Olympus*, landed the army's XXIV Corps comprising the U.S. 7th and 96th Infantry Divisions, with eventually 51,500 men and 85,000 tons of supplies and equipment. Wilkinson's III Phib was split between his deputies, Rear Admirals Dick Conolly in *Appalachian* and Forrest B. Royal in *Rocky Mount*. The Northern force's bombardment and gunfire support group was led by Rear Admiral George Weyler in *Mississippi*, while the Southern force's bombardment group was commanded by Rear Admiral Oley Oldendorf in heavy cruiser *Louisville*, with Rear Admiral Theodore Chandler in battleship *Tennessee*.

The landings went off satisfactorily. Japanese land commander, Lieutenant General Sosaku Suzuki, decided to defend Leyte from the hills rather than at the beaches. In the afternoon of October 20, Douglas MacArthur made his long-heralded and much-publicized return, debarking from a landing craft from cruiser *Nashville*. He strode into the calf-high water with Philippines President Sergio Osmeña, and with many cameramen in attendance.

There was one casualty among the flag officer ranks. Rear Admiral William Sample, an early aviator who commanded a division of escort carriers in the Taffy 2 group, decided to observe the air support for the landings. He boarded a TBM bomber on his flagship, *Marcus Island*, and rode in the belly gunner's position. He not only observed, but also had the pilot make a strafing run on Japanese positions. After, they were circling at 5,000 feet when an anti-aircraft shell crashed into the plane, wounding Sample with shrapnel. The pilot managed skillfully to make it back to the carrier. The plane was considered a total loss and pushed over the side.

Commodore Ralph Bates, in his analysis, called the flight unwarranted. "This points up the battle lesson," he said, "that it is unwise for a naval commander, who is conversant with the present and planned future operations of his command, and possible of other commands as well, to expose himself in such a manner unnecessarily for, were he captured by the enemy, he might be forced to give away information of vital importance to the successful conduct of the operation." Word got back to Admiral King in Washington who wanted to know whether Sample was joyriding (for which he could be relieved of command) or on a legitimate mission (for which he could be decorated). Sample's reply must have satisfied his superiors, for he remained in command of a carrier division until October 1945, when his plane failed to return from a flight over Japan.

There were sporadic attacks from Japanese aircraft. One torpedo plane managed to get a fish into the bow of the light cruiser *Honolulu* with Rear Admiral Pug Ainsworth aboard. The famed Blue Goose, a veteran of the Solomons battles, had lived a charmed life until then. She suffered sixty officers and crewmen killed in action, but was saved by prompt and effective damage control. As the skipper, Captain Ray Thurber—who had issued orders to Arleigh Burke while on Halsey's Nouméa staff—said, "It was a matter of everyone doing the right thing at the right time in the first half hour."

Hard fighting lay ahead on Leyte before the island was secured. The army troops would fight in torrential rain and mud, swamps and rice fields. Since Leyte was a big island, which could not be isolated by the sea and airpower, Japanese landed reinforcements. By October 24, General Kruger moved his 6th Army headquarters ashore and the assault phase of the invasion was finished.

But the Japanese navy was not going to give up Leyte without a fight. The stage was set for the Battle for Leyte Gulf, the largest naval action in history.

Twenty-eight
THE GREATEST
SEA BATTLE

October 1944

The Japanese seagoing admirals were itching to take on the U.S. fleet. When it became clear where the Americans were landing, the Japanese high command ordered its forces into action. The complex plan was called Sho-Go, meaning "victory operation." It consisted of three main elements. Vice Admiral Jisaburo Ozawa, commanding the carriers *Zuikaku*, *Zuiho*, *Chitose*, and *Chiyoda*, would approach from Kure, Japan, to the northeast side of Luzon to lure Admiral Halsey's Third Fleet away from Leyte Gulf.

Vice Admiral Kurita's Central Force including the super-battleships *Yamato* and *Musashi* departing Ligga Roads off Singapore, refueling at Brunei in Borneo, would head north and turn east through the Sibuyan Sea. Then, passing through the San Bernardino Strait between Samar and Luzon, it would head south to attack shipping in Leyte Gulf. The Southern Force led by Vice Admiral Nishimura would depart Brunei northeast through the Sulu Sea, passing through the Mindanao Sea along the northern coast of Mindanao. Then it would turn north through the Surigao Strait into Leyte Gulf. Another force from Japan under Vice Admiral Kiyohide Shima would link up with the southern group heading through the Surigao Strait, supporting Admiral Nishimura. By October 22, all the Japanese forces were at sea converging on the Philippines.

The Japanese plan first went awry when Kurita's battleship-cruiser force was sighted by two U.S. submarines, *Darter* and *Dace*, off Palawan

Island bordering the Sulu Sea. *Darter*, commanded by David McClintock, sent an invaluable contact report to Commander, Submarines Southwest Pacific. In the half-light of dawn on October 23, McClintock fired torpedoes into heavy cruiser *Atago*, Kurita's flagship, sinking her. Kurita eventually transferred his flag to the mighty *Yamato*. McClintock then fired *Darter*'s stern tubes, hitting the heavy cruiser *Takao* with two fish. She was badly damaged and had to return to port.

Dace's skipper, Bladen Claggett, drew a bead on the heavy cruiser *Maya* and hit her with four torpedoes sending the big ship to the bottom. *Darter* and *Dace* had been navigating these shoal-ridden waters by dead reckoning, and *Dace* ran aground on an uncharted reef, Bombay Shoal. In a daring rescue, *Darter* approached, took off all *Dace*'s crew, and destroyed all secret documents and sensitive gear. Claggett and McClintock had sunk two heavy cruisers, one being a flagship, and badly damaged a third. More importantly, they sent timely reports on the movements of the Japanese fleet toward the Sibuyan Sea.

As the Japanese advanced, Halsey deployed his three carrier groups on a broad front: Ted Sherman's TG 38.3 to the north, Gerry Bogan's TG 38.2 off San Bernardino Strait, and Ralph Davison's TG 38.4 east of Leyte. Before the U.S. submarine sightings, Admiral Halsey leaned toward the view that the Japanese were not coming out to fight. His men were tired and he decided to begin a schedule of rotating one carrier group at a time to Ulithi for rest and replenishment. On October 22, Admiral Halsey detached Slew McCain's TG 38.1 to Ulithi, for re-supply, much to Gerry Bogan's disgust, for he thought they should remain on station. Halsey's was a strange decision considering that the Leyte landing operation was far from complete, Japanese fleet units were reported in the Philippines, and every U.S. ship and plane was needed. By dispatching McCain to Ulithi, Halsey deprived Task Force 38 of its strongest carrier group on the eve of a historic battle.

In Leyte Gulf itself, General MacArthur was aboard the cruiser *Nashville* while his fleet commander, Admiral Kinkaid, was nearby in the amphibious command ship *Wasatch*. The gulf was filled with shipping, mainly amphibious craft of all descriptions with attendant cargo ships unloading supplies. Under Kinkaid's control, and leant to him by the Pacific Fleet, was a gunfire support group. It was led by Rear Admiral Oley Oldendorf, a meticulous, far-sighted commander, in the heavy cruiser *Louisville*, with seven other cruisers and many destroyers. The force was augmented by the Pacific Fleet's old, slow battleships: *West Virginia, Maryland, Pennsylvania, Tennessee, Mississippi*, and *California*. The battleships were headed by Rear Admiral George Weyler in *Mississippi*. Weyler's second in command in *Tennessee* was Theodore Chandler, who had served earlier in the Mediterranean. Five of the six battlewagons had been sunk or badly damaged at Pearl Harbor.

Also under Admiral Kinkaid's command were three groups of escort carriers stationed just outside Leyte Gulf. These comprised TG 77.4 and were commanded by Rear Admiral Tommy Sprague. But they were better known by their call signs: Taffy 1 with six jeep carriers under Tommy Sprague; Taffy 2, six carriers under Rear Admiral Felix Stump; and Taffy 3, six escort carriers commanded by Rear Admiral Ziggy Sprague (no relation to Tommy), who had been commanding officer of the seaplane tender *Tangier* at Pearl Harbor, the first ship to open fire at the Japanese. The Taffies were deployed north to south: Taffy 3, Taffy 2, and Taffy 1, respectively.

By the afternoon of October 23, with reports of the oncoming Japanese pincer movement becoming clearer, Admirals Halsey and Kinkaid foresaw that a fleet action was imminent. Halsey ordered intensive air searches from his fast carrier force, which were launched at daybreak on October 24. The planes flew over the west coast of Luzon and the Sibuyan, Sulu, and Mindanao seas. At 0812, a plane from *Intrepid* sighted the massive battleship *Yamato* in the Sibuyan sea and immediately reported back.

Nimitz had given Halsey orders not to send ships into the Sibuyan Sea without his expressed approval. Halsey issued instructions to the carrier task group commanders to attack, bypassing the authority of Vice Admiral Pete Mitscher—so very unlike Raymond Spruance's method of ceding tactical control to his carrier task force commander. Halsey ordered Admirals Bogan, Davison, and Sherman to concentrate their forces and belatedly recalled Admiral McCain from his trip to Ulithi, arranging a mobile refueling rendezvous at sea. Halsey was deployed for the first of the four great engagements that comprised the Battle for Leyte Gulf.

Japanese land-based planes drew first blood. In a large-scale strike, many enemy aircraft attacked Third Fleet ships, but many were lost to

U.S. carrier pilots. Commander David McCampbell shot down nine Japanese aircraft that morning. A bomb struck light carrier *Princeton*, part of Ted Sherman's group, setting off a blazing fire that roared through the hanger deck. Captain Buracker ordered Salvage Control Phase 2, which meant that most of the crew should prepare to abandon ship, leaving 240 firefighters behind to save the vessel.

Admiral Sherman instructed three destroyers to come alongside the almost-stopped *Princeton* and take off the crew that had mustered forward. The light cruiser *Birmingham* came to *Princeton's* aid, under the command of Captain Thomas B. Inglis, an expert ship-handler. Inglis was senior officer of the small group of ships, now that the carrier group had moved off. He ordered cruiser *Reno* to provide anti-aircraft protection while the destroyers picked up survivors. Then he brought his ship alongside *Princeton* to fight the fires with his powerful hoses.

Just as it appeared *Princeton's* fires were under control, an enormous explosion in the carrier's torpedo stowage compartment blew apart her stern. The force of the explosion rained steel debris on the exposed starboard side of the cruiser, riddling the superstructure and wreaking a deadly toll. Nearly every man on deck was hit. A total of 237 of *Birmingham's* crew were killed, and 426 were wounded, most of them seamen on deck assisting *Princeton*. *Birmingham's* losses were greater than *Princeton's*. The wounded cruiser made it to port for repairs. But the carrier could not be saved. The cruiser *Reno* was ordered to put two torpedoes into *Princeton*, sending her to the bottom.

Task Force 38 had its revenge. Throughout the day, planes attacked the Japanese Central Force in the Sibuyan Sea. *Intrepid*, *Essex*, *Lexington*, *Enterprise*, *Franklin*, and *Cabot* put nineteen torpedoes and seventeen bombs into the super-battleship *Musashi*, which sent the world's largest battlewagon under the sea. Two bombs hit *Musashi's* sister-ship *Yamato*. They also struck the battleship *Nagato*. The heavy cruiser *Myoko* had her propeller shafts damaged by an aerial torpedo and was forced to return to Brunei.

Admiral Kurita milled about with his ships for some time, but was still determined to head for Leyte Gulf, though by now he knew his appointed rendezvous with Admiral Nishimura's Southern Force would be delayed. At 1714, Admiral Kurita once again headed his ships toward the San Bernardino Strait, leading to the open Pacific and Leyte Gulf.

At 1935, a night-capable plane from *Independence* spotted Kurita's force heading eastward toward San Bernardino Strait and radioed the vital contact report with accurate course and speed. Halsey received the message at 2006, which was relayed to Kinkaid at 2024.

As the Battle of the Sibuyan Sea was underway, Nishimura's force was steaming north out of the Mindanao Sea toward Surigao Strait into Leyte Gulf. He didn't bother to wait for the backup force of Admiral Shima. Aware that he was sighted by Allied planes, he continued to steam toward Surigao Strait, which told Admiral Kinkaid that Nishimura would most likely enter it on the night of October 24. Kinkaid ordered Oldendorf, who commanded all fire-support ships at Leyte, to deploy his forces across the northern neck of the strait, which is 15 miles wide. Oley consulted his subordinate admirals and decided on a plan of action.

Surigao Strait runs north and south. The Japanese were entering from the southern mouth. Russell Berkey's three-cruiser force would guard the west side of the strait. Oley's own five-cruiser group would patrol across the center and eastern parts of the strait. His second in command of the cruisers was Rear Admiral Bob Hayler in *Denver*, who had captained *Honolulu* in the Solomons. Behind his cruisers, some 7,000 yards to the north, the six-ship battle line, under Rear Admirals Weyler and Chandler, would patrol. Farther to the south, destroyer divisions would be stationed on both sides of Surigao to launch torpedo attacks at the northbound Japanese, and get out of the way. Even farther to the south, U.S. PT boats would be placed at random to attack at will with torpedoes. Oldendorf was setting up a splendid trap by placing his warships in position to accomplish every admiral's dream: crossing the enemy's T.

Shortly before midnight, U.S. PT boats encountered Nishimura's force and radioed its position to Admiral Oldendorf. The boats launched several attacks until 0200 on October 25, but their torpedoes failed to score. As Nishimura steamed due north in a single column, he next ran into Captain Jesse G. Coward's Destroyer Squadron 54. Coward launched torpedoes at 0300 from three ships on the eastern side of the strait at a range of 8,500 yards at Nishimura's flagship, battleship *Yamashiro*; another battle wagon, *Fuso*; and heavy cruiser *Mogami*. One fish hit *Fuso*, which turned out of the column and began burning fiercely. *Yamashiro* was hit but carried on.

Meanwhile, Coward's second division under Commander Richard H. Phillips made a similar attack from the western side of the strait at 0309. Three enemy tin cans were hit: *Yamagumo* and *Michishio* sank, and *Asagumo*'s bow was blown off. Next, the Japanese force was struck by another U.S. destroyer force, Captain K. M. McManes' DesRon 24, whose torpedoes sank the disabled *Michishio*, and again struck battleship *Yamashiro*. Admiral Nishimura steamed on, now down to battleship *Yamashiro*, cruiser *Mogami*, and destroyer *Shigure*. Ahead waited the battleships and cruisers of Admiral Oldendorf, capping the T, the action Oley had studied so assiduously at Annapolis and the Naval War College.

At 0323, the radar screens on the American battleships began picking up the enemy formation. Admiral Oldendorf, his cruisers closer to the enemy, ordered all ships to open fire at 0351. *West Virginia*, *Tennessee*, and *California*, all with the latest radar, got off the most salvos. Battleship *Yamashiro* and cruiser *Mogami* were pummelled by dozens of shells, while the elusive *Shigure* managed to dodge most of the gunfire. Finally, Admiral Nishimura ordered retirement at about 0400. Captain Roland Smoot's DesRon 56 got into the battle and launched torpedoes, which hit *Yamashiro*, spelling her doom. About 0420, she capsized and went down, taking almost all of her crew and Admiral Nishimura.

About this time, Admiral Shima was arriving with his backup force at the southern end of Surigao Strait. His light cruiser *Abukuma* was hit by a PT boat torpedo and fell out of the column. Unlike his fellow admiral, Shima decided that discretion was the better part of valor and, as he passed the wrecks of the Japanese vanguard, he decided to pull back. But his cruiser *Nachi* collided with southbound *Mogami* of the retreating force. Admiral Oldendorf pursued with *Louisville*, *Portland*, and *Denver* and shelled the hapless *Mogami*. But she continued onward.

Bob Hayler's *Denver* and *Columbia* caught up with destroyer *Asagumo*, whose bow had been severed earlier, and sank her. The light cruiser *Abukuma*, which had been hit by a PT boat, was later sunk by army bombers. Avenger bombers from Tommy Sprague's escort carriers spotted the valiant *Mogami* in the Mindanao Sea and sank her, too. That ended the battle. The U.S. Navy made nearly a clean sweep of Admiral Nishimura's force, at a cost of 39 sailors killed and 114 wounded.

The Battle of Surigao Strait was to be the last time in naval history that two battle lines opposed each other.

It was now sunup. At 0732, Rear Admiral Oldendorf was flashed the stunning news that Tommy Sprague's Taffy escort carriers just outside Leyte Gulf were under attack by a Japanese battle force. He was ordered by Kinkaid to steam to its rescue, even though his warships were low on fuel and armor-piercing ammo, and the crews—and flag staff officers— were exhausted. The staff had to plan immediately for a new and unexpected battle.

While Nishimura's force was heading for disaster, Vice Admiral Ozawa's carrier force, seventeen ships in all, was moving south toward northern Luzon to play its role in the attempt to crush American forces at Leyte by acting as a decoy to attract Halsey's Third Fleet. His four carriers had only 116 planes, about half the normal complement because of the devastating losses to Japanese air groups. His force was expendable.

During the daylight hours of October 24, U.S. search planes spotted Ozawa's flattops, and these reports were forwarded to Admiral Halsey in his flagship *New Jersey* off Luzon. Halsey was obsessed with taking on the Japanese carrier force. As a measure of his thinking, Halsey had told a group at the Naval Academy: "Missing the Battle of Midway was the greatest disappointment of my life—but I'll sink those damned Jap carriers yet!" He was now determined not to let the Japanese carriers get away, as he believed Spruance had at the Battle of the Philippine Sea. He accepted his pilots' claims of extensive damage to the Central Force in the Sibuyan Sea, and reports that the Japanese turned back in apparent retreat. Pete Mitscher tended to be more sceptical of pilots' claims, but Halsey chose not to consult Mitscher.

Having sent Slew McCain's TG 38.1 to Ulithi, Halsey was left with three carrier groups, but they were powerful. They comprised eleven fast carriers, six fast battleships, nine cruisers, and forty-four destroyers—a formidable force indeed. Halsey planned to form a separate battle line, consisting of four fast battleships, which would be pulled out of their escort role with the fast carriers to take on the Japanese carriers or anything else afloat. This, when formed, was to be Task Force 34.

Halsey had his orders from Nimitz, but they could be read in conflicting two ways: "to cover and support" the landing forces of the Seventh Fleet, and "destruction of a major portion of the enemy fleet." Nimitz never intended Halsey to abandon his responsibilities for protecting the beachhead. Halsey could have easily done both by splitting his task groups, leaving one—either carriers or battlewagons—behind at the San Bernardino Strait to take on the Japanese if they came. But that was not Bill Halsey's all-or-nothing style.

At 1512, October 24, Halsey issued a battle plan, including the possibility of breaking off Task Force 34, to all his task force and group commanders, with Admirals King and Nimitz as "information" addressees, as opposed to "action" addressees, who are expected to respond. Halsey did not include Admiral Kinkaid as an information addressee. But Kinkaid's sharp communicators intercepted the message. This was against regulations but a widely practiced form of radio eavesdropping of major messages to stay informed. Kinkaid thought Admiral Lee was blocking the San Bernardino Strait with Task Force 34, as Oldendorf had plugged Surigao.

Halsey's battle plan declared that the fast battleships "will be formed as Task Force 34." This grammatical usage could be read two ways. In the future indicative, it meant the formation would be created when Halsey gave the word. But in the present imperative, often used for military orders, "will be formed" meant "do it now."

This was a critical difference. Halsey later sent a clarifying voice message to his admirals, instructing: "If the enemy sorties [through the San Bernardino Strait] Task Force 34 shall be formed when directed by me."

But this voice transmission, which clarified Halsey's intentions, was not received by anyone outside the task force area. Admiral Kinkaid, Admiral Nimitz, and Admiral King's staff all read the original message as meaning that an independent Task Force 34 had been formed. The deep flaw was that the divided command precluded Kinkaid and Halsey staking out clear sectors of responsibility or communicating directly. MacArthur ordered Kinkaid not to have "direct" communications with Halsey, so Kinkaid had to route his messages through the standard "Fox schedule," or fleet transmissions through Southwest Pacific channels, in this case the radio station at Manus in the Admiralty Islands. Manus, in turn, would forward messages to the Third Fleet. This led to severe delays and misunderstandings. Kinkaid could only make assumptions about Halsey's plans. Because of these delays, Kinkaid's messages to Halsey were received out of sequence, leading to more confusion.

On the early evening of October 24, Halsey made a fateful decision. He had recalled McCain's task group short of Ulithi, but it was still hundreds of miles away. Halsey decided to turn his three carrier groups north to take on Ozawa's carriers. He had talked it over with his staff and if any disagreed, the staff officer was overruled.

Just after 2000, Halsey turned to Admiral Carney and ordered: "Mick, start them north." Carney sent a message to Admiral Kinkaid, with copies to Admirals King and Nimitz and the Third Fleet. "Strike reports indicate enemy force Sibuyan Sea heavily damaged. Am proceeding north with three groups to attack enemy carrier force at dawn." Kinkaid and the other addressees all believed the message meant the three carrier groups were heading north, while Task Force 34 battleships blocked San Bernardino Strait. They could not believe that Halsey would leave the strait totally unguarded.

What about the Japanese Central Force heading for the San Bernardino Strait? Halsey believed this force had been so heavily damaged that it posed no threat to the Seventh Fleet ships in Leyte Gulf. He thought that it would be "childish" to guard the San Bernardino Strait "statically," that is, with warships. Yet Halsey had the information that the Central Force remnants—and they must constitute a threat—were heading for the strait and the open ocean. Halsey decided he needed all of his ships to ensure an overwhelming victory against the Japanese carriers to the north. It was a strange decision, and one wonders why his astute chief of staff Mick Carney did not use his intellect and powers of persuasion to modify this crucial decision. The revised battle plan could have left one carrier air group (or Task Force 34), the battle line, or even a destroyer division to guard the strait. Even a single tin can could have sounded a warning to Sprague's carriers and Kinkaid's force if the Japanese battlewagons were sighted.

Later, Carney said, "When Halsey reached his decision, there was no question in anybody's mind. When he pointed his finger at you, when he pounded on the table and said, 'All right, I've made up my mind,' why, you went ahead and did it." Carney said that Halsey and his staff in the flag plot decided that the principle objective should be the enemy carrier air whose destruction would destroy their fleet's effectiveness. "It was almost an obsession."

Certainly, Halsey's Third Fleet admirals were concerned, even disturbed, by his decision. Halsey's responses—or lack of them—to their urgent queries seemed to reflect a strange indifference on the part of the admiral's staff.

Rear Admiral Gerry Bogan, tough minded, aggressive, and admired by his aviators, thought about protesting Halsey's decision to leave the San Bernardino Strait uncovered. Over TBS radio in *Intrepid*, he discussed the Central Force's movements with Captain E. C. Ewen of *Independence*, whose night pilots spotted the Japanese move toward the strait. Ewen confirmed the sightings and added that the navigational lights in the strait had been turned on, an unusual and ominous sign.

Bogan incorporated this information in a message to Halsey, and he read it over the TBS. A Halsey staff officer said in an impatient voice, "Yes, yes, we have that information." Bogan was about to recommend that his TG 38.2 be combined with Ching Lee's battleship Task Force 34 to handle the Central Force, while Halsey continued north with Sherman and Davison's carrier task groups, more than enough to take care of Ozawa. But after getting what he considered the brush-off from Halsey's staff, he let the matter drop.

Vice Admiral Lee in *Washington*, his flagship at Guadalcanal, was one of the most astute flag officers in the fleet. Pouring over the data that reached his flag plot, he deduced that the Northern Force was a decoy to draw the Third Fleet away from Leyte Gulf, leaving the Southern and Central Forces to wipe out the ships and beachhead. (Nobody knew the outcome of Surigao.) He wanted to station his battlewagons off the San Bernardino Strait and cross the Japanese T as the enemy came through. At sunset, Lee sent Halsey in *New Jersey* a message by flashing light with his views and recommendations. He received no reply other than the routine "roger," meaning, "transmission received." After Lee digested the reports from *Independence* planes, he sent Halsey a TBS message indicating that he was convinced Kurita was heading out of San Bernardino. He received a perfunctory "roger." Ching Lee gave up. Captain Ray Thompson, his staff gunnery officer, commented, "We told Admiral Lee to tell Halsey to leave something out there watching the strait, because they were bound to come out and everyone seemed to know that. But the reaction was, if you tell Halsey to do something, that's the one thing he won't do. . . . In my opinion it was the greatest tactical blunder of the war."

In the flag plot of *Franklin*, Rear Admiral Ralph Davison studied the reports and the radar screen with his chief of staff, Captain James Russell. They believed the battle line should be heading south rather than north. Davison said, "Jim, we're playing a helluva dirty trick on the transports in Leyte Gulf." Russell agreed. He asked, "Do you wish to say anything to Admiral Mitscher?" Davison shook his head negatively. "Maybe they have more information than we do. But this doesn't look right to me."

On his flagship Lexington, the expert tactician Vice Admiral Pete Mitscher had been virtually ignored for days by Halsey, who acted as OTC, issuing orders directly to the carrier group commanders. Halsey made it clear from the start that he considered himself the fast carrier commander, a dangerous position since he lacked the experience of Mitscher in handling large carrier groups. Mick Carney was a surface officer with little carrier experience. The battle experience lay with Pete Mitscher, Arleigh Burke, Ted Sherman, Gerry Bogan, and Ralph Davison. Mitscher thought he was no more than a passenger with Halsey. Both Halsey and McCain had a freewheeling style, which verged on sloppiness. Rather than issuing detailed operation orders like Spruance, he preferred to command by dispatch, often impromptu and vague. Both Halsey and McCain were loved by their staffs and sailors, but did not enjoy the professional respect from their admirals and captains that Spruance and Mitscher did.

When he received Halsey's order to turn north at 2029, Mitscher assumed he was being given tactical command for the following day's action. He headed for bed. He left Commodore Arleigh Burke in charge of the flag plot, and as he departed, he said to Burke, "We'd better see where that [enemy] fleet is." Burke suspected that the Northern Force carriers were decoys to draw the Third Fleet away from Leyte Gulf. Mitscher went to bed. Burke received the intelligence from Independence that the Central Force was moving to San Bernardino. Burke and his operations officer, Commander Jimmy Flatley, believed it was vital to detach the battle line to take on Kurita's Central Force. They woke Mitscher to "tell Halsey" to do so.

"Admiral, we'd better tell Halsey to turn around," Flatley said.

On one elbow, Mitscher asked, "Does Admiral Halsey have that information?"

"Yes, he does," Flatley said.

"If he wants my advice, he'll ask for it." Mitscher went back to sleep.

The Third Fleet was heading north at 16 knots with sixty-five warships to face Ozawa's seveteen, while leaving the strait wide-open to Kurita's heavy force. Thus, nothing was between it and Leyte Gulf, which was exactly what Ozawa had intended. And while Mitscher technically was the OTC, Bill Halsey—in his impulsive way and unlike Raymond Spruance—sometimes contradicted Mitscher's orders as to fleet speed. For Mitscher and Arleigh Burke, it was a confusing night. Halsey's inexperience showed up again when he decided to form his battle line into Task Force 34, 10 miles ahead of the rest of the task force. But pulling six battlewagons out of three separate carrier formations in the dark and getting them together underway was a very tricky and time-consuming business, which neither Admirals Mitscher nor Lee cared for. Mitscher appreciated Spruance's foresightfulness at the Philippine Sea to form the battle line before the action.

For his part, Kurita was amazed to find the strait unguarded as he transited at 0035 on October 25 and headed south for his expected rendezvous in Leyte Gulf with Nishimura's Southern Force. The stage was set for the Battle Off Samar.

About fifteen minutes after sunrise on October 25, Rear Admiral Ziggy Sprague ordered the jeep carriers of northernmost Taffy 3 to stand down from General Quarters, so the deck crews could eat breakfast. All was calm. The three Taffies had spent the previous days covering the Luzon landings and providing close air support for the ground forces. At 0647, the pilot of an aircraft on anti-submarine patrol reported to Ziggy Sprague's flagship *Fanshaw Bay* that he was being fired on by a force of battleships, cruisers, and destroyers at a position about 20 miles to the northwest.

"Air plot," Sprague called into his squawk box from his cramped flag bridge at the rear of the jeep carrier's tiny navigation bridge, "tell that pilot to check identification," assuming the aviator may have stumbled on units of the Third Fleet. But even before this could be done, lookouts on the "Fanny B" observed an astonishing sight: the tall, pagoda masts of Japanese battleships on the horizon.

At 0648, the Japanese ships opened fire, with shell splashes falling among the carriers and destroyers of Taffy 3. As surprised as Sprague was, Admiral Kurita believed he had stumbled into Pete Mitscher's fast carrier force. Kurita had led a charmed life, surviving the Battle of the Sibuyan Sea, and steaming unobserved down the Samar coastline during the past seven hours. Kurita's force had 18.1-inch guns of battleship *Yamato* and 16-inch guns of his other battleships, plus the 8-inch guns of his cruisers.

Sprague's largest guns on his carriers and destroyers were only 5-inch, mere popguns by comparison. Caught by surprise, Sprague was in deep trouble. With six small carriers and seven destroyer escorts, he faced Kurita's four battleships, six heavy cruisers, and many destroyers.

But Sprague remained remarkably cool, as he correctly ordered his carriers to turn east and increase the speed to a maximum of 17 1/2 knots—pitiable compared to the fast, powerful Japanese warships. Ziggy Sprague ordered all his planes launched and requested help from Admirals Tommy Sprague and Felix Stump, whose Taffy groups were well to the south. Ziggy Sprague was assisted by Kurita's mistakes. Instead of organizing his powerful force into a proper battle line, with his destroyers launching torpedo attacks, Kurita let his ships shift for themselves and they went into action piecemeal. Sprague had his destroyers make smoke, which with rainsqualls obscured the view. He turned his ships to the south and west, hoping to close Leyte and get assistance from Oldendorf's battlewagons. But these were replenishing after the Battle of Surigao Strait and were too far away to help.

At 0716, Ziggy Sprague ordered his destroyers to attack the Japanese main body. The tin cans launched one of the most gallant attacks of the whole war. They were *Hoel*, flying the pennant of Commander W. D. Thomas, *Heermann*, and *Johnston*. The latter laid down a smoke screen and closed to 10,000 yards to launch torpedoes at the heavy cruisers. One hit *Kumano*. At 0730, *Johnston* was struck by three 14-inch and three 6-inch shells. Having expended torpedoes, *Johnston* opened fire with a 5-inch gun on the battleship *Kongo*. It was a futile fight and soon several Japanese ships poured fire on the stricken *Johnston*. At 0950, Commander Ernest Evans, skipper of *Johnston*, ordered Abandon Ship, and soon the plucky tin can went down. Evans was posthumously awarded the Medal of Honor.

Heermann, skippered by Commander A. T. Hathaway, fired at four battleships then launched six torpedoes, forcing *Yamato* to turn away for ten minutes, which took her huge guns out of action and gave the baby carriers breathing room. *Hoel*, whose captain was Commander L. S. Kintberger, took forty hits before going down. Her brave crew, said Captain Kintberger, "performed their duties coolly and efficiently until their ship was shot from under them."

Admiral Sprague ordered a second torpedo attack by the destroyer escorts in his screen against heavy odds. One of them, Samuel B.

Roberts, fired on several heavy cruisers before being smothered by the foe's heavier shells and began sinking.

Taffy 3's ships stuck together in and out of rainstorms as they traced a wide arc to the southwest. Their planes continued to attack the Japanese force, assisted by those from Taffy 2 and Taffy 1. The courageous attack by Taffy 3's screen enabled the slower carriers to maintain their distance from the superior Japanese force. But finally the Japanese heavy cruisers closed the range on the small carriers.

Kalinin Bay was hit by several shells, suffering heavy damage, but managed to keep in formation. Flagship Fanshaw Bay and White Plains were bracketed by shellfire. Gambier Bay and St. Lo were hit several times, slowing them down. In return, the baby carriers got off 5-inch fire at enemy ships when they could. Heavy cruiser Chikuma zeroed in on Gambier Bay. The jeep carrier dodged the heavy shells for twenty-five minutes, until Chikuma found the range and battered the thin-skinned carrier, as did the other heavy cruisers. Finally, Gambier Bay was mortally stricken and Captain W. V. Vieweg ordered Abandon Ship. She capsized and sank at 0907.

In Taffy 2, Felix Stump, from his flagship Natoma Bay, had been planning to support Taffy 3 but realized that since all his planes were just finishing their launch, it would be a futile effort. To a staff officer, he misquoted John Paul Jones, as making the famous Nelson statement, "No captain can do very wrong in laying his ship alongside the enemy." Just then, as the Fox flag dropped from the yardarm, signaling the launch was complete, Stump stared at the direction of the Japanese fleet and commented, "John Paul Jones to the contrary, notwithstanding, the time has come to get the hell out of here." He ordered his task group to make flank speed in the opposite direction.

In a counterattack, U.S. planes from Taffy 2 scored ten hits on Chokai, which quickly sank. Other air attacks sank cruisers Chikuma and Suzuya. At 0911, Admiral Tommy Sprague was surprised and relieved to see Admiral Kurita breaking off the attack and turning away. Sprague heard a signalman on the bridge of flagship Fanshaw Bay yell, "Goddammit, boys, they're getting away!"

Admiral Kurita was beset by poor communications and by his own misdirection of his fleet in helter-skelter fashion. He did not know how near his battleships were to the baby carriers, which they could have exterminated. Kurita intended to withdraw and regroup, but once he did, he pondered Admiral Shima's message that the southern force was in retreat, and there was to be no rendezvous. Fearing reprisals from U.S. planes on Leyte and Admiral Halsey's fleet, he decided to continue his withdrawal to the San Bernardino Strait.

Toward the end of the battle, the Taffies underwent the first attack of the Kamikaze (Divine Wind) Corps. One crashed into division commander Rear Admiral Ralph Ofstie's flagship *Kitkun Bay* but skidded into the ocean, while two more hit the ship, causing minor damage. But a suicide plane slammed into the deck of *St. Lo* and broke into the hanger bay, setting off bombs and torpedoes. The enormous explosions quickly sank *St. Lo*.

The Battle off Samar was over, but at a cost of two escort carriers, two destroyers, and a destroyer escort, which all fought valiantly. The United States lost 1,130 seamen and aviators, but sank three Japanese heavy cruisers and protected the vulnerable dozens of ships and thousands of men in Leyte Gulf.

Meanwhile, Admiral Halsey was taking the Third Fleet north, having spotted Admiral Ozawa's carrier force 200 miles off Cape Engaño on northeast Luzon. Halsey again turned over tactical control to Pete Mitscher, who ordered all his carriers to arm planes for a massive launch at first light.

Halsey had Carney order an air search from the night carrier *Independence*. Arleigh Burke recommended against this tactic because he feared the presence of search planes would tip off the Japanese.

"Have you any information we don't have?" Mick Carney asked Burke.

"No, sir," Burke said.

"Launch the search," Carney said abruptly, in effect countermanding the staff of the OTC.

When Mitscher returned to the flag bridge from a nap in his sea cabin, he told Burke to get full deckloads of planes ready to take off at first light. The first air strike approached the Japanese at about 0800, and was coordinated by Commander David McCampbell, Medal of Honor pilot and commander of the *Essex* Air Group. He had shot down a record nine enemy planes the day before.

Helldivers bombed and Avengers dropped torpedoes. The carrier *Chitose* and a destroyer were sunk. The large carrier *Zuikaku*, which fought at Pearl Harbor, the Coral Sea, and the Philippine Sea, was hit by a torpedo, knocking out communications and forcing Admiral Ozawa to shift his flag to the light cruiser *Oyodo*. Nearby, the destroyer *Akitsuki* was sunk.

The next U.S. carrier strike bombed *Chiyoda*, starting fires and damaging her engines. *Chiyoda* began abandoning ship and was later sunk by Rear Admiral Larry DuBose's cruisers. The third strike from Ted Sherman and Ralph Davison's carriers, mounting two hundred planes, hovered over Ozawa's ships. Three torpedoes hit *Zuikaku*, sealing her fate and she slipped to the bottom. The fourth carrier, *Zuiho*, absorbed much punishment and finally went down. But the two so-called "hermaphrodite" battleship-carriers—*Ise* and *Hyuga*—which were equipped with a flight deck at their sterns, got away in what was designated the Battle Off Cape Engaño, the fourth and final phase of the Battle for Leyte Gulf.

As Bill Halsey was occupied with his fight, the high-priority message traffic was crackling from Tom Kinkaid. Late on October 24, Kinkaid had ordered air searches for early next morning toward the Sibuyan Sea, with emphasis on San Bernardino Strait, to determine the location and course of the Japanese Central Force. The first was by night-flying PBY Catalinas. Three planes took off from Leyte Gulf but missed sighting the Japanese ships.

Kinkaid at 0156 also ordered Tommy Sprague to send out a dawn search to locate the Central Force. Sprague instructed at 0430 Felix Stump to carry out a search from Taffy 2. Stump in turn ordered *Ommaney Bay* to do the job. But the jeep carrier was painfully slow to respond. She had to re-spot her deck and did not launch her ten planes until 0658, a near fatal mistake. By then the Japanese warships were nearly in visual contact. Kinkaid did not know the carrier search was so long delayed. In any event, he thought that Halsey would be searching for the Central Force and was covering San Bernardino.

"I had good reason to think Task Force 34 was guarding San Bernardino Strait," Kinkaid said. "It was such a logical, perfect plan that I couldn't believe [Halsey] had not carried it out."

Kinkaid's staff officers convinced him to double-check with Halsey as to the location of Task Force 34, and at 0412 on October 25, Commander Seventh Fleet informed Commander Third Fleet of the results of the Battle of Surigao Strait, inquiring whether Task Force 34 was near the Strait.

Because of the persistent radio delays in transmitting through Manus, Halsey did not receive this message until 0648. He was miffed because Kinkaid had not been included in the original message about Task Force 34, but had to have copied it. Otherwise, how would he have known about Task Force 34? At 0705, Halsey replied: "Negative. Task Force 34 is with carrier groups now engaging enemy carrier force."

Kinkaid did not receive this reply until six minutes after getting the startling news from Ziggy Sprague that his carriers were under surface gunfire attack. Kinkaid lost no time in diverting all the planes he could to assist Taffy 3. He also sent a plain language dispatch to Halsey at 0707, which was received at 0822, spelling out his plight and asking for assistance. Ziggy Sprague messaged Halsey directly that he was under attack by battleships and cruisers. Kinkaid followed up by additional pleas to Halsey to send battleships and carrier planes.

Halsey was surprised at the normally low-keyed Kinkaid's pleas for help. After all, he had six battleships, cruisers, dozens of destroyers, and eighteen escort carriers with fighters and bombers. That should have been plenty. Halsey replied that he was engaging Ozawa's northern force and had ordered Admiral McCain's carrier task group immediately to come to aid the Seventh Fleet. But McCain was still hundreds of miles to the east. "Where is Lee?" Kinkaid messaged Halsey. "Send Lee!"

Kinkaid ordered Oldendorf's old battleships to prepare to assist the Taffies. These battleships had expended shells at Surigao but still had enough to fight. At 0800 Oley was 65 miles from the action, which meant three hours steaming. Kinkaid ordered Oldendorf at 0850 to move to block the mouth of Leyte Gulf. Then Kinkaid ordered Oley to assist Sprague but almost immediately countermanded the order when he learned Kurita had broken off contact.

In Pearl Harbor, Admiral Nimitz and his staff were monitoring the radio traffic from and to Kinkaid. Nimitz, too, believed Halsey must have left Task Force 34 behind to cover the strait. Raymond Spruance, on temporary duty at headquarters, looked at the command chart and, placing his hand just east of San Bernardino Strait, remarked, "If I were there, I would keep my force right there."

Nimitz was shocked at the news of Kurita's surprise attack off Samar. He sent an urgent dispatch that was one of the most controversial of the war. His message to Halsey was: "Where is Task Force 34?" Naval urgent messages sent in code contain padding, usually meant to be nonsensical, at the beginning and end of the text in order to confuse enemy decoders. The rule was that padding should never be mistaken for the message.

Assistant Chief of Staff Captain Bernard "Count" Austin, who served in Arleigh Burke's Little Beaver squadron, dictated the short message to a yeoman, who typed it for transmission. Austin emphasized the words "where is," and the yeoman mistakenly put the emphasis in print by repeating it. Then a young ensign coding communicator devised the padding, which was always separated from the text by any two consonants. So the dispatch read: "From CinCPac action com Third Fleet info Cominch [King] CTF 77 [Kinkade]," with the fore-and-aft padding, "Turkey trots to water gg where is rpt [repeat] where is Task Force 34 rr the world wonders."

The unfortunate choice of rear padding—similar to a line from Tennyson's "The Charge of the Light Brigade"—was compounded when a yeoman onboard *New Jersey* at 1000 included the rear padding before handing it to Halsey's staff. Normally the padding would be deleted. It now read: "Where is rpt where is Task Force 34. The world wonders." The padding made a certain sense and Halsey's inefficient communicators did not recognize it as such, separated by the "rr." The admiral was handed the message. He went white. He tore off his cap and threw it to the deck. He broke into sobs. He thought Nimitz was publicly humiliating him by including Admirals King and Kinkaid as addressees. Carney grabbed him by the shoulders. "Stop it," he said. "What the hell's the matter with you? Pull yourself together!"

Halsey seethed for an hour, uncertain what do to. But believing Nimitz's intent was clear, at 1055 he ordered Ching Lee's battleships to detach and speed south to come to Sprague's rescue, along with Gerry Bogan's TG 38.2. He was riding in *New Jersey* with Lee's force. It was a rash decision made in the heat of anger, since his force could not reach Leyte Gulf for hours, long after any battle would be over. And Halsey's battleships would miss the Japanese carriers. Pete Mitscher was left behind to clean up the Northern Force. But Halsey arrived several hours after Kurita steamed westward through San Bernardino Strait, a bitter disappointment to Halsey and Lee. They were able to catch the laggardly Japanese destroyer *Nowaki*, which had been picking up survivors, and sink it.

To the north, Pete Mitscher at 1415 ordered his cruisers and destroy-ers under Rear Admiral Larry DuBose to search for Japanese surviving warships. Once found, they sank abandoned carrier *Chiyoda* and, after dark, caught up with and sank destroyer *Hatsuzuki*, which had lingered to pick up survivors. But the rest of the Japanese force was too far away for DuBose to pursue through the night, and such action would bring him too close to land-based planes at Formosa in the morning. So ended the Battle Off Cape Engaño, the fourth and last of the four engagements that constituted the historic Battle for Leyte Gulf.

Japanese admirals, for the most part performed poorly. Admiral Nishimura had failed to wait for Admiral Shima to mass his force for the run up Surigao Strait. Admiral Kurita—despite his aggressive determina-tion to get through San Bernardino Strait—had failed to press his attack on the Taffies when victory was within his grasp. But the behavior of Admiral Jisaburo Ozawa, a fine carrier commander, was commendable. He was ordered to sacrifice his flattops as part of a strategy to win at Leyte Gulf. Bill Halsey never would have believed Ozawa's force was used as bait to draw him away from Leyte Gulf. But in a rare reflective moment, Halsey later suggested that the battles might have gone better if he had commanded at the Philippine Sea and Spruance at Leyte Gulf.

Twenty-nine

BATTLE OF THE ADMIRALS

November–December 1944

Controversy over Admirals Halsey and Kinkaid's actions at Leyte Gulf simmered in naval circles. Having left San Bernardino Strait unguarded, was Halsey responsible for the loss of the ships in the Battle Off Samar? Then having made his decision to go north, did he allow the Japanese heavy surface ships to get away, when he was almost within big-gun range, but then headed south?

What was Admiral Kinkaid's role? Should he have made sure proper air searches were conducted around the San Bernardino Strait? And should he have pulled back his battle line sooner and sent it full steam to assist the Taffies? In Washington, Admiral King was at first furious with Halsey's leaving the strait uncovered, but later tempered his anger and did not publicly criticize Halsey. When King met Halsey several months later, Halsey brought up Leyte Gulf, but King cut him off: "You don't have to tell me any more. You've got a green light on everything you did."

Admiral Nimitz in Pearl Harbor was equally perplexed by Halsey's all-or-nothing tactics. He, too, refrained from criticizing the national naval hero. But he wrote King that he regretted that the "fast battleships were not left in the vicinity of Samar when Task Force 38 started after the striking force reported to be in the north." CinCPac added, "It never occurred to me that Halsey, knowing the composition of the ships in the Sibuyan Sea, would leave the San Bernardino Strait unguarded, even though the Jap detachments in the Sibuyan Sea had been reported seriously damaged."

Possibly in an attempt to spike his critics' guns, Halsey himself messaged Nimitz on October 25, "I believed the Center Force had been so heavily damaged in the Sibuyan Sea that it could no longer be considered a menace to the Seventh Fleet."

There the matter officially rested until after the war when Bill Halsey published his account in the *Saturday Evening Post* magazine. In his story, he attempted to vindicate himself. In doing so, he made public a sensitive subject that had not been known to the general public. Halsey refused to acknowledge he made any mistakes. He blamed the root of the problems on the divided command. He shifted the blame to his old friend, Tom Kinkaid, Commander of Seventh Fleet, with phrases like, "I wondered how Kinkaid had let Ziggy Sprague get caught like this."

After pointing the finger at Kinkaid, though, Halsey reversed himself in the same article, writing, "I have attempted to describe the Battle for Leyte Gulf in terms of my thoughts at the time, but on rereading my account, I find that this results in an implication grossly unfair to Tom Kinkaid. True, during the action, his dispatches puzzled me. Later, with gaps in my information filled, I not only appreciate his problems, but frankly admit that had I been in his shoes, I might have acted precisely as he did." Even so Halsey, by leaving the earlier account stand in print, appeared to be trying to have it both ways.

Admiral King entered the fray with a letter to Halsey: "Personally, I must say that I did not like the tenor of the [*Post*] installment, neither as to Kinkaid . . . nor as to the command setup. . . . You would do well to review—and rewrite—the matter . . ."

Halsey had made an enemy of Tom Kinkaid, and now had alienated another friend and supporter, Ernie King. Halsey replied to King: "I have given your letter and my article much thought and study, and have asked for and received counsel. I regret your point of view and mine do not coincide."

In a final fillip, Halsey admitted he gave the orders to turn south while "in a rage," but blamed his anger on the phrase "the world wonders," which was written by an encoder who was either "drowsy or smart-alecky" and that Nimitz "tracked down the little squirt and chewed him to bits." This may have been true but hardly seems the way a gallant admiral shouldered responsibility.

*

Admiral Leahy was quoted in the *New York Herald Tribune* article critical of Halsey's decisions, "Halsey went off on a little war of his own." Other officers made their views known. Gerry Bogan said, "I'm clear in my own mind that it was a great mistake on Halsey's part." Captain Jimmy Thach, later to become a full admiral and who was Slew McCain's air operations officer (but, with McCain, missed the battle), defended Halsey and said with all that had been written "if I were Halsey . . . I'd still go after the carriers."

Tom Kinkaid's friends knew that he was deeply upset by Halsey's remarks and refusal to put Leyte Gulf in the past. He maintained a dignified public silence, but wrote Ernie King, "I believe Halsey made a serious mistake and I regret that he did not acknowledge it in his book instead of his shabby references to me. I have refused to be drawn into a controversy on the subject because no good could come of it."

Finally, Kinkaid spoke out publicly in an interview with Hanson W. Baldwin, military editor of the *New York Times* and a graduate of the U.S. Naval Academy. The admiral declared that Halsey "apparently overlooks the fact that the absence of TF [Task Force] 34 from San Bernardino Strait precluded the total destruction of Kurita's force on the spot, to say nothing of the loss of American lives and ships of the CVE force." Later, Kinkaid said, "Halsey spent ten years or more trying to justify his action. . . . Some of his efforts to justify it were at my expense. I don't mind that so much, but I don't think his logic was very good."

Still, Halsey's actions were a result of his boldness, and the other flag officers performed well indeed: Kinkaid handling the overall invasion force with aplomb, Oley Oldendorf almost flawless in winning the Battle of Surigao Strait, and Ziggy Sprague coolly making the best of a dreadfully bad tactical situation.

With Task Force 38, Admiral Halsey resumed air operations over the Philippines designed to knock out enemy air and protect the army troops running up against tough opposition on Leyte. But his ships were facing the new threat of kamikazes, which was escalating from random, single attacks to more concentrated raids on the task force. Halsey would have liked to pull his ships out of range, but the army's Fifth Air Force was not able to provide the planes for adequate cover. MacArthur requested the help of what was sometimes called "The Big Blue Fleet," since many ships wore a dark-blue paint. In response, the Third Fleet remained nearby.

The single airstrip at Tacloban on Leyte was inadequate and heavy tropical rains slowed the building of new ones.

On October 29, a kamikaze plane plowed into Gerry Bogan's flagship *Intrepid*, killing ten crewmen and wounding six. The next day,
another suicide plane struck Admiral Ralph Davison's flagship *Franklin*,
and another blasted into the nearby carrier *Belleau Wood*.

That same day, in Ulithi Lagoon, Slew McCain formally relieved
Pete Mitscher as Commander Task Force 38, and the veteran air admiral returned to the United States for a well-earned rest. Then he joined
up with Raymond Spruance and Kelly Turner in Pearl Harbor to plan the
invasion of Iwo Jima, which had been ordered by the Joint Chiefs of Staff
for early 1945. Admiral Nimitz decided that it would be a good idea to
keep McCain with Halsey and Mitscher with Spruance. Monty
Montgomery turned up to take over TG 38.1 from McCain.

McCain led Task Force 38 to sea again to support the troops on
Leyte and work over the Japanese bases in the Philippines. But on
November 5, east of Luzon, a land-based kamikaze smashed into the
island of McCain's flagship *Lexington*. The blast killed 50 crewmen and
wounded 132.

On November 11, McCain's planes sank a large convoy transporting
eleven thousand troops to the western shore of Leyte. And on November
25, the unlucky *Intrepid* with Gerry Bogan aboard was battered by another
suicide plane. Close by, *Cabot* was also hit, killing thirty-five and
wounding sixteen. Ted Sherman's flagship *Essex*, too, was struck by the
"divine wind," leaving fifteen men dead. Two days later, Japanese
planes damaged a battleship and two cruisers in Leyte Gulf, part of
Tom Kinkaid's Seventh Fleet. On November 29, it was the turn of battleship *Colorado* and two tin cans to suffer damage from kamikaze
blows. It seemed admirals were as much at risk in the fleet as the lowliest seaman. Halsey and McCain's ships were given a ten-day break to
replenish at Ulithi and give the exhausted crews some rest and relax-
ation on Mog Mog Island.

It was in the officers club on Mog Mog that conversation frequently
turned to discussions of the relative merits of the Halsey-McCain team
versus Spruance-Mitscher. Naturally, the outgoing, gregarious Halsey
captured the affection of many sailors with his impetuous style of leadership. Officers who supported him said that his impromptu brand of
command was perhaps confusing to his subordinates, but think how it

bewildered the enemy. Those who favored the Spruance-Mitscher method of careful advance planning—where everyone knew what was expected of him—tended to brand Halsey and his staff work as reckless, sloppy, and catch-as-catch-can.

After observing the quiet, expert Pete Mitscher in action, many did not know what to make of the unkempt, casual Slew McCain. The highly professional skipper of the light cruiser *Astoria*, Captain George Dyer, who served under both Halsey and Spruance and was destined to become a flag officer, summed up the view of many ship captains: "My feeling was one of confidence when Spruance was there. When you moved into Admiral Spruance's command from Admiral Halsey's . . . you moved from an area in which you never knew what you were going to do in the next five minutes or how you were going to do it, because the printed instructions were never up to date. . . . He never did things the same way twice. When you moved into Admiral Spruance's command, the printed instructions were up to date, and you did things in accordance with them."

The pugnacious Gerry Bogan was harsher on the commander of Task Force 38: "Pete Mitscher was a consummate master of naval airpower. When he ran it, it was a professional outfit, doing a professional job, in a professional way. When McCain ran it, it was a goddamn circus. He'd come up with one screwy idea after another. One night we changed the bomb load three times for morning strikes. Those kids had been working 24 hours on the flight deck, and when you have to change a load of bombs on 47 planes three times during the night, because he thought that different bombs might be better on the targets we were going to hit, it was disgusting to me, but there was nothing you could do about it."

Another fighting air admiral and skilled tactician, Raddy Radford, seconded Bogan's complaints. "When Admiral Spruance was in command," he said, "you knew precisely what he was going to do. But when Admiral Halsey was in command you never knew what he was going to do." Radford also said that Halsey often switched signals in his night orders, which were also many times unclear. Since his messages to air group commanders were so complicated and puzzling, the air group flag staffs often were in a quandary as to exactly what actions Halsey was going to take and what was expected of them.

For his next offensive step, General MacArthur planned to mount an invasion of Mindoro Island, and then the main Philippine island of

Luzon. But General Kenney had not yet established enough airfield bases on Leyte to support the ships. Admiral Kinkaid asked for a postponement, and MacArthur reluctantly agreed.

On December 15, while heading for the invasion of Mindoro Island, the venerable cruiser *Nashville*, flagship of General MacArthur at Leyte and carrying the flag of Rear Admiral Arthur D. Struble, was hit by a kamikaze. It killed 133 sailors and wounded another 190, many seriously. Among the dead were Admiral Struble's chief of staff, Captain E. W. Abdell, Colonel Bruce C. Hill, chief of staff to Brigadier General William C. Dunckel, the army troop commander, and Colonel John T. Murtha, Commander of the 310th Bombardment Wing. General William Dunckel and several other staff members were wounded. The crash destroyed the flag bridge, the combat information center, and the communications office. The kamikaze threat was turning into a real menace, with the ship's bridges the most likely target.

But with Halsey's Third Fleet at sea, again steaming to support MacArthur's forces in the Philippines, a storm was building up in the western Pacific that would cast another dark shadow on Bill Halsey's tactical reputation.

On December 17, Halsey's ships, having launched three days of strikes, were steaming east to make a fueling rendezvous, before returning to action on December 20 to support MacArthur's requests for air strikes. A storm was brewing, and belatedly Halsey and his staff realized that it was not an ordinary one; it had the prospects of building up to a typhoon. On the advice of his fleet aerographer, Halsey decided to avoid the eye of the storm by changing course to the northwest. But the aerographer was wrong; the storm center was 200 miles closer than predicted. Instead of avoiding the worst of the weather, the fleet was crossing the path of the typhoon.

Halsey changed fleet course to the southwest and worriedly watched the barometer in flag plot continue to drop. By now, his destroyers were running short on fuel, and some managed to ballast their tanks with seawater, but some did not. In a storm, a fully ballasted ship is normally the safest. All day December 17 and into December 18, the seas became mountainous, and the destroyers struggled to maintain fleet course and speed. Riding in his flagship, mighty *New Jersey*, the four-star admiral did not experience the worst of the typhoon's force, as did the small destroyers and the unwieldy carriers.

In the typhoon, the winds became stronger, the waves higher. The distance between crest and trough became greater. The wind sliced off the tops of waves, creating a world of rain and spray with visibility reduced to next to nothing. It was impossible to differentiate between night and day, sea and sky. The vessels began shipping water through ventilators, stacks, blower intakes, and every topside opening. Electrical circuits were drowned out, causing fires, power breakdowns, and steering failures. Lighting and propulsion equipment failed. The sea tore at deck equipment washing it overboard. Radar and radio and other communications equipment broke down. Ships lost internal communications and the ability to contact one another. Men were sick and exhausted. In a typhoon, never is the sea so cruel.

On bucking aircraft carrier decks, planes broke loose from their lashings, smashing into one another and starting fires from ruptured fuel tanks. The intense wind blew many aircraft overboard. Carriers nosing into the massive seas saw their flight deck overhangs carried away. The tin cans bobbed around like corks. Worse, they began listing from side to side: 30 degrees, 45 degrees, 60 degrees, and even farther from the vertical. Ships heeled over on their beam-ends with their stacks almost horizontal and struggled to teeter back.

Halsey sent messages to Admirals McCain and Bogan asking their assessments of where the typhoon was centered and where it was heading. Their own aerologists were closer to the mark than Halsey's, but misjudged course and distance. McCain was OTC but sent out a message to his commanders mislocating the typhoon. He changed course several times, incorrectly trying to find a way out of the typhoon. For a time, McCain tried to make a fueling rendezvous, before realizing the sea made it impossible.

Halsey, when he had a better idea of the typhoon's course, did not correct his earlier misinforming fleet message. He failed to listen to his task group commanders, who had better aerologists and information. When Halsey finally recognized he was in a typhoon, he still did not notify Nimitz until 1345 on December 18. Admiral Carney, Halsey's chief of staff, recalled that the Third Fleet commander was determined to keep his air strike schedule on behalf of MacArthur's forces until the last minute. "This was his decision and nobody was disposed to argue with it," Carney said.

December 18 was a black one for the U.S. Navy. Three destroyers, *Hull, Monaghan,* and *Spence,* rolled over in the tumultuous seas and sank with heavy loss of life. Serious damage was incurred by the light cruiser *Miami*; the light carriers *Monterey*, *Cowpens*, and *San Jacinto*; the escort carriers *Cape Esperance*, *Altamaha*, *Nehenta Bay*, and *Kwajalein*; and the destroyers *Aylwin*, *Hickox*, and *Dewey*—flagship of Captain Preston Mercer, commodore of Destroyer Squadron 1 and Nimitz's former flag captain. Lesser damage was inflicted on two dozen other ships, ranging from heavy cruisers to destroyer escorts. The carrier force lost 146 planes, and a total of 790 sailors died in the typhoon. Admiral Nimitz said the navy had suffered its worse loss without recompense.

Nimitz ordered a Board of Inquiry aboard the destroyer tender *Cascade* in Ulithi Lagoon. The senior members were Vice Admiral John Hoover, Vice Admiral George Murray, and Rear Admiral Glenn Davis. The court found that large errors were made in forecasting the storm's location and severity. They blamed Halsey for not issuing more detailed information and instructions on the storm on the morning of December 18. Once the severity of the storm was realized, orders should have gone out to ship commanders revising instructions to maintain fleet speed and course in order to protect their vessels. The findings faulted Halsey and McCain for steering an erratic course that did not take the force away from the typhoon. No blame was attached to any of the ship commanders. The court commended the skippers of *Cape Esperance* and *Altamaha* for taking independent action, without reference to superiors, to find the best course to ride out the storm.

The court decided: "The preponderance of responsibility falls on Commander Third Fleet, Admiral William F. Halsey, U.S. Navy. In analysing the mistakes, errors, and faults included therein, the court classifies them as errors in judgment under stress of war operations and not as offenses . . ." The sour Admiral Hoover privately thought that Halsey should be court-martialed. In his testimony, the outspoken Gerry Bogan reported that he had advised McCain and Halsey of a northerly course to miss the heart of the storm. Later, Bogan commented, "Halsey had a date to support MacArthur two days later. I felt it was just plain goddamn sloppiness and stupidity. All the information was available that this area we went to was going to be the heart of the typhoon. I thought it a needless tragic loss of life and materiel."

The Court of Inquiry passed its judgment to the convening authority, Admiral Nimitz, CinCPac. On January 22, Nimitz approved the court's findings. Regarding Admiral Halsey, Nimitz said, "The convening authority is of the firm opinion that no question of negligence is involved, but rather that the mistakes made were errors in judgment committed under stress of war operations and stemming from a commendable desire to meet military commitments. No further action is contemplated or recommended." Admiral King concurred. After all, Admiral Halsey was a national hero.

The Board of Inquiry confirmed to many senior naval officers in the Pacific what they privately had observed. Halsey lacked the experience and skill to handle the massive number of ships and complicated structure of a major fleet. His casual and impetuous style fitted his earlier command of small carrier forces, but was unsuited for the complexities of the Third Fleet. His improvising and failure to keep his subordinates fully informed of his plans left doubt and confusion. Still, he had won the hearts of his seamen; Bill Halsey was the sailor's admiral, while Raymond Spruance was the admiral's admiral.

In December, Congress authorized that four generals and four admirals be given a special five-star rank to correspond to the British Field Marshal and Admiral of the Fleet. The army chose Generals Marshall, Eisenhower, MacArthur, and Arnold for the honor of General of the Army. The navy picked Admirals Leahy, King, and Nimitz for the rank of Fleet Admiral, leaving one place vacant. Presumably, there was a question of whether to award it to Halsey or Spruance. The decision was left until after the war, when Bill Halsey received his fifth star, which many thought should have rightfully gone to Raymond Spruance.

Thirty

LINGAYEN, IWO JIMA, AND OKINAWA

January–June 1945

The liberation of the Philippines would be a long, laborious process since the Japanese occupied so many islands. But the main U.S. target after Leyte was the big island of Luzon with the capital of Manila. Like the Japanese, the United States decided to regain Luzon by first landing in Lingayen Gulf, halfway up the western shore of the island. The Luzon Attack Force comprised many of the ships that participated in the Leyte invasion.

Leading the Seventh Fleet once again was Vice Admiral Tom Kinkaid in his command ship *Wasatch*. He carried aboard Lieutenant General Walter Krueger, Commanding General U.S. Sixth Army. There were two amphibious groups, one commanded by Vice Admiral Dan Barbey and the other by Vice Admiral Ping Wilkinson. Vice Admiral Oley Oldendorf led the bombardment and fire support group of battleships, cruisers, and destroyers. Rear Admiral Calvin Durgin, a veteran of Operation Dragoon, commanded an escort carrier group providing air support for the ground troops.

The operation began ominously, for Japan now was mounting full-scale attacks by the Kamikaze Corps. Oldendorf's force moved from Leyte Gulf through the Sulu Sea to arrive in Lingayen before the amphibious transport ships. En route, on January 4, 1945, Japanese suicide planes attacked and sank the jeep carrier *Ommaney Bay*, with the loss of one hundred sailors. On January 5, planes crashed and damaged heavy cruiser *Louisville*, Australian cruiser *Australia*, escort carrier

Manila Bay, and destroyer escort *Stafford*. Oley's force arrived in Lingayen Gulf, and on January 6 when battleship *New Mexico* was bombarding the enemy shore batteries, a kamikaze crashed on the bridge, killing her skipper, Captain R. W. Fleming, Lieutenant General Herbert Lumsden, Winston Churchill's liaison officer at General MacArthur's headquarters, and *Time* magazine correspondent William Chickering. There were twenty-six other men killed and eighty-seven wounded. Unscathed on the offside of the bridge were Rear Admiral George Weyler, and the Royal Navy observer, Admiral Sir Bruce Fraser. *New Mexico* remained in action.

That same day, kamikazes smashed into and sank destroyer-minesweeper *Long*, and damaged destroyer-minesweeper *Southard* and tin cans *Walke*, *Barton*, and *Sumner*. Another suicide plane crashed into the main deck of the light cruiser *Columbia*, setting off severe fires. But prompt damage control, which flooded the magazines, prevented a full-scale explosion. Vice Admiral Oley Oldendorf's flagship *California* was hit at the base of her foremast, killing 45 men and wounding 151 aboard the battleship, which remained in the formation. (Oley was uninjured.) The unlucky *Australia* was hit for the second time, adding 14 dead and 26 wounded to earlier casualties.

A serious blow to the force came when a kamikaze crashed into *Louisville* for the second time, this time hitting the bridge of the heavy cruiser, which had served as Oldendorf's flagship at the Battle of Surigao Strait. Now it was the flagship of Rear Admiral Chandler. Ted Chandler was fifty years old, born in Annapolis and the son of a rear admiral. He was a graduate of the Naval Academy Class of 1915, which included fellow admirals Arthur Struble, Lynde D. McCormick, Richard W. Bates, Forrest B. Royal, and John L. McCrea. He commanded a phib group in Operation Dragoon in France, and a battleship division at Surigao Strait and was now in charge of a bombardment cruiser division. He was a quiet and efficient officer who was admired by one and all. Standing on his bridge when the suicide plane hit, he was enveloped in flaming gasoline. He tried to help with the firefighting hoses, but was soon overcome by the flames that scorched his lungs. He died the next day aboard *Louisville*, the fifth U.S. flag officer to be killed in action in the war. Thirty-one other sailors died with him, and fifty-six more were wounded. "Lady Lou" was so badly damaged that she had to pull out of the formation for repairs.

Then the amphibious groups under Vice Admirals Barbey and
Wilkinson arrived to debark the Sixth Army. Rear Admiral Dick
Conolly's reinforcement group brought up an additional infantry division. Cruiser *Boise* steamed into the gulf with General MacArthur, now
wearing five stars, aboard. *Boise* was attacked but not hit. However, Rear
Admiral Ralph Ofstie's flagship *Kitkun Bay* was struck and disabled. On
January 9, *Columbia* was hit by another suicide plane and suffered ninety-
two more casualties. On January 10, the kamikazes returned to damage
the destroyer escort *Belknap* and four Liberty ships. Finally, the next day,
the Japanese were running out of planes but managed to get in a last hit
on the escort carrier *Salamaua*. For the moment, the U.S. fleet rested, but
there would be more to come.

The Japanese did not oppose the landings at Lingayen Gulf, but
tough fighting lay ahead for the Sixth Army on the advance to Manila.
The navy assisted with secondary landings nearer the capital, but Manila,
after hard and destructive fighting, was not secured until March 4.

MacArthur was determined—he insisted obligated—to liberate the
rest of the Philippine Islands, though they could now be strategically
bypassed. So the Seventh Fleet amphibious groups were pressed into
service in the central and southern Philippines. The alternating teams
were led by amphibious Rear Admirals William Fechteler, Arthur
Struble, Albert G. Noble, and Forrest B. Royal—all under the supervi-
sion of Vice Admiral Barbey. The covering and support groups were
commanded by Rear Admirals Russell Berkey and Ralph Riggs. From
February to July, they made ten good-sized landings in the Philippines
and in Borneo. In routing out Japanese defenders from mountains and
jungles, the U.S. Eighth Army suffered thousands of casualties. Some
questioned the strategic value of the operations.

Rear Admiral Forrest Royal was a bright new rear admiral and
landed Australian troops on Borneo with dispatch. As he departed for
Leyte, the Australian commanding general messaged him: "I wish to
express admiration and appreciation of the thorough, efficient and gallant
and successful manner in which the naval force under your command
carried out its vital role in the Borneo operations."

On June 18, returning to Leyte in his flagship *Rocky Mount*, Forrest
Royal, having worked long, strenuous hours, died of a heart attack on his
flag bridge.

*

As the liberation of the Philippines, with the help of the Seventh Fleet, continued well into 1945, the Fifth Fleet went ahead with its plans to take Iwo Jima. In February, Fifth Fleet's Raymond Spruance replaced the Third Fleet's Bill Halsey.

The small island of Iwo Jima was 4 1/4 miles long and 2 1/2 miles wide, lying about halfway between the Marianas and Tokyo. It was needed as a base by the U.S. Air Force to serve as an emergency field for the new B-29 raids on Japan, based in the Marianas, and for fighters to provide escorts for the new super-bombers on the flights over Japan. The first B-29s landed on Saipan on October 12, 1944. By November 24, they launched the first big bomber attack on the Japanese homeland. The Japanese hit back with attacks on the B-29 fields with planes that staged through Iwo Jima.

Admiral Nimitz selected his familiar Fifth Fleet team to plan and take Iwo Jima: Raymond Spruance, fleet commander; Kelly Turner, amphibious force commander; and Pete Mitscher, commander of the carrier Task Force 58. The U.S. Marines would provide three divisions to invade the island. Lieutenant General Howlin' Mad Smith was named Commander Expeditionary Troops, which comprised the V Amphibious Corps under Major General Harry Schmidt. That meant H. M. Smith had no direct-command responsibility.

Harry Hill thought his old battlemate, Howlin' Mad Smith, at Iwo seemed a "different man." He was bitter, dejected, morose, and "mad at everyone: Nimitz, Spruance, Turner." It was in this spirit, Hill said, that Smith was to write his postwar memoir, *Coral and Brass*, which castigated everyone except his treasured marines. Under Turner were two veteran amphibious group commanders, Rear Admirals Harry Hill and Spike Blandy. The landing force was composed of the 3rd Marine Division commanded by Major General Graves B. Erskine, which had fought at Guam; the 4th Marine Division, led by Clifton B. Cates, training at Maui; and the new 5th Marine Division headed by Major General Keller E. Rockey in Hawaii.

Between December 8 and February 15, land-based U.S. bombers performed at least one strike daily against Iwo. A heavy cruiser force with destroyers headed by Rear Admiral Allan E. Smith bombarded the island in December. The battleship *Indiana* with Rear Admiral Oscar Badger aboard also shelled Iwo. Yet after each attack, the Japanese quickly resumed operations on the island's two airfields. Once the Americans

invaded the Mariana Islands, Lieutenant General Tadamichi
Kuribayashi, a tough, diligent and resourceful officer, was assigned to
build underground defenses under Iwo Jima's volcanic rock. The general
concentrated his defenses in and around Mount Suribachi in the southwest corner of the island. So industrious and skillful was he that his
defenses were almost impregnable, and the bombardments did not do as
much damage as American admirals presumed.

D-day was set for February 19 and opened with the heaviest sea bombardment of the war by Spike Blandy's battleships, cruisers, and destroyers. At 0645, Kelly Turner gave the order: "Land the Landing Force."
After forming up around the transports, the first waves hit the beach at
0900. The troops were not opposed at the waterline, but they had trouble moving across the soft volcanic sand. The Japanese were well dug in
inside hundreds of bunkers and opened up on the marines and the landing
craft from slightly higher positions. The enemy mortar fire was rapid and
accurate. There was little protection for incoming marines.

Still, some thirty thousand troops went ashore on the first day, supported by call fire from the warships. At nightfall, the gunfire support
forces moved well out to sea, leaving cruiser *Santa Fe* and ten destroyers
to supply star shells for illumination for the marines. General
Kuribayashi had no intention of launching suicidal banzai charges during the night. He knew he was cut off, that the Japanese fleet was not
bringing in reinforcements, but he was determined to fight from his
entrenchments to the last man.

The conquest of Iwo was most difficult and took much longer than
expected because of the defensive capabilities of the Japanese troops.
The marines were supported by planes from the escort carrier group commanded by Rear Admiral Calvin Durgin. But the Kamikaze Corps reared
its dangerous head again. One struck venerable old *Saratoga* about 35
miles offshore, killing 132 men and wounding 192, while destroying
forty-two planes. Plucky Sara made it back to port. Escort carrier
Bismarck Sea was less fortunate. On the evening of February 21, a
kamikaze crashed into the escort carrier, which set off explosions and
fires that sent the vulnerable flattop to the bottom, with 218 of her crew.

Joe Rosenthal, the *Associated Press* photographer, took the famous
shot of five marines and a navy medic raising the flag atop Mount
Suribachi. Secretary of the Navy James Forrestal, onboard Turner's

flagship *Eldorado* as an observer, remarked to General Smith, "Holland, the raising of that flag on Suribachi means a Marine Corps for the next five hundred years."

Iwo Jima was not declared secure until March 16. Admiral Nimitz said that on Iwo Jima "uncommon valor was a common virtue." General Smith called Iwo Jima "the most savage and most costly battle in the history of the Marine Corps." The marines lost nearly 6,000 men, with some 16,500 wounded. The Japanese suffered more than 20,000 killed, including General Kuribayashi. The airfields were soon used by P-51 fighters to escort the bombers and, by war's end, some twenty-four thousand B-29 landings were made on the island. One B-29 pilot, who made an emergency landing, said, "Whenever I land on this island, I thank God and the men who fought for it."

The next major leap for Admiral Nimitz's command was the capture of Okinawa, the centerpiece of the Ryukyu Islands. Okinawa was strategically placed in the Western Pacific: 340 miles from Japan, 360 miles from China, and 340 miles from Formosa. About 70 miles long with an area of 800 square miles, the island has landing beaches and a fine harbor, while the limestone structure provides for good defenses.

The Fifth Fleet team remained in harness: Spruance, Turner, and Mitscher. This time the ground forces were headed by Lieutenant General Simon Boliver Buckner, commanding the U.S. Tenth Army. It comprised the army's XXIV Corps, headed by Major General John R. Hodge, with four army infantry divisions, and the Marine Corps III Phib Corps led by Major General Roy Geiger, with three marine divisions—the 1st, 2nd, and 6th—the last going into action for the first time.

The northern attack force was commanded by Rear Admiral Lawrence Reifsnider in *Panamint*, who had served with Turner in the Solomons. Rear Admiral Jimmy Hall, a veteran of Sicily, Normandy, and Southern France, would command the southern landing force in *Teton*, while the Amphibious Support Force was commanded by Spike Blandy.

The size of the fleet was enormous. Where once a carrier task force would have a couple of admirals at most, the number of flag officers in the Fifth Fleet aboard all the ships at sea in the operation numbered forty-four, not including five others in the British Carrier Force. They served in such roles as battleship, cruiser, and carrier division commanders, amphibious units, the mine flotilla, and service force leaders. It was massive fleet to keep track of, but Spruance, Turner, and Mitscher were the admirals who could do it.

This enormous body of ships converged from Ulithi, Manus, Hawaii, and Saipan on Okinawa for the D-day landings on April 1, 1945, Easter Sunday, preceded by five days of air and sea bombardment. Admiral Hall closed in near the beach and his flagship, conned by Captain D. R. Tallman, prepared to drop anchor. Hall noticed Kelly Turner's flagship *Eldorado* steaming past and anchoring closer in, despite occasional enemy artillery rounds landing in the water. Hall told Captain Tallman if he let Turner's flagship get closer to the beach than *Teton*, he would fire him. Tallman steamed *Teton* past *Eldorado* before dropping the hook.

The landings went off with few hitches after dawn on one of the island's few level stretches. The marine III Corps hit the northern sector beaches halfway up the west side of Okinawa near the Yonton airfield, which was a preliminary target. The army XXIV Corps landed tle or no opposition at the beaches. According to the plan, the two marine divisions would head across the island and then head north. The army divisions would also drive across the island and turn south aiming at the more populous areas and the capital Naha. By April 4, the marines had cut the island in two, reaching the east coast. On April 12, the marines attacked the northern stronghold of the Motobu Peninsula, a rugged redoubt, which they cleared in a week. Then they turned south to assist the army divisions.

On May 4, the Japanese mounted a major counterattack, but it was repelled. Still, hard fighting continued, and the 6th Marine Division entered the outskirts of Naha on May 23. Bitter struggles raged around the Japanese position at the southern end of Okinawa. On June 18, near the end of the long battle, General Buckner was killed by enemy shellfire. He was succeeded by General Geiger, who remained in command until Okinawa was secured a few days later. American losses in the land battle were 7,374 killed and 31,807 wounded with 239 missing, the highest casualty total in any Pacific battle. The Japanese lost more than 100,000 dead.

But for the U.S. Navy, the battle off Okinawa was turning into the bloodiest chapter in its history.

Thirty-one
THE LAST DANGEROUS DAYS

March–August 1945

The "Divine Wind" Corps hit the Fifth Fleet off Okinawa like a typhoon. The attacks on the ships began even before the invasion, as the fast carriers maneuvered while launching air strikes against the Japanese home island of Kyushu.

On March 18, the kamikazes headed for Rear Admiral Radford's carrier group TG 58.4 and one hit Raddy's flagship *Yorktown*. The plane passed through the signal bridge and exploded near the ship's side, killing five sailors and wounding twenty-six. Another suicide plane tried to crash into *Intrepid* but was shot down. It exploded so close to the ship that two men aboard were killed and forty-three were wounded. *Enterprise* was another target, but the bomb that landed was a dud.

The following evening, the kamikazes aimed for Ralph Davison's TG 58.2. One dropped a bomb on *Wasp* that penetrated to the hanger deck then to the crew's quarters, and exploded in the galley where cooks were preparing breakfast. Fires broke out on several decks, however, expert damage control brought them under control in fifteen minutes. But 101 sailors died in the attack and 269 were wounded. *Wasp* continued to operate for several days before retiring to Ulithi for repairs.

The worst hit was Davison's flagship *Franklin*. The crew called her "Big Ben" after Benjamin Franklin, but the carrier was actually named after a Civil War battle. She was conducting the morning launch on March 19, when an undetected enemy plane dropped two bombs. The first exploded on the hanger deck ruining the forward elevator. Fires quickly spread to the parked planes, sparking a massive blaze. Everyone in the area was killed. The second bomb hit the after part of the flight deck, wrecking the aft elevator and spreading destruction among the planes lined up for the launch. The entire ship was wreathed in flames and smoke.

On the bridge, Captain Leslie H. Gehres was knocked down by the first blast. When he got back on his feet, he ordered the huge carrier to steer to starboard to bring the wind sweeping over the deck and keep the flames from the carrier island, the ship's nerve center. But fires touched off rockets on some of the planes on deck. Admiral Pete Mitscher on *Bunker Hill* heard the tremendous explosions while still over the horizon.

Admiral Davison, who had Rear Admiral Gerry Bogan onboard as an observer, ordered the light cruiser *Santa Fe* to come alongside to assist. After more than an hour fighting fires, Davison instructed a destroyer to take off the flag staff. As Davison departed, he advised Captain Gehres that he would probably have to order Abandon Ship, but the plucky skipper replied that he thought he could save his ship.

Gehres ordered key officers and men to remain aboard to save *Franklin* but gave permission for others to depart the stricken carrier. *Santa Fe* transferred aboard wounded and more than eight hundred men of Franklin's crew. By 1000, *Franklin* was dead in the water. The heavy cruiser *Pittsburgh*, in a masterly bit of seamanship by Captain John E. Gingrich, took *Franklin* under tow and began moving at 6 knots, while the combat air patrol hovered overhead. Shortly after noon the next day, March 20, *Franklin* was able to restore power and make 15 knots on her own.

"Down by the tail but reins up!" Gehres reported.

Admiral Spruance sent a signal on March 24 praising the captain and crew for their magnificent job in saving their carrier, which earlier in the war would have been a dead loss. *Franklin* had much more serious damage than *Lexington* at Coral Sea and *Yorktown* at Midway, both of which went under. Casualties amounted to 724 killed or missing and 265 wounded. *Franklin* steamed all the way to Pearl, and then to New York for major repairs and national acclaim for the feat.

Mitscher's carriers continued their mission to prepare Okinawa for invasion by striking Japanese air bases. Spruance and Nimitz praised Mitscher for his offensive stance and the efforts expended to save his carriers.

Having survived kamikazes, Ralph Davison fell victim to his own penchant for living it up on the beach. The brilliant air tactician was, in the words of historian Clark Reynolds, "a jovial but not obnoxious drinker when relaxing had managed to miss an important airplane flight and was forthwith removed from command for his error." So the courageous but momentarily irresponsible Ralph Davison spent the rest of his career in training commands. Gerry Bogan took over the task group.

After the Okinawa landings, the Fifth Fleet remained to provide support and cover with gunfire and airpower. The brunt of the attack by the Kamikaze Corps was absorbed by the "small boys," the code name for destroyer types on radar picket duty between the main body of the fleet and the Japanese airbases, which dispatched the suicide planes. In the course of the campaign, thirty-four destroyers and smaller craft were sunk and many more were damaged, some almost beyond repair. These destroyermen fought a long, valiant fight, and the punishment the tin cans took attested to the heroic qualities of their crews and the toughness of the ships themselves.

But the prime target of the kamikazes was the big carriers and other capital ships. For Task Force 58, carriers were hitting Japanese ports and airfields from their steaming position, north of Okinawa.

In early April, a surface special attack force sortied from the Inland Sea intending to disrupt Kelly Turner's amphibious force off Okinawa. The main element of this flotilla was the super-battleship *Yamato*, whose sister-ship *Musashi* was sunk by U.S. carrier aircraft in the Sibuyan Sea. Pete Mitscher anticipated this move and deployed the planes of two carrier groups to stop Vice Admiral Seiichi Ito's ships. The Japanese had made the grave mistake of hurling all their airpower at the Okinawa warships, leaving no air cover for the *Yamato* force.

Vice Admiral Oley Oldendorf had been injured when his motor launch, from flagship *Tennessee*, rammed a harbor buoy in Ulithi. He was replaced as battleship commander by Rear Admiral Mort Deyo, who prepared his battle line to meet the threat from the massive battlewagon, the world's largest—nearly 73,000 tons with 18.1-inch main guns—and the pride of the Imperial Japanese Navy. Pete Mitscher's planes reached the Japanese force first, having been alerted of the sightings by two American submarines, *Threadfin* and *Hackleback*.

Yamato was moving south from Kyushu. Aboard were Vice Admiral Ito and Rear Admiral Kosaku Ariga. Another sighting of the enemy ships was made by planes from *Essex*. Mitscher launched a full-scale bomber and torpedo plane attack from two carrier groups. Carrier *Bennington* claimed first blood with bomb hits on *Yamato's* mainmast and a torpedo in her side. Torpedoes also hit light cruiser *Yahagi* and destroyer *Hamakaze*, the latter of which sank immediately. For the next two hours *Yamato* was under constant attack. Bombs and torpedoes slammed into the battleship, ruining her steering gear and turning her into a flaming hulk. Internal explosions added to *Yamato's* woes, and at 1423 on April 7 she went down. With her went Admirals Ito and Ariga and most of her crew. Also sunk were destroyers *Hamakaze*, *Isokaze*, *Asashimo*, and *Kasumi*. The remaining four destroyers in the force were damaged but made it back to Sasebo in the Inland Sea.

Japan's fleet was in tatters and the Kamikaze Corps sought vengeance. Rarely, it seemed, were admirals themselves under such personal peril than when on their exposed bridges, which were a natural target for the suicide planes.

On April 7, a plane dropped a bomb on the forward flight deck of the fast carrier *Hancock* then plunged into the aft end of the deck, setting fires among the waiting planes. Seventy-two sailors were killed and eighty-two wounded. On April 11, a suicide plane crashed into battleship *Missouri* but caused little damage to the heavily armored ship. On the same day, two kamikazes hit *Enterprise* again with glancing blows, but fires were quickly brought under control. On April 11, *Essex* was the target of a near miss that caused severe damage to fuel tanks, killing thirty-three sailors, with the same number wounded.

After the *Yamato* sinking, Kelly Turner sent Chester Nimitz a jesting dispatch declaring: "I may be crazy but looks like the Japs have quit the war, at least in this section."

CinCPac messaged back: "Delete all after 'crazy'!"

April 11 was a black date for the U.S. Navy, though the day itself was beautiful. The Japanese mounted a major air attack: 185 kamikazes with 145 fighters and 45 torpedo planes. Destroyer *Abele* was hit by a suicide plane and a radio-controlled bomb which Americans called a "baka," sinking the tin can with seventy-nine men lost and thirty-five wounded. The minesweeper *Gladiator*, destroyer escort *Rall*, and destroyer *Zellars* were badly damaged and out of action. *Tennessee*, Admiral Deyo's flagship, was also a target, as a plane crashed near the flag bridge, spraying burning fuel over the gun crews, with its bomb exploding in the warrant officers quarters. A total of 23 officers and men were killed and 106 were wounded, many of whom were burned horribly. Three other destroyer escorts—*Whitehurst*, *Riddle*, and *Wann*—were hit or suffered damage from near misses.

In the next stage of the Divine Wind attacks, the Japanese aimed for the radar picket destroyers, which were individually positioned well forward of the main body of the task groups to provide early warning. On April 16, the Japanese launched an attack of 165 planes. The kamikazes first singled out destroyer *Laffey*, inflicting perhaps the heaviest damage ever on a ship without sinking it. In an eighty-minute period, twenty-two separate attacks were counted, and *Laffey* was hit by six suicide planes, as well as being bombed and strafed. Her crew lost thirty-one killed or missing and seventy-two wounded. Gunners managed to shoot down nine enemy planes.

The destroyer *Pringle* was sunk by an exploding kamikaze. The tin can *Isherwood* took a bad wound from an incoming plane, losing forty-two men killed or missing and the same number wounded. Destroyer *Hobson* was also damaged in an attack, as was *Bowers*, which suffered forty-eight killed or missing and fifty-six badly wounded after a plane crashed the flying bridge. A kamikaze exploded so close to destroyer-minesweeper *Harding* that it blew a hole in her side, leaving twenty-two dead and ten wounded.

There was a brief respite until April 27–28, when destroyers *Ralph Talbot* and *Rathburne* were damaged by kamikazes. An ammo-laden Canadian-built merchant Victory ship was sunk. On April 28, two destroyers, *Daly* and *Twiggs*, were damaged. That evening, a plane crashed into the hospital ship *Comfort* carrying wounded to Saipan under a full moon. It demolished the ship's surgery room. Six army nurses and seven patients were among the dead. On May 3, destroyer *Aaron Ward* took a beating with repeated hits. The crew worked to save the tin can amid exploding ammunition, and forty-five were killed and forty-nine were wounded. After a valiant struggle, the crew made it into port to receive a message from Admiral Nimitz: "We all admire a ship that can't be licked. Congratulations on your magnificent performance."

Another destroyer type, *Little*, wasn't as lucky. She was struck five times by suicide planes and sank within minutes, with thirty dead and missing and seventy-nine wounded. In early May, other tin cans manning the radar picket line were hit in the Divine Wind attacks. Then the kamikazes turned their attacks from the small boys to the bigger ships, often flagships with admirals aboard.

On the cloudy morning of May 11, 1945, Vice Admiral Mitscher was called into the flag plot on the flag bridge of USS *Bunker Hill*, his large flagship steaming 100 miles east of Okinawa.

At 1004, the radio speaker crackled, "Alert! Alert! Two planes diving on *Bunker Hill*."

The wizened Mitscher and his chief of staff, the bluff Arleigh Burke, peered at the vast flight deck below. *Bunker Hill*, leading the carrier strike force, carried nearly ninety warplanes. The flattop and other warships of the task force had been in continuous combat, operating at sea, for more than two months supporting the Okinawa invasion. Pete Mitscher's planes were also pounding enemy warships and bombing Japan's home islands.

The sailors in the task force were worn out from constant action with no respite. Mitscher, never robust, was down to scarcely 100 pounds. The leathery admiral looked skeletal in his long-billed cap. He appeared exhausted. Not Commodore Burke, though, who was still bouncy and ebullient. The two flag officers, who had become friends, watched intently as kamikazes approached their ships, despite the curtain of anti-aircraft fire sent up by the force: battleships, cruisers, destroyers, the carriers themselves.

An enemy fighter, a "Zeke" (code name for the Zero plane), made a shallow dive at *Bunker Hill*, dropped a 500-pound bomb, and skidded across the flight deck, spewing gasoline among the ready U.S. aircraft, then flipped over the side into the sea. A second kamikaze aimed an explosive at the flight deck, and then flew into the base of the carrier's island—the nerve center of the huge ship—scarcely 30 yards from Admiral Mitscher's position on the flag bridge. The plane's engine slammed into the flag office, killing three officers and eleven enlisted men on Mitscher's staff. The bomb penetrated the flight deck, exploding in the gallery deck, killing many more men, including flagstaff members. Among the dead were the Admiral Mitscher's flight surgeon, Captain

Ray Hege; Lieutenant Commander Charles Steele, his devoted flag secretary; and Lieutenant Commander Frank Quady, assistant operations officer. Commander Jimmy Flatley, a brilliant fighter pilot who was Mitscher's air operations officer, had his back scorched with flame.

When he heard the first blast, Mitscher moved with Burke to the edge of the flag bridge and saw that flames had enveloped the radio room at the base of the island superstructure. Burke helped Mitscher up the ladder one deck to the navigation bridge to confer with *Bunker Hill's* Captain George A. Seitz. The one-star Commodore Burke dashed down the ladders, several levels, to the radio room. He assisted Lieutenant Commander Frank Dingfelder, the staff communications officer, in leading half-conscious radiomen to safety up the ladder. Burke reached the flag plot as the smoke gushed up the stairwell. He ordered everyone out to the open flag bridge area. A cruiser, USS *Wilkes-Barre*, and destroyers came alongside *Bunker Hill* to pour water through their hoses onto the blazing hanger deck.

Burke instructed a senior officer, Captain Gus Read, to round up members of the staff because Mitscher would want to know everyone's status immediately. Mitscher considered his staff his naval family, the modern counterpart—as historian E. B. Potter put it—of Horatio Nelson's "band of brothers." Captain Read found that half the staff had been killed or wounded, some by blast and fire, others by smoke inhalation. Mitscher's own sea cabin was gutted, his clothing destroyed, his official papers all burned.

In an instinctive maneuver, Captain Seitz turned his ship sharply to starboard, which threw burning aircraft off the ship and sloshed flaming gasoline off the hanger and flight decks. He then turned into the wind to shift the flames to the rear and allow his damage controlmen to fight the fires.

It was clear to Mitscher and Burke that *Bunker Hill* could no longer serve as the flagship of Task Force 58. Mitscher sent a visual signal to Rear Admiral Ted Sherman, aboard the carrier *Essex*, turning over to him temporary command of Task Force 58. Burke ordered twenty staff members to assemble on the hanger deck to transfer by high-line, a kind of breeches buoy, to the destroyer USS *English* alongside. The ladder from the bridge to the hanger deck was still ablaze, so Burke managed to lift the weakened Mitscher over a hastily rigged Jacob's ladder to the flight deck and then to the destroyer.

The tin can steamed away from the stricken *Bunker Hill*. It transferred Mitscher and his remaining staff to the Big E. Behind, in *Bunker Hill*, 396 sailors were dead and 264 were wounded. Most of the ship's fighter squadron pilots, awaiting orders in their ready room, were killed from asphyxiation. Through superb damage control efforts, the carrier remained afloat, and her skipper, Captain Seitz, steered her toward safety and then eventually to Pearl Harbor.

The next day, May 12, Mitscher resumed command of Task Force 58 from the flag bridge of *Enterprise*. He ordered a new round of carrier air strikes against Japanese airfields on the home islands of Kyushu and Shikoku. Two days later, a group of Japanese planes headed for *Enterprise*'s task group. Commander Flatley shouted for everyone to hit the deck. One plane managed to fly through the anti-aircraft fire and strike *Enterprise*, crashing into the after aircraft elevator, badly damaging the rear section of the carrier, and sending up lethal bits of debris. A metal fragment hit a man standing next to Commodore Burke on the open bridge, killing him. Frank Dingfelder had his glasses shattered by a splinter. A half dozen of Admiral Mitscher's staff were wounded. Mitscher remained standing and imperturbable during the attack: his arms folded, a frown on his face.

"Flatley," Mitscher said, "tell my task group commanders that if the Japs keep this up they're going to grow hair on my head yet."

Commander Dingfelder stumbled in, bleeding from a cut near his eye. He was reeling. Commodore Burke led him to Mitscher's sea cabin behind the bridge, and gave him a shot of whiskey from an emergency supply in the admiral's safe. Burke restored order on the flag bridge, but *Enterprise*'s flight deck was shattered; the carrier needed serious repairs. To maintain effective command of the force, Mitscher was forced again to transfer his flag to the carrier *Randolph*, which had earlier been hit by a kamikaze but had been patched up in Ulithi atoll. During all the drama, Mitscher was not once heard to raise his wispy voice, or even show excitement. Burke was quick to point out that the admiral never *did* show excitement.

Mitscher wasn't the only flag officer having problems. Off Okinawa, the morning before the invasion, the heavy cruiser *Indianapolis* was steaming in to resume an offshore bombardment with her nine 8-inch guns. Aboard was Admiral Spruance, commander of the Fifth Fleet.

Spruance was on his flag bridge supervising the activities of the fleet, the largest ever assembled. Through the clouds, a solitary plane broke into the clear and crashed into *Indianapolis* near the stern. The explosion was deafening and acrid smoke engulfed the ship. Spruance gave his flag lieutenant two orders; determine the damage from the ship's captain, and find out if the kamikaze pilot carried a codebook. The officer returned with the information that the ship's propellers were damaged and there was flooding in the after compartments. Nine sailors were killed and twenty wounded. The damage would affect steering on the warship. This compelled Raymond Spruance, as quiet mannered as Pete Mitscher, to abandon his favorite flagship, which was under the command of Captain Charles V. McVay III, and shift to the battleship *New Mexico*, which had the necessary communications for a fleet commander.

But *New Mexico*, too, was the target of a suicide plane, which struck near the bridge on the evening of May 12, narrowly missing the admiral. Spruance's staff feared for his safety and frantically searched the ship. The four-star admiral was found manning a fire hose, along with ordinary seamen. Spruance had been in his aft cabin and was heading for the bridge when the kamikaze struck along the deck the admiral would normally walk to reach his flag bridge. Fifty-four sailors were killed in the attack and 119 were wounded.

This time, *New Mexico* was able to make repairs at anchor while Admiral Spruance remained aboard. The cool Spruance noted in a letter to his wife, Margaret, "I have gotten very good at sleeping through five- and fourteen-inch gunfire and Jap hecklers at night."

In another letter to Margaret, Spruance informed her of the suicide of the commanding officer they had both known. He had a mental breakdown in the Pacific. "Some people can't take a war," Spruance remarked, "and others thrive on it."

Raymond Spruance and his staff were nearing the limits of their endurance after the months at sea in the invasions of Iwo Jima and Okinawa. Spruance was dissatisfied with the work of General Kenney's Fifth Air Force because of its lackluster performance from Luzon in hitting kamikaze airfields on Formosa. Spruance and others believed General Buckner's plan of attack was too slow. Again, it was the fast, take-your-losses-and-secure-the-island tactics of the U.S. Marines versus the step-by-step approach of the army.

Admiral Nimitz was worried that the dragged-out Okinawa campaign was costing the Fifth Fleet heavily. He wanted to pull the ships out of harm's way. On a visit to Okinawa, General Buckner asserted to the impatient Nimitz that the land campaign was an army affair. Nimitz replied sharply, "Yes, but ground though it may be, I'm losing a ship and a half a day. So if this line isn't moving within five days, we'll get someone here to move it so we can all get out from under these stupid air attacks."

Spruance wrote to Carl Moore: "I doubt if the Army's slow, methodical method of fighting really saves lives in the long run. The longer period greatly increases naval casualties when Jap air attacks on ships is a continuing factor. However, I do not think the Army is at all allergic to losses of naval ships and personnel. There are times when I get impatient for some of Holland Smith's drive, but there is nothing we can do about it."

Spruance's comments were probably unfair because of the rugged nature of the terrain on Okinawa and he wisely never made any public comments about the army's performance. Nobody wanted a rerun of the Smith-versus-Smith episode in the Marianas.

At one point Jimmy Flatley, Pete Mitscher's operations officer, was worried about the high losses of carrier air group commanders who usually led their planes into battle against heavily defended targets. He instructed Commander Hank Miller—commander of *Hancock*'s air group and the aviator who trained Jimmy Doolittle's pilots for the Tokyo raid—to stand off and direct the attack from afar. Miller ignored Flatley's directive. As Miller explained, "If a CAG [carrier air group] or squadron commander says, 'Okay, now, kids, you go in there and give it the old college try, and I'll stay out here and watch,' well, you can't fight a war that way."

In late May, Bill Halsey took over from Raymond Spruance, and the Third Fleet was back on line. Slew McCain replaced Pete Mitscher, who went to Washington as Deputy CNO for Air and an extended rest. Kelly Turner handed over to Harry Hill, now a vice admiral. Turner was promoted to four stars and went to work with Spruance planning the invasion of Japan. Spruance sailed away from Okinawa in *New Mexico*.

Spruance remained almost unknown to the American public. But that's the way he wanted it. As he put it privately, possibly with his friend Bill Halsey in mind:

> Personal publicity in war can be a drawback because it may affect a man's thinking. A commander may not have sought it; it may have been forced on him by zealous subordinates or imaginative war correspondents. Once started, however, it is hard to keep in check. In the early days of the war, when little about the various commanders is known to the public, and some admiral does a good or spectacular job, he gets a headstart in publicity. Anything he does thereafter tends toward greater headline value than the same things done by others, following the journalistic rule that 'names make the news.' Thus his reputation snowballs; and soon, probably against his will, he has become a colorful figure, credited with fabulous characteristics over and above the competence in war command for which he has been conditioning himself all his life.
>
> His fame may not have gone to his head, but there is nevertheless danger in this. Should he get to identifying himself with the figure as publicized, he may subconsciously start thinking in terms of what this reputation calls for, rather than of how best to meet the action problem confronting him. A man's judgment is best when he can forget himself and any reputation he may have acquired, and can concentrate wholly on making the right decisions.

Bill Halsey and Slew McCain resumed their carrier attacks on Japan, and the carrier group commanders remained much the same: Jocko Clark commanding TG 38.1, Ted Sherman TG 38.3, and Raddy Radford TG 38.4. In another change, Ching Lee was due for a long rest and was reassigned to head a special group based in Casco Bay, Maine, to work out effective anti-kamikaze tactics. There, Lee died of a heart attack in a motor launch in the harbor. Oley Oldendorf was named to head a special battleship task force and was wounded aboard his flagship *California* by an enemy torpedo plane.

On June 3 and 4, Halsey sent air strikes against the southern Japanese island of Kyushu. On June 5, a typhoon slammed into Halsey's Third Fleet for the second time. Raddy Radford recommended to his immediate boss, Slew McCain, that the task force should steer clear of the heavy weather. McCain replied that Halsey had to decide. Halsey was intent on holding to his air strike and refueling schedule. He and his aerologist, Commander George Kosko, who had been in the first storm, again drew inaccurate conclusions as to the direction of the typhoon. Halsey ordered Radford and Clark's carrier groups into the path of the typhoon.

Jocko Clark's group was refueling from the replenishment ships and oilers of Rear Admiral Donald B. Beary's Service Squadron Six and signaled McCain: "Believe this course is running us back into the storm." McCain changed course to due north, which was fine for Radford's group containing both Halsey's flagship *Missouri* and McCain's flagship *Shangri-La*. But Clark's carrier group was 15 miles to the south and nearer to the storm, which was overtaking his ships.

At 0420 June 5, Clark signaled McCain: "I can get clear of the center of the storm quickly by steering 120 degrees. Please advise."

McCain replied: "We have nothing on our scope to indicate storm center."

"We definitely have," Clark answered. "We have had one for one and a half hours."

McCain waited for fifteen minutes before asking Clark for his storm data. He continued to hold the northern course, but he finally and belatedly gave Jocko permission to use his own judgment on evading the eye of the typhoon. By the time Clark was able to break off refueling and steer away, it was too late. The storm caught his ships. No ships were sunk but *Pittsburgh* lost 100 feet of her bow, torn off by the force of the waves. Flight deck overhangs on *Bennington* and *Hornet* collapsed. Every ship in the task group was damaged, some severely. Six men were lost overboard, and seventy-six planes were destroyed. Clark managed to avoid more damage by ordering his ships to lie to, thus riding out the storm. The next day, the fleet tug *Munsee* under Lieutenant Commander J. F. Pingley messaged: "Have sighted the suburb of *Pittsburgh* and taken it in tow."

Halsey's handling of the Third Fleet in the second typhoon came close to wrecking his career. Nimitz called a Board of Inquiry on Guam headed again by Vice Admiral Hoover. The court was tough on Halsey and McCain. It pointed out that Nimitz's advice to the fleet on the lessons of the first December typhoon was not followed. As well, there was a "remarkable similarity between the situations, actions and results" of the two storms. The court placed most of the blame on Halsey and McCain.

Court member Vice Admiral Charles Lockwood commented privately, "The whole matter certainly is a mess and indicates that nobody ever heard of a guy named Bowditch," referring to Nathaniel Bowditch, who wrote classic treatises on navigation. Halsey blamed the weather-reporting service for the disaster. The court recommended that Halsey and McCain be assigned to "other duties." Navy Secretary Forrestal wanted to retire Halsey, but Admirals King and Nimitz talked him out of it, arguing once again that Halsey was a national hero and his removal would damage national morale and boost Japan's. Halsey remained in command.

The Third Fleet spent the month of July off Honshu, Japan's main island, launching air strikes at ships in the Inland Sea and closing in on the coast to bombard industrial plants with the fast battleships' big guns. The war was near its end. U.S. submarines, which had done so brilliantly during the war, were running out of targets. Raymond Spruance in Pearl Harbor and Kelly Turner in Manila, planning the invasion of Kyushu, were worried about the prospective American losses in taking on the Japanese army in its homeland. Their fears vanished with the dropping of the atomic bomb at Hiroshima and Nagasaki. The last air strike was launched from Task Force 38 on August 15. Then Admiral Halsey received word from Admiral Nimitz to "cease all offensive operations against Japan." The great sea war was at an end.

EPILOGUE

The war ended in total victory for the U.S. Navy and the fighting admirals who led it into action. Hostilities had hardly ceased when admirals (in their memoirs), their adherents, and some historians began assessing the strengths and weaknesses of the wartime flag officers. Often an admiral's performance depended on the kind of command he held, which could determine the opportunity an admiral had to fight and to win battles.

Three admirals of unparalleled ability did not, because of the nature of their commands, go to sea. Ernie King, the human blowtorch, ran the navy with an iron fist from Washington; Chester Nimitz, the wise CinCPac, directed strategy and operations at Pearl Harbor; and Charles Lockwood, the highly effective Commander Submarines Pacific, conducted the successful submarine war against Japan.

As the conflict progressed, the fleet increased almost exponentially in size and complexity. Some fighting admirals like Tip Merrill and Pug Ainsworth, who defeated enemy cruiser-destroyer formations in mano-a-mano combat in the South Pacific, were assigned to lead cruiser screens in large carrier formation. As such, they performed valuable services to the Third and Fifth Fleets, but they had little chance for the sort of independent action that once had allowed them to distinguish themselves.

Battleship admirals like Ching Lee became bombardment group commanders for island invasions or escorts for the fast carriers. American and Japanese battleships came to direct grips only twice: at the Battle for Guadalcanal and the Battle of Surigao Strait. The battlewagon admirals found they were often under the command of amphibious group commanders, a kind of operation that was unknown before the war.

Some of the brilliant young air admirals, after being blooded in the Pacific, showed excellent planning and administrative skills. Rear admirals like Wu Duncan and Raddy Radford were sidetracked for important jobs in Washington or naval air commands. And distinguished combat commanders like Soc McMorris and Forrest Sherman proved too valuable to Chester Nimitz as senior aides, thus they never got sea commands again.

Yet some fighting admirals stayed in the forefront of the action throughout the war. Chief among these was Admiral Raymond Spruance, commander of the Fifth Fleet, whose flagships were hit by enemy planes' bombs more than once in the thick of action. From his early days as a cruiser-division commander with Bill Halsey's carrier task force, to heading the mightiest naval force ever assembled, Spruance proved to be the finest all-around fighter and tactician the U.S. Navy ever produced. Calm and unruffled, modest and publicity shy, Spruance led hundreds of ships and dozens of subordinates with unfailing efficiency and courage, with a clear perception of a battle situation, and with orders that were models of speed and clarity.

Spruance was the outstanding U.S. fleet commander, whose responsibilities extended to sea, air, and land. As the foremost naval tactician, Raymond Spruance was always less concerned about what the enemy was *going* to do than what the enemy *could* do. And in battle after battle, he followed this principle. Through the war, Spruance remained largely unsung and unappreciated by the American public. Yet he was the victor at the crucial Battle of Midway, and he had overall command of the Central Pacific Force—both planning and execution—from the Gilberts to the final struggle for Okinawa (except for the invasion of the Philippines). In his direction of the fleet, Spruance had that rare quality of the greatest captains: the ability to make swift, correct decisions in a rapidly changing situation under the heaviest combat pressure.

In looking back, Spruance explained his view on his role as admiral: "Things move so fast in naval actions, and the consequences that hang on the results of these actions are often so momentous that fast teamwork is essential. Teamwork is something that comes best from association, training, and indoctrination. There are too many variables possible in war for everything to be foreseen and planned ahead of time. Our plans can be made out in great detail up to the time we hit the enemy. After that, they have to be flexible; ready to counter what the enemy may try to do to us and ready to take advantage of the breaks that may come to us. To do that, the man on the spot must know where he fits into the operation, and he must be able to act on his own initiative, either without any orders at all because radio silence may be in effect, or on very brief orders because there is no time for long instructions."

The relationship between Spruance and Halsey was curious. Spruance was cool, quiet, introspective, and almost aloof. Halsey was excitable, profane, and gregarious. Yet both men shared rare qualities: devotion to duty, absolute integrity, determination to fight, and the ability to command the respect of those below and above them, thus getting the best out of everyone. Though they were of totally different temperaments with vastly differing styles, they remained close friends over the years.

Raymond Spruance had as subordinates two of the ablest, most aggressive admirals in history, each being a master of a new form of warfare, which became paramount in World War II. Admiral Richmond Kelly Turner was the amphibious commander without equal, from the first, tentative landings on Guadalcanal—when the issue was in doubt—to the massive operation on Okinawa thousands of miles from friendly bases. Turner proved to be a brilliant planner and a tenacious fighter: irascible, abrasive but hugely effective. Turner's opposite number under Spruance was Pete Mitscher, the finest air admiral ever. As understated as Turner was domineering, Mitscher was beloved by his aviators as he pioneered and developed the carrier air tactics that—along with devastating scores of U.S. submarines under Admiral Charles Lockwood—would mark the end of the Japanese navy.

The fighting admiral with perhaps the most varied career in the Pacific war was Tom Kinkaid, who commanded cruiser divisions, carrier task forces, the North Pacific Force, and finally the Seventh Fleet, working in a difficult job under General MacArthur. Quiet and determined, he fought a complex war, making few mistakes. In the end, he was saddened over his falling out with Bill Halsey concerning the responsibilities involved in the controversial Battle for Leyte Gulf.

After Kelly Turner, the top amphibious commanders were Kent Hewitt and Alan Kirk in the Atlantic, and Ping Wilkinson, Harry Hill, Dick Conolly, Jimmy Hall, and Uncle Dan Barbey in the Pacific. The top air admirals were, by and large, superb in commanding carrier formations. The most talented and aggressive were Ted Sherman, Jocko Clark, Raddy Radford, Black Jack Reeves, Gerry Bogan, Monty Montgomery, and Ralph Davison. Others were tried in action and found wanting.

As for surface ship fighters, Tip Merrill, Pug Ainsworth, Norman Scott, and Oley Oldendorf were the best combat cruiser formation commanders. Ching Lee was an outstanding leader of battleships, though he was never to repeat his victory off Guadalcanal. In a class of his own, Arleigh Burke made a spectacular reputation as a destroyer squadron commodore, and then as probably the finest chief of staff (to Pete Mitscher) in the Pacific.

So varied were the personalities and individual styles of the top admirals that it was a source of wonder that they meshed together in such a relatively smooth-running overall team. The arguments between Kelly Turner and Howlin' Mad Smith were legendary—but they got the job done.

The career of the charismatic Bill Halsey took a strange midwar turn. The undeniable hero of the early carrier strikes, when aggressiveness was in short supply, his morale-building operations proved an indispensable boost to naval and national morale. That vitality suffused the faltering South Pacific forces, when he assumed command in late 1942, and led the successful offensive up the Solomons.

Unfortunately, by the time he was appointed to head the Third Fleet in 1944, it seemed that the war had passed him by, in the sense that he seemed no longer up to exercising proper control over his vast carrier groups with new tactics. He was as aggressive as ever, but his impulsive judgment came into question, particularly in his actions during the Battle for Leyte Gulf and in the two typhoons, into which he led the Third Fleet. However, in the knowing eyes of Admirals Ernest King and Chester Nimitz, Bill Halsey remained an authentic naval hero, the sailors' admiral.

In postwar years, a handful of World War II fighting admirals made it to the top post of CNO, though they were all not necessarily the stars in the war: Louis Denfield, Forrest Sherman, William Fechteler,

Mick Carney, and Arleigh Burke. Raddy Radford jumped the CNO job to be appointed by President Eisenhower as chairman of the Joint Chiefs of Staff.

The rigors of war were hard on American admirals. Many flamed out or proved to be less than effective under gruelling combat conditions. They were, in most cases, quietly removed to shore jobs where their administrative or training talents could be utilized. Five admirals—Ike Kidd, Dan Callaghan, Norman Scott, Henry Mullinix, and Ted Chandler—were killed in action on their flag bridges. A dozen more were wounded. With victory in sight, the last months of the war—and the constant threat of suicide planes—were perhaps the most dangerous days for flag officers exposed on their bridges. But they persevered, many changing flagships as their ships were damaged.

Raymond Spruance was once asked, what was the most important attribute a commanding admiral needed? He replied, "You need to be a good judge of people. There's one thing you don't know in a war—who is going to fight and who isn't. A man himself doesn't know beforehand. So you have to get the right people." Spruance found the right people, trusted them, and let them do their jobs.

In the end, the fighting admirals proved themselves in the crucible of combat and became the pride of the U.S. Navy. They were truly "men who fought in gallant actions as gallantly as ever heroes fought."

CAST OF FLAG OFFICERS

Rear Admiral Walden L. "Pug" Ainsworth: genial but tough cruiser division commander under Halsey in the South Pacific. His aggressive tactics in night bombardment missions and engagements with the Japanese led to a turnaround in the fortunes of the navy in battles in the Slot. Later he commanded cruisers in carrier screens and Destroyers Pacific.

Commodore Bernard L. "Count" Austin: a dashing destroyer commander who served with Arleigh Burke's famous Destroyer Squadron 23 in the South Pacific. As a captain, he led DesRon 14 in the Central Pacific offensive before being assigned to Admiral Nimitz's staff in Pearl Harbor as a commodore in charge of administration.

Vice Admiral Daniel E. "Uncle Dan" Barbey: Commander Seventh Fleet Amphibious Force. Began as the phib commander in MacArthur's Navy, operating on a shoestring, and moved Southwest Pacific troops in leapfrogging operations along the coast of New Guinea, and finally into the Leyte Gulf landings. He then supervised landings which liberated all the Philippine Islands.

Rear Admiral Gerald F. "Gerry" Bogan: a hotshot pilot who became one of the most aggressive air admirals in Task Force 38 and 58. He was a natural air tactician who handled his task group with superior ability and dedication. Highly regarded by both senior air admirals and his carrier pilots.

Commodore Arleigh A. "31-Knot" Burke: the superb commander of Destroyer Squadron 23 racking up victories in the Solomons, who— against his wishes—was assigned chief of staff to Vice Admiral Pete Mitscher, commander of Task Force 58. He became Mitscher's strong right arm in guiding the fast carriers to a decisive victory in the Pacific.

Rear Admiral Daniel J. "Dan" Callaghan: cheerful, silver-haired, popular naval officer who was aide to President Roosevelt. He was captain of *San Francisco* in the war's early months, then chief of staff to Admiral Ghormley, Commander South Pacific, before being assigned to lead a task force aboard *San Francisco*. He was killed on the heavy cruiser's bridge during the night naval Battle of Guadalcanal in November 1942.

Rear Admiral Robert B. "Mick" Carney: began the war as a convoy and anti-submarine specialist in the Atlantic Fleet, when he was promoted to captain and given command of the new light cruiser *Denver*. Taking the ship to the South Pacific, he bombarded Japanese positions and covered landings in the Solomons. He was promoted to flag rank and made chief of staff to Admiral Halsey, with whom he went to sea with the Third Fleet until the end of the war.

Rear Admiral Theodore E. Chandler: specialized in gunnery and was skipper of the light cruiser *Omaha*. He commanded a landing force in the invasion of Southern France and later was a battleship division commander in the Battle of Surigao Strait in October 1944. He shifted his flag to the heavy cruiser *Louisville* for the invasion of Luzon at Lingayen Gulf and was mortally wounded on his flag bridge by a suicide plane in January 1945—the last U.S. admiral killed in action.

Rear Admiral Joseph J. "Jocko" Clark: the most aggressive of the carrier air admirals. Pete Mitscher picked him as his "point" man to lead Task Force 58 sweeping across the Central Pacific. Part Cherokee, the pugnacious Clark was an early naval aviator and a master ship-handler among carrier skippers before winning flag command.

Rear Admiral Richard L. "Dick" Conolly: destroyer squadron commander in the Pacific when assigned to Admiral King's staff in

Washington. He was given amphibious commands in the Mediterranean and Central Pacific. Effective and personable, he earned the nickname "Close-In Conolly" for bringing his gunfire support ships close to the beach to help invasion troops.

Rear Admiral Ralph E. Davison: an expert pilot who became a gifted escort carrier group commander before graduating to a fast carrier group in Mitscher's Task Force 58. He was an intellectual and a superb carrier tactician, whose one weakness was a fondness for drink while on the beach.

Rear Admiral Donald B. "Wu" Duncan: a bright naval aviation expert who helped devise the Tokyo raid. He commanded the new *Essex* and was an expert ship-handler, who soon was in demand for both his administrative and fighting skills. He was aviation adviser in Admiral King's command in Washington.

Vice Admiral Aubrey W. "Jake" Fitch: while a latecomer to naval aviation, proved to be an aggressive carrier admiral in the war's early days. He became Commander Air Forces South Pacific directing the successful Solomon Islands air campaign. Genial and well liked, he returned to Washington as Deputy CNO for Air, and later became the first aviator superintendent of the Naval Academy.

Vice Admiral Frank Jack Fletcher: a non-aviator who was placed in command of carrier task forces in the early days of the Pacific War. Admiral Kimmel directed him to lead forces in relief of Midway, but Fletcher used up precious time refueling destroyers, thus the operation was called off by Admiral Pye. Fletcher was in command at the Battle of the Coral Sea and the Battle of Midway, though he turned over control to Admiral Spruance when his flagship *Yorktown* was mortally stricken. He prematurely withdrew his carriers from support of the troops on Guadalcanal to the disgust of Admiral Kelly Turner. He was shunted to the quiet of the North Pacific command for the remainder of the war.

Vice Admiral Robert L. Ghormley: as a rear admiral, he was assigned to London for secret talks on naval coordination with the British. He was then named Commander South Pacific before the invasion of

Guadalcanal. The strain of the tropical command sapped Ghormley's energy, and he was replaced by Vice Admiral Bill Halsey in October 1942. Ghormley served as an adviser to Admiral Nimitz and Commander Hawaiian Sea Frontier, before becoming Commander U.S. Naval Forces in Germany.

Rear Admiral Samuel P. "Si" Ginder: commanding officer of *Enterprise* who seemed unsuited for higher combat command. Though a good administrator and planner, as a fast carrier air group commander in Task Force 58, Ginder was a worrier and suffered an apparent nervous breakdown during combat operations and was shifted to other duties.

Rear Admiral John L. "Jimmy" Hall: was chief of staff to Rear Admiral John Wilcox, who was lost overboard on USS *Washington* in the Atlantic, but saved. He commanded amphibious groups in the Mediterranean, at Normandy, and Southern France. An outspoken, forceful leader, Admiral Hall then led an amphibious group during the struggle for Okinawa in the Pacific.

Admiral William F. "Bill/Bull" Halsey: commander carrier task forces, Commander South Pacific, Commander Third Fleet. A latecomer to naval aviation, winning wings at age fifty-two, he was charismatic, impetuous, aggressive, the quintessential fighter, and beloved by his sailors despite serious flaws in tactical judgment.

Rear Admiral William Keen Harrill: a veteran pilot and a polished naval officer, he was also beset by worries and indecision. He was a fast carrier group commander during the Marianas campaign, his first. However, neither Jocko Clark nor Pete Mitscher thought he was up to the job and he was shifted to shore duties.

Admiral Thomas C. Hart: commanded the U.S. Asiatic Fleet from 1939 to 1942 shortly before it was disbanded. He led the fleet from its base in Manila, which General MacArthur failed to protect, to the Dutch East Indies. There, the combined American, Australian, British, and Dutch naval forces proved to be no match for the Japanese. He served on the General Board until February 1945 when he became a

U.S. Senator for Connecticut.

Admiral Henry Kent Hewitt: commander of U.S. forces in the Mediterranean, he led the U.S. assaults on North Africa, Sicily, and Southern Italy. He was commander of the re-designated Eighth Fleet and was a superb organizer and leader, blessed with the diplomatic skills to get along with British and French allies.

Vice Admiral Harry W. Hill: a leading amphibious group commander in the Fifth Fleet who became Kelly Turner's right-hand man. A gunnery specialist on battleships, Hill was cheerful, affable, and energetic, a natural fighter who consistently turned in outstanding performances in all the Central Pacific invasions.

Rear Admiral Isaac C. "Ike" Kidd: a veteran surface ship commander who was captain of the battleship *Arizona* before the war. He was Commander Battleship Division One, with his flag aboard *Arizona*, when struck by the Japanese air attacks at Pearl Harbor and killed in action on the bridge. He was the first U.S. flag officer to die in combat.

Admiral Husband E. Kimmel: those in Washington had jumped him over senior admirals and made him commander in chief of the U.S. Fleet in 1941. At Pearl Harbor, when the Japanese attacked, he maintained he was not informed of the diplomatic developments, but he was blamed for the unreadiness of the fleet to resist the attack. He was replaced by Admiral Nimitz in late December 1941 and spent the rest of the war trying to clear his name.

Fleet Admiral Ernest J. King: commander in chief of the U.S. Fleet and Chief of Naval Operations. Carbon hard, abrasive, and brilliant, he was a master strategist who, from Washington, fiercely and successfully pursued his wartime policies, which led to the U.S. Navy becoming second to none. He was generally considered the most forceful of the U.S. Joint Chiefs of Staff and was cordially detested by his British counterparts.

Admiral Thomas C. "Tom" Kinkaid: cruiser and carrier task force commander, Commander North Pacific Force, Commander Seventh Fleet. A tense chain smoker, he was cool under fire and had the ability to weld disparate air and ground elements in his Aleutians command into a fine fighting force. He had the difficult job of getting along with the imperious General MacArthur, who had fired two previous U.S. Navy commanders.

Vice Admiral Alan G. Kirk: Director of Naval Intelligence in 1941, he clashed with Kelly Turner, and was reassigned to the Atlantic Fleet Amphibious Force, commanding an attack group at Sicily and later head of the American invasion force at Normandy. He then took over command of U.S. naval forces in France.

Fleet Admiral William D. Leahy: the personal chief of staff to President Roosevelt throughout the war. Leahy presided over the Joint Chiefs of Staff in Washington, the highest U.S. policymaking body. He conveyed the views of the service heads to the president, and quietly and effectively implemented Roosevelt's decisions within the military.

Vice Admiral Willis A. "Ching" Lee: a cool, brainy battleship force commander who won the night naval battle of Guadalcanal, and became Commander Battleship Pacific in the Fifth Fleet under Admiral Spruance. He died of a heart attack in Maine while heading a group assigned to develop anti-kamikaze tactics.

General of the Army Douglas MacArthur: Commander in Chief Southwest Pacific Area. Haughty, domineering—worshiped by some, despised by others—he was in command of an area that included New Zealand, Australia, the upper Solomons, New Guinea, the Dutch East Indies, and the Philippines. He opposed the Central Pacific strategy and insisted the road to Japan lay through the Philippines. The U.S. Seventh Fleet came under his command.

Vice Admiral John S. "Slew" McCain: latecomer to naval aviation who commanded land-based air in the South Pacific before being assigned to head BuAer in Washington. In late 1944, he was named to command the carrier force of Halsey's Third Fleet, alternating with Pete Mitscher. He led Task Force 38 in the final air strikes against Japan's home islands.

Vice Admiral Charles H. "Soc" McMorris: a bright student at the

Naval Academy, where he received the nickname "Soc" for Socrates. McMorris was skipper of the heavy cruiser *San Francisco* at the Battle of Cape Esperance and, as a rear admiral, led the U.S. task force, which stood off heavier Japanese opposition in the Battle of the Komandorskis. He relieved Admiral Spruance as Admiral Nimitz's chief of staff, a post he held for the rest of the war.

Rear Admiral Aaron Stanton "Tip" Merrill: a lively, charming, and exceedingly able cruiser division commander in the South Pacific. After commanding the battleship *Indiana*, he took over a division of the first *Cleveland*-class light cruisers. Handling them like destroyers, he rang up an enviable record against Japanese surface ships. He fought the last of the Solomons' night-running engagements against the Japanese navy.

Vice Admiral Marc A. "Pete" Mitscher: an early-day naval aviator who held a variety of air commands and was skipper of USS *Hornet* in the Tokyo raid. Commanded land-based air at Guadalcanal and headed the Central Pacific carrier air task force. He also became commander of all fast carriers in the Fifth Fleet. The finest air tactician in the navy, Pete Mitscher, scarcely raising his voice above a whisper, and was beloved by his pilots.

Rear Admiral Alfred E. "Monty" Montgomery: after heading naval air training commands in the United States, Montgomery took over a fast carrier air group in the Central Pacific offensive and was one of Pete Mitscher's top air admirals. Sometimes irascible because of migraine headaches, he was respected, if not loved, and calm and efficient in battle.

Rear Admiral Henry M. Mullinnix: first in his class at Annapolis and an expert naval aviator, who helped in the development of modern aircraft engines. Mullinnix was captain of the *Saratoga* before making flag rank and being assigned command of an escort carrier group in the Gilberts operation. He had a bright future, until he was killed when his flagship *Liscombe Bay* was torpedoed by a Japanese submarine off Makin Island in November 1943.

Fleet Admiral Chester W. Nimitz: commander in chief of the U.S. Pacific Fleet and Pacific Ocean Areas, who was calm, avuncular, understanding, but with a will of steel. A good judge of naval talent, he held together a temperamental mix of flag officers in his determination to win the Pacific war. Next to Admiral King, he was the finest wartime naval strategist.

Vice Admiral Jesse B. "Oley" Oldendorf: a cruiser bombardment commander in the Marshalls, the Carolines, the Marianas, and Leyte Gulf. He also led the battle line—cruisers and battleships—against Japanese battleships in the night action of the Battle of Surigao Strait. It was history's last toe-to-toe combat of battleships in action. The easygoing Oldendorf succeeded Admiral Lee as the senior battleship commander in the Pacific.

Vice Admiral Charles A. "Baldy" Pownall: a veteran pilot who commanded the carrier *Enterprise* shortly before the war's outbreak. He later was selected to command the Fifth Fleet's fast carriers, but his leadership lacked punch and was criticized by some of his air admirals. Nimitz decided to beach Pownall and made him Commander Air Pacific (replacing Jack Towers who became Nimitz's number two), where Pownall's administrative skills were valuable.

Vice Admiral William S. Pye: Commander Battleships Pacific at Pearl Harbor, who took over briefly from Admiral Kimmel. He recalled the task force sent to relieve the embattled marines on Wake Island. Criticized for this in some quarters, he maintained that he wished to preserve the precious Pacific Fleet carrier force. He was shifted to the navy's General Board and then served as president of the Naval War College in Newport, Rhode Island.

Rear Admiral Arthur W. "Raddy" Radford: a natural pilot and fighter and among the most brilliant of the air admirals. When commanding a fast carrier group in Task Forces 38 and 58, he proved to be as capable and accomplished in combat as he was as an administrator in naval aviation training and development.

Rear Admiral Dewitt C. "Duke" Ramsey: an early pilot, naval aviator No. 45 in 1917, who was both a splendid pilot and a keen administrator. He was skipper of *Saratoga* during the Guadalcanal operation, the aggressive commander of a fast carrier division in 1942–1943, before being called back to Washington to be chief of BuAer.

Rear Admiral John W. "Black Jack" Reeves: a latecomer to naval aviation, yet proved to be a fine skipper of the carrier *Wasp*, then fast carrier group commander in Task Force 58, which swept across the Pacific. He was calm but tough, and eager to make contact with the enemy. Due for a rest and shore duty, in late 1944, Reeves became head of the new Naval Air Transport Service, based in San Francisco.

Rear Admiral Norman Scott: a veteran gunnery officer on surface ships and a respected staff officer. He was captain of the heavy cruiser *Pensacola* and served in Washington in Admiral King's office, before taking over a task force in the South Pacific. He participated in the landings on Guadalcanal, was the victor at Cape Esperance, and was killed in action aboard his flagship *Atlanta* in the night Battle of Guadalcanal.

Rear Admiral Forrest P. Sherman: an early aviator and considered among the most brilliant of the air admirals, Sherman was captain of the carrier *Wasp*, sunk in the South Pacific, before becoming chief war plans officer for Admiral Nimitz in Pearl Harbor. He was perhaps Nimitz's closest and most influential adviser in the latter stages of the war, with a keen mind for strategy and tactics. He was an ambitious master of bureaucracy.

Vice Admiral Frederick C. "Ted" Sherman: hotheaded and egocentric, a latecomer to aviation who was one of the most blooded of the air admirals. As captain of *Lexington*, and a carrier group commander in both the South Pacific and Central Pacific, he was sometimes at personal odds with superiors and was thought to have something of a chip on his shoulder. Sherman nevertheless turned in outstanding performances as an aggressive air tactician.

Lieutenant General Holland M. "Howlin' Mad" Smith: marine commander in the Pacific from the Gilberts to Iwo Jima. Smith's dedication to the marines led to his frequent quarrels with Kelly Turner and other admirals. But his relief of army Major General Ralph Smith on Saipan led to a severe breach with the army command and calls that he would never be allowed to command army forces in the Pacific.

Rear Admiral Clifton A. F. "Ziggy" Sprague: a jovial longtime naval aviator who commanded an escort carrier group, Taffy 3, off Leyte Gulf when surprised by a Japanese battleship-cruiser force. Sprague acquitted himself well, maneuvering his vulnerable jeep carriers and destroyers, courageously taking on the Japanese battlewagons, which eventually broke off contact.

Rear Admiral Thomas L. "Tommy" Sprague (no relation to Clifton Sprague): commanded the Taffies off Leyte Gulf in October 1944 when attacked by the Japanese battleship-cruiser force coming through the San Bernardino Strait. He backed up Ziggy Sprague and later supported many Philippine landings of the Seventh Fleet.

Admiral Raymond A. Spruance: commander of cruisers and the carrier task force at Midway, Commander Fifth Fleet. Quiet, unflappable, intellectual, Spruance led his enormous Fifth Fleet with smooth efficiency and with a strong sense of sticking to and achieving his overall mission in the various operations.

Admiral Harold R. Stark: CNO at the time of Pearl Harbor, Stark escaped serious censure and was reassigned as senior U.S. naval flag officer in England. The outgoing and friendly flag officer served as nominal head of U.S. naval forces in Europe through the war.

Rear Admiral Felix B. Stump: an early naval aviator who commissioned the new fast carrier Lexington. After several operations, he was promoted to rear admiral in charge of escort carrier groups in the Pacific. He was in command of the escort carrier group Taffy 2 at the Battle of Leyte Gulf and continued as a jeep carrier admiral until mid-1945 when he was made Chief of Naval Air Technical Training in the United States.

Rear Admiral Robert A. "Fuzzy" Theobald: intelligent, argumentative officer who as Commander, North Pacific Force, was out of position when the Japanese attacked the western Aleutians. He failed to get along with his army and air force counterparts in the North Pacific command and was replaced by Admiral Kinkaid. Theobald spent the rest of the war at shore commands.

Vice Admiral John H. Towers: a naval aviation pioneer, who was a fine administrator and ran the BuAer before being assigned to Pearl Harbor as Commander Air Pacific under Admiral Nimitz. Courteous and wellmannered, Towers nevertheless was a heated defender of naval aviation. His sometimes truculent attitude offended Admirals King and Nimitz, who denied him the seagoing command he desired during the war. Nimitz made Towers his deputy in 1944, and he took over many burdens of that widespread command. Only after the war did Towers get the fleet command he so wanted.

Admiral Richmond Kelly Turner: the 1941 war plans officer in Washington, who led landing operations at Guadalcanal. He was Commander South Pacific Amphibious Force, and Commander Fifth Fleet Amphibious Force. Brainy, intellectually arrogant, determined, and aggressive—he developed and perfected the amphibious techniques that landed marines and soldiers on Pacific islands in the successful strategy to win the war.

Vice Admiral Theodore S. "Ping" Wilkinson: first in his Annapolis class, prewar Chief of Naval Intelligence, succeeded Kelly Turner as III Amphibious Force commander in the South Pacific, and landed troops at Leyte and Lingayen in the Philippines. One of the top amphibious commanders.

SOURCES

Barbey, Daniel. *MacArthur's Amphibious Navy: Seventh Amphibious Force Operations, 1943–1945.* Annapolis, MD: Naval Institute Press, 1969.

Beach, Edward L. *Salt and Steel: Reflections of a Submariner.* Annapolis, MD: Naval Institute Press, 1999.

———. *The United States Navy: 200 Years.* New York: H. Holt, 1986.

Beigel, Harvey M. *Battleship Country: The Battle Fleet At San Pedro-Long Beach, California, 1919–1940.* Missoula, MT: Pictorial Histories Pub. Co., 1983.

Bischof, Gunter. *The Pacific War Revisited.* Baton Rouge: Louisiana State University Press, 1997.

Blair, Clay Jr. *Silent Victory: The U.S. Submarine War Against Japan.* Annapolis, MD: Naval Institute Press, 2001.

Blumenson, Martin, and James L. Stokesbury. *Masters of the Art of Command.* Boston: Houghton Mifflin, 1975.

Bradlee, Ben. *A Good Life: Newspapering and Other Adventures.* New York: Simon and Schuster, 1995.

Brodie, Bernard. *A Guide to Naval Strategy.* New York: Praeger, 1965.

Bryan, J. *Aircraft Carrier.* New York: Ballantine Books, 1954.

Buell, Thomas. *Master of Sea Power: A Biography of Fleet Admiral Ernest J. King.* Boston: Little, Brown, 1980.

———. *The Quiet Warrior: A Biography of Admiral Raymond A. Spruance.* Annapolis, MD: Naval Institute Press, 1987.

Calhoun, C. Raymond. *Typhoon, The Other Enemy: The Third Fleet and the Pacific Storm of December 1944.* Annapolis, MD: Naval Institute Press, 1981.

Carver, Michael. *The War Lords: Military Commanders of the Twentieth Century.*

Boston: Little, Brown and Co., 1976.

Casey, Robert. *Torpedo Junction: with the Pacific Fleet from Pearl Harbor to Midway.* Indianapolis: The Bobbs-Merrill Company, 1943.

Clark, J. J., and Clark Reynolds. *Carrier Admiral.* New York: D. McKay Co., 1967.

Crenshaw, Russell. *Naval Shiphandling.* Annapolis, MD: Naval Institute Press, 1974.

Cutler, Thomas J. *The Battle of Leyte Gulf, 23–26 October, 1944.* New York: HarperCollins, 1994.

Dull, Paul. *The Imperial Japanese Navy.* Annapolis, MD: Naval Institute Press, 1978.

Dyer, George C. *The Amphibians Came to Conquer: The Story of Admiral Richmond Kelly Turner.* Washington: U.S. Dept. of the Navy, 1972.

Fahey, James J. *Pacific War Diary: 1942–1945.* Westport, CT: Greenwood Press, 1963.

Forrestel, Emmet Peter. *Admiral Raymond A.Spruance, USN: A Study in Command.* Washington: U.S. Government Print Office, 1966.

Gailey, Harry A. *"Howlin' Mad" vs. the Army: Conflict in Command Saipan, 1944.* Novato, CA: Presidio Press, 1986.

Grove, Eric. *Big Fleet Actions: Tsushima, Jutland, Philippine Sea.* London: Arms and Armour, 1995.

Hammel, Eric. *Guadalcanal.*

Hattendorf, John. *Sailors and Scholars: The Centennial History of the U.S. Naval War College.* Newport, RI: Naval War College Press, 1984.

Heathcote, T. A. *British Admirals of the Fleet 1734–1995: A Biographical Dictionary.* Barnsley, South Yorkshire: Pen and Sword Military Classics, 2004.

Holmes, W. J. *Double-Edged Secrets: U.S. Naval Intelligence Operations in the Pacific during World War II.* Annapolis, MD: Naval Institute Press, 1979.

Honan, William H. *Great Naval Battles of the Twentieth Century.* London: Robson Books, 1998.

Howarth, Stephen, ed. *Men of War: Great Naval Leaders of World War II.* New York: St. Martin's Press, 1993.

Hoyt, Edwin P. *How They Won the War in the Pacific: Nimitz and His Admirals.* New York: Weybright and Talley, 1970.

———. *The Kamikazes: Squadron Suicides of World War II.* New York: Arbor House, 1983.

———. *MacArthur's Navy: The Seventh Fleet and the Battle for the Philippines.* New York: Orion Books, 1989.

Hughes, Wayne P. *Fleet Tactics: Theory and Practice.* Annapolis, MD: Naval Institute Press, 1986.

Humble, Richard. *U.S. Fleet Carriers of World War II.* Poole, Dorset: Blandford Press, 1984.

————. *Flights of Passage: Reflections of a World War II Aviator*. Annapolis, MD: Naval Institute Press, 1988.

Keegan, John. *The Price of Admiralty: The Evolution of Naval Warfare*. New York: Penguin, 1988.

Kernan, Alvin. *Crossing the Line: A Bluejacket's World War II Odyssey*. Annapolis, MD: Naval Institute Press, 1994.

Kilpatrick, C. W. *Night Naval Battles of the Solomons*. Pompano Beach, FL: Exposition Press, 1987.

Kimmett, Larry, and Margaret Regis. *The Attack on Pearl Harbor: An Illustrated History*. Seattle: Navigator Publishing, 1991.

King, Adm. Ernest J., and Walter Muir Whitehill. *Fleet Admiral King: A Naval Record*. New York: Da Capo Press, 1976.

Kurzman, Dan. *Left to Die: The Tragedy of the USS* Juneau. New York: Pocket Books, 1994.

Larrabee, Eric. *Commander in Chief: Franklin Delano Roosevelt, His Lieutenants, and Their War*. Annapolis, MD: Naval Institute Press, 2004.

Layton, Edwin, Roger Pineau and John Costtello. *"And I Was There": Pearl Harbor and Midway—Breaking the Secrets*. Annapolis, MD: Naval Institute Press, 2006.

Leary, William, ed. *We Shall Return!: MacArthur's Commanders and The Defeat of Japan, 1942–1945*. Lexington, KY: University Press of Kentucky, 1988.

Lockwood, Charles A. and Hans Christian Adamson. *Tragedy at Honda: One of America's Greatest Naval Disasters*. Philadelphia: Chilton, Book Division, 1960.

Lockwood, Charles A. *Sink 'Em All: Submarine Warfare in the Pacific*. New York: Dutton, 1951.

Love, Robert W. *The Chiefs of Naval Operations*. Annapolis, MD: Naval Institute Press, 1980.

Macksey, Kenneth. *Military Errors of World War Two*. London: Arms and Armour Press, 1987.

Manchester, William. *American Caesar: Douglas MacArthur 1880–1964*. Boston: Little, Brown, 1978.

Mason, John T., Jr., ed. *The Atlantic War Remembered: An Oral History Collection*. Annapolis, MD: Naval Institute Press, 1990.

————. *The Pacific War Remembered: An Oral History Collection*. Annapolis, MD: Naval Institute Press, 1986.

Miller, Nathan. *War at Sea: A Naval History of World War II*. New York: Oxford University Press, 1996.

Morison, Samuel Eliot. *History of United States Naval Operations in World War II, Vol. 1: The Battle of the Atlantic, September 1939–May 1943*. Boston: Little,

Brown, 1947.

———. *History of United States Naval Operations in World War II, Vol .2: Operations in North African Waters, October 1942–June 1943*. Boston: Little, Brown, 1947.

———. *History of United States Naval Operations in World War II, Vol. 3: The Rising Sun in the Pacific, 1931–April 1942*. Boston: Little, Brown, 1948.

———. *History of United States Naval Operations in World War II, Vol. 4: Coral Sea, Midway and Submarine Actions, May 1942–August 1942*. Boston: Little, Brown, 1949.

———. *History of United States Naval Operations in World War II, Vol. 5: The Struggle for Guadalcanal, August 1942–February 1943*. Boston: Little, Brown, 1949.

———. *History of United States Naval Operations in World War II, Vol. 6: Breaking the Bismarcks Barrier, 22 July 1942–1 May 1944*. Boston: Little, Brown, 1950.

———. *History of United States Naval Operations in World War II, Vol. 7: Aleutians, Gilberts and Marshalls, June 1942–April 1944*. Boston: Little, Brown, 1951.

———. *History of United States Naval Operations in World War II, Vol. 8: New Guinea and the Marianas, March 1944–August 1944*. Boston: Little, Brown, 1954.

———. *History of United States Naval Operations in World War II, Vol. 9: Sicily-Salerno-Anzio, January 1943–June 1944*. Boston: Little, Brown, 1954.

———. *History of United States Naval Operations in World War II, Vol. 10: The Atlantic Battle Won, May 1943–May 1945*. Boston: Little, Brown, 1956.

———. *History of United States Naval Operations in World War II, Vol. 11: The Invasion of France and Germany, 1944–1945*. Boston: Little, Brown, 1957.

———. *History of United States Naval Operations in World War II, Vol. 12: Leyte, June 1944–January 1945*. Boston: Little, Brown, 1958.

———. *History of United States Naval Operations in World War II, Vol. 13 : The Liberation of the Philippines—Luzon, Mindanao, the Visayas, 1944–1945*. Boston: Little, Brown, 1959.

———. *History of United States Naval Operations in World War II, Vol. 14: Victory in the Pacific, 1945*. Boston: Little, Brown, 1960.

———. *The Two-Ocean War: A Short History of the United States Navy in the Second World War*. Boston: Little, Brown, 1963.

Murphy, Francis X. *Fighting Admiral: The Story of Dan Callaghan*. New York: Vantage Press, 1952.

Musicant, Ivan. *Battleship at War: The Epic Story of the USS Washington*. San Diego: Harcourt Brace Jovanovich, 1986.

Newcomb, Richard F. *Abandon Ship!* New York: Holt, 1958.

———. *The Battle of Savo Island*. New York: H. Holt, 2002.

O'Callahan, Joseph T. *I Was Chaplain on the Franklin*. New York: Macmillan, 1956.

Potter, Elmer Belmont, and Chester Nimitz, eds. *The Great Sea War: The Story of Naval Action in World War II*. Englewood Cliffs, NJ: Prentice-Hall, 1960.

———. *Admiral Arleigh Burke*. New York: Random House, 1990.

———. *Bull Halsey*. Annapolis, MD: Naval Institute Press, 1985.

———. *Nimitz*. Norwalk, CT: Naval Institute Press, 1976.

Regan, Geoffrey. *Geoffrey Regan's Book of Naval Blunders*. London: A. Deutsch, 2001.

Reynolds, Clark G. *Famous American Admirals*. New York: Van Nostrand Reinhold, 1978.

———. *Admiral John H. Towers: The Struggle for Naval Air Supremacy*. Annapolis, MD: Naval Institute Press, 1991.

———. *Navies in History*. Annapolis, MD: Naval Institute Press, 1998.

———. *The Carrier War*. Alexandria, VA: Time-Life Books, 1982.

———. *The Fast Carriers: The Forging of an Air Navy*. Annapolis, MD: Naval Institute Press, 1992.

———. *The Fighting Lady: The New* Yorktown *in the Pacific War*. Missoula, MT: Pictorial Histories Pub. Co., 1986.

Roscoe, Theodore. *United States Destroyer Operations in World War II*. Annapolis, MD: United States Naval Institute, 1953.

———. *United States Submarine Operations in World War II*. Annapolis, MD: United States Naval Institute, 1949.

Roskill, Stephen. *Churchill and the Admirals*. New York: Morrow, 1977.

Sherman, Fredrick C. *Combat Command: The American Aircraft Carriers in the Pacific War*. New York: Dutton, 1950.

Smith, Holland M., and Percy Finch. *Coral and Brass*. New York: C. Scribner's Sons, 1949.

Spector, Ronald. *At War, at Sea: Sailors and Naval Combat in the Twentieth Century*. New York: Viking, 2001.

———. *Eagle Against the Sun: The American War with Japan*. New York: Vintage Books, 1985.

Stephen, Martin. *The Fighting Admirals: British Admirals of the Second World War*. Annapolis, MD: Naval Institute Press, 1991.

Sweetman, Jack. *The U.S. Naval Academy: An Illustrated History*. Annapolis, MD: Naval Institute Press, 1979.

Talyor, Theodore. *The Magnificent Mitscher*. Annapolis, MD: Naval Institute Press, 2006.

Taussig, Betty C. *A Warrior for Freedom*. Manhattan, KS: Sunflower University Press, 1995.

Van der Vat, Dan. *The Pacific Campaign: The U.S.-Japanese Naval War, 1941–1945*.

London: Hodder and Stoughton, 1992.

Von der Porten, Edward P. *The German Navy in World War II*. New York: T. Y. Crowell, 1969.

Wheeler, Gerald E. *Kinkaid of the Seventh Fleet: A Biography of Admiral Thomas C. Kinkaid*. Annapolis, MD: Naval Institute Press, 1996.

Winton, John. *Ultra in the Pacific: How Breaking Japanese Codes and Cyphers Affected Naval Operations against Japan 1941–1945*. Annapolis, MD: Naval Institute Press, 1993.

Wooldridge, E. T. *Carrier Warfare in the Pacific*. Washington: Smithsonian Institution Press, 1994.

Wyld, Lionel. *Images of America: The Naval War College*. Collingdale, PA: Diane Pub. Co., 1999.

———. *The Navy in Newport*. Charleston, SC: Arcadia Pub., 2004.

Y'Blood, William. *The Little Giants: U.S. Escort Carriers Against Japan*. Annapolis, MD: United States Naval Institute, 1999.

CHAPTER NOTES

One: The Raid from Shangri-La

Books: Morison, *Naval Operations, Vol. 3*; Buell, *King*; Buell, *Spruance*; Forrestel, *Spruance*; Howarth, *Men of War*; Potter and Nimitz, *The Great Sea War*; Potter, *Nimitz*; Taylor, *Mitscher*.

Oral Histories: Conolly, Richard; Doolittle, James; Duncan, Donald; Miller, Henry.

Articles: Cagle, Malcolm. "Mr. Wu, Part I and Mr. Wu, Part II." *Naval Aviation Museum Foundation Magazine*, 1987.

Two: The Education of an Admiral

Books: Beach, *Salt and Steel*; Beach, *United States Navy*; Buell, *Spruance*; Dyer, *Turner*; Potter, *Burke*; Potter, *Halsey*; Taylor, *Mitscher*; Potter, *Nimitz*; Sweetman, *The U.S. Naval Academy*; Taussig, *Warrior for Freedom*, Wheeler, *Kinkaid*.

Oral Histories: Baldwin, Hanson; Burke, Arleigh; Duncan, Donald.

Three: Naval War College

Books: Beigel, *Battleship Country*; Blair, *Silent Victory*; Buell, *King*; Buell, *Spruance*; Dyer, *Turner*; Forrestel, *Spruance*; Hattendorf, *Sailors and Scholars*; Hughes, *Fleet Tactics*; Lockwood and Adamson, *Tragedy at Honda*; Keegan, *Price of Admiralty*; King and Whitehill, *King*; Potter, *Halsey*; Potter, *Nimitz*; Reynolds, *Towers*; H. M. Smith, *Coral and Brass*.

From the Naval War College: The Naval War College Curriculum: An Historical Overview, 1914–1988. Prospectus of Lectures, Presentations, Theses, Reading Courses, International Law Courses, Senior and Junior Classes, 1936–37. Prospectus of the Naval War College Courses in Strategy and Tactics, 1935.

Four: Rise of the Air Admirals

Books: Buell, *Master of Sea Power*; Clark, *Carrier Admiral*; Taylor, *Mitscher*; Dyer, *Turner*; King and Whitehill, *King*; Potter, *Nimitz*; Reynolds, *Towers*; Reynolds, *Carrier War*; Reynolds, *Fast Carriers*; Reynolds, *Fighting Lady*; Sherman, *Combat Command*; Wooldridge, *Carrier Warfare*.

Oral Histories: Anderson, George; Bogan, Gerald; Clark, J. J.; Duncan, Donald; Hedding, Truman; Miller, Henry; Pownall, Charles; Russell, James; Thach, John; Stump, Felix.

Articles: *Naval Aviation Museum Foundation Magazine*. Admiral Duncan profile, 1987.

Five: Admirals in Action

Books: Buell, *King*; Buell, *Spruance*; Carver, *War Lords*; Dyer, *Turner*; Heathcote, *British Admirals*; Holmes, *Double-Edged Secrets*; Honan, *Great Naval Battles*; King and Whitehill, *Fleet Admiral King*; Larrabee, *Commander in Chief*; Layton, *"And I Was There"*; Miller, *War at Sea*; Morison, *Naval Operations, Vol. 1*; Roscoe, *Destroyer Operations*; Roskill, *Churchill and the Admirals*; Spector, *At War, at Sea*; Stephen, *British Fighting Admirals*; Von der Porten, *German Navy in World War II*.

NHC Biographies: Adms. Ainsworth, Bristol.

Six: America Enters the War

Books: Beach, *United States Navy*; Buell, *King*; Buell, *Spruance*; Carver, *War Lords*; Casey, *Torpedo Junction*; Dull, *Japanese Navy*; Dyer, *Turner*; Holmes, *Double-Edged Secrets*; Hoyt, *How They Won the War*; Kimmett and Regis, *Attack on Pearl Harbor*; King and Whitehill, *King*; Larrabee, *Commander in Chief*; Layton, *"And I Was There"*; Leary, *We Shall Return!*; Lockwood, *Sink 'Em All*; Manchester, *American Caesar*; Mason, *Pacific War Remembered*; Miller, *War at Sea*; Morison, *Naval Operations, Vol. 3*; Morison, *Two-Ocean War*; Potter, *Burke*; Potter, *Halsey*; Potter, *Nimitz*; Reynolds, *Towers*; Reynolds, *Famous American Admirals*; Roscoe, *Destroyer Operations*; Roskill, *Churchill and the Admirals*; Sherman, *Combat Command*; Spector, *At War, at Sea*; Spector, *Eagle against the Sun*; Smith, H. M., *Coral and Brass*; Taussig, *Warrior for Freedom*; Wheeler, *Kinkaid*; Winton, *Ultra in the Pacific*.

Oral Histories: Baldwin, Hanson; Carney, Robert; Clark, J. J.; Conolly, Richard; Dyer, George; Hedding, Truman; Hewitt, Kent; Jurika, Stephen; Kinkaid, Thomas; Kirk, Alan; McCrea, John; Nimitz, Chester; Rochefort, Joseph.

Seven: The Carriers Strike Back

Books: Beach, *United States Navy*; Bischof, *Pacific War Revisited*; Blair, *Silent Victory*; Brodie, *Guide to Naval Strategy*; Buell, *King*; Buell, *Spruance*; Carver, *The War Lords*;

Casey, *Torpedo Junction*; Clark, *Carrier Admiral*; Dull, *Japanese Navy*; Dyer, *Turner*; Forrestel, *Spruance*; Holmes, *Double-Edged Secrets*; Hoyt, *How They Won the War*; Kernan, *Crossing the Line*; Larrabee, *Commander in Chief*; Layton, *"And I Was There"*; Manchester, *American Caesar*; Mason, *Pacific War Remembered*; *Naval Operations, Vol. 3*; Morison, *Strategy and Compromise*; Morison, *Two-Ocean War*; Potter, *Great Sea War*; Potter, *Halsey*; Potter, *Nimitz*; Reynolds, *Towers*; Reynolds, *The Carrier War*; Reynolds, *The Fast Carriers*; Sherman, *Combat Command*; Spector, *At War, at Sea*; Spector, *Eagle against the Sun*; Taylor, *Mitscher*; Van der Vat, *The Pacific Campaign*; Wheeler, *Kinkaid*; Wooldridge, *Carrier Warfare*.

Oral Histories: Anderson, Clark, Conolly, Dyer, Hedding, Hill, Jurika, Kinkaid, Nimitz, Pownall, Rochefort, Thach.

Eight: Coral Sea Clash

Books: Beach, *United States Navy*; Buell, *King*; Casey, *Torpedo Junction*; Clark, *Carrier Admiral*; Dull, *Japanese Navy*; Dyer, *Turner*; Honan; *Great Naval Battles*; Howarth, *Men of War*; Hoyt, *How They Won the War*; Humble, *Fleet Carriers*; Keegan, *Price of Admiralty*; Larrabee, *Commander in Chief*; Mason, *Pacific War Remembered*; Morison, *Naval Operations, Vol. 4*; Potter, *The Great Sea War*; Potter, *Nimitz*; Reynolds, *Towers*; Reynolds, *Carrier War*; Reynolds, *Fast Carriers*; Sherman, *Combat Command*; Van der Vat, *Pacific Campaign*; Wheeler, *Kinkaid*; Wooldridge, *Carrier Warfare*.

Oral Histories: Baldwin, Clark, Dyer, Hedding, Kinkaid, Nimitz, Pirie, Rochefort, Thach.

Nine: Prelude to Midway

Books: Beach, *United States Navy*; Blair, *Silent Victory*; Brodie, *Guide to Naval Strategy*; Buell, *King*; Buell, *Spruance*; Dull, *Japanese Navy*; Dyer, *Turner*; Forrestel, *Spruance*; Holmes, *Double-Edged Secrets*; Honan, *Great Naval Battles*; Howarth, *Men of War*; Hoyt, *How They Won the War*; Kernan, *Crossing the Line*; Layton, *"And I Was There"*; Lockwood, *Sink 'Em All*; Mason, *Pacific War Remembered*; Miller, *Naval History*; Morison, *Naval Operations, Vol. 4*; Potter, *Great Sea War*; Potter, *Halsey*; Potter, *Nimitz*; Reynolds, *Fast Carriers*; Roscoe, *Destroyer Operations*; Sherman, *Combat Command*; Spector, *At War, at Sea*; Spector, *Eagle against the Sun*; Taylor, *Mitscher*; Van der Vat, *Pacific Campaign*; Wheeler, *Kinkaid*; Winton, *Ultra in the Pacific*; Wooldridge, *Carrier Warfare*.

Oral Histories: Anderson, Baldwin, Dyer, Hedding, Russell.

Ten: Triumph at Midway

Books: Beach, *Salt and Steel*; Beach, *United States Navy*; Blair, *Silent Victory*; Brodie, *Guide to Naval Strategy*; Buell, *King*; Buell, *Spruance*; Casey, *Torpedo Junction*; Dull, *Japanese Navy*; Forrestel, *Spruance*; Holmes, *Double-Edged Secrets*; Honan, *Great Naval Battles*; Howarth, *Men of War*; Hoyt, *How They Won the War*; Humble, *Fleet Carriers*; Keegan, *Price of Admiralty*; Kernan, *Crossing the Line*; King and Whitehill, *King*; Layton, *"And I Was There"*; Mason, *Pacific War Remembered*; Miller, *War at Sea*; Morison, *Naval Operations, Vol. 4*; Potter, *Great Sea War*; Potter, *Halsey*; Potter, *Nimitz*; Reynolds, *Carrier War*; Roscoe, *Destroyer Operations*; Roscoe, *Submarine Operations*; Spector, *At War, at Sea*; Spector, *Eagle against the Sun*; Taylor, *Mitscher*; Van der Vat; *Pacific Campaign*; Wheeler, *Kinkaid*; Winton, *Ultra in the Pacific*; Wooldridge, *Carrier Warfare*.

Oral Histories: Baldwin, Hedding, Jurika, Kinkaid, Pirie, Rochefort.

Eleven: Landings at Guadalcanal

Books: Beach, *United States Navy*; Buell, *King*; Dyer, *Turner*; Hammel, *Guadalcanal*; Howarth, *Men of War*; Hoyt, *How They Won the War*; Kilpatrick, *Night Naval Battles in the Solomons*; Larrabee, *Commander in Chief*; Mason, *Pacific War Remembered*; Miller, *War at Sea*; Morison, *Naval Operations, Vol. 5*; Potter, *Halsey*; Potter, *Nimitz*; Roscoe, *Destroyer Operations*; Spector, *At War, at Sea*; Spector, *Eagle against the Sun*.

Oral Histories: Baldwin, Dyer, Kinkaid, Nimitz.

Twelve: Defeat at Savo

Books: Buell, *King*; Dull, *Japanese Navy*; Dyer, *Turner*; Hammel, *Guadalcanal*; Hoyt, *How They Won the War*; Hughes, *Fleet Tactics*; Kilpatrick, *Night Naval Battles in the Solomons*; Miller, *War at Sea*; Morison, *Naval Operations, Vol. 5*; Newcomb, *Battle of Savo*; Potter, *Halsey*; Potter, *Nimitz*; Reynolds, *Carrier War*; Roscoe, *Destroyer Operations*; Spector, *At War, at Sea*; Spector, *Eagle against the Sun*; Van der Vat, *Pacific Campaign*.

Thirteen: Action around the Canal

Books: Buell, *King*; Dull, *Japanese Navy*; Dyer, *Turner*; Hammel, *Guadalcanal*; Hoyt, *How They Won the War*; Kilpatrick, *Night Naval Battles in the Solomons*; Larrabee, *Commander in Chief*; Mason, *Pacific War Remembered*; Miller, *War at Sea*; Morison, *Naval Operations, Vol. 5*; Potter, *Great Sea War*; Potter, *Halsey*; Potter, *Nimitz*; Reynolds, *Carrier War*; Reynolds, *Famous American Admirals*; Spector, *At War, at Sea*;

Spector, *Eagle against the Sun*; Van der Vat, *Pacific Campaign*; Wheeler, *Kinkaid*; Wooldridge, *Carrier Warfare*.

Fourteen: Death of Admirals

Books: Dull, *Japanese Navy*; Dyer, *Turner*; Hammel, *Guadalcanal*; Hoyt, *How They Won the War*; Kilpatrick, *Night Naval Battles in the Solomons*; Kurzman, *Left to Die*; Miller, *War at Sea*; Morison, *Naval Operations, Vol. 5*; Murphy, *Fighting Admiral*; Potter, *Great Sea War*; Potter, *Halsey*; Potter, *Nimitz*; Reynolds, *Famous American Admirals*; Roscoe, *Destroyer Operations*; Spector, *At War, at Sea*; Van der Vat, *Pacific Campaign*.

Fifteen: Duel of the Battlewagons

Books: Dull, *Japanese Navy*; Dyer, *Turner*; Hammel, *Guadalcanal*; Hoyt, *How They Won the War*; Kilpatrick, *Night Naval Battles of the Solomons*; Miller, *War at Sea*; Morison, *Naval Operations, Vol. 5*; Musicant, *Battleship at War*; Potter, *Great Sea War*; Potter, *Halsey*; Potter, *Nimitz*; Reynolds, *Famous American Admirals*; Spector, *At War, at Sea*; Van der Vat, *Pacific Campaign*.

Sixteen: Long-Lance Menace

Books: Buell, *King*; Dull, *Japanese Navy*; Dyer, *Turner*; Hammel, *Guadalcanal*; Hoyt, *How They Won the War*; Hughes, *Fleet Tactics*; Kilpatrick, *Night Naval Battles of the Solomons*; Mason, *Pacific War Remembered*; Miller, *War at Sea*; Morison, *Naval Operations, Vol. 5*; Potter, *Great Sea War*; Potter, *Halsey*; Potter, *Nimitz*; Roscoe, *Destroyer Operations*; Sherman, *Combat Command*; Van der Vat, *Pacific Campaign*; Wheeler, *Kinkaid*; Y'Blood, *Little Giants*.

Seventeen: Fighting Flags: Pug, Tip, Arleigh

Books: Barbey, *MacArthur's Amphibious Navy*; Beach, *United States Navy*; Buell, *King*; Dull, *Japanese Navy*; Dyer, *Turner*; Fahey, *Pacific War Diary*; Howarth, *Men of War*; Hoyt, *How They Won the War*; Hoyt, *MacArthur's Navy*; Hughes, *Fleet Tactics*; Love, *Chiefs of Naval Operations*; Manchester, *American Caesar*; Mason, *Pacific War Remembered*; Miller, *War at Sea*; Morison, *Naval Operations, Vol. 6*; Potter, *Great Sea War*; Potter, *Burke*; Potter, *Halsey*; Potter, *Nimitz*; Reynolds, *Famous American Admirals*; Roscoe, *Destroyer Operations*; Sherman, *Combat Command*; Taussig, *Warrior for Freedom*; Van der Vat, *Pacific Campaign*.

Eighteen: MacArthur's Admirals

Books: Barbey, *MacArthur's Amphibious Navy*; Beach, *United States Navy*; Buell, *King*; Howarth, *Men of War*; Hoyt, *MacArthur's Navy*; Manchester, *American Caesar*; Miller, *War at Sea*; Morison, *Naval Operations, Vol. 6*; Potter, *Great Sea War*; Potter,

Halsey; Potter, *Nimitz*; Spector, *At War, at Sea*; Van der Vat, *Pacific Campaign*.

Nineteen: War in the Cold and Mist

Books: Buell, *King*; Hoyt, *How They Won the War*; Miller, *Naval History*; Morison, *Naval Operations, Vol. 7*; Potter, *Great Sea War*; Potter, *Nimitz*; Reynolds, *Famous American Admirals*; Spector, *At War, at Sea*; Van der Vat, *Pacific Campaign*; Wheeler, *Kinkaid*.

Twenty: U.S. into the Med

Books: Beach, *United States Navy*; Buell, *King*; Carver, *War Lords*; Clark, *Carrier Admiral*; Heathcote, *British Admirals*; Howarth, *Men of War*; Keegan, *Price of Admiralty*; King and Whitehill, *King*; Larrabee, *Commander in Chief*; Mason, *Atlantic War Remembered*; Miller, *Naval History*; Morison, *Naval Operations, Vols. 1, 2 and 9*; Morison, *Two-Ocean War*; Potter, *Great Sea War*; Reynolds, *Famous American Admirals*; Reynolds, *Navies in Histories*; Roscoe, *Destroyer Operations*; Roskill, *Churchill and the Admirals*; Spector, *At War, at Sea*; Stephen, *Fighting Admirals*.

Oral Histories: Baldwin, Conolly, Hall, Hewitt, Kirk, Wellborn.

Twenty-one: Central Pacific Cranks Up

Books: Beach, *United States Navy*; Buell, *King*; Buell, *Spruance*; Clark, *Carrier Admiral*; Crenshaw, *Naval Shiphandling*; Clark, *Carrier Admiral*; Dyer, *Turner*; Forrestel, *Spruance*; Gailey, *"Howlin' Mad" vs. the Army*; Howarth, *Men of War*; Hoyt, *How They Won the War*; Humble, *Fleet Carriers*; Hughes, *Fleet Tactics*; Kernan, *Crossing the Line*; King and Whitehill, *King*; Larrabee, *Commander in Chief*; Mason, *Pacific War Remembered*; Miller, *War at Sea*; Morison, *Naval Operations, Vol. 7*; Potter, *Great Sea War*; Potter, *Halsey*; Potter, *Nimitz*; Reynolds, *Famous American Admirals*; Reynolds, *Fast Carriers*; Sherman, *Combat Command*; Smith, *Coral and Brass*; Spector, *At War, at Sea*; Spector, *Eagle against the Sun*; Taylor, *Mitscher*; Van der Vat, *Pacific Campaign*; Wooldridge, *Carrier Warfare*; Y'Blood, *Little Giants*.

Oral Histories: Anderson, Clark, Dyer, Hedding, Hill, Jurika, King, Moore, Nimitz, Pirie, Pownall, Russell.

Twenty-two: Marshalls Breakthrough

Books: Beach, *United States Navy*; Buell, *King*; Buell, *Spruance*; Clark, *Carrier Admiral*; Dyer, *Turner*; Forrestel, *Spruance*; Gailey, *"Howlin' Mad" vs. the Army*; Howarth, *Men of War*; Hoyt, *How They Won the War*; Hughes, *Fleet Tactics*; Humble,

Fleet Carriers; King and Whitehill, *King*; Mason, *Pacific War Remembered*; Miller, *War at Sea*; Morison, *Naval Operations, Vol. 7*; Musicant, *Battleship at War*; Potter, *Great Sea War*; Potter, *Nimitz*; Reynolds, *Towers*; Reynolds, *Carrier War*; Reynolds, *Fast Carriers*; Reynolds, *Fighting Lady*; Sherman, *Combat Command*; Smith, *Coral and Brass*; Spector, *At War, at Sea*; Spector, *Eagle against the Sun*; Taylor, *Mitscher*; Y'Blood, *Little Giants*.

Oral Histories: Anderson, Clark, Dyer, Hedding, Hill, Jurika, Moore, Nimitz, Pirie, Pownall, Russell.

Twenty-three: South Pacific Roll-Up

Books: Barbey, *MacArthur's Amphibious Navy*; Beach, *United States Navy*; Bradlee, *A Good Life*; Buell, *King*; Dull, *Japanese Navy*; Fahey, *Pacific War Diary*; Howarth, *Men of War*; Hoyt, *How They Won the War*; Hoyt, *MacArthur's Navy*; King and Whitehill, *King*; Larrabee, *Commander in Chief*; Leary, *We Shall Return!*; Manchester, *American Caesar*; Mason, *Pacific War Remembered*; Miller, *War at Sea*; Morison, *Naval Operations, Vols. 4 and 7*; Potter, *Great Sea War*; Potter, *Burke*; Potter, *Halsey*; Potter, *Nimitz*; Reynolds, *Carrier War*; Reynolds, *Famous American Admirals*; Roscoe, *Destroyer Operations*; Sherman, *Combat Command*; Spector, *At War, at Sea*; Spector, *Eagle against the Sun*; Taussig, *Warrior for Freedom*; Van der Vat; *Pacific Campaign*; Wheeler, *Kinkaid*; Wooldridge, *Carrier Warfare*.

Oral Histories: Austin, Baldwin, Burke, Carney, Nimitz, Smedberg, Smoot, Tarbuck.

Twenty-four: West to the Marianas

Books: Buell, *King*; Buell, *Spruance*; Clark, *Carrier Admiral*; Dyer, *Turner*; Fahey, *Pacific War Diary*; Forrestel, *Spruance*; Gailey, *"Howlin' Mad" vs. the Army*; Howarth, *Men of War*; Hoyt, *How They Won the War*; Hughes, *Fleet Tactics*; King and Whitehill, *King*; Mason, *Pacific War Remembered*; Miller, *War at Sea*; Morison, *Naval Operations, Vol. 8*; Potter, *Great Sea War*; Potter, *Burke*; Potter, *Nimitz*; Reynolds, *Towers*; Reynolds, *Carrier War*; Reynolds, *Famous American Admirals*; Reynolds, *Fast Carriers*; Reynolds, *Fighting Lady*; Sherman, *Combat Command*; Smith, *Coral and Brass*; Spector, *At War, at Sea*; Spector, *Eagle against the Sun*; Taylor, *Mitscher*; Van der Vat, *Pacific Campaign*; Winton, *Ultra in the Pacific*; Wooldridge, *Carrier Warfare*; Y'Blood, *Little Giants*.

Oral Histories: Anderson, Bogan, Carney, Clark, Conolly, Dyer, Hedding, Hill,

Moore, Nimitz, Russell, Stump, Thach, Wellborn.

Twenty-five: Marianas Turkey Shoot
Books: Bradlee, *A Good Life*; Buell, *King*; Buell, *Spruance*; Clark, *Carrier Admiral*; Dyer, *Turner*; Forrestel, *Spruance*; Gailey, *"Howlin' Mad" vs. the Army*; Grove, *Big Fleet Actions*; Howarth, *Men of War*; Hoyt, *How They Won the War*; Humble, *Fleet Carriers*; King and Whitehill, *King*; Mason, *Pacific War Remembered*; Miller, *War at Sea*; Morison, *Naval Operations, Vol. 8*; Potter, *Great Sea War*; Potter, *Burke*; Potter, *Nimitz*; Reynolds, *Towers*; Reynolds, *Carrier War*; Reynolds, *Fast Carriers*; Reynolds, *Fighting Lady*; Sherman, *Combat Command*; Smith, *Coral and Brass*; Spector, *At War, at Sea*; Spector, *Eagle against the Sun*; Taylor, *Mitscher*; Van der Vat, *Pacific Campaign*; Wooldridge, *Carrier Warfare*.

Oral Histories: Anderson, Bogan, Clark, Conolly, Dyer, Hedding, Hill, McCrea, Moore, Nimitz, Russell, Stump, Thach, Wellborn.

Twenty-six: The Invasion of France
Books: Beach, *United States Navy*; Blumenson, *Masters of the Art of Command*; Buell, *King*; Carver, *War Lords*; Heathcote, *British Admirals*; Howarth, *Men of War*; Keegan, *Price of Admiralty*; King and Whitehill, *King*; Larrabee, *Commander in Chief*; Mason, *Atlantic War Remembered*; Miller, *War at Sea*; Morison, *Naval Operations, Vols. 10 and 11*; Potter, *Great Sea War*; Roscoe, *Destroyer Operations*; Stephen, *British Admirals*.

Oral Histories: Baldwin, Hall, Hewitt, Kirk McCrea.

Twenty-seven: Return to the Philippines
Books: Barbey, *MacArthur's Amphibious Navy*; Bischof, *Pacific War Revisited*; Buell, *King*; Buell, *Spruance*; Clark, *Carrier Admiral*; Cutler, *Battle of Leyte Gulf*; Fahey, *Pacific War Diary*; Forrestel, *Spruance*; Hoyt, *How They Won the War*; Hoyt, *MacArthur's Navy*; Humble, *Fleet Carriers*; King and Whitehill, *King*; Leary, *We Shall Return!*; Manchester, *American Caesar*; Mason, *Pacific War Remembered*; Miller, *War at Sea*; Morison, *Naval Operations, Vol. 12*; Potter, *Burke*; Potter, *Great Sea War*; Potter, *Halsey*; Potter, *Nimitz*; Reynolds, *Towers*; Reynolds, *Carrier War*; Reynolds, *Fast Carriers*; Reynolds, *Fighting Lady*; Sherman, *Combat Command*; Spector, *At War, at Sea*; Spector, *Eagle Against the Sun*; Taussig, *Warrior for Freedom*; Taylor, *Mitscher*; Van der Vat, *Pacific Campaign*; Wheeler, *Kinkaid*; Wooldridge, *Carrier Warfare*; Y'Blood, *Little Giants*.

Oral Histories: Austin, Bogan, Burke, Carney, Clark, Conolly, Dyer, Hedding, Hill, Jurika, Kinkaid, Moore, Nimitz, Russell, Stump.

Twenty-eight: The Greatest Sea Battle
Books: Barbey, *MacArthur's Amphibious Navy*; Beach, *United States Navy*; Bischof, *Pacific War Revisited*; Buell, *King*; Clark, *Carrier Admiral*; Cutler, *Battle of Leyte Gulf*; Dull, *Japanese Navy*; Honan, *Great Naval Battles*; Howarth, *Men of War*; Hoyt, *How They Won the War*; Hoyt, *MacArthur's Navy*; Hughes, *Fleet Tactics*; Macksey, *Military Errors*; Mason, *Pacific War Remembered*; Miller, *War at Sea*; Morison, *Naval Operations, Vol. 12*; Musicant, *Battleship at War*; Potter, *Burke*; Potter, *Great Sea War*; Potter, *Halsey*; Potter, *Nimitz*; Regan, *Naval Blunders*; Reynolds, *Towers*; Reynolds, *Carrier War*; Reynolds, *Fast Carriers*; Roscoe, *Destroyer Operations*; Sherman, *Combat Command*; Spector, *At War, at Sea*; Spector, *Eagle Against the Sun*; Taussig, *Warrior for Freedom*; Taylor, *Mitscher*; Van der Vat, *Pacific Campaign*; Wheeler, *Kinkaid*; Wooldridge, *Carrier Warfare*; Y'Blood, *Little Giants*.

Oral Histories: Baldwin, Bogan, Burke, Hedding, Carney, Clark, Conolly, Kinkaid, Moore, Smedberg, Smoot, Stump Wellborn.

Twenty-nine: Battle of the Admirals
Books: Buell, *King*; Calhoun, *Typhoon*; Clark, *Carrier Admiral*; Cutler, *Battle of Leyte Gulf*; Howarth, *Men of War*; Hoyt, *How They Won the War*; Hughes, *Fleet Tactics*; Mason, *Pacific War Remembered*; Morison, *Naval Operations, Vol. 12*; Potter, *Burke*; Potter, *Halsey*; Potter, *Nimitz*; Reynolds, *Towers*; Reynolds, *Fast Carriers*; Spector, *At War, at Sea*; Taussig, *Warrior for Freedom*; Taylor, *Mitscher*; Van der Vat, *Pacific Campaign*; Wheeler, *Kinkaid*.

Oral Histories: Bogan, Burke, Carney, Clark, Kinkaid, Moore, Stump.

Thirty: Lingayen, Iwo Jima, and Okinawa
Books: Barbey, *MacArthur's Amphibious Navy*; Bischof, *Pacific War Revisited*; Bryan, *Aircraft Carrier*; Buell, *King*; Buell, *Spruance*; Clark, *Carrier Admiral*; Dull, *Japanese Navy*; Fahey, *Pacific War Diary*; Forrestel, *Spruance*; Howarth, *Men of War*; Hoyt, *How They Won the War*; Hoyt, *Kamikazes*; Hoyt, *MacArthur's Navy*; Humble, *Fleet Carriers*; Hynes, *Flights of Passage*; Kernan, *Crossing the Line*; King and Whitehill, *King*; Larrabee, *Commander in Chief*; Leary, *We Shall Return!*; Manchester, *American Caesar*; Mason, *Pacific War Remembered*; Miller, *War at Sea*; Morison, *Naval Operations, Vols. 13 and 14*; O'Callahan, *I Was Chaplain on the* Franklin; Potter,

Burke; Potter, *Great Sea War*; Potter, *Halsey*; Potter, *Nimitz*; Reynolds, *Towers*; Reynolds, *Carrier War*; Reynolds, *Fast Carriers*; Sherman, *Combat Command*; Smith, *Coral and Brass*; Spector, *At War, at Sea*; Spector, *Eagle Against the Sun*; Taylor, *Mitscher*; Van der Vat, *Pacific Campaign*; Wheeler, *Kinkaid*; Wooldridge, *Carrier Warfare*; Y'Blood, *Little Giants*.

Oral Histories: Austin, Bogan, Burke, Carney, Clark, Conolly, Hall, Hill, Hustvedt, Jurika, Kinkaid, McCrea, Pirie, Russell, Stump, Thach, Wellborn.

Thirty-one: The Last Dangerous Days

Books: Bryan, *Aircraft Carrier*; Buell, *King*; Buell, *Spruance*; Calhoun, *Typhoon*; Clark, *Carrier Admiral*; Dull, *Japanese Navy*; Dyer, *Turner*; Fahey, *Pacific War Diary*; Forrestel, *Spruance*; Howarth, *Men of War*; Hoyt, *How They Won the War*; Hoyt, *Kamikazes*; Humble, *Fleet Carriers*; Hynes, *Flights of Passage*; Kernan, *Crossing the Line*; Larrabee, *Commander in Chief*; Mason, *Pacific War Remembered*; Miller, *War at Sea*; Morison, *Naval Operations, Vol. 14*; Musicant, *Battleship at War*; Newcomb, *Abandon Ship!*; O'Callahan, *I Was Chaplain on the* Franklin; Potter, *Burke*; Potter, *Halsey*; Potter, *Nimitz*; Reynolds, *Towers*; Reynolds, *Carrier War*; Reynolds, *Fast Carriers*; Roscoe, *Destroyer Operations*; Sherman, *Combat Command*; Spector, *At War, at Sea*; Spector, *Eagle Against the Sun*; Taussig, *Warrior for Freedom*; Taylor, *Mitscher*; Van der Vat, *Pacific Campaign*; Wooldridge, *Carrier Warfare*; Y'Blood, *Little Giants*.

Oral Histories: Anderson, Bogan, Dyer, Carney, Clark, Hall, Hill, Jurika, McCrea, Pirie, Thach, Stump.

Epilogue

Books: Beach, *United States Navy*; Bischof, *Pacific War Revisited*; Buell, *King*; Buell, *Spruance*; Carver, *War Lords*; Dyer, *Turner*; Forrestel, *Spruance*; Howarth, *Men at War*; Hoyt, *How They Won the War*; Larrabee, *Commander in Chief*; Morison, *Naval Operations, Vol. 14*; Morison, *Two-Ocean War*; Potter, *Halsey*; Potter, *Nimitz*; Reynolds, *Towers*; Reynolds, *Fast Carriers*; Wheeler, *Kinkaid*.

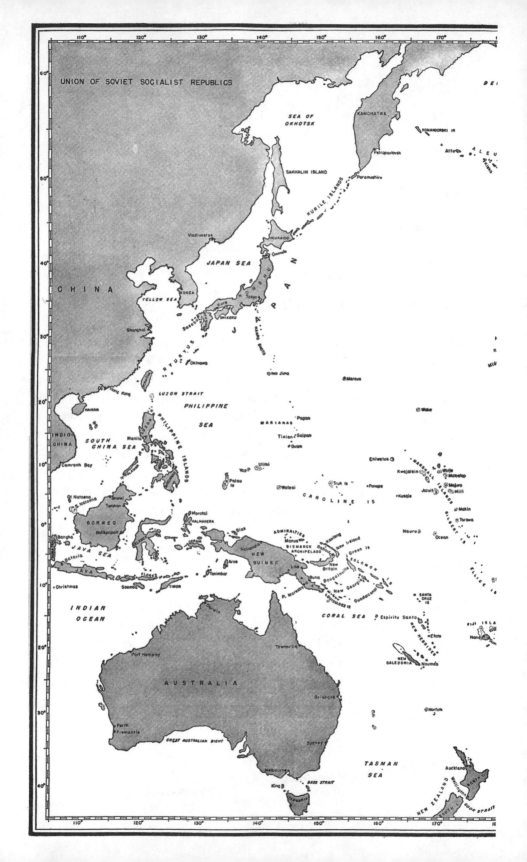

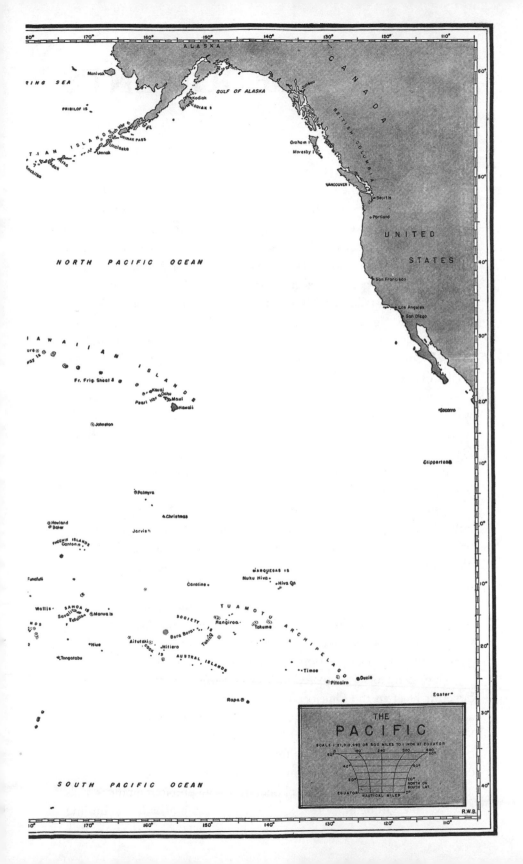

ACKNOWLEDGMENTS

The first admiral I knew was my father-in-law, the two-starred RADM George J. Dufek, who was the commander of the Antarctic expedition Operation Deep Freeze. George was an impressive figure, a versatile naval officer who first earned submariner's dolphins before going to flight school and winning gold wings as a naval aviator. In World War II, he commanded an escort carrier group in *Bogue*, which was credited with destroying the last German submarine in the war. In the Korean War, he captained the big carrier *Antietam*. In between he participated in polar expeditions. As Commander of Deep Freeze he was the first man to land and set foot at the South Pole—aboard a ski-equipped Navy R4D, the civilian DC-3.

George was a strikingly handsome, gregarious charmer. When he walked into the Matador bar in San Francisco in his dress blues—gold wings and dolphins topping his rows of ribbons—he turned every head. He was a wonderful raconteur who drank and smoked like an aviator. He was fun to be with and brightened some of my nights as a reporter for the *San Francisco Chronicle*.

Later, as a correspondent for *Newsweek*, I had lunch with Rear Admiral (Ret.) Samuel Eliot Morison at his home in Boston on the occasion of completing his 14-volume work, the magisterial *History of Naval Operations in World War II*. He was witty and insightful regarding the naval strategy and tactics of flag officers. During one *Newsweek* trip to the West Coast during the 1964 Presidential campaign, I managed to fit in a visit to Admiral Raymond Spruance at his home in Pebble Beach, California. He was modest, yet a store of information on Midway and the great Central Pacific operations—and his own role in them.

During my four years based in Vietnam in the sixties, I flew to the Seventh Fleet in the Gulf of Tonkin, usually to a carrier with a rear admiral, commander of Task Force 77. On my first trip I landed on *Coral Sea*. It was the flagship of Rear Admiral Henry L. "Hank" Miller, who trained Jimmy Doolittle's pilots for their 1942 raid on Tokyo from the carrier *Hornet*. He was a pilot's pilot and a fascinating flag officer.

I covered various other naval operations: amphibious landings with U.S. Marines; firing missions aboard the battleship *New Jersey*, hurling

16-inch shells into North Vietnam; I accompanied supporting destroyers; and rode with the riverine patrol boats in the Mekong Delta. I became intrigued with the mechanics of the job of a flag officer, an interest that led to this book.

Sadly, none of the principals of this work are still alive, nor are their senior staff officers. But their vivid memories live on in the invaluable *Oral History Collections*—extensive interviews with retired senior officers by John T. Mason Jr. and Paul Stillwell—at the Naval Historical Center in Washington, Columbia University in New York, and the Nimitz Library at the Naval Academy in Annapolis. These institutions are a repository of written memories, after-action reports and war diaries of the wartime flag officers. I would like to thank the curators and assistants at these institutions for their generous help, as well as to the research staff of the U.S. Naval Institute and the Naval War College.

My thanks also to author and former war correspondent A. J. (Jack) Langguth for his advice and suggestions, and Professor Clark J. Reynolds, perhaps the foremost expert on U.S. World War II carrier warfare. His *The Fast Carriers* is a classic work on naval combat.

My deepest appreciation goes to my agent, Tom Wallace, for his support and keen advice and for shepherding this book through to my publisher, Richard Kane, head of Zenith Press. I found Zenith acquisitions editor Steve Gansen to be a thorough professional and a delight to work with.

Finally, I'd like to extend my deepest gratitude to my understanding wife, Rose Marie, for her help in proofreading the manuscript and for her many cogent suggestions.

INDEX